D1544524

The Foreign Aid Programs
of the Soviet Bloc and
Communist China

The Foreign Aid Programs of the Soviet Bloc and Communist China

KURT MÜLLER

Translated by Richard H. Weber
and Michael Roloff

WALKER AND COMPANY
NEW YORK

Preface

This book is the first comprehensive result of my work in the Research Institute of the Friedrich-Ebert-Stiftung about the East bloc and the underdeveloped countries. I have tried to show the principles and objectives of the East bloc policies in Asian, African and Latin American countries, and to document the background and interconnections of communist activity in the underdeveloped countries.

"To reach Paris you have to go by way of Peking and Calcutta." These words, which only Western publications ascribe to Lenin, quite accurately describe the general communist objectives toward winning or neutralizing the young national states. We had to investigate this approach—that is, the strategy and tactics of the East bloc, to be specific—for the following reasons.

1. Today, Moscow—as we know it—is not at all prepared to go "by way of Peking." In addition to the center of communism in Moscow, there exists the center in Peking which will continue to exist. That is why it should be emphasized at once that our investigation is dealing with the influence of Moscow when it mentions the Soviet bloc; China is treated separately. We use East bloc as a comprehensive term for the whole communist realm.

2. The Soviet ideologists claim today that in the matter of the national liberation movements the communists already deviated from the Leninist way in 1920.

3. The concept of the way to national liberation which was held by Moscow until 1955 proved to be erroneous. By far the greater majority of the young Asian and African national states achieved their national independence in a way that had not been foreseen by any

communist program, which even stood in conflict with the communist conceptions. The events in Asia and Africa took Moscow by surprise.

4. Nor did the "new way via Calcutta" which Khrushchev propagated after the Bandung Conference of 1955, the attempt to bind the neutral Asian and African countries to the East bloc by creating a "zone of peace," produce the hoped for results, and

5. That is why the Moscow Central Committee has proclaimed a new, differentiated class strategy and tactics for Asia, Africa and Latin America since 1959-1960. This strategy was formulated in the "declaration of the conference of representatives of the Communist and Workers Parties" of November 1960 in Moscow, and particularly in Section VI of the new party program of the CPSU. Thus there were and still are several ways that had to be investigated. We not only had to analyze the intentions and projects, but also the successes and failures of communism in the underdeveloped countries; for while implementing our own developmental plans we encounter the activity of the communist bloc in Africa and Asia. A more precise knowledge of communist objectives, projects, strengths and weaknesses is therefore indispensable.

Although the national and colonial question, or the "doctrine of the national liberation movement," is firmly part of communist ideology, the East bloc to this day lacks a comprehensive presentation or textbook on this problem. Lenin's selected essays and speeches about this matter have been collected in a volume entitled *Concerning the National and Colonial National Question*. However, until a few years ago the standard work on this subject for the whole East bloc was Joseph Stalin's omnibus volume, *Marxism and the National and Colonial Question*. The last German edition of this book was published in 1955 in East Berlin.

In 1960 the textbook *Foundations of Marxism-Leninism* was published. It comprises 840 pages, of which forty are devoted to the doctrine of "the national liberation movement." It is significant that the "national liberation movement of the peoples against colonialism" is treated as a subsection in the main section, *The Theory and Tactics of the International Communist Movement*. In this section we also find for the first time a discussion of economic aid as a part of the theory and tactics of international communism.

However, since 1956 a great deal has been published in the East bloc about the underdeveloped countries. Until 1962 alone 180 titles (only books and omnibus volumes) were published in the USSR about the previously neglected African countries. Even more numerous and more comprehensive is the material that has been published in newspapers and journals.

It was impossible for me to exhaust these sources completely. I was only able to draw on the most important of them. The interested reader will find a list of the most important source material in the bibliography of the Research Institute of the Friedrich-Ebert-Stiftung, *Literature about Underdeveloped Countries II & IV*, which includes the titles of East bloc books and magazine articles about the underdeveloped countries. This bibliography is supplemented periodically.

The first part of this book examines the strategy and tactics from Lenin to Fidel Castro; the second part, the East bloc's foreign trade and its economic and training aid.

I am aware that much of the data in this book is of a temporary nature. The economic and trade figures will soon have to be supplemented again, for they change from year to year. New loans, and the conclusion of further agreements between the Soviet bloc and China with the young national states, will also have to be added. A running supplementation of the dates, figures and documents of this book becomes necessary in order to remain up to date. This is done in *Vierteljahresberichte des Forschungs-instituts der Friedrich-Ebert-Stiftung*, which the Friedrich-Ebert-Stiftung has published since 1960.

This manuscript was completed in March 1963. The first edition of this book appeared in 1964 in German. It was revised, supplemented and brought up to date for the American edition.

N.B. The conversion rate of rubles into US-$ as it is used in this book, particularly in the tables, is based on the official Moscow quotation (Statebank of the USSR, Moscow) and the official New York quotation (The Chase Manhattan Bank). Until December 31, 1960 the exchange rate quoted respectively by both banks was: 4 Ruble = 1 US-$; 1 Ruble = 0.25 US-$. For the conversion of the value of foreign trade and credits as of January 1, 1961 and after we used the new conversion rate quoted by both banks as of that date: 100 US-$ = 90 rubles; 100 rubles = 111.12 US-$.

Contents

Preface v

List of Tables ix

PART ONE
STRATEGY AND TACTICS
From Lenin to Fidel Castro

Up to the Bandung Conference 2

The New Course in Asia, Africa and Latin America 28

The "Peace Zone" and "Positive Neutrality" 34

Coexistence Strategy and Underdeveloped Nations 39

The Concept of State Capitalism 57

Communism and the One-Party Systems in Africa and Asia . . 64

The Strategy of Mao Tse-tung 83

Focal Point Africa 98

The Latin American Center of Communism 116

PART TWO
WITHIN THE VORTEX OF COEXISTENCE
Foreign Trade, Economic Aid and Training Assistance

Handbook for Action 132

Foreign Trade Ties with Underdeveloped Nations 136

The Development of Foreign Trade 143
The Policy of the Unfavorable Balance of Trade 170
Export of Machine Tools and
    Plant Equipment to Backward Nations 175
The Indian Example 181
Ideology and Reality of Soviet Bloc Foreign Trade 186
The Foreign Aid Program of the Soviet Bloc 192
Comments on Some Propaganda Claims
    about Backward Nations 194
Principles of the Foreign Aid Policy 201
Forms and Terms of Soviet Bloc Loans 208
East Bloc Loans and Nonrepayable Aid 214
USSR Loans to the Countries of the "Third World" 218
USSR Gifts 230
China's Financial Aid 233
Loans Made by European Soviet Bloc Nations 240
Industrialization Aid 255
The Soviet Bloc and the UN Foreign Aid Program 272
The Training of Functionaries
    and Development of a National Elite 277
Party Schooling 279
Training of Trade Union Cadres 283
Schooling the National Elite 292
Study at Universities and Polytechnic Institutes 296
The Patrice Lumumba People's Friendship University . . . 301
The University of 17 November 308
The Herder Institute in Leipzig 312
New Methods in the Political Education and
    Indoctrination of Academic Youth 317
On-the-Job Training Program 323
Schools in the Underdeveloped Countries 327

List of Tables

1   Membership of Communist Parties   80
2   USSR Trade Agreements with Underdeveloped Nations   138
3   Share of "Third World" Countries in the Total Foreign Trade Turnover of the Western and Eastern Countries in 1964   144
4   The Distribution of Foreign Trade in the Developing Countries   144
5   Developing Countries' Share in Total Foreign Trade Turnover of the USSR   146
6   USSR Foreign Trade Turnover According to Groups of Countries, and Its Increase   147
7   The Development of Soviet Foreign Trade with Several Asian Countries   148
8   The Balance of Soviet-Indian Foreign Trade   149
9   The Development of USSR Trade with Several African Countries   150
10 The Development of Soviet Trade with the UAR   151
11 The Share of Machinery and Equipment in the USSR Export to the UAR   151
12 USSR Foreign Trade with the Latin American Countries   152
13 CSSR Foreign Trade According to Groups of Countries   153
14 CSSR Foreign Trade with the Individual Developing Countries   154
15 Polish Foreign Trade According to Groups of Countries   155
16 Polish Foreign Trade with Asia, Africa and Latin America   155
17 Hungary's Foreign Trade According to Groups of Countries (Export & Import)   156
18 Hungary's Foreign Trade with the Developing Countries   157
19 Bulgaria's Foreign Trade According to Groups of Countries   158

20 Bulgaria's Foreign Trade with Several Developing Countries 158

21 Rumania's Foreign Trade Turnover with Its 10 Principal Partners in the "Third World" 160

22 DDR Trade According to Groups of Countries 162

23 DDR Trade with Its Principal Partners in the "Third World" 163

24 Yugoslavia's Foreign Trade According to Groups of Countries 166

25 Yugoslavia's Trade with the Developing Countries According to Continents 167

26 The People's Republic of China's Foreign Trade Turnover According to Groups of Countries 168

27 China's Trade with Afro-Asian Nations 169

28 USSR Rubber Purchases in Malaysia 171

29 USSR Cotton Imports from the UAR 172

30 1958 Soviet and East European Imports of Tropical Products 172

31 1965 and 1980 Tropical Fruit Import Forecast for USSR and East Europe 173

32 USSR Imports of Tropical Goods from the Developing Countries 173

33 USSR Machine Tool and Equipment Export 176

34 Soviet Machine Tool Deliveries to "Third World" Countries 176

35 USSR Export of Complete Industrial Plants 178

36 USSR Export of Complete Industrial Plants to the Developing Countries 178

37 Soviet Bloc Share in India's Foreign Trade 181

38 Share of Soviet Bloc Nations in India's Export and Import 182

39 A Comparison of Indo-Soviet Statistics 182

40 Soviet and Chinese Aid to the Developing Countries 214

41 Soviet Loans to the "Third World" from 1953 to 1966 219

42 China's Loans and Nonrepayable Aid to Other Countries Between 1953-61 234

43 Loans by the People's Republic of China to the Developing Countries from 1956 to 1965 239

44 Yugoslav Investment Loan Grants to the Developing Countries from 1957 to March 1965 248

45 Czechoslovak Financial Assistance to the Developing Countries 250

46 Financial Aid of Several European Comecon Countries to the "Third World" 253

47 Total Grants and the Share of Each Soviet Bloc Country and of China in Supplying Them 254

48 East Bloc Industrial Facilities Scheduled for 1966 256

49 USSR Projects for Young National States 256

50 USSR vs. East Bloc Credits 257

51 USSR Projects in the Developing Countries and Their Completion 259

52 Contributions of Soviet Bloc and Selected Backward Nations to UN Expanded Program of Technical Assistance 276

53 The Number of Students from the "Third World" at Universities and Institutions of Higher Learning of the Comecon Countries 293

54 Students Enrolled at Patrice Lumumba University During First Year 304

PART I

Strategy and Tactics

From Lenin to Fidel Castro

Up to the Bandung Conference

The question of nationalism and colonialism has been part of communism's world revolutionary program at least since 1916, when Lenin wrote the pamphlet *Imperialism, the Highest Stage of Capitalism*. Therefore, it is wrong to assume that Lenin only discovered the national liberation movement when the world revolution of the West's industrial proletariat failed to materialize—to serve as the world revolution's surrogate, as it were. Rather, Lenin regarded the national liberation movement as one of the main streams of world revolution, as a "strategy of creating 'a second front' against Imperialism." [1] Immediately after the 1917 Revolution, the Soviets began to take an active part in the national liberation movements of the peoples of Asia and North Africa. One of their first acts was an "Appeal to all Mohammedan Workers of Russia and the East," issued 3 December 1917, a few weeks after the Bolshevik take-over, in which they asked the Eastern Moslems, the Persians, Turks, Arabs, and Hindus to support the Russian Revolution and its government. "On our banners," the appeal read, "is inscribed the liberation of the world's suppressed peoples." Significantly, this appeal is considered a foreign policy document today.[2]

The Soviets, who gathered their first experiences between 1917 and 1928, won over some of today's Asian leaders during that time, only to lose them again later.

---

[1] Richard Löwenthal, *Kommunismus und nachkoloniale Revolution, Das Parlament* (Bonn), Beilage No. 10/1963, 6 March 1963.
[2] *USSR Foreign Policy Documents*, Ministry of Foreign Affairs, USSR, Vol. 1 (Russ.), Moscow 1957, pp. 34-35.

THE 1920 BAKU "CONGRESS
OF THE EASTERN PEOPLES"

After the Second Party Congress of 1920 had formulated the "Theses on the National and Colonial Questions," the Comintern endeavored to translate these into action by convening the Congress of the Eastern Peoples at Baku from 1-7 September 1920.[3] The Congress was attended by 1891 delegates from twenty-six countries and included 235 Turks, 192 Persians, 157 Armenians, fourteen Hindus, and eight Chinese, and "was composed in almost equal parts of communists and political independents. The latter were again split into two factions: those who really belong to no party, such as the peasants and semi-proletarian urbanites, and those who merely called themselves independents but were in fact members of bourgeois parties." [4]

The hope during those first turbulent years was to achieve world revolutionary objectives—objectives the Soviets now believe can only be reached gradually; whereas the Chinese feel they can realize them quickly by changing Africa and Asia into a "storm center of the world revolution."

The former Russia correspondent of the *Christian Science Monitor,* William H. Chamberlain, describes the political atmosphere of this Congress of the Peoples of Asia:

"Zinoviev brought a long speech to a passionate oratorical climax with the following outburst: 'The real revolution will blaze up only when the 800,000,000 people who live in Asia unite with us, when the African continent unites, when we see that hundreds of millions of people are in movement. Now we must kindle a real holy war against the British and French capitalists . . . We must say that the hour has struck when the workers of the whole world are able to arouse tens and hundreds and millions of peasants, to create a Red Army in the East, to arm and organize uprisings in the rear of the British, to poison the existence of every impudent British officer who lords it over Turkey, Persia, India, China.'

"At this moment the audience, mostly clad in colorful Oriental costumes, sprang up. Swords, sabres and revolvers were flourished in the air, while the vow of *jehad,* or holy war, was pronounced. Radek endeavored to conjure up the spirit of Tamerlane and Ghengis Khan.

---

[3] This "Congress of the Eastern Peoples" should not be confused with the "All-Russian Congress of Communist Organizations of Eastern Peoples" sitting in Moscow from 22 Nov.-3 Dec. 1919. This Congress was a gathering of Communist organizations of Tatar, Bashkir, and Turkestan at which Lenin also discussed the winning of the Oriental peoples.

[4] *Sovetskoe vostokovedenie* (Moscow), No. 5/1957, pp. 114-120.

After saying that the East, under capitalist oppression, created a philosophy of patience, he added: 'We appeal, comrades, to the spirit of struggle which once animated the peoples of the East when they marched against Europe under the leadership of their great conquerors. And when the capitalists of Europe say that there is a menace of a new wave of barbarism, a new wave of huns, we reply: Long live the Red East which, together with the workers of Europe, will create a new culture under the banner of communism.' " [5]

A Council for Propaganda and Action was formed at the congress, with a membership of forty-seven and a presidium of nine. As its first attempt toward setting up a nationalist-revolutionary front organization the Council, under the title *Peoples of the Orient* (*Narody Vostoka*), issued a periodical in Arabic, Persian, Turkish, and Russian. Of this, however, only one issue appeared. This Council ceased to function even before it was officially dissolved in 1922.

This first effort to gain the support of the Oriental races failed because of a contradiction in Soviet theory and practice in the matter of the "national question." During the sessions of the Congress of the Peoples of the East, delegates from the Russian part of Central Asia had complained to the presidium about the cruelties, maladministration, and repressive measures of Soviet representatives, causing the Congress presidium to dispatch a grievance committee to Moscow,[6] something still possible at that time. Doing violence to the spirit of the Baku Congress, the Soviets applied a policy of national suppression in Armenia, Bukhara, and Khiva, and with the help of the Red Army forcibly liquidated the independent Social-Democrat "Georgian Democratic Republic" in early 1921.

THE FIRST CONGRESS OF COMMUNIST AND REVOLUTIONARY ORGANIZATIONS OF THE FAR EAST OF 1922

The political orientation of the Congress of the Peoples of the East was as follows: The national liberation movement can lead to victory only under the leadership of the industrial proletariat of the progressive nations and within the framework of world revolution. This viewpoint, disproved by subsequent historical developments, also figured in the decisions made at another conference, that of the First Congress of Communist and Revolutionary Organizations of the Far East, held in Moscow from 21-27 January 1922. A resolution of this Congress, attended by 127 voting and seventeen advisory dele-

---

[5] William H. Chamberlain, *Die russische Revolution*, Frankfurt/Main, Vol. II, pp. 369-70.

[6] *The First Congress of the Peoples of the East* (*Russ.*), Moscow 1961, p. 14.

gates from Korea, China, Japan, India, Mongolia, Java, and the Asiatic Soviet Republics, states:

"The Congress of the workers of the Far East . . . especially emphasizes the need for thoroughly understanding the interrelationships of the national-revolutionary movements on the one hand, and the struggle of the workers for their social liberation on the other. The Congress is convinced that the working masses, enslaved by imperialism, will achieve national and social liberation only in league with the international proletariat." [7]

THE SPREAD OF WORLD REVOLUTION TO THE ORIENT

The "policy of direct action," or attempts to propagate world revolution in the Orient with Soviet support, which had been applied in Persia (Soviet Republic Gilan) as early as May 1920, achieved results after the Baku Congress only in Outer Mongolia and in tiny Tannu-Tuva, in both of which the czarist government had already sought to achieve hegemony. In Outer Mongolia, traditional arena of Sino-Russian rivalry and vassal state of China until 1911, the Soviets, in March 1921, mounted an "attack against the White Guard formations of Ungern-Sternberg and the *hetman* Semenov." Soviet troops remained in Mongolia until February 1925. During this time the "Mongolian People's Party," established with Soviet assistance in March 1921, proclaimed the independence of Mongolia at Urga (present-day Ulan Bator) on 10 July 1921.

On 13 June 1924 the "Mongolian People's Republic" was founded, initiating the first steps in this country's move towards the evolution of a type of state now called "people's democracy." In Tannu-Tuva, which belonged to China from 1757 until 1912 and which became a czarist protectorate in 1914, the Soviets, in 1921, organized the "Revolutionary People's Party of Tannu-Tuva" which, in August 1921, proclaimed this region, bordering on Mongolia, an independent republic. "With fraternal Soviet assistance"—thus claims the *Small Soviet Encyclopedia*—"Tannu-Tuva started on the road to gradual transition from feudalism to socialism." On 11 October 1944 Tannu-Tuva, on its "own volition," was incorporated in the USSR as an autonomous region.

INITIAL FOREIGN POLICY RESULTS

The trend of the times was propitious for the Soviet endeavor to enlist the nationalist movement, gripping the colonial and semicolonial Asiatic countries, in the service of Soviet foreign policy, and

---

[7] *Der Ferne Osten, der Erste Kongress der Kommunistischen und revolutionären Organisationen des Fernen Ostens*, Hamburg 1922, p. 124.

to assure the influence of the Communist International over the movement. The 1917 Russian Revolution cast a profound spell over the national liberation movement of the peoples of the Orient, and as early as 1919 the "Father of the Turks," Kemal Ataturk, approached Lenin with the proposal of a "united front against imperialism." On 16 March 1921, close on the heels of signing its first treaties with Oriental nations in which it renounced czarist prerogatives (Persia, 26 February 1921, and Afghanistan, 28 February 1921), the Russian Soviet Federated Socialist Republic concluded a "treaty of friendship and fraternity" with the young Turkish Republic.[8] This Russo-Turkish friendship and fraternity treaty reads in part:

"Both signatories confirm that the national liberation movement of the peoples of the Orient is closely linked with the struggle of the Russian workers for a new social order, and they solemnly acknowledge the right of these peoples to liberty and independence, as well as their right to choose an administration in accordance with their wishes." [9]

Turkey was the first country to welcome Russian advisory personnel (Borodin).

The "Father of the Chinese Revolution," Sun Yat-sen, also was an admirer of the Russian Revolution. From early 1918 he corresponded with Lenin and the Soviet Government.[10] It was in China that Soviet politics initially gained its greatest successes in the years 1923 to 1927. In January 1923 were concluded the well-known agreements between Soviet Ambassador Joffe and Dr. Sun Yat-sen which, as the alliance between Russian Bolshevism and Chinese Nationalism, assumed historical importance. The Soviets committed themselves to assist Sun Yat-sen's national-revolutionary movement by reorganizing the Nationalist People's Party—Kuomintang—along the lines of the CPSU, and to help organize a national-revolutionary Chinese army modeled on the Red Army. Also agreed on at the time were the working rules between the Kuomintang and the fledgling Communist Party of China, which counted only 432 members in 1923. The Chinese communists, in becoming members of the Kuomintang, were the first example of the political Trojan horse.

China in those days served as the great proving grounds for the Soviets. With the exception of Mongolia and North Korea, the Soviets never again were able to send as high a number of political advisors and military experts to an Oriental country as they did in the years

---

[8] *Das Parlament* (Bonn), No. 34/35 of 24 August 1960; *Sovetskoe vostokovedenie* (Moscow), No. 5/1957, pp. 13-14.

[9] *Geschichte der Diplomatie*, Moscow 1957, Vol. III, p. 142.

[10] *Sino-Soviet Relations* (*Russ.*), Moscow 1959-Documentary Collection.

after 1923 to organize the Kuomintang and the Nationalist Chinese army, and during the time of the Chinese national-revolutionary Northern Campaign of 1926-27. While it is true that Mao Tse-tung required thousands of Soviet engineers and technicians,[11] he evolved his own military doctrine and, after assuming leadership of the Chinese Communist Party (1935), showed a greater tendency to hand out political advice than to take it from others.

MAIN THESES OF THE SECOND CONGRESS
OF THE COMMUNIST INTERNATIONAL

The aforementioned Soviet agreements with Persia, Afghanistan, Turkey, and China were partially dictated by the will to break through the *cordon sanitaire* that isolated Russia from the rest of the world. On the other hand, the Soviets also endeavored to put into practice in Turkey and China the tenets on the national and colonial questions, evolved at the Second Congress of the Communist International (July-August 1920), which led to early failure and defeat in Turkey and also, after some initial successes in 1927, in China.

The thinking underlying the tenets on the national and colonial questions as resolved by the Second Congress of the Communist International on 28 July 1920 is as follows:

1. All communist parties must support the revolutionary liberation movements in the backward countries.

2. Relentless battle is to be waged against the reactionary and medieval influence of the church, its missions, and similar elements.

3. *It is necessary to fight Pan-Slavism and Pan-Asiatic movements and similar efforts.*

4. It is also necessary to have the support of the peasant movement against landlords and all forms and vestiges of feudalism. An attempt must be made to lend a highly revolutionary character to the peasant movement, organizing the peasants and all those exploited into soviets if at all feasible.

5. Furthermore, it is necessary to take a decisive stand against the attempt to conceal a revolutionary liberation movement that is not truly communist-oriented under a false guise of communism. "It is the duty of the Communist International to support the revolutionary movement in the colonies and backward countries *solely for the purpose* of collecting the constituent elements of future proletarian parties—those that are in reality and not in name only communistic —in all backward countries, in order to arouse in them a consciousness of their special tasks; that is, of the tasks of *fighting the bourgeois-*

---

[11] According to Chou En-lai's *Das grosse Jahrzehut,* Peking 1959, p. 40, 10,800 Soviet specialists were active in China from 1950 to 1959.

democratic trend within their own country. The Communist International is to establish temporary union, even an alliance, with the revolutionary movement in the colonies and the backward countries but *must not, however, amalgamate with it.* The independent character of the proletarian movement must at all costs be maintained, even if only in an embryonic state." [12]

6. In his report on these tenets, Lenin emphasized: "The supposition that the backward countries must inevitably go through a capitalist stage will be disproved if the victorious proletariat [i.e., the USSR; today the Soviet bloc] systematically propagandizes the underdeveloped countries and if the Soviet republics lend all possible assistance . . . The Communist International must also advance—and furnish theoretic proof for—this thesis: *that the backward nations, assisted by the proletariat of the progressive countries, may arrive at the Soviet order of things and, after going through certain evolutionary steps, at communism without going through a capitalistic stage.*" [13]

Our further analysis will bring us back to these tenets of the Second Congress of the Communist International, and we shall see which guidelines have retained their validity, and which were strategically and tactically adapted to a new set of circumstances. It must be mentioned, however, that the tenets on the national and colonial questions of the Second Comintern Congress represent a compromise of two arguments that are still noticeable in communism.

M. N. ROY OF INDIA AS FORERUNNER OF MAO TSE-TUNG

The commission at the Second Party Congress that dealt with the national and colonial questions found itself confronted with two conflicting views: on the one hand, Lenin's *Original Draft of the Tenets on the National and Colonial Questions,* and on the other, the *Supplement to the Tenets on the National and Colonial Questions* of the Indian Communist M. N. Roy.

M. N. Roy opposed Lenin in two decisive questions at the Second Congress, and voiced opinions that somewhat resemble those later expressed by Mao Tse-tung.

First of all, it was a question of world revolution. Whereas Lenin still hoped for a world revolution in the West, and considered the national liberation movement a "second front," Roy felt, as Mao does today, that the colonial countries would have to make the decisive

---

[12] *Protokoll des II. Kongresses der Kommunistischen Internationale,* Hamburg 1921, pp. 224-232. Italics are the author's.
[13] Lenin, *Sämtliche Werke,* Vol. XXV, Vienna-Berlin 1930, pp. 437-38. Italics are the author's.

contribution to the world revolution. He reasoned: "European capitalism does not draw its main support from the European industrial countries but from its colonies . . . The extra profit derived from the colonies is the main source of the strength of present-day capitalism. The European working class will only succeed in overthrowing the capitalist order when this source has been cut off," and the colonies have been separated from their mother countries through revolutions.

Secondly, there was disagreement on the question whether communists should temporarily—as Lenin originally phrased it—support the "bourgeois democratic national movement" (which would be called "national bourgeoisie" today) during the first phase of the revolution, or only the "national-revolutionary movement in the struggle against the bourgeois-democratic trend"—as Roy formulated it.

Essentially, it was a question of the "two-phase theory": May the communists in the initial *national phase of the revolution* support the national bourgeoisie so as to consolidate their own forces for the time when they will take over the leadership during the *second phase of the social revolution*—thus Lenin and also Khrushchev after 1955—or must the communists assume leadership in the very first phase of the national revolution and isolate the national bourgeoisie from leadership, which was Roy's point of view, shared then as now, in theory and in practice, by Mao Tse-tung?

At the time of the Second Party Congress, Lenin adopted Roy's formulation of the basic tenets. The congress also accepted Roy's supplementary tenets, although they are deleted from more recent publications of documents of the Second Party Congress.[14] At that time Lenin found a "way out" of the impasse by disparaging Roy's views and by telling the congress delegates: "There can be no doubt whatever that any national movement can only be a bourgeois-democratic one" (which Roy aimed to fight at the very outset). Today, every communist movement is in the position to draw on the Second Party Congress for supporting arguments; for it has a choice among Lenin's original draft, the tenets of the congress itself, and Roy's supplementary tenets. A study of the latter reveals formulations that the Chinese Communists prefer today.

"To support the struggle for the destruction of foreign overlordship," Roy declared, "does not therefore mean to underwrite the nationalistic aspirations of the homegrown bourgeoisie, but to open the road to liberty for the proletariat of the colonies . . . There are two distinct movements that grow farther apart every day. One is the bourgeois-democratic national movement, whose program calls

---

[14] *Der I. und II. Kongress der Kommunistischen Internationale*, East Berlin, 1959.

for political independence within a capitalistic order. The other is
that of the poor and backward peasants and workers . . . In its
initial phase the revolution in the colonies will not be a communistic
one. But if at the very outset a communist vanguard moves to the
forefront, the revolutionary masses . . . will reach the set goal . . .
The leadership of the revolution in the colonies must not be in the
hands of a democratic bourgeoisie." [15]

We note here only that today's Sino-Soviet polemic over the question of policy apropos "national bourgeoisie" has its precedent in the
divergent viewpoints of 1920. Beyond this, the communist attitude toward the bourgeois order during the past decades has been subject to
constant vacillations, changes, and endless backing and filling. Since
1955 alone, dozens of conferences of communist theoreticians in Moscow, Prague, and East Berlin have struggled with this problem. Pre-
dictably, these theoreticians will face new headaches as the young
national states and their leadership gain political and economic
strength and, in their development, follow yet another, a "third road."

THE "LEAGUE AGAINST IMPERIALISM
AND COLONIAL RULE" OF 1927

Following their initial success in China, the Soviets endeavored to
gather together all national leaders of liberation movements everywhere. For this purpose the Congress of the "League Against Imperialism, Against Colonial Rule, and For National Independence,"
chaired by George Lansbury and organized by Willi Münzenberg,
was called from 10-15 February 1927 at Brussels' Palais Egmont. Except for some temporary successes of the Communist Party of France
in West and Equatorial Africa after World War II, it may be said
that this 1927 Congress, which the Soviets inspired, was their last
great success in influencing the nationalist leaders of Asia and North
Africa before the new turn in Soviet policy of 1955. The People's Republics of Korea and also of North Vietnam arose under different
auspices. And even Stalin did not dare claim Mao Tse-tung's takeover
in China in 1949 to be a result of his own policies.

In his opening comments at the 1955 Bandung Conference, Sukarno
recalled the Brussels congress. He said: "Only a few decades ago it
was often necessary for the spokesmen of our nations to travel to
other countries, even other continents, to confer with each other. In
this connection I think of the conference of the League Against Imperialism and Colonialism in Brussels about thirty years ago. Many
of those present here today met at that conference and found renewed

---

[15] *Protokoll des II. Kongresses der Kommunistischen Internationale,* Hamburg
1921, pp. 145-152.

strength in their struggle for independence." [16] The Soviets were unable to listen to these words, for the inspirers of Brussels in 1927 were excluded from Bandung in 1955.

The Dutch cultural historian Jan Romein reports: "In the first half of February 1927 in Brussels' Palais Egmont—the name recalls the Dutch hero during the "colonial" struggle against Spain—was held the Congress Against Colonial Subjugation and Imperialism, which was organized by a small revolutionary group of the League Against Imperialism and For National Independence. Nehru and Hatta will recall the event, for both spoke at the congress. Those who read the report on this congress today realize the better that freedom calls for sacrifices, many sacrifices. For all of the other twenty-five who held forth at the time are either dead or at least out of power." [17]

The concluding remark is particularly pertinent to the communist organizers of that congress: all fell victim to Stalin's purges.

The Brussels Congress Against Imperialism and National Repression produced an organization which may be considered the precursor of the Solidarity Organization, founded in Cairo as an outcome of the Solidarity Conference of the Peoples of Asia and Africa held at Cairo in December 1957 and January 1958. The new Moscow Friendship-Among-Nations-University, opened in 1960, also had its models in the Sun Yat-sen University and the University of the Workers of the Orient, both dating back to the 1920s.

The elimination of the national leaders who, in contrast to the Communist Party, were influential in their respective countries, began a few years after the Brussels Congress Against Imperialism. After the defeat of Soviet policy in China, the radical course against the "nationalist bourgeoisie" gained the upper hand.

Stalin's assessment of national leaders such as Nehru, Hatta, and others, began to dominate. As early as 1925 Stalin denigrated these leaders by commenting:

"Since this well-to-do and influential bourgeois faction fears the revolution more than imperialism, since it is more concerned over its own advantages than over the fate of the country, it stands foursquare in the camp of the intractable enemies of the revolution and unites with imperialism against the workers and peasants of its own homeland." [18]

This view of the "reactionary role of the bourgeois-nationalist leaders" in the colonial and semicolonial states became intensified at the

[16] Horst Sasse, *Die asiatisch-afrikanischen Staaten auf der Bandung-Konferenz,* Frankfurt/Main-Berlin 1958, p. 40.
[17] Jan Romein, *Das Jahrhundert Asiens,* Berne 1958, p. 414.
[18] Stalin, *Werke,* Vol. 7, Berlin 1952, p. 128.

Sixth Party Congress in the summer of 1928. Here it was emphasized that victory in the struggle for national liberation can come only under the leadership of the proletariat with the Communist Party in the vanguard. Based on the thesis of the inevitable downfall of capitalism, the congress also asserted the impossibility of technical progress and development of the means of production in the colonies. Not until the Twentieth Party Congress were these assertions revised. But meanwhile these nationalist leaders (some of whom still play a role in Asia today) who had been adversely "assessed" could scarcely be retained as members of the anti-Imperialist League. Nehru commented on his expulsion in his inimitable manner:

"In later years the League Against Imperialism drifted toward communism, even though, as far as I know, it never lost its independent character. I was able to maintain only loose contact with it through correspondence. In 1931 the League became extraordinarily angry with me because I took part in concluding the Truce of Delhi between the National Congress and the Government of India. I was excommunicated in grand style, actually the League expelled me on the basis of some resolution. I confess there was reason to be angry with me, but I should have been afforded an opportunity to present my side." [19]

In those days the Soviets ill-advisedly removed from the anti-imperialist movements, which they themselves inspired, those national forces which they woo today. Stalin's policy of "socialism in one country" and the doctrine of the "leading role of the working class with the Communist Party in the vanguard" in the struggle for national freedom, led to the isolation of the Soviets from the events in Asia and Africa.

THE EASTERN DESK OF THE "RED INTER-NATIONAL OF LABOR UNIONS" (RILU)

The "leading role of the working class in the struggle for national freedom" was to be assured, as was already brought out in the tenets of the Second Party Congress, through the buildup of communist parties and also through activation of trade union movements in Asia, Africa, and Latin America. For the latter purpose, the Executive Bureau of the Moscow "Red International of Labor Unions" (RILU, also known as "Profintern") maintained, since the middle of 1927, a Pacific Secretariat, with temporary headquarters in Hankow and Wuhan. Also organized during the 1920s was a Latin American Sec-

---

[19] Nehru, *Indiens Weg zur Freiheit*, Berlin-Zurich 1957, p. 185.

retariat of the RILU, from which emerged the presently involuntarily dormant *Confederación de Trabajadores de America Latina* (CTAL). Guidance of the entire activity of the RILU in the Orient came from the Eastern Section (also called "Eastern Desk") of the RILU in Moscow. This office had been in existence since 1925.

There exists a highly interesting report that covers the activities of this Eastern Desk until 1927. Today, at a time when the union activities of the Soviet bloc in underdeveloped countries have assumed entirely different proportions, such reports are no longer made public. Since the report furnishes insight into the system and working methods of such Eastern Desks, some excerpts from it are given:

The Eastern Section of the RILU is active in the two areas of organization and information.

Organizational activity included:

1. Examination of material for the reports of the Executive Bureau of the RILU concerning questions pertaining to Eastern countries. Number of reports submitted: China, 37; Japan, 11; Korea, 2; India, 10; Indonesia, 9; the Philippines, 1; Australia, 5; Pacific States, 10; Turkey, 5; Syria, 3; Palestine, 8; Egypt, 2; Persia, 1; North Africa, 4; South Africa, 4; the Far East, 1.

2. Collaboration with the several commissions on questions concerning Oriental countries. The material in the hands of these commissions served the Executive Bureau of the RILU as basis for resolutions, programs of action, or guidelines for the Eastern Sections of the RILU.

3. Conferring with comrades from the Eastern countries, as with the comrades from China, Japan, India, Indonesia, Turkey, Persia, Egypt, Palestine.

4. Collaboration with the Chinese and Japanese commissions during the session of the Central Council of the RILU in March 1926, in which the action programs for the trade union movements in China and Japan were drawn up.

5. Autonomous correspondence with the sections of the RILU in the East. Counseling the latter in diverse questions of the trade union movement.

6. Continuous contact with the international professional secretariats, and supplying them with information on all Eastern countries.

7. Participation at the meetings of the individual secretariats of the Communist International, the Sports International, the International Red Aid, and other international organizations, if the agenda included Eastern questions.

8. Organization of trade union courses (1926-27) for students of Eastern universities. Additionally, in February and March 1927,

courses for the Chinese trade union delegation during its stay in Russia.

Informational activity included:

Readers have been recruited for the various Eastern countries (Japan, China, India, Indonesia) and Near East colonies and dominions, who daily peruse over a hundred Eastern foreign-language newspapers and periodicals, among them eighteen in Japanese, Chinese, Arabic, and Turkish. These readers also follow up new foreign-language literary publications that treat Eastern problems.

The Eastern Desk issues a Russian language "Weekly Digest on the Economic Situation and Workers' Movement in Eastern Countries." Until March 1927 this digest appeared for internal use only. After that it was built up to press service size (*The East and the Colonies*).

In August 1927 began the publication of a semimonthly, also under the title *The East and the Colonies,* in English and French (a German edition appears in slightly altered form in Berlin). The magazine contains articles dealing with diverse Eastern questions only and is dispatched to 175 foreign newspaper and magazine editors who frequently reprint material from it.

In addition the Eastern Desk also informed the RILU Executive Bureau on special matters, as for example the delegations of the RILU and of the Central Council of the trade unions of the USSR on the Pacific Conference and on the 1927 Chinese Trade Unions Congress.

In 1927 the Eastern Desk prepared brochures for the RILU press in Turkish, Persian, and Arabic. At the same time, it assisted the international professional secretariats in the publication of brochures in Eastern languages for workers of diverse trades employed in the USSR.[20]

THE NEGRO QUESTION AND THE INTERNATIONAL TRADE UNION COMMITTEE OF NEGRO WORKERS

The "liberation of the Negroes," which in the communist vernacular of the day meant the peoples of Dark Africa, was to be achieved by winning over the American Negro. The Fourth Party Congress of November-December 1922 had the "Negro Question" as item number 10 on its agenda. The speaker on this question, Billing, emphasized that the American Negroes "because of their history" assumed an "important role in the liberation of the whole race." The congress resolved to call a "Conference of Negro Workers" for the purpose of

---

[20] *Die internationale Gewerkschaftsbewegung in den Jahren 1924 bis 1927,* Berlin 1928.

"organizing the Negro movement on a worldwide basis." However, six years were to pass before events proved propitious for preparing such a conference. The opportunity arose in 1928 at the Sixth Party Congress, at which the American communist delegation included several prominent Negroes, among them James W. Ford, repeatedly Presidential candidate of the United States Communist Party, and George Padmore, who upon Ghana's independence became President Kwame Nkrumah's advisor on foreign policy. The Executive Bureau of the Red International of Labor Unions invited the Negro delegates of the Sixth Party Congress to a nonscheduled meeting on 31 July 1928. "Following a lively discussion in which the comrades Losovsky, Heller, Wilson, Engdahl, Foster, Johnstone, Philipps, Jones, Delobelle, Germanetto, Roux, Bunting, Haywood, Hardy, Carleton, and others took part," the RILU Executive Bureau adopted resolutions of which it was said at the time that "they were of the highest importance for the entire Negro proletariat of America and Africa."

It was decided:

1. To establish within the RILU an "International Trade Union Committee of Negro Workers," to consist of two representatives of the Negro workers of the United States (Ford and Padmore) and one representative each of the Negro workers of South Africa, Guadalupe, Martinique, and Cuba. At the time, there were as yet no representatives within reach from Haiti, East Africa, Brazil, Colombia, and Venezuela. These were, it was stated, to be added later to the Negro Trade Union Committee.

2. To direct the Negro Trade Union Committee to organize the Negro workers, to establish trade union alliances, and "to work toward uniting the colored workers of the world on a class struggle basis."

3. To direct the committee to issue a magazine specifically aimed at Negro workers.

4. To prepare for and call an international conference of Negro workers.[21]

Early in 1929 this International Trade Union Committee of Negro Workers issued an elaborate action program couched in class struggle idiom.[22] Both Comintern and Profintern made available also the services of the aforementioned Brussels "League Against Imperialism" in the preparation of the RILU-planned international conference of colored workers. At the Second Congress of this League (July 1929, in Frankfurt/Main) James W. Ford announced the First International Conference of Negro Workers for 1 July 1930 in London. However,

---

[21] *Internationale Presse-Korrespondenz* (*Inprekorr*) (Berlin), No. 84/1928, p. 1532.
[22] *Inprekorr*, No. 38/1929, pp. 913-15.

"in May 1930 the conference organizers were informed by the British Labor Government that no permission for the conference would be granted." Thus the attempt at creating an organization for communist influence in Africa was shifted to Hamburg, where the International Conference of Negro Workers was opened 7 July 1930. Originally planned for ten days, it came to an end after only three. The response was also less than expected. Participating in the conference were "delegates from seven important United States Negro unions including a Negress, as well as delegates from Jamaica, Nigeria, Gambia, Sierra Leone, the Gold Coast, from the former German Cameroons, and a white delegate from the Negro workers' organizations of South Africa. Because of the absence of representatives from the French colonies, from East Africa, the Belgian and Portuguese areas, and Latin America, this first gathering of Negro workers was essentially a preparatory conference." But another conference of this type never did take place.

At this Hamburg International Conference of Negro Workers of the RILU a new International Trade Union Committee of Negro Workers was elected. Its composition was as follows: James W. Ford (chairman—USA), J. Hawkins (USA), George Padmore (USA), F. Macauley (Liberia), G. Small (Gambia), Albert Nzula (South Africa). Spaces were reserved on the committee for representatives from Haiti, Liberia, and East Africa. With Hamburg as its base, this committee, assisted by the RILU, endeavored to propagandize the colored workers of America and Africa. Following the Hamburg conference, the committee issued an English language propaganda magazine *The Negro Worker*, which was disseminated in American and African harbor cities with the help of the "International Propaganda and Action Committee of the Transport Workers of the RILU" (Seamen's and Dockworkers' International—SDI) and Hamburg's "International Seamen's Club." [23]

This attempt to gain influence in Africa by means of an international trade union committee of Negro workers failed largely for three reasons:

1. The committee's battle slogan of "class against class" as propagandistic rallying cry was ill-suited for Africa. As recently as 1963, even left-oriented union leaders such as Sékou Touré rejected, among other things, the communist doctrine of class warfare, insisting that African society is classless.

2. While the Second Party Congress had already underscored the necessity of firmly opposing Pan-Slavic and Pan-Asiatic movements,

---

[23] *Inprekorr*, No. 57/1930, p. 1290; No. 59/1930, p. 1382; No. 60/1930, pp. 1417-18.

the Trade Unions Committee of Negro Workers of the RILU saw its main task in fighting the "Garvey Movement," and Pan-Africanism. The latter, however, then as now had strong roots among the African intelligentsia. Thus it was not by chance that one of the organizers of the International Trade Unions Committee of Negro Workers, George Padmore, put Pan-Africanism in contraposition to Communism when he broke with the latter in 1934. He called the book containing his basic tenets *Pan-Africanism or Communism?—The coming struggle for Africa.*[24]

3. The plan to win over the population of Africa with the help of the Negro workers of the United States proved illusory. A communist commentary noted soon after the Hamburg Conference of Negro Workers: "The Negro conference revealed a distinct difference between the Negroes from the United States, who are industrial workers with pronounced proletarian habits, and the African delegates, who think like peasants. The special circumstances surrounding the Negro problem in Africa necessitate divergent methods and special tactics for the American Negro workers. Possibly, the latter show a tendency to see the African Negro question too much from the American viewpoint."[25]

THE POPULAR FRONT IN AFRICA: THE FRENCH COMMUNIST PARTY AND THE "RASSEMBLEMENT DÉMOCRATIQUE AFRICAIN"

Until the 1950s, the affairs of the national movements in the countries of Asia and Africa—with the exception of China and a few other countries—were put in the hands of the Communist parties of the "mother countries." Only the Communist Party of France was able to score considerable temporary gains after World War II. It, too, was required to follow the general Party line, which held that the national liberation movement can be successful only under leadership of the proletariat, with the Communist Party in the vanguard. But because there was only a feeble working class south of the Sahara, and no Communist Party at all, the Communist Party of France propagated "an alliance between the working class of the exploiter country and the peoples of the exploited colonies." This alliance was to put political leadership safely in the hands of the (French) working class and, with the assistance of the African affiliates of the communist *Confédération Générale du Travail*, leave ultimate control with the French Communist Party. From 1946 to 1950, this policy bore results in West and Equatorial Africa.

---

[24] George Padmore, *Pan-Africanism or Communism?* London-Accra 1956.
[25] *Inprekorr,* No. 60/1930, p. 1418.

"With active assistance from the Communist Party of France, the democratic movement in the French colonies of the Sudan region reached broad segments of the population after World War II. At the head of this movement was the Popular Front organization, the *Rassemblement Démocratique Africain* (RDA), established at a Founding Congress held in Bamako, 19-21 October 1946. The following joined the RDA: the *Parti Démocratique de la Côte d'Ivoire*, the *Sénégalaise Fédération des Indigénes Démocratique* (SFID), the *Parti Progressive du Niger* (PPN), the *Union des Populations du Cameroun* (UPC), and other national democratic organizations that now became sections of the RDA. All these parties were founded during or soon after World War II. In the wake of the Founding Congress of 1946, sections of the RDA were established in those colonies that up to this time had no political parties whatsoever (Guinea, Upper Volta, Dahomey). The RDA, which united all colonies in Equatorial Africa and the Western Sudan, was guided by a *Comité de Coordination* that contained representatives of all ten sections." [26]

The RDA resulted from the collaboration of African national leaders, such as Felix Houphouet-Boigny and Gabriel d'Arboussier, with the French communists. In the light of our present knowledge, it is understandable that the French communists applied every trick in the rule book of communist organization, including the cell system in the villages and democratic centralization, in building RDA. Here were applied the same principles and practices that the Soviet bloc currently brings to bear in the underdeveloped countries: RDA functionaries were trained by the Communist Party of France, newspapers for the African movement were printed in Paris, and communist instructors dispatched to Africa. Funds were made freely available to the African ally, and the African RDA delegates in the French National Assembly sat with the communist faction. Even the World Peace Council included RDA representatives. And as with many an African pilgrim to Peking and Moscow of today, the West considered the RDA functionaries of those days communists.

But in October 1950 this alliance foundered. A majority of RDA leaders under Houphouet-Boigny declared their intention to assume control of the communist-built RDA and thus take struggle for freedom into their own hands. On 19 October 1950 the RDA representatives severed their relation with the communist government faction. Five years later Sékon Touré and his friends also broke with the communist *Conféderation Générale du Travail* and the *Weltgewerkschaftsbund*.

The cause of this break, comparable in some ways with the split

---

[26] *Narody Afriki*, Moscow 1954, p. 353; *Die Völker Afrikas*, Berlin 1961, Vol. I, p. 424.

between the Kuomintang and the Chinese communists of 1927, was that the French communists used the alliance between the Communist Party of France and the RDA first and foremost to strengthen their own inner political position in France itself. In line with official doctrine, they considered the African national leaders incapable of independently conducting the struggle for freedom. The historic truth is that the Communist Party of France, at the time of its participation in the government after 1945, did not in any way sponsor the right of the people of Africa for *selfdetermination to the point of separation from France*. Tunisia, Morocco, and the Sudan achieved independence in opposition to the conception of the French communists. Even the status of the Ivory Coast and other African nations as members of the French community goes beyond the solution propagated at the time by the French communists. It was the intent of the Communist Party of France to retain the former French colonies in Africa with equal rights and duties *within the configuration of the French Union!* In this regard a comment, based on documentary proof, may be cited. The former secretary general of the Tunisian labor union *Union Générale Tunesienne du Travail*, Ahmed Tlily, writes: "At the time [January 1946], we tried to gain the attention of the world for our struggle for freedom. Our application for membership in the [then still united] *Weltgewerkschaftsbund* was sabotaged at the behest of the French communists, then in power in France. For they sponsored the French Union and opposed all movements for independence." [27]

The French communists and communist labor leaders at the time considered themselves the appointed guardians of the people of Africa, to whose own leaders they denied the right and ability to defend their own interests before the international organizations. As recently as early 1956, the French communist CGT expelled from its ranks those African union functionaries who, together with Sekou Touré, had founded the *Confédération Générale des Travailleurs Africains*, an African labor union independent of Paris. [28] In this the French communists followed Lenin's dictum that the right of nations to unrestricted separation must not be confused with the question of opportuneness. [29] In 1945 they considered the separation of the French

---

[27] *Freie Gewerkschaftswelt* (Brussels), May 1960.
[28] Franz Ansprenger, *Politik im Schwarzen Afrika,* Cologne-Upladen 1961, p. 222; *"Vierteljahresberichte der Friedrich-Ebert-Stiftung,"* (Hannover), No. 4/5, September 1961, p. 30.
[29] Thus at a time when the peoples of Africa have achieved the right to make their own decisions, the "thesis of opportuneness" remains an unlaid ghost in French communist literature. See, among others, Elie Mignot, *Der Kampf der Kommunistischen Partei Frankreichs gegen Kolonialismus und für den Frieden in Algerien.* Berlin 1959, p. 13.

colonies from France "not opportune," and wished to incorporate the latter in a "people's democratic France."

It is not within the scope of this book to examine the stand of the Communist Party of France on Indo-China during the "People's Front" years of 1935-38, or its governmental and especially its budgetary policies concerning Algeria, Morocco, and Tunisia at the time of its participation in the government after 1945. This requires a separate analysis which would undoubtedly supply interesting information on the problem of the attitude of the Communist Party of France regarding the colonial and national questions. As late as 1948, the Party, in Point I of the action program of the *Rassemblement Démocratique Africain,* unequivocally asked for "battle for political, economic, and social liberation of Africa *within the framework of the French Union* on the basis of equal rights and duties." [30] For many African nationalists this was neither fish nor fowl.

It may be said that at the time many of the African leaders showed greater foresight than the French communists, just as Sukarno in 1945 and Nehru in 1947, judged developments more accurately than did the Soviets.

SOVIET MISJUDGMENT OF THE YOUNG NATIONAL STATES AND THEIR LEADERS PRIOR TO THE BANDUNG CONFERENCE

When in the wake of World War II the first independent states appeared in Asia, the Soviet bloc, as did the entire communist movement, lacked all experience in coping with this new departure in global politics. The majority of the newly independent nations subscribed to a neutralist foreign policy and remained outside the two major power blocs. The Soviet concept of "two world camps," promulgated at the 1947 Comintern conference and further strengthened in 1952 by Stalin in his *Economic Problems of Socialism,* allowed no place for third forces, neutralism, or freedom from bloc alignment. Soviet theoreticians saw in this "neutralism" a maneuver to disguise "incorporation into the imperialist camp." Until the mid-1950s, Soviet bloc publications contended that the national bourgeoisie could not effectively represent national interests. Soviet theoreticians proclaimed that the national-bourgeois leaders, once governmental powers are in their hands, will cease "their oppositional role and become the obedient tools of the ruling circles of the colonial power." [31]

A few examples from the plethora of material should amply demon-

---

[30] *Narody Afriki, loc. cit.,* p. 353. Italics are author's.

[31] *Der imperialistische Kampf um Afrika und die nationale Befreiungsbewegung der Völker* (Russ.), Moscow 1951, p. 258.

strate how lacking in realism was the Soviet estimate of Afro-Asian developments as late as 1955.

Since Lenin's time the Soviets had paid particular attention to developments in India. The *Great Soviet Encyclopedia* writes as follows about the growth of India's national-revolutionary movement under leadership of the Congress Party during the years 1918-22: "The Indian bourgeoisie and big landowners sought to canalize the burgeoning uprising among the people and, by assuming leadership and control over it, use it to gain concessions from the English imperialists. Gandhi and his Gandhism gained even greater popularity among the Indian middle-class nationalists. Gandhism, the doctrine of nonviolence towards the oppressors, was used by the bourgeois, nationalist-reformist politicians to weaken the revolutionary energies of the masses and to gain control over them." [32]

And in another volume of the *Great Soviet Encyclopedia* Gandhi is characterized as follows: "Gandhi's role in the evolution of the national liberation movement reflects the traitorous attitude of India's upper classes and of the liberal landowners. These made common cause with the imperialists against the people and looked upon their own people as their chief enemy. They tried to enlist the national liberation movement in their own service in order to obtain concessions from the imperialists . . . Gandhi paid lip service to the condemnation of big business and England's colonial policy, and in demagogic fashion called himself a spokesman for Indian independence and an enemy of England . . . The English imperialists used Gandhi and his influence over the masses for their own purposes. In his political report before the Central Committee of the Sixteenth Party Congress Stalin, speaking of the swelling tide of the revolutionary movement among the Eastern peoples, stated: 'The bourgeois gentlemen seek to drown these countries in blood, relying on police bayonets, and calling on people of Gandhi's type for help.' " [33]

In August 1947 India achieved independence and sovereignty, and in January 1950 the Republic of India was established. To the Cominform, this world-important event was meaningless. The India expert of the earlier Comintern, R. Palme Dutt, in his 1951 book *India Today* sketched the attitude of the new Cominform toward an independent India under Nehru's leadership. This book shows how unrelated the Soviet bloc policies were to reality. Palme Dutt wrote:

"The new regime has not solved the Indian crisis. It has not brought freedom to India's masses. It has not removed India from the sphere of imperialist influence. The 'transition of power' brought indeed an

[32] *Great Soviet Encyclopedia* (Russ.), Moscow 1953. Vol. 18, p. 68.
[33] *ibid.*, Moscow 1952, Vol. 10, p. 203.

important political change. It has shifted imperialist rule from a direct to an indirect role. It has changed the former vacillatory, semi-oppositional and compromise-prone role of the Indian upper class at the head of the people's mass movement to that of the junior partner of imperialism." [34] "Indian bourgeoisie nationalism burgeoned into Indian neo-imperialism," [35] claimed Palme Dutt, labeling "India the Asian policeman of imperialism." [36] It is no wonder that after these "determinations," Dutt reaches the conclusion: "The change signifies that the leaders of India's upper class have ceased to play the leading role in the national freedom movement, that they have joined the counterrevolutionary camp and formed a bloc with imperialism." [37]

In like vein A. M. Diakov, the Soviets' India expert who plays a role to this day, wrote in 1951: "India, whose government party is the Congress Party, which allegedly adheres to Gandhi's teaching of nonviolence, today is a country in which the dictatorship of bourgeoisie and landowners appears in its most flagrantly terroristic form." [38] Today, such "evaluations" of India may be found again in the *Peking People's Paper*.

Similar commentaries about national-revolutionary freedom movements in other countries, about their leaders, and about the new nations recently become sovereign and independent, were compiled by the Soviet experts at the very time of preparation for the Bandung Conference. The Arab League was described in Soviet literature as a "reactionary and nationalistic agency, a creature of British imperialism." In her 1953 article "The Imperialistic Battle over Africa and the Peoples' Liberation Movement," the Soviet Egyptologist L. N. Vatolina assessed Naguib, the Egyptian leader of the coup d'état against the corrupt Farouk regime, as a brutal reactionary. She called the land reform, initiated by Naguib, a "measure in support of the Kulaks."

Most bitterly attacked of all during these years was Southeast Asia's most radical national leader, Sukarno, and the young Indonesian Republic. The recently deceased Soviet authority on Africa, I. I. Potekhin, claimed that the national struggle for independence, which led to the establishment of Indonesia in 1945, "because of the cynical sellout of the national bourgeoisie, led by the clique Sukarno-Hatta, ended in abject defeat and the imposition of an American-Dutch imperialistic dual yoke, disguised by the hypocritical signboard 'Republic.' " [39]

---

[34] R. Palme Dutt, *Indien heute,* Berlin 1951, pp. 648-49; an English edition *India Today* appeared in Bombay in 1949.

[35] *ibid.,* p. 648.

[36] *ibid.,* p. 648.

[37] *ibid.,* p. 649.

[38] A. M. Diakov, *Indien und Pakistan,* Berlin 1951, p. 70.

[39] *Sovetskaya etnografiya* (Moscow), No. 3/1950, p. 235.

A. A. Guber, Soviet specialist for Southeast Asia, commented similarly about Indonesia.[40] Kwame Nkrumah's Convention People's Party fared no better than India's Congress Party at the hands of Soviet evaluators. The first election success of this party, in February 1951, earned the comment that it "mirrors the interests of the upper classes and does not justify the confidence of the people." The party was accused of collaborating with British agents and of having supported the latter against labor leaders friendly to the *Weltgewerkschaftsbund.* Nkrumah was charged with opportunism and readiness to compromise.[41] In 1959 the Soviet Africa specialists D. A. Olderogge and I. I. Potekhin wrote about Africa in general: "On the whole, the evolution of the concepts of the African national bourgeoisie confirms the general rule that with the growth of political independence of the masses the national bourgeoisie moves closer to imperialism." [42]

Following Yugoslavia's bolt from the Soviet bloc and Tito's promulgation of "positive neutrality," the Cominform turned sharply against the nonaligned and neutralistic stand of the young national states. Since a latter-day Soviet press often puts a positive interpretation on Nehru's neutralism, it is interesting to note that R. Palme Dutt in 1951 still could say the following about neutralism: "At the time when India achieved its new Dominion status its foreign policy was often proclaimed by India's leaders to represent a policy of neutrality toward the two Western blocs. It is obvious that this interpretation of neutrality already tacitly admitted a separation from the anti-imperialistic camp with which Indian nationalism had been formerly allied." And Dutt adds: "The thin veneer of 'neutralism' was only to cloak the lineup with imperialism and the Anglo-American bloc." [43]

It should be mentioned that at the same time Soviet theoreticians considered the nationalist leaders of Asia as "agents of imperialism" and the proliferation of new national states as an "imperialistic stroke of genius," Moscow unreservedly supported Mao Tse-tung's thesis that national liberation and independence are possible only along lines of the Chinese model. Applying Mao's partisan strategy, however, the communists now led the "battle for genuine independence" against the new national governments of India, Burma, Indonesia, the Philippines, and other countries. The result was that the communists became com-

---

[40] *Die Krise des Kolonialsystems—der nationale Befreiungskampf der Völker Ostasiens,* Essay Collection (Russ.), Moscow 1949, pp. 178ff.

[41] *Narody Afriki, op. cit.,* pp. 350-52.

[42] *ibid.* A lucid picture of the change in the Soviet Africa policy emerges by comparing the Russian issue of *Narody Afriki* of 1954 with its German translation, *Die Völker Afrikas,* Vols. I and II, Berlin 1961.

[43] R. Palme Dutt, *Indien heute, op. cit.,* pp. 647-48.

pletely isolated in these countries, a position from which they have not been able to escape to this day in Burma and Malaya.

This condensed survey was all the more necessary since this aspect of Soviet Afro-Asian policy is also being forgotten in the underdeveloped countries during the current Soviet propaganda wave about their unselfish aid programs. The survey shows how unwarranted the claim is that "Moscow had a hand" in the national-revolutionary movement that led to the inception of new states in Asia and Africa. To Moscow, the events in Asia and Africa came as *faits accomplis*. Developments in the Afro-Asian region itself, made plain for all to see in the preparation for and conduct of the Bandung Conference, forced Moscow to a change in attitude and policy, and to a revision of its theory concerning the new states and the leaders of the national movements of this region. It must be recalled that Sukarno proclaimed Indonesia's independence in 1945, and that India was granted its sovereignty in 1947. Burma, Ceylon and other countries became independent in 1948. But neither in the decisions of the Cominform meetings of 1947 and 1948, nor in the resolutions and speeches of the Nineteenth Party Congress in October 1952 were these new departures assessed. They were not even deemed worthy of notice. The Soviet bloc politicians considered only Mongolia, North Korea, North Vietnam and, since 1949, China as countries that had "achieved independence."

The first revision of Soviet policy concerning the underdeveloped countries began in 1955. But the official announcement of a new approach to the new national states of Asia and Africa came only at the Twentieth Party Congress in February 1956. On the international level, the session of the Communist and Workers' Parties, held November 1957 in Moscow, defined the new problems.[44]

However, it should be mentioned that the entire political and theoretical arsenal of the Soviet bloc is still incapable of providing answers to all problems created by the new situations in the individual countries and continents—Asia, Africa, Latin America. Above all, today's Soviet theoreticians must come to grips with the "third course," the "nonviolent course," the diverse concepts of socialism in Asia, and with "African socialism." Past Soviet research only considered North Africa, disregarding the rest of the continent. The Soviet bloc's specialists for underdeveloped areas thus were also caught unawares when "Africa's hour" dawned. Today they are all the more eagerly trying to catch up. Indicative of and applicable to the entire Soviet bloc are the statements made by Professor Walter Markov at

---

[44] *Erklärung der Beratung von Vertretern der Kommunistischen und Arbeiterparteien der sozialistischen Länder,* Berlin 1957.

East Germany's Africa Conference, held in Leipzig on 17-18 April 1959. He commented:

"It must be admitted in all honesty that the successful breakthrough of the African freedom movement has run ahead of its statistical and theoretical digestion by our historians—as far as I can see, and not only here in Leipzig. Once again Marx was proved right in saying that a revolutionary deed outweighs a dozen programs. At the same time, the development has thoroughly tweaked our historians' noses and exhorts us to immediate action and not to wait until the dust has settled and the time is ripe for easy acknowledgement and reflection." [45]

THE UNDERDEVELOPED STATE OF SOVIET BLOC INSTITUTES AND RESEARCH CENTERS UP TO 1955

As is to be expected from the kinds of assessments the Soviet bloc institutes and research centers for analysis of the problems of underdeveloped countries made, the institutes themselves were underdeveloped until 1955. Discounting the small number of feeble communist parties, a few sections of the *Weltgewerkschaftsbund,** and the World Peace Movement which maintained branches in India, Indonesia, and Egypt, the Soviet bloc had practically no organizations, institutions, or procedures for operating in the countries of Asia, Africa, or Latin America before the Bandung Conference. Thus Mikoyan complained at the Twentieth Party Congress in 1956: "There still exists an institute at the Academy of Sciences which devotes itself to Eastern problems. But of this institute it may be said that, whereas the whole East has awakened in our time, the institute blissfully slumbers on. [movement in the audience, laughter.] Hasn't the time come for this institute to concern itself with the needs of our times? Just as difficult to understand is the dissolution of the 139-year-old Moscow Institute of Oriental Studies, precisely when our bonds with the East are growing stronger; when increased political, economic and cultural contacts with the Eastern peoples have enormously increased Soviet public interest in these peoples, as it has raised the demand for people who are familiar with the languages, economy, and cultures of these peoples." [46] At the same Party Congress the recently deceased veteran communist Otto Kuusinen admitted that the tenets of the Sixth Party Congress (1928) and the criticism of Gandhi had been in error. Symptomatic also was the fact that the First Con-

---

[45] *Geschichte und Geschichtsbild Afrikas—Studien zur Kolonialgeschichte und Geschichte der nationalen und kolonialen Befreiungsbewegung,* East Berlin 1960, Vol. 2, p. 25.
[46] *Protokoll des XX Parteitages der KPdSU,* Vol. II, Düsseldorf 1956, p. 118.
* *World Federation of Trade Unions (WFTU).*

gress of Soviet Orientalists was held only in June 1957, in Tashkent, forty years after the founding of the Soviet Union.[47]

Once more on Africa: A plan to establish a homogeneous Center of African Studies—an African Institute—was first broached in mid-February 1958 at a coordinating conference of the Soviet Institute of Oriental Studies and the Institutes of Ethnography, World Economy and International Relations, and Geography. The new institute was not founded until late 1959.[48]

A Latin America Institute was not established at the Soviet Academy of Sciences until the end of 1961, whereas the Chinese have maintained an Institute for Latin American Affairs in the Central Committee of the Communist Party of China since 1959.

The Soviet's pre-1955 concepts of Afro-Asiatic problems make it clear why Soviet bloc economic aid to underdeveloped countries is only of recent date. Thus the USSR extended its first credit to an Asiatic nation outside the Soviet bloc in 1954. This was a credit of 5.6 million dollars to Afghanistan. Other members of the Soviet bloc extended sizeable credits only after 1956. Therefore it is wrong to assume that the International Conference of World Economy (called by a Soviet-inspired committee, with the assistance of the World Peace Council, in Moscow from 3-12 April 1952) initiated the Soviet bloc to the idea of rendering economic aid. Nor should it have been expected of the Soviet Union to come to the aid of countries whose governments were deemed "agencies of imperialism." Actually, the International Conference of World Economy served only one purpose: to attract Western businessmen and help the Soviet bloc break out of its isolation from world trade. Of the 471 delegates at this conference, 122 came from Asian, African, and Latin American countries (excluding Soviet bloc countries). The majority of delegates were minor industrialists, representatives of private business firms, and functionaries of unions and cooperatives. Entirely absent were representatives of those governments especially wooed by the Soviets today. Only a small number of delegates from underdeveloped countries came from official or semiofficial state economic agencies. A working group for backward countries was nevertheless appointed by the conference. Chairman of this group was India's Professor Gyan Chand, whose report confirms that at the time of the conference the USSR had no program for economic aid for the underdeveloped countries. On the contrary, the same recommendations which Chand submitted are again advanced today for the elimination of East-West competi-

[47] *Pravda*, June 5-14, 1957.
[48] *Sovetskoe vostokovedenie* (Moscow), No. 2/1958, p. 214; *Problemy vostokovedeniya* (Moscow), No. 6/1959, p. 221.

tion in the field of economic aid. He suggested a coordinated approach between advanced and underdeveloped countries, buttressed by a mutual fund from which, in accordance with an international time-table, the underdeveloped nations would draw technical know-how.[49]

In summary, it should be stressed that an evaluation of the degree and depth of the policy change that occurred in the Soviet bloc in this all-important sector of international politics is only possible with a thorough knowledge of the Sovet bloc's pre-Bandung position in rela-tion to events and problems in underdeveloped countries.

Much has been written since the 1956 Twentieth Party Congress about a change in course, about a turning away from the Stalinist past, about reforms in West and East. The Soviet change in policy toward the national freedom movements and the newly independent nations is certainly one of history's most decisive turnabouts.

[49] *Die Internationale Wirtschafts Konferenz—Reden und Materialien*, Berlin 1952, pp. 229-33.

The New Course in
Asia, Africa and Latin America

Eugen Varga, the recently deceased Soviet economist of Hungarian extraction, writes in the chapter "Disintegration of the Colonial System and the National Struggle for Freedom" of his book *The Basic Questions of the Economics and Politics of Imperialism:* "In the past twenty years many of us believed that the colonial nations' struggle for independence would not be victorious unless the proletariat, with the Communist Party in the vanguard, played the leading role. Postwar experience has disproved this opinion." [50]

Here Varga admits that experience dictated the change in policy. He explains the change of attitude as follows: "The bourgeoisie is, of course, less consistent than the proletariat or even the peasantry. This is because individual strata of the bourgeoisie share common interests with the imperialist bourgeoisie in the exploitation of labor. On the other hand, the national industrial bourgeoisie is greatly handicapped by the economic policies of the imperialists which interfere with the industrialization of the colonies. This dual character of the national bourgeoisie accounts for the latter's frequent political vacillations. As a rule, the national bourgeoisie leads the battle against the imperialists but is, under certain conditions, ready to compromise. Yet the experience of recent years has been that such compromising is of temporary nature, and after certain intervals the struggle for freedom is resumed, to be carried on until full political sovereignty is achieved. In all this the ideological factors play an important role. The bour-

---

[50] Eugen Varga, *Grundfragen der Wirtschaft und Politik des Imperialismus* (Russ.), 2nd ed., Moscow 1957, p. 339.

geoisie, the civil servants, above all, the intelligentsia, as well as all peoples of the colonies and semicolonies can never forget the political and moral degradations to which the conquerors and colonizers subjected them. It is for this reason that a large segment of the colonial bourgeoisie strives for full national independence, often even to the detriment of immediate personal material interests." [51]

In a footnote, Varga underscores what is contrary to all prior doctrine: "The above explains why the national liberation struggle was often led by men from well-to-do families. Nehru's father was an affluent lawyer, Ceylon's Bandarenaike is a landowner, in Cambodia Prince Norodom Sihanouk came to the fore, and so on." [52]

Varga characterizes here the Soviets' new attitude toward the national leadership corps of Asia and Africa. The Soviet magazine for Oriental studies now even includes some of the big estate owners in the progressive movement, for we read: "A characteristic of the national struggle for freedom is that it has united the patriots and anti-imperialists of all social strata, from the workers and peasants, the core of the movement, to the national bourgeoisie and even a segment of the large landowners. [53]

THE DIALECTICS OF A SOVIET ASIA EXPERT

In 1957 the Soviet Asia expert J. M. Zhukov bluntly declared that all nationalistic and religious organizations that fight for their country's freedom are progressive and merit Soviet support. Also included in this appraisal were anticommunist organizations whose anticommunism—as Zhukov put it—was only a "state of mind" and amenable to other evaluations. From an historical viewpoint, anticommunist groups were to be evaluated as being objectively progressive as long as they fought for national independence.

One might think that time has outdated Zhukov's appraisal. Soviet reaction to communist persecution in Egypt, and to the bloody suppression of communism after the *coup d'état of* 8 February 1963 in Iraq, and their reaction to the dismemberment of Indonesia's Communist Party after the "Movement of September 30, 1965" had failed, show that the appraisal is still in effect. In each of these cases the Soviets protested the persecution of the communists but, to the annoyance of the Chinese, continued their foreign aid programs. Despite his persecution of communists, they regard Nasser as an anti-imperialist whose "progressive role is not yet finished."

Obviously, the Soviets were not merely concerned with an academic

---

[51] *op. cit.*, p. 340.
[52] *op. cit.*, p. 340.
[53] *Sovetskoe vostokovedenie* (Moscow), No. 5/1956.

appraisal of historic processes but with hardheaded politics. It was developments in Africa and Asia that forced the Soviets to abandon their erstwhile standpoint in order to jockey for position in movements from which they were isolated.

FOUNDING OF THE AFRO-ASIAN BLOC

Historically, events show that the Soviets initially sought to gain influence in Afro-Asian affairs by applying well-worn methods and procedures. Efforts had been afoot since early 1954 to call an all-embracing conference of African and Asian nations. Ali Sastroamidyoyo, Prime Minister of Indonesia at the time, publicly submitted such a proposal on 12 January 1954.[54] Informal discussions were held on the subject at the so-called Colombo Conference of 28 April-2 May 1954, called by the five prime ministers: Sastroamidyoyo (Indonesia), Nehru (India), U Nu (Burma), Mohammed Ali (Pakistan), and Sir John Kotelawala (Ceylon). Final decision to call the Bandung Conference for April 1955 came at a meeting of the same prime ministers in Bogor in December 1954.

Between the Colombo and Bogor conferences both the Chinese and the Soviets bestirred themselves. In Point Four of their Colombo communiqué the prime ministers had supported admission of the People's Republic of China to the UN.[55] The Chinese in turn glibly adapted to the new situation. Thus they stole a march on the Soviets at the time, from the right as it were, for at that time the Chinese were going through a rightist phase, of which more anon. In the now abrogated so-called Tibet Treaty of 29 April 1954, which was a Sino-Indian agreement on Tibetan trade, the Chinese were the first to accept Nehru's five principles of peaceful coexistence. Chou En-lai, then China's Premier and Foreign Minister, used the lull of the Geneva Conference of Foreign Ministers (26 April-21 July 1954) to visit Nehru, and in a mutual communiqué (28 June 1954) to reaffirm the five principles. This assured China a seat at the Bandung Conference. Despite all current Soviet bloc interpretations, however, there should be no misunderstanding that the five principles, the *Pancha Shila*, are rooted in Indian thought and were formulated by Nehru on the basis of ancient Indian principles:

1. Mutual respect of territorial inviolability and sovereignty.
2. Mutual nonaggression.
3. Mutual nonintervention in the internal affairs of the other.

---

[54] Horst Sasse, *Die asiatisch-afrikanischen Staaten auf der Bandung-Konferenz*, p. 8.
[55] *Schlusskommunique der Colombo-Konferenz*, p. 34.

4. Equality and common benefits.

5. Peaceful coexistence.[56]

The Soviet Union, under the official explanation that it was not an "Asiatic Power," was not invited to the Bandung Conference. In 1955 India also opposed Soviet participation at the Bandung Conference. But the Soviet-Chinese and Chinese-Indian conflict had altered this situation by 1965, and India actively supported Soviet participation at a Second Bandung Conference which had been scheduled for late 1965 in Algiers but which failed due to Chinese tactics.

The exclusion of the Soviets from the Bandung Conference in 1955 revealed their isolation from the events in Africa and Asia. The Soviets reacted to the preparation for Bandung by still applying the old, familiar method of counteraction. For this the World Peace Movement was enlisted to do yeoman service.

The "World Peace Council" held a Conference for Easement of International Tension in Stockholm from 19-23 June 1954. At this conference the Asian "friends of peace" were separately brought together to lay the groundwork for their own Afro-Asian conference. This parallel Conference of Asian Nations for the Easement of International Tension, called by the Stockholm Indian peace delegation, the feminist Rameshwari Nehru and Congressman Dr. Anup Singh, was held at New Delhi from 6-10 April 1955, immediately preceding the Bandung Conference. Participants included the Bandung-absent Soviet Union, as well as Mongolia, North Korea, North Vietnam, and China. Politically, this conference of lost opportunities was meaningless and, overshadowed by Bandung, soon passed into oblivion. Organizationally, however, it gave birth to the Cairo-centered solidarity movement of the Afro-Asian nations.

During 1956 and 1957 the Soviets skillfully evoked the "Spirit of Bandung" and transposed it propagandistically to the new organization, causing even some Western publications frequently to mention Cairo as a second Bandung.

Thereupon the First Solidarity Conference of the Peoples of Asia and Africa was held in Cairo in December 1957-January 1958, at which the Soviets and Chinese as yet did not oppose each other openly. At the Second Solidarity Conference in 1960 at Conakry the first signs of tension between the Soviets and Chinese became apparent, tensions that affected the entire organization. The Third Solidarity Conference in February 1963 in Moshi, and the Fourth Solidarity Conference in May 1965 in Winneba, were dominated by

---

[56] *Die Verträge der Volksrepublik China mit anderen Staaten*, Frankfurt/M— Berlin 1957, p. 78.

the Soviet-Chinese conflict and struggle for control of the organization, a conflict that was augmented by various nationalistic movements that lacked any party direction.

The long-planned First Solidarity Conference of the Peoples of Asia, Africa and Latin America finally took place in Havana from 3-15 January 1966. Despite the multitude of threats of imminent revolution and actions against the Latin American governments, the conference was lacking in unity. The Soviets sought to retain only one organization (the one of the three continents) but were thwarted by Chinese opposition. So now there are two organizations, the Afro-Asian-Latin American Solidarity Organization with its headquarters in Havana, and the Afro-Asian Solidarity Organization with its seat in Cairo. Neither the Soviets nor the Chinese succeeded in winning a place on the presidium of the new tricontinental organization. The leadership of the organization is in the hands of Cuba, which is presently Soviet-oriented. But let us return to Soviet policies after the Bandung Conference of April 1955.

One could cite several examples to prove that the change in Soviet policy toward the new events in Asia and Africa occurred while the Bandung Conference took place. The Soviet Orientalists became active and, as of April 1955, began to reissue their periodical *Sovetskoe vostokovedenie.*

In the summer of 1955, immediately following the Bandung Conference, Nehru was invited to Moscow. He received a welcome never before witnessed by the Russian people. Among Soviet leaders, travel fever for Asia set in. In November and December 1955 Bulganin and Khrushchev visited India, Burma and Afghanistan. This, too, was an unprecedented event, quite unthinkable under Stalin. Nehru's five co-existence principles, not yet mentioned at the parallel conference in New Delhi of April 1955, but included in the Ten Points of the Bandung Conference, were made part of the resolutions of the Twentieth Party Congress of February 1956 almost *verbatim.* Today, the Chinese and the so-called "enemies of the Party" like Molotov claim with some right that Khrushchev's coexistence policy can hardly be founded on Lenin. As with other concepts, the Soviets took over Nehru's five coexistence principles solely to serve Soviet purposes.

Our analysis is primarily concerned with answering the question: What are the goals of Eastern bloc policies concerning the under-developed nations, and in which direction are the growing number of different organizations to be committed in the underdeveloped nations? To appraise strategy and tactics of the Eastern bloc in the underdeveloped countries, it is necessary to consider five interrelated problems:

1. The role of the backward nations' "positive neutrality" in Soviet politics of coexistence, and competition of the two systems.

2. The Soviet concept of strengthening national sovereignty through economic autonomy for the backward nations.

3. The Soviet view of national independence as a first step, and the concept of the gradual growth of a people's democracy in Phase Two.

4. The new role of the communist parties in the backward nations within the framework of the Soviet bloc's overall design.

5. Peking's strategy and the role of the Latin American center of communism in Havana.

The "Peace Zone"
and "Positive Neutrality"

At the 1956 Twentieth Party Congress Khrushchev summarily declared those uncommitted backward nations that opted for neutrality as constituting a "peace zone." He reasoned at the time:

"The appearance in the arena of international affairs of a group of peace-loving Asian and European nations that have made independence of bloc politics the basis of their foreign policy has greatly increased the forces of peace. The leading political elements in these states rightfully believe that membership in self-centered militarist-imperialist groupings only increases the danger of these states becoming involved in the military adventures of aggressive powers, and of being sucked into the destructive maelstrom of an arms race. Thus there arose in the world an extensive 'zone of peace' that includes socialist as well as nonsocialist Asian and European states. This zone contains vast territories in which live almost one and a half billion people, the greater part of our planet's population." [57]

Since the West at the time showed scant understanding for the neutralist stand of the leaders of Asia and Africa, Khrushchev saw in his "peace zone" move an easy means of pulling the neutralists into the Soviet orbit. This policy, though it did not reap the hoped-for great success, has not been abandoned, either; and the new Party program of the Soviet Union contains references to an "extended peace zone." This zone-of-peace concept is currently applied above all toward a group of underdeveloped states, with India at the head. In these states the Soviet bloc conducts long-range politics, hoping for the future to bring about social-revolutionary changes.

[57] *Protokoll des XX Parteitages der KPdSU, op. cit.*, Vol. I, p. 18.

This political masterstroke of engineering a "peace zone" that for political propaganda purposes admits the inclusion of both the Soviet bloc and the nonaligned states, does not at all represent a recognition of the right of intermediate powers to stand between the two world powers. Rather, it is an adaptation of Soviet politics to the end of gaining allies for Soviet foreign policy and for Soviet peace, disarmament, and coexistence propaganda. By the same standards that Professor Zhukov applied to his appraisal of religious organizations, the neutralists are considered progressive, provided they shun Western entanglements. They are vilified and fought if they oppose the Soviet bloc or the Warsaw Pact.

DUAL NEUTRALITY

It cannot be overemphasized that in the neutrality question there exist very basic differences between the viewpoints of Soviet theoreticians and those of the leaders of the young national states. To Nehru, as to Sekou Touré, neutrality means avoiding politico-military entanglements with East and West alike. But within the "peace zone," in which Khrushchev and his successors included the uncommitted African and Asian nations, there is not and cannot be any neutrality. In a turnabout of their quondam claim that any neutrality is a step toward a "lineup with the imperialist camp," the Soviet bloc today, for tactical reasons, approves of neutrality insofar as it is anti-West. In this the Soviets hope to speed up the process of separation of the former colonies from their mother countries, attempting at the same time to bind the developing nations to the Soviet bloc.

Leaving no dialectic trick untried, Professor Walter Markov sets out to prove that neutral zones or third forces in contraposition to the Soviet bloc are unthinkable. He states: "The qualitative leap forward being made by the African masses in their struggle for freedom does not only reconstruct their own continent. As an active African contribution to world progress, as a return gift to the latter, this forward leap is perforce changing *the relation of the international class forces to each other*. This is the true import of the African peoples' choosing the creative New against the putrescent Old in the entire world. But no one alone may thus creatively intervene in the course of history: *the bipolarity of death and birth knows neither neutral zones nor third forces*. Whoever, in good or bad faith, undertakes the like does in fact side with the colonial imperialists by breaking through the Popular Front, which alone is able to defy and defeat them. Though diverse imperialist nations exist, there is only one imperialist world system, led by the U.S. monopolists. The World Peace Camp includes the socialist states, with the Soviet Union at the head, and the majority of the Bandung nations, the freedom and peace fighters of the countries under capitalistic colonial subjugation. This camp therefore contains a variety of anticolonial and anti-imperialistic movements, but these also stand united in global action to end the colonial-imperialistic outrage." [58]

Communist theoreticians see two sides to neutralism: a positive one to be exploited tactically, and a pernicious, negative one; namely, neutrality toward the Soviet bloc, a neutrality to be fought as a matter of principle. This is brought out clearly in *The African Communist*, which writes:

"At Pan-African conferences and meetings the concepts of 'neutrality,' 'positive neutrality,' and 'nonparticipation in the blocs of the big powers' are popular. *These concepts have a positive side.* They reflect the separation of the former colonies from their respective mother country and from imperialism . . . Thanks to these concepts, the Afro-Asian bloc is able to play a positive role at the United Nations, and many nations of this bloc have taken up the closest contacts with socialist states at diplomatic, economic, cultural, and other levels. *At the same time, there are negative and pernicious sides to this concept of 'neutrality.'* It suggests the identification of the Soviet Union, of the People's Democracy of China, and of other socialist countries, with the imperialist as 'foreign powers' that rule over the peoples of Africa and desire to exploit them. It suggests that for the African nations to retain their independence, they must shun not only the imperialist countries, but the socialistic world system as well, since both forces threaten the African revolution. Under cover of the catchword 'Resist Foreign Ideologies,' imperialist agencies such as Moral Rearmament and the International League of Independent Labor Unions penetrate Africa to spread poisonous slogans and anticommunist political ideas among African nationalists and labor functionaries. These 'neutralists' are not neutral! They are constantly tuned in to imperialism, ready to listen to its recommendations and to keep Africa under its influence, albeit under application of new methods . . . Even though 'neutralism,' if regarded objectively, played, and in the immediate future will continue to play, a necessary role as catchword during the transitory stage away from colonialism, in the future it will change more and more into a reactionary *parole,* put in the service of antisocialistic and pro-imperialistic political aims." [59]

This blunt statement must surely be judged as an answer to the voice of Africa; that is, as a communist polemic against the proponents of genuine neutrality in the Afro-Asian countries. It also refutes the

---

[58] *Geschichte und Geschichtsbild Afrikas, op. cit.,* p. 22. Italics are this writer's.
[59] *The African Communist* (London), No. 3/1960. Italics are the author's.

crudely simplified claim of Western political writers that "all countries, already infected by communism but unwilling as yet to publicly join it, look upon themselves as 'neutral.' [60] It is obvious that the tactical exploitation of neutralism and the proclaimed "peace zone" represents a new propaganda stage of the Soviet bloc for the commitment of its functionaries and organization within the developing countries, as well as for participation of Soviet bloc nations themselves in the various organizations, committees, and meetings in Asia and Africa. On the international level, the USSR seeks to effectuate its "peace zone" policy; that is, to enlist the desire for peace and neutrality of the developing countries in the service of its own proposals and propaganda.

V. Nachimin, in an article dedicated to "the new role of the Eastern nations in the international arena," writes: "The people and the governments of the independent Afro-Asiatic nations decisively oppose the military imperialistic blocs. Today, of the twenty-two states of Southeast Asia and the Near and Middle East only five are members of SEATO and the Baghdad Pact. The many attempts at extending these aggressive alliances all ended in failure. In addition, after Iraq's victorious revolution and that country's withdrawal from the Baghdad Pact, meantime renamed CENTO, this aggressive agglomeration of states plunged into a deep crisis." [61]

In the UN membership of the uncommitted nations, the Soviet Union sees increased political possibilities of operation. Thus, the request of the underdeveloped nations for an increase in foreign aid is linked with disarmament propaganda. In his UN address of 18 September 1959, Khrushchev already proposed that all monies spent on armament be put into an international development fund. *Pravda* commented on the same subject: "Another matter is the establishment of an international aid fund for the underdeveloped areas, with the monies that could be obtained from a reduction in military forces and a curtailment of military budgets. All nations, including the Soviet Union, are burdened with such expenses today. If, in addition, the Cold War could be ended, the armed forces reduced, and the military budgets diminished, the means thus made available could in all justice be turned over to the international aid fund for poorly developed countries." [62]

The new attitude of the Soviets toward the uncommitted nations

---

[60] Thus Suzanne Labin, *Die politische, wirtschaftliche und taktische Tätigkeit der Sowjetregierung in den Entwicklungs ländern.* (Russ.), XIII. *Konferenz des Instituts zur Erforschung der UdSSR,* Munich 1961, p. 27.
[61] *Mezhdunarodnaya zhizn* (Moscow), No. 5/1960, pp. 54-55.
[62] *Pravda,* 22 October 1959.

in the underdeveloped areas, the "peace zone" policy, is, it should be noted, far more flexible and versatile and tailored to the mental processes of the Afro-Asian leaders than the Soviet politics of the past. Foremost in the ranks of the uncommitted nations, and assiduously wooed by the USSR under the new policy, stands India. "The Republic of India, in territory and population the largest nonsocialist state in the East, deserves a prominent role in the struggle of the Afro-Asian countries for peaceful coexistence." [63]

The *touchstone* that determines not only the attitude of the Soviet bloc, and of the Communist Party in each underdeveloped country toward the government and the national leaders of that country, but also Soviet foreign aid, is whether in Moscow's view the country fits into the "peace zone." As a rule, only "peace zone" countries are included in the Soviet bloc foreign aid program. The exceptions that prove the rule are cases where the Soviet bloc either wants to outdo the West—highly advantageous oil concession offers made by the USSR to Iran—or where an aid offer tends to strengthen forces that strive for separation from the West (Pakistan). Even ideological differences between Soviet bloc leaders and the leaders of Africa and Asia are subordinated to this touchstone. To Nasser's well-known attacks on communism in 1958, Khrushchev reacted in these words:

"We admit to ideological differences between us and several individuals in the United Arab Republic. But on questions of the struggle against imperialism, the consolidation of political and economic independence of countries newly liberated from colonialism, and the fight against war, there is agreement among us. Ideological differences must not impede the development of friendly relations between our countries, nor our common battle against imperialism." [64]

---

[63] *Mezhdunarodnaya zhizn* (Moscow), No. 5/1960, p. 55.
[64] *Concerning the Control Indices of the Development of USSR National Economy 1959-1965* (Russ.), Moscow 1959, pp. 90-91.

Coexistence Strategy
and Underdeveloped Nations

The Twentieth Party Congress of February 1956 did little more than register the new events in Asia and Africa. It merely arrived at final conclusions for the politico-diplomatic as well as foreign aid activities of the Soviet Union and the Soviet bloc. Additionally, it conceived the policy of collaboration with the national leadership corps in the developing nations, in order to exploit their uncommitted and neutral stand. The Congress did not engage in the otherwise customary appraisals of the class composition and driving forces of the national liberation movements, of the character of the new nations, and of the means to further the national and social revolution in the developing countries.

The "peace zone" policy—that is, the strategy of Soviet diplomacy and foreign aid—brought only limited, in part only temporary, results for the Soviet bloc. Reaction was favorable in Indonesia until 30 September 1965, largely because of the internal power structure of that country, and in Cuba. But no gains could be registered in those countries, whose leadership professed "positive neutrality," who ranked foremost in the Soviet foreign policy concept, and who had first call on Soviet credits. In India, communist rule in the state of Kerala was a fleeting episode; Nasser, while offering Cairo as head-quarters for the Soviet-inspired Afro-Asian Solidarity Organization and as switchboard for Soviet bloc activity in the rest of Africa, for years suppressed the communists in his own country and, following the establishment of the UAR in 1958, in Syria as well. Following the *coup d'état* of 14 July 1958, the Communist Party of Iraq gained mass influence, including control of the newly-created trade unions.

Kassem, in his struggle with the Pan-Arabic Nasser supporters, at first leaned on the communists. But when the latter demanded a voice in the government in summer 1959, Kassem turned on the Communist Party and the communist trade unions. After the February 1963 *coup,* the Communist Party of Iraq was destroyed. Nor did the communists realize their goals in Algeria.

AFRO-ASIA'S "THIRD WAY" FORCES POLICY REVISION

More important than all else, the national leadership corps of Asia and Africa once again stole a march on the Soviet theoreticians. The Afro-Asian leaders and statesmen had early begun to develop their own, independent concepts. Nehru proclaimed a "state along socialistic patterns" and emphasized that "the concept of communism is inapplicable in India, because communism speaks with the voice of force." Sukarno's "just society" is to be "socialism, Indonesian style." For Burma, U Nu conceived a "Burmese socialism," since made the program of Nu Win's Revolutionary Council. Nasser's Pan-Arabism and "cooperative socialism" served him as a bulwark against West and East. In Africa, progressively becoming decolonized, many concepts of a "third way," of "African socialism," have been proclaimed.

For the Soviet bloc the new dilemma "arises out of the attempt of a number of nationalist leaders and movements of ex-colonial and semicolonial countries to solve post-independence developmental problems with their own revolutionary methods, which will differ sharply from both the classic road of liberal capitalism and the path of communism." [65] These facts forced the Soviet bloc theoreticians to a reappraisal and revision of their policy and theory. Since 1959 this revision has proceeded in the direction of a reactivation of the proletarian class components within the underdeveloped countries, at the same time retaining, however, the "peace zone" diplomacy. The New Program of the CPSU states:

"Political independence does not end the revolution of national liberation. Independence remains feeble and becomes a fiction if the revolution does not lead to fundamental social and economic changes, if it does not solve the most urgent tasks of national rebirth."

Here we are informed that according to communist thought, the problems of the so-called First Phase of the national revolution as Lenin saw it are still to be solved. In his essay "National Democracy —the way to Social Progress," A. Sobolev emphasizes: "Because of

[65] Richard Löwenthal, *Kommunismus und nachkoloniale Revolution, op. cit.,* p. 25.

poorly developed production capacities and because of the international requirements, most underdeveloped countries are incapable of immediately creating a socialistic society." [66]

According to the statement of the eighty-one communist parties of November 1960, the following tasks remain to be accomplished for the completion of Phase One of the national revolution: consolidation of political autonomy; agrarian reform to benefit the peasantry; eradication of vestiges of feudalism; extirpation of the economic roots of imperialistic rule; restriction and gradual removal of foreign monopolies from the national economy; buildup and development of the national industry; raising the standard of living; democratization of public affairs; an uncommitted and peace-oriented foreign policy; furthering of economic and cultural collaboration with socialist countries. To carry out these tasks, and to serve in a sense as an answer to the Afro-Asian leaders' concept, the communist parties in conclave worked out the following strategy to be embodied in the party program:

1. Organization of a four-class alliance of workers, peasants, the nationalist bourgeoisie, and the democratic intelligentsia, in which the Communist Party must strive for sole leadership.

2. Pursuit of the "noncapitalistic road of development." "This road does not guarantee the immediate transition to socialism but initiates the socio-economic evolution that leads to socialism." [67]

3. Formation of a transition state, the "state of national democracy," under the aegis of the four-class alliance.

More will be said later about the "noncapitalistic road of development" and the "state of national democracy." Here we mention only that this strategy is designed to bring about in Phase One of the national revolution those conditions that are a prerequisite to its completion in Phase Two. However, there seems as yet no complete agreement among Soviet theoreticians on the new developmental theory. Sobolev underscores that the "state of national democracy" is a specific form of the noncapitalistic way. At the same time he polemicizes: "In this connection I should like to declare my utter disagreement with those comrades who equate the noncapitalistic way with socialism itself, divorcing national democracy from noncapitalistic development." [68] Yet the author points out that in individual countries, "at a certain level of their economic development and under a favorable constellation of the class forces," the national democratic state "may also be a form

---

[66] *Probleme des Friedens und des Sozialismus* (East Berlin—Prague), No. 2/1963, pp. 126-27.
[67] *ibid.*, p. 127.
[68] *ibid.*, p. 128.

of transition that leads directly to the techno-material basis of socialism." [69] This comment indicates a differentiated political approach by the Soviet bloc to the individual underdeveloped countries and areas, an approach geared to socio-economical development and inter-class relations. The Party program states that in the liberated areas the developmental process of Phase One "may well be complicated and may require a *series of stages.*" Thus in some countries [Burma, Congo (Brazzaville), Guinea, Mali] the Soviet bloc operates for immediate gains; in others (India, Iraq), for future profits. And so we read: In many cases the duration of the noncapitalistic stage of development will be "an episode in the life of society. In other cases, long years of qualitative changes in the socio-economic conditions will be required." [70]

Before we consider the Soviet analysis of the class structure and class groupings of the underdeveloped countries as bases for the differentiated approach, it behooves us to examine the inter-relationship between Soviet bloc strategy in the developing areas, and the general strategy of the Moscow doctrinal center.

First, in the new concept the "noncapitalistic road to development" plays a decisive role. Lenin, as has been mentioned, at the Second Party Congress had already advanced the thesis that under certain circumstances backward nations might arrive at communism without passing through a capitalistic stage. Yet, though the Soviet theoreticians claim that in Stalin's time the Mongolian People's Republic and Tannu Tuva took the "noncapitalistic developmental way," the latter played no role in Stalin's concept and is not even mentioned in his *Marxism and the National and Colonial Questions.* Thus Potekhin writes: "Without the world-embracing socialist system there could be no question of a socialistic evolution of nations that skips the capitalistic stage." [71] There is a causal relationship between the Soviet concept of the "noncapitalistic way," applied in underdeveloped areas, and the general Party doctrine, expressed by the coexistence policy.

Second, Lenin's thesis that "the national liberation movement is one of the streams of world revolution" has again become part of Soviet doctrine. The new Party program states: "The socialist revolutions, the anti-imperialistic libertarian revolutions . . . , as well as all of the democratic movements against national enslavement—all fuse into a homogeneous, world-embracing revolutionary process that undermines and destroys capitalism." Other sources emphasize: "The nationalist libertarian revolution is one of the most vital components of

---

[69] *ibid.,* p. 128.
[70] *ibid.,* p. 128.
[71] *Mezhdunarodnaya zhizn* (Moscow), No. 1/1963, p. 99.

the world-revolutionary process of our time." [72] The strategy that underlies this "world-revolutionary process," that is, to undermine and destroy capitalism, is the policy of coexistence.

WHAT IS COEXISTENCE?

The Twentieth Party Congress of February 1956 raised peaceful coexistence to the position of general Party line and to the basic principle of Soviet foreign policy for the prevention of war as a means of solving international disputes. Beyond this, herein reversing Clausewitz, coexistence since the end of 1959 "is at bottom nothing but continuance of war, only with peaceful means, nothing else but *a type of class warfare* occasioned by the transition from capitalism to socialism." [73] Since 1959, coexistence is therefore "class"-defined. Even in point of time this interpretation of coexistence coincided with the class-oriented reappraisal of Soviet policy in the underdeveloped areas!

Even though the new Soviet leaders, in comparison with Khrushchev, handle the coexistence propaganda line more carefully and de-emphasize their predecessor's claim that the Soviets would shortly catch up with and outstrip the West economically, coexistence nonetheless remains the general policy line of Soviet policy. Several of Khrushchev's exaggerations were modified but his theses on coexistence are still valid. Coexistence, according to the Soviets, is:

1. *The living in peace with each other of states with different social systems* in order to prevent war and to improve mutual economic and cultural relations. Khrushchev said: "We are for peaceful coexistence, not because we are weak, not because we fear the imperialists, but because another war, fought with the frightful weapons systems of today, such as thermonuclear bombs and means for their delivery like the ICBM, would mean the death of untold millions and the destruction on a colossal scale of material wealth that was the work of many generations." [74]

2. *Economic competition between the two systems* in order to overtake the leading capitalist power, the U.S., in the next ten to twelve years in per capita as well as absolute production, and politically to push the West against the wall. These goals are at the core of the Soviet Seven-Year and Twenty-Year Plans. On this, Khrushchev commented: "Our country is now approaching that stage of development

---

[72] *Mirovaya ekonomika i mezhdunarodnie otnosheniya* (Moscow), No. 3/1962, p. 20.

[73] *Probleme des Friedens und des Sozialismus* (East Berlin—Prague), No. 11/1959, p. 11.

[74] N. S. Khrushchev, *Für dauerhaften Frieden und friedliche Koexistenz*, East Berlin 1959, pp. 214-15.

where our well-functioning economy shall permit us to create a surplus of consumer goods. Then our example, and not the study of Marxism-Leninism, will make the meaning of communism plain to many people. The working people of the world will see that only communism guarantees an abundance of material and spiritual goods. This is why victory will be ours! And then those who sneer at the word "communism" today, will also join us." [75]

3. *Reinvigorated ideological struggle*, for—as the new Party program puts it—"the world today is the theater of a bitter struggle between two ideologies, the communist and the bourgeois."

4. *Peaceful coexistence as a specific form of class warfare on an international scale*. On this the new Party program comments: "Peaceful coexistence is the basis of the peaceable competition between socialism and capitalism on an international scale, and as such exemplifies a specific form of class struggle. Through their consistent support of peaceful coexistence, the socialist nations strive to strengthen the position of world socialism in its contest with capitalism. Peaceful coexistence improves the fighting chances of the working class in capitalistic countries, and aids the people of the colonial and dependent areas in their struggle for freedom."

In summary, the four components add up to: *Peaceful coexistence is the strategy of world revolution in the atomic age under leadership of the industrial giant USSR.* Even in the question of leadership, a basic and qualitative difference from Lenin's views is apparent here. In this new concept of coexistence as the strategy underlying the world-revolutionary process, leadership can rest only with a modern industrial power and certainly not with a developing country such as China. It needs hardly be mentioned that neither Lenin nor Stalin can be quoted in support of a coexistence strategy, or that Mao Tse-tung holds decidedly different views.

Lenin spoke of "peaceful coexistence among peoples." By taking up economic ties with the capitalist countries, he tried to gain a breathing spell for further revolutionary struggles ahead. To Stalin, the "peaceful existence of both systems side by side" meant safeguarding the USSR as "refuge of world revolution" for "the establishment of socialism in one country." Mao also accepts coexistence as a means of Chinese foreign policy; he denies, however, that war is evitable. The idea of economic competition was also adopted by the Chinese. As late as 1958 they boasted of catching up to Great Britain's level of raw material production in fifteen years at the latest—to be sure, with the economic help of the USSR. But Mao is completely unwilling to

---

[75] N. S. Khrushchev, *Für den Sieg im friedlichen Wettbewerb mit dem Kapitalismus,* East Berlin 1960, pp. 259-60.

accept coexistence as the strategy of world revolution; coexistence as a diplomatic game on the one hand, and class warfare as well as revolutionary acts in every country on the other, are two fundamentally different things for him. The Soviet coexistence strategy as a general foreign policy line is a long-range proposition. Khrushchev himself spoke of ten to twelve years, once even of twenty years. "Strategy today refers to the Party line for an entire epoch . . . Today, communists speak of strategy, or the strategic line, when referring to the general Party line, the goal of which is to find solutions to the problems of a particular historic stage, and whose base point is the existing interrelationship of the class forces." [76]

Whether, and to what extent, the Soviets will succeed in realizing their ambitious goals is not the concern of our survey. We can only affirm it to be their intent in a "historic stage" to alter favorably the "interrelationship of the class forces in the world" by means of the coexistence strategy. The effect of this strategy on Soviet bloc policy in the developing countries means:

1. Success in the developing countries is tied intimately to a successful outcome of the ambitious internal and external plans. Thus, it is emphasized in *Foundations of Marxism-Leninism:* "Future communist victories will decisively determine which road in their historic evolution the peoples of the liberated areas will take." [77]

2. The Soviet bloc will continue its policy of foreign aid and friendly relations with the national leadership corps also in those underdeveloped countries which promise no immediate results other than failure. The Soviet bloc theoreticians see ultimate control in these countries as a long-range objective, achieved only after shifts in the "internal class interrelationships" as a result of industrialization, after a successful outcome of the overall strategy, and in the hope of "future world victories." This idea is not new; Stalin already mentioned that in the event of a successful "socialist encirclement of the world many countries, because of the 'unfavorable' international constellation, will deem it practical 'voluntarily' to make serious concessions to the proletariat." [78]

In other respects the Soviet strategists are prisoners of their own doctrine. They endeavor to keep the developing nations in a neutral position in order to reduce the number of opponents in the struggle between East and West. This forces them to continue foreign aid to, and maintain friendly relations with, those neutralist states whose internal politics are sharply anticommunist. One of Khrushchev's

---

[76] *Grundlagen des Marxismus-Leninismus*, East Berlin 1950, pp. 402-03.
[77] *ibid.*, p. 804.
[78] Stalin, *Probleme des Leninismus*, Moscow 1938, p. 47.

greatest worries was that India at the time of the Indo-Chinese border conflict would give up its neutrality and ally itself with the West. Nor is it unilaterally true any longer, as the communists claim, that the West was forced to make concessions to the underdeveloped countries because of the political and economic policies of the Soviet bloc. The fact that a great many Afro-Asian nations have chosen a "third road of development" has forced the Soviet bloc, through mere recognition of neutrality alone, to make foreign policy concessions to this "third road," although Soviet theory is sharply opposed to it. But it is Western foreign aid policy that assures these nations their own "third road of development."

What role does the class struggle concept of the Soviet bloc envision for the neutralists?

THE COEXISTENCE STRATEGY OF CLASS STRUGGLE

The meeting of Communist and Worker Parties in Moscow (November 1960) expounded that "contrary to the revisionists' claim, peaceful coexistence by no means implies renunciation of class struggle. The coexistence of states with different social orders is a form of class struggle between socialism and capitalism. Peaceful coexistence creates conditions favorable to the spread of class struggle in capitalist countries and to the national liberation movement among the peoples of the colonies and dependent areas itself." [79]

Many sources confirm coexistence as "a specific form of class struggle on an international scale." Thus the new Party program requires that the nonaligned nations in the "peace zone" be won over as allies, or at least be kept neutral or be neutralized. As Soviet bloc theoreticians explain it, there are *two kinds of coexistence:*

1. Coexistence with the Western Powers as a form of class struggle on a world scale in order to gain the lead on them.

2. Coexistence with the developing nations as a "common, anti-imperialistic front," aimed at defeating the West.

Professor Robert Schulz comments on this tactic as follows: "Our policy toward all nonsocialistic states is determined by the principles of peaceful coexistence. We must *differentiate*, however, between imperialistic and anti-imperialistic states. The young African national states and freedom movements are anti-imperialistic and therefore our friends and allies in the struggle against world imperialism. With them we form a *common, anti-imperialistic front*. Coexistence contains within itself this battle alliance, this anti-imperialistic, anti-colonial oneness." [80]

---

[79] *Die Presse der Sowjet-union* (East Berlin), No. 144/1960, p. 3187.
[80] *Geschichte und Geschichtsbild Afrikas, op. cit.,* p. 174. Italics are this writer's.

But there is yet a third variant of coexistence. For the Soviet bloc experts also count the developing nations in the capitalist camp. And in these nations as well, coexistence, via the common front or second variant, is to furnish favorable bases for the spreading of internal class struggle.

CLASS STRUGGLE REQUIREMENTS IN THE AFRO-ASIAN COUNTRIES

In the spring of 1962, immediately following the Twenty-Second Party Congress, a conference of the Soviet Institute of World Economy and International Relations dealt with the requirements of spreading class struggle in the underdeveloped areas. Of the fourteen published addresses of the conference, the general theme of which was "the current epoch and the roads to development of the liberated nations," no less than three considered the role of the national bourgeoisie after the power takeover. Dzhagunenko spoke on "Trends in societal development of the liberated countries in the present epoch," R. Avakov and G. Mirsky on "Class structure in the underdeveloped countries." [81] The meeting's analysis of the proletarian forces that are to be educated to spur the transition to the noncapitalistic road of development bore very meager results. As was pointed out, the class structure of Afro-Asian and Latin American countries still bears the imprint of different epochs and is therefore extraordinarily complicated.

"The weakness of the industrial proletariat lies in its fragmentation among many small enterprises. The level of concentration of the proletariat, an important factor in determining the latter's role in the socio-political development of the nations, is pitifully low. This is particularly true of businesses in the hands of indigenous capital. A far higher degree of proletarian concentration exists in the mining industry, and in other branches of industry owned by foreign monopolies. The low number of skilled workers also impedes the growth of class consciousness among the proletariat. An important segment of today's working class in these countries are yesterday's peasants, who have not severed all ties with the land but return to the village periodically. These are the causes for the broad inroads made by petite-bourgeois ideology in the ranks of the workers." [82]

With few exceptions, the working class in all of Asia is found to be relatively weak in comparison to the national middle class. In Africa south of the Sahara, however, where all modern social classes are weak, the communist theoreticians reached an opposite conclu-

---

[81] *Mirovaya ekonomika i mezhdunarodnie otnosheniya* (Moscow), No. 3-6/1962.
[82] *loc. cit.*, No. 4/1962, p. 73.

sion in their evaluation of the relation between proletariat and bourgeoisie. The conference found: "The national bourgeoisie as a clearly defined class does not exist in the majority of African nations south of the Sahara. This does not mean that capitalistic conditions are entirely absent in these nations. Such conditions have arisen and continue to develop in the cities, and there is a small number of African entrepreneurs and merchants. But the level of indigenously owned private capital is still extremely low. Even though the working class of several countries is still feeble and numerically small, in almost every case it has formed or is forming into a class. In view of the fact that in many African countries there is no, or almost no, urban or agrarian bourgeoisie nor a feudal class, the above situation is of tremendous importance for the fate of Africa." [83] And for the communist strategy on this continent, one might add.

Though the new Party program boldly declaims "The working class is the most consistent champion of the national revolution, of the national interests, and of social progress," in view of the present debility of this class, it prudently adds: "Industrial development will increase its strength and enhance its role in public and political life." This clearly is counting chickens not yet hatched. In view of their appraisal of the present strength of the working class, the Soviet bloc theoreticians are understandably reluctant to offend the present national leadership corps. True, they claim that today's national bourgeoisie differs from that of the pre-liberation days, that it is now a "class with two faces." "Never in the past have the two political faces of the exploiter class been exposed so clearly and distinctly as in the case of the national bourgeoisie of the underdeveloped countries in our stormy epoch of the two embattled world systems." [84] However, the national bourgeoisie must be granted a probationary period. The congress emphasized: "During the first phase of the liberating revolution the task of the proletariat was relatively simple, being no more than to effect a separation between the main body of the bourgeoisie, which participates in the national freedom movement, and the small handful of indigenous underlings and their cohorts who stand aloof from the struggle or openly support the imperialists and colonizers. The situation changes once the former colonies gain independence. In addition to its attitude toward imperialism, the bourgeoisie's reactionary or progressive character may currently also be judged by how consistently it carries out agrarian reforms and other forms of social reconstruction; by its sincerity, or lack of it, in developing economic and cultural contacts with the socialist coun-

[83] *ibid.*, pp. 72-73.
[84] *Asiya i Afrika segodnya* (Moscow), No. 3/1962, p. 6.

tries; by its stand on questions of war and peace, and so on. Knowing the position of the different bourgeois groups [today divided into upper, middle, and lower middle class] on this or that subject, the proletariat can easily determine which of these groups might cooperate with it in a given situation, which forces must be neutralized, and whom it must relentlessly oppose." [85] Based on this criterion— this is specifically pointed out—even feudalistic forces may be progressive in some ways, insofar as they promote USSR foreign policy or establish relations with the Soviet bloc (Afghanistan).

Soviet bloc theoreticians devote special attention to the intelligentsia of the undercapitalized backward countries. Its social position is deemed feeble and uncertain, while education of the new generation is handicapped by lack of financial support. Here the inference is that this new generation is still malleable, and it is this appraisal that is at the back of the Soviet bloc's increase in educational aid for the training of a national elite.

The new Party program states that the "nationalist bourgeoisie is dualistic in nature" and, insofar as it is objectively interested in prosecuting the anti-imperialistic and antifeudalistic revolution, "its progressive role is not yet ended, nor its capacity exhausted to help solve urgent problems of general national concern." [86] But, the document continues, "to the degree that friction between wage earners and property owners increases and the class struggle intensifies, the national bourgeoisie tends more and more to accommodate itself with imperialism and the indigenous reactionary element." [87] The national leadership corps is here plainly seen as a temporary ally only, thus reverting to the theses of the Second Party Congress which stated that "the revolutionary movement in the colonies and backward countries is to be supported solely for the purpose of collecting the constituent elements of the future proletarian parties."

The new Party program warns against a stereotyped and dogmatic approach toward revolution for national independence. This means that the overall strategy requires careful consideration of the exploitative possibilities inherent in the different Afro-Asian movements and trends. It also means the simultaneous application of "amity and enmity" tactics. These new tactics, which underly the "battle against the reactionary trends of the national bourgeoisie," could easily lead to a strengthening of the Chinese communists who, on the basis of their experiences with Chiang Kai-shek, deny the national leadership corps any revolutionary capabilities whatsoever.

[85] ibid., No. 5/1962, pp. 99-100.
[86] Izvestia, 2 November 1961.
[87] ibid.

This view is not shared by the Moscow theoreticians, who emphasize that "attempts to deny the anti-imperialistic role of the bourgeoisie have been made for a long time, since 1920 as a fact." Here it is admitted for the first time that such was the case even in Lenin's time. What is meant, of course, is the Soviet campaign against Nehru's Congress Party until 1955.

Soviet criticism of the Chinese communists' position is as follows: "The dogmatic, leftist-sectarian denial of anti-imperialist components in the character of the national bourgeoisie greatly circumscribes the national front to which belong—as is known—the working class, the peasants, the national bourgeoisie, and the democratic intelligentsia. This dogmatism artificially divorces the working class from its nonproletarian allies and throws the revolutionary forces into ill-founded strategic and tactical adventures. The leftist-sectarian, dogmatic approach to the national bourgeoisie question is in effect pouring oil on reactionary fires." [88]

In their concept of a "world-revolutionary process" with the Soviet bloc in the lead, the Soviets divide the underdeveloped countries into several groups "on the basis of class evolution and class relation." Each group is carefully analyzed, and a variety of approaches, each applicable to a particular group, is then worked out.

THE COMPOSITION OF THE NATIONAL GROUPINGS

Professor Walter Markov particularized at a scientific conference in Leipzig held 5-8 April 1961: "Internal class relations determine the structure of the anticolonial and anti-imperial popular front, as well as the tempo, thoroughness, and timeliness of the liberation struggle. In some countries the reins are still tightly in reactionary hands; in others, the commanding heights are in undisputed possession of the national bourgeoisie; while national democracies were able to form where the government is firmly allied with the urban and rural working people." [89] A. A. Arsumanyan, director of the Soviet Institute for World Economy and International Relations, also speaks of these three groups of nations in the underdeveloped areas.[90] Countries where "the reins are still tightly in reactionary hands" clearly are those that are Western-aligned, in addition to the eighteen African Common Market-associated states. The Soviet bloc attitude toward these countries is known. Countries whose "commanding heights are in undisputed possession of the national bourgeoisie" include,

---

[88] *Aziya i Afrika segodnya* (Moscow), No. 4/1962, p. 8.
[89] *Probleme des Neokolomismus und die Politik der beiden deutschen Staaten gegenüber dem nationalen Befreiungskampf der Völker*, East Berlin 1961, p. 9.
[90] *Mirovaya ekonomika i mezhdynarodnie otnosheniya* (Moscow), No. 12/1961, p. 13.

among others, India and Iraq; in short, nations that, while important in the "zone of peace" concept, have thus far proved impervious to internal communist influence. It is in these countries that the Soviet bloc applies its long-range policies, and it is these countries (especially India and Iraq) that prove most expensive to the USSR in terms of foreign aid. In the third group of nations Markov includes the "national democratic states."

At the aforementioned meeting of the Soviet Institute of World Economy and International Relations, R. Avakov and G. Mirsky, arguing that "outlook and further growth of the revolutionary independence movement are dependent on the class structure of the underdeveloped countries," arrived at a further differentiation of the latter. They list six nation groups that are partly congruent with Markov's enumeration, but in other cases resulted from a more differentiated view of the "national bourgeoisie states" and the independent African states. These six groups are:

1. Countries with relatively well-developed capitalistic background and a national bourgeoisie in power: India, Ceylon, Lebanon, Tunisia, Brazil, Mexico. India is said to have evolved a big-business class with monopolistic tendencies.

2. A group of nations of less developed capitalistic background with a weak national bourgeoisie that frequently shares power with those feudalists who took part in the national independence movement, as, for example, Morocco, Iraq, Somalia, Sudan, Cambodia. Both these groups adhere to a neutralist policy and are actively engaged in achieving economic independence.

3. In the third group the authors include the Philippines, Turkey, Malaya, Thailand, Pakistan, and many of the Latin American countries, said to be ruled by a pro-imperialistic bourgeoisie or a coalition of the latter with the feudalistic class of landowners. Here independence exists only pro forma, and the battle for economic self-sufficiency and political autonomy is still to be fought.

4. Ghana (during Nkrumah's time), Guinea, Mali and Indonesia (until 30 September 1965) were placed into a special category. The UAR, Algeria (under Ben Bella), Burma and Congo (Brazzaville) have also been part of this category since 1963. The authors' own comment is: "The class structure in these countries is characterized by the fact that capitalism is still in its embryonic stage. A national bourgeoisie does not exist or is very weak, as is also true of a feudal class. But there exists a proletariat that is becoming class-conscious. Development of class relations and political power is such that the forces that work for the noncapitalist road to development are increasing their strength."

Until 1963 Soviet theoreticians claimed that the "national bourgeoisie" held the reins of power also in these countries. Now, however, they realized that such countries [like the UAR, Burma, Guinea, Mali, Congo (Brazzaville), Algeria (under Ben Bella) and Ghana (under Nkrumah)] were also being led by representatives of the petite bourgeoisie, members of the free professions, the democratic intelligentsia, and the military intelligentsia, who are now called revolutionary democrats. The Soviet theoreticians claim that these leaders have entered the noncapitalist road to development, and are solving problems in their countries which the communists too would have had to solve if they had taken over the governments.

5. "Generally speaking, the class structure of the fifth group of nations, among which one may include the former French colonies of West and Equatorial Africa, Madagascar, the Congo (Leopoldville) and others, in many ways resembles the preceding group. But, with the exception of the Congo, Tanganyika, and Senegal, the proletariat in nearly every other country is extremely weak and only beginning to take shape as a class. The chief criterion here is that political power in these countries is still largely in the hands of those who are subservient to imperialism." [91]

Thus the Soviet theoreticians have relinquished the designation "national bourgeoisie" for the fifth group of nations also. According to the present Soviet view, these countries are headed by a "bureaucratic bourgeoisie," a "bourgeoisie that receives a salary." The communists regard the internal conditions of these countries as very unstable.

6. The sixth group contains the feudal nations with a minuscule proletariat, an extraordinarily low state of capitalistic development, and the almost complete absence of a national bourgeoisie: Nepal, Yemen, Saudi Arabia, Ethiopia, and Afghanistan. Yet it is claimed that these nations, "because of historic and international reasons, belong in their foreign political orientation to the neutralist camp." The separate listing in a special group of these nations seems to emphasize that, though an adverse internal power configuration offers little chance for communism in these countries, they nevertheless play an important part in the Soviet foreign policy concept. This applies especially to Afghanistan and also Ethiopia, both of which were of foreign political interest even to czarism.

This division into six groups does not occur fortuitously. Rather, it is to serve as a guideline for the Soviet bloc's differentiated political approach to each delineated group. The nations ranked as the most promising from the standpoint of Soviet bloc policy are the UAR, Burma, Guinea, Mali and Congo (Brazzaville). The Soviet theoreti-

---

[91] *Mirovaya ekonomika i mezhdunarodnie otnosheniya*, No. 4/1962, pp. 76-77.

cians say of the leaders of these countries that they are "constructing a national democratic nation." However, after Ben Bella's and Nkrumah's downfall, and after the failure of the "Movement of the 30th of September," the Soviets also had to strike Algeria, Ghana and Indonesia from among the list of "progressive countries." So far the Soviets have not given an appraisal of these most recent developments.

THE NATIONAL DEMOCRATIC STATE

As early as the November 1960 Moscow meeting of the Communist and Worker Parties, a new type state had been discovered for the developing countries: the "autonomous state of national democracy." This state is also mentioned in the Party program, which says broadly: "Presently, several sovereign states show important preconditions for the creation of a national democracy. In some countries, these are the great advances made in curtailing foreign capital investment; in others, the relatively strong government apparatus; in still others, the increasingly strong alliance between peasantry and working class, the people's determination to prevent the formation of reactionary dictatorships of big business and big landowners." [92]

"What are the earmarks of an autonomous state of national democracy?" asked the head of the international section and secretary of the Soviet Communist Party's Central Committee, B. N. Ponomaryev. He lists four. First, such a state consistently defends its political and economic independence, and resolutely opposes war alliances and military bases. Second, this state fights against new patterns of colonialism and the influx of foreign capital. Third, "this state rejects dictatorial and despotic rulership methods. It guarantees far-/reaching democratic rights and freedoms: freedom of speech, of assembly, of demonstration, and of the founding of political parties and other social organizations." Fourth, this state excels in safeguarding agrarian reforms, in democratic and social reconstruction, and in the participation of the masses in determining government policy. [93] The demand for "founding of political parties and other social organizations" refers, of course, to the legalization and buildup of communist parties and front organizations. Executive power in a national democracy is to be vested in the aforementioned national front of workers, peasants, national bourgeoisie, and democratic intelligentsia. "The uniqueness and transitory character of the state of national democracy rest on the fact that it will not be a one-class state, not even a two-class state of workers and peasants. Nor will it be the dictatorship of one

[92] *Aziya i Afrika segodnya* (Moscow), No. 11/1961, p. 13.
[93] *The Labor Movement in Capitalistic Countries* (Russ.), Moscow 1961, p. 24.

or two classes. Rather, it will be a state that acts in the interest of the entire patriotic segment of the nation and that suppresses the overthrown reactionary classes." [94]

The national front as a bulwark of this state is to exemplify "a lasting alliance and at the same time a common struggle," to be "fought primarily with peaceable and democratic means." This means that communist influence is to be increased on a step-by-step basis within the framework of this alliance.

In view of the proletariat's weakness and the Communist Party's nonexistence in many underdeveloped countries, the communist strategists are willing to retreat two steps in order to gain one.

Is it possible to establish national democracies in countries where the working class is weak? How is the leadership problem solved in a national democracy? Sobolev poses and answers these questions.

1. "A national democracy may originate under the leadership of any democratic class: the working class, the peasantry, the urban petite bourgeoisie. In some countries the intelligentsia, the revolutionary officer corps included, may become the leading force." Here the question is specifically about the *origin* of a national democracy; the consummation of its tasks is reserved for another force. Other authors are of the opinion that such a state may be formed under the leadership of some of Africa's unity parties, "led by the democratic intelligentsia."

2. "In a number of countries that lack any Marxist parties the class organizations of the proletariat—the trade unions—may up to a certain degree take over the role of the revolutionary vanguard. Simultaneously, the process of growth and development of Marxist forces sets in."

3. Sobolev sees in the Soviet bloc "an objective embodiment of the principle of proletarian leadership" that is also to serve "those countries that lack a proletariat as a solid ideological base." [95] According to this new concept, "any democratic class" may give a national democracy its initial start, but society can "travel the whole road, and make the transition to socialism, only under leadership of the working class." The new state of national democracy, which is to carry out the tasks of the national revolution's first phase, was inserted as a first step and transitional stage toward the people's democracy. The new Party program states that the "people's democracy is a form of dictatorship of the proletariat." Indonesia's Communist Party leadership labeled national democracy a "dictatorship of the people."

---

[94] *Probleme des Friedens und des Sozialismus* (East Berlin—Prague), No. 2/1963, p. 129.

[95] *ibid.*, p. 130.

All existing Communist Parties in the underdeveloped countries to-day propagate the founding of a national front of workers, peasants, national bourgeoisie, and democratic intelligentsia, as well as the struggle for establishment of a national democracy. Even the Communist Party of Basutoland, founded 5 May 1962, and willing to collaborate with the tribal chiefs in the national popular front, concluded "that the people, led by the Communist Party, can defeat imperialism, found a national democracy, and march along the non-capitalistic road to socialism and later communism." But the Soviet bloc theoreticians, as their national grouping shows, see the most promising signs for the formation of a national democracy in the fourth group (Guinea, Mali, Burma and the UAR). This appraisal received support from the delegations to Moscow's Twenty-Second Party Congress and to other Soviet bloc party conferences by the political parties of the three African nations—Mali's *Union Soudanaise,* Ghana's *Convention People's Party* under Nkrumah, and Guinea's *Parti Démocratique de Guinée.* After the events of December 1961, the *Parti Démocratique de Guinée* also sent representatives to Bulgaria's Party Congress in November 1962. The *Union Soudanaise* was represented at East Germany's most recent SED Party Congress. Its spokesman, Tidyane Traoré, proclaimed before the Moscow Forum that Mali "has started on the road to a national democracy."

Although in Guinea the Soviet bloc operates more circumspectly since the publicized incidents of December 1961 that led to the recall of Soviet Ambassador Solod, several Soviet authors nevertheless report rapid progress in that country's socio-economic reconstruction in the direction of noncapitalistic development. In October 1962 the organ of the Soviet Afro-Oriental experts claimed: "It is necessary to note that in those countries [Ghana, Guinea, Mali] where capitalism is not yet strongly developed nor the concept of private property widespread, the prerequisites for the building of a national democracy are most favorable." [96]

Khrushchev, at the Twenty-Second Party Congress, also counted Cuba in this new category of states. Cuba, however, was a very short-lived example of this new statehood experiment. Still, the intent of this type of state showed up plainly. G. Kim, the Soviet expert for underdeveloped countries, who specifically points out the transitional nature of a national democracy, says: "The experience of the Cuban Revolution shows that here the national democratic phase was short-lived. After the removal of conservative elements from the government and the strengthening of the revolutionary Marxist forces in it,

[96] *Aziya i Afrika segodnya* (Moscow), No. 10/1962, p. 3.
[97] *ibid.,* p. 5.

the revolution moved from the nationalistic into the socialistic phase of democracy." [97]

The erection of a national democracy would have far-reaching consequences. It must not be overlooked that the aim of the land-grouping strategy is to create Cuban-style bridgeheads in several countries through establishment of national democracies that could then serve to roll up the entire Afro-Asian front.

The Concept of State Capitalism

The Soviet theoreticians developed the theory of state capitalism in the underdeveloped countries in answer to the Afro-Asian leaders' request to buttress their country's political independence through industrialization. Soviet literature had indeed mentioned state capitalism before, in connection with the state capitalism of the advanced industrial states, which was dismissed and fought as reactionary. The state capitalism of the NEP period, the so-called concession policy, was looked upon as a progressive transitional step and a control and directional device over private enterprise; above all, over the temporarily state-authorized foreign concessionaires. With considerable amusement the Soviet theoreticians took note of China's state capitalism—the "policy of buying off the national bourgeoisie" through temporary capital investment and payment of dividends, which is now coming to an end—and China's method of "re-educating the capitalists into socialist wage earners" (*Liu Shao-chi*). This Chinese variant of state capitalism did eventually become part of the CPSU's new party program, albeit only as a future possibility. Should these plans succeed, it is hoped that in several countries "the bourgeoisie will find it advantageous to sell its most important means of production, and the proletariat, to 'buy itself free.' " [98]

---

[98] Prof. M. Rubinstein, "Möglichkeiten eines nichtkapitalistischen Weges für schwachentwickelte Länder," in *Neue Zeit* (Moscow), No. 28/1956; "The Role of State Capitalism in Burma, in Economic Development in Southeast Asia" (Russ.), Moscow 1959; M. J. Losyuk, *The Struggle of Latin America for Economic Independence* (Ukrain.) Kiev 1959; W. Shamin, "Concerning the Transition of Economically Weak Countries to Socialism (Russ.), in *Voprosy Ekonomiki*, No.

But the state capitalism of the developing countries is considered to be a transitional stage "between capitalism and socialism" of the Chinese and Soviet varieties. Yet it is a fact that Soviet initiative had nothing to do with state capitalism in these countries; that is, with the state's overseeing the country's industrialization, the creation of a centralized state economy, the foreign trade monopoly, and economic planning and control. Because of the magnitude of the task of industrializing, of the lack of capital, and of the impotence of indigenous private capital, the state itself performed these measures as soon as independence had been achieved; at a time, that is, when the Soviets were still isolated from these countries. The Soviets only started to exploit this situation and evolve their own concepts in 1956. The voluminous Soviet bloc literature that exists on this problem, therefore, is also of recent date. Dr. Walter Markov makes these general comments:

"The newness lies especially in the primary importance of a state capitalism that differs from the neomonopolistic state capitalism which results from direct fusion of monopolistic finance capitalism with the imperialistic state. In those Afro-Asian national states where the bourgeoisie is too weak to accumulate private capital for the large-scale investment necessary to eliminate economic retardation and thus effect a breakaway from foreign monopolies, state capitalism shows progressive traits. It contains elements amenable to further development." [99]

THE GOAL: ISOLATION OF NATIONAL STATES FROM WORLD MARKETS

Soviet experts believe that an increase of economic power in the hands of the governments of the underdeveloped countries might effect a separation and dissolution of the young national states from the system of the capitalist world economy, and might strengthen their political neutrality. Regarding these countries, the new Party program states that politically they "are aligned with neither the imperialist nor the socialist bloc, but that the majority of them have

---

6/1959; P. A. Ulyanovsky, "Concerning the Peculiarities of Development and Character of State Capitalism in Independent India" (Russ.), in *Problemy Vostokovedeniya*, No. 3/1960; S. N. Rostovsky, "Lenin's Teaching on the Noncapitalistic Road to Development" (Russ.), in *Problemy Vostokovedeniya*, No. 2/1960; *Industrialization Problems of the Underdeveloped Sovereign Nations of Asia* (Russ.), Moscow 1960; I. V. Vassilyev, *State Capitalism in Modern Burma* (Russ.), Moscow 1961; J. Bragina and O. Ulrich, *State Capitalism in the Industry of Eastern Countries* (Russ.), Moscow 1961.
[99] *Geschichte und Geschichtsbild Afrikas*, pp. 22-23.

not yet loosened their economic ties with the capitalistic system of international trade in which they hold a special position." For this reason two measures rank foremost in the Soviet concept of state capitalism:

1. Buildup and strengthening of the political economy through outright expropriation and nationalization of foreign capital and foreign-owned firms, which at the same time serves to intensify the conflict between the developing nations and the West's industrial powers.

2. Preference to the buildup of heavy industry, partly to make the developing countries economically independent of the industrial nations, partly to kindle competition between them. But in the communist viewpoint, state capitalism truly unfolds its progressive capabilities only when nationalization of industry and banking is complemented by a corporate agriculture and by control over, and later nationalization of, private business.

The resolution of the Soviet bloc-influenced First Afro-Asian People's Solidarity Conference, held in Cairo December 1957 to January 1958, calls nationalization of foreign investments for the purpose of capital accumulation and in support of the national economy a legitimate move and the just prerogative of a sovereign state. At the above conference the director of the Soviet Institute for World Economy and International Relations, A. A. Arsumanyan, declared: "The question of using profits and capital of foreign enterprises in the underdeveloped countries for this industrialization is of great importance. It would be advisable in this connection to remember the recent experience of Egypt, which discontinued the use of the Suez Canal by French, British and other foreign monopolists for their own profits, and is now using these profits to expand its own economy. The Republic of Indonesia has taken the same path. The Indonesian patriots are now fighting to nationalize the Dutch banks and other enterprises so that the riches extracted by the toil of the Indonesians in the course of ages can be used by the people . . .

"Today in some countries considerable funds remain in the hands of the state, and the enterprises built with them are state-owned. We think that this is a progressive phenomenon. The more state-owned enterprises there are, the greater will be the profits of the state. It will have more funds with which to expand construction, and the lesser the need for it to resort to taxes." [100]

V. Shamin emphasizes the other side of state capitalism by stating: "The prerequisite for the transition of all countries to socialism is the creation and uninterrupted strengthening of the state's economic

---

[100] *Afro-Asian People's Solidarity Conference* (Russ.), Moscow 1958, pp. 148-50. Also Eng. ed., Moscow 1958, pp. 180-82.

power. This general causative principle is also in full effect in the development of economically backward countries." [101]

State capitalism, the communists hoped, would give them access to positions in the economic apparatus and in the economic life of the underdeveloped countries. In this endeavor they succeeded only in Cuba, and to some degree in Indonesia in connection with the confiscation of Dutch firms and Dutch capital. The creation of large government-owned concerns is to provide a modern industrial proletariat whose numerical strength and "role in the public and political life" —so the Party program—will grow. Also, the communists consider it a preparation for the "noncapitalist developmental road" if the governments of the backward countries try to ensconce themselves in every sector of their nation's economy.

At a discussion by Marxist theoreticians, held December 1962 in Prague, the aforementioned Arsumanyan tried to sell the communists from the underdeveloped nations on the Soviet concept of state capitalism. He claimed that government guidance over the economy of the underdeveloped nations, sponsored by the communist parties:

a) represents a logical continuation of the struggle against imperialism and is in many cases a direct means of attacking the positions of imperialist monopolies;

b) could be, and in many cases already is, an effective way of mobilizing the national resources for their commitment in the most important sectors of the national economy;

c) curtails the influence of private capital in the national economy;

d) protects the national economy (especially in the event of a foreign trade monopoly) against the dire consequences facing the underdeveloped nations through international trade participation in the capitalist world markets;

e) creates and develops the means of production in such organizational manner as best suits the transition of private property to socialist ownership; and

f) creates the conditions that permit the experiences gathered by the socialistic states in the field of planning, industrialization, small producers' cooperatives, and so on, to be applied to national progress. [102]

Arsumanyan found few buyers for these ideas among his colleagues from the underdeveloped countries. "Many of the debaters" were of the opinion that such "global assessment would prove wanting under empiric testing."

---

[101] *Voprosy ekonomiki* (Moscow), No. 6/1959, p. 64.

[102] *Probleme des Friedens und des Sozialismus*, (East Berlin—Prague), No. 3/1963, p. 233.

CONCEPTUAL CONTRADICTIONS

The indigenous communists were as unreceptive to the Soviet theoreticians' concept of "state capitalism" as they had been to Soviet strategy of "collaborating with the national leaders." Until then, the Soviet bloc had maintained that the West's industrial nations opposed industrializing the underdeveloped countries, and would fight government influence over the economy in these countries. But Mohamed Ennafaa, general secretary of Tunisia's Communist Party, at the Prague meeting found that "It is not true, at least not any longer, that U.S. capitalists aid only private capitalism in the African countries. Often, they have no objection to the establishment of state agencies or state-owned concerns. Why? Because in some countries there are no private capitalists to come to the aid of." [103]

In contradiction of his own assessment of state capitalism as a "logical continuation of the struggle against imperialism" and as a "direct means of attack," Arsumanyan was obliged to admit: "The imperialists have adopted a new tactic *vis-à-vis* the state as a business partner. They do not deny the need of industrializing and declare themselves ready to assist the state sector, only they strive to consign this sector to an insignificant position in the political economy." [104]

The dilemma also arose because the national leaders of the backward nations are loath to take over the communist system of a state-controlled economy, preferring to practice their own admixture of state and private economics, of government planning and private initiative. Thus Ennafaa came to see that the Soviet bloc recipe does not work in Tunisia and that something must be wrong with the theory. He noted: "State capitalism at first appears to be a means of furnishing an economic basis for the national bourgeoisie." Government interference in economic affairs is "caused by the weakness of the national capitalist resources, not by the government's desire to lead the country's development into noncapitalistic paths." This is certainly true not only of Tunisia, but of the majority of the backward nations. Actually, said Ennafaa, the state became a manufacturer of production tools only "where Tunisia's bourgeoisie proved incapable of action; it leaves the bourgeoisie a free hand where the latter is particularly adept at developing—in agriculture and trade. In some state-owned or semistate-owned enterprises the exploitation of the workers is more brutal than in private businesses." His conclusion was: "We do not go along with those who see nothing but good in

[103] *ibid.*, pp. 233-34.
[104] *ibid.*, p. 233.

state capitalism . . . nor do we believe that state capitalism or state control is *always* anti-imperialistic." [105]

This criticism comes close to Peking's views. The Chinese accept as progressive only that form of state capitalism whose credo is exploitation of the capitalists and their abilities by the communist state.

The Prague discussion made the role state capitalism is to play from now on dependent on the struggle of the masses, on class warfare, and on the purpose and character of the state itself. Here, too, we notice an adapting to the new class strategy and an indication that the "national democratic state" is to guarantee a progressive form of state capitalism. Analogous to the "grouping of nations," a distinction is now also being made between the state capitalism of those countries "whose power is mainly in the hands of the national bourgeoisie, and the state capitalism of countries ruled by a reactionary, pro-imperialistic bourgeoisie and by feudalistic elements." The communists in the underdeveloped countries are charged with transmuting those forms of state capitalism "which might still be exploited by private capital or, worse yet, by foreign private capital, into a form that may more fully serve the interests of a developing national economy and aid the struggle for economic independence." [106]

The shrewd Soviet theoreticians had, by 1964, reached the conclusion that one could no longer apply the designation "state capitalism" to countries—such as the UAR, Burma, Guinea, Mali and Congo (Brazzaville)—that execute the program of a national democratic state and have entered on a noncapitalist road to development. In these countries, the theoreticians claim, there exists a governmental economic sector with socialist objectives.

STATE CAPITALISM AND FOREIGN AID

However, the above guidelines for state capitalism apparently do not apply to the Soviet foreign aid policy as a component of the policy of collaboration with the national leaders. For USSR foreign aid is made available also to anticommunist governments. The Soviet Union cooperates also with underdeveloped countries in working out economic plans for state-owned, as well as private, enterprises (India).

Peking claims that Russia's foreign aid policy "strengthens the reactionary forces in the underdeveloped countries." Oddly enough, the Iraqi Aziz al Hadsh rebutted the Chinese claim: "Many people think that Soviet aid to some Afro-Asian countries, especially to those *ruled by bourgeois-nationalist forces that suppress the democratic*

[105] *ibid.*, p. 233.
[106] *ibid.*, p. 235.

movement, strengthens the position of the ruling bourgeois cliques and helps them to intensify their repressive policy against the wage earners. Such views, it seems to me, prove an inability to link the interests of the national freedom movement of an individual country with those of the international revolutionary movement. In its aid to those bourgeois governments that oppose socialism, the Soviet Union banks on the fact that this aid underpins the political autonomy of the country in question . . . and thereby serves the interests of the wage-earning masses." [107]

It may be assumed that this "dialectic" carries little weight, least of all in Iraq.

---

[107] *ibid.*, p. 232. *Italics are this author's.*

Communism and the One-Party

Systems in Africa and Asia

When the young national states achieved their independence, many of them adopted constitutions that had been negotiated in the Western capitals and which envisioned the introduction of multi-party systems. Just as the West sought to transfer its system of parliamentary democracy to the countries of Asia and Africa, the Soviet bloc too wanted to transplant its conception to the young national states: it wanted to bring communist parties onto the scene in the Asian and African countries, communist parties that would gradually play a dominant role and eventually displace the existing national parties so as to "complete the national revolution" and "the transition to a higher level of development." However, in the majority of cases communism had no decisive success in founding communist mass parties in the developing countries.

The Western parliamentary form of government with its multi-party system prevailed in several Asian countries such as India and Ceylon, countries which also have legal communist parties. At first Indonesia too chose the parliamentary form of government, but this was replaced later by the politically and economically "directed democracy." Several African countries also adopted a multi-party system; among them are Congo (Leopoldville) with all its internal difficulties and a number of groups that are communist-influenced, where the military have since taken over the government; until the recent military coup, Nigeria, a country in which a new Marxist-Leninist "Socialist Workers and Farmers Party" has come into existence; also Madagascar (with a small legal communist Party); Somalia (relatively strong communist group); and Sierra Leone. After the most recent government turnover a multi-party system was also introduced in the Sudan. Here the Sudanese Communist Party was made legal again, only to be prohibited again shortly afterward.

But here we already reach the end of our list of African countries with a multi-party system. For it has become evident that the tendency to introduce one-party systems, which are also legally codified, and to eliminate any form of organized opposition, has prevailed particularly on this continent. The most recent examples of the introduction of one-party systems were Algeria and Tunisia. In Algeria the Communist Party was prohibited and the "Front de Liberation Nationale" (FLN) was declared the unity party. The "Parti Socialiste Destourien" is Tunisia's unity party. The Tunisian Communist Party was also prohibited. Discounting the countries where the military have taken over, twenty-three African states have unity parties and the majority of them profess no adherence to any social-revolutionary program. Some countries with one-party systems are even associated with the Common Market. The tendency toward the adoption of one-party systems in Africa has been strengthened by the decision of the "Organization for African Unity" (OAU) to support only representative unity fronts in the countries as yet not independent.

The majority of the unity parties came into existence in a variety of ways: in a few countries (such as Guinea and Mali, but also the Ivory Coast) the unity parties were the only extant parties before the respective countries achieved independence. Once independence had been declared they simply took over the entire administrative and governmental apparatus and sought to thwart the appearance of competitive opposition parties.

Some other countries had a multi-party system when the first elections were held. The victorious parties then became unity parties— the functionaries of what had been the opposition went over to the government party; the opposition parties themselves dissolved more or less voluntarily and were absorbed by the victorious party, or the victorious party codified the one-party system through its parliamentary majority. Examples of this were Ghana and Mali, but also Kenya and Tanganyika. Not very long ago the "Kenya African Democratic Union" (KADU) dissolved itself and its leading functionaries became members of the governing "Kenya African National Union" (KANU) which automatically made the latter into a unity party. In Tanganyika the "Tanganyika African National Union" (TANU) was declared a unity party by an act of parliament. Although Tanganyika and Zanzibar form a union, the law that established TANU as a unity party has not been extended to cover the "Afro-Shirazi Party" of Zanzibar which is communist influenced, at least not as of this writing.

Political parties at first played no role in the UAR where independence was achieved under leadership of "free officers." Here the attempt to establish a unity party was made, so to speak, after the fact. It is called the "Arab-Socialist Union" and Nasser uses it to create social support for himself.

A variation on the UAR example is the founding of the "Burma Sócialist Programme Party." This party too was inspired by officers, namely by the "Revolution-Council of Burma." On 28 March 1964 General Nu Win prohibited the political parties, among them three communist parties, and the "Party of the Burmese Socialist Program" became a unity party. All other parties had the option of joining this new party.

It should be mentioned that military dictatorships with a strong popular following can occasionally and temporarily exercise the function of a unity party in these countries. After the unity parties were prohibited in countries such as Dahomey, Upper Volta and the Central African Republic, the military have exercised the same function.

What is characteristic of these new regimes is 1) that unions, women, youth, students and other mass organizations are either made part of these unity parties or are controlled by them. As is evident from the events in several countries, this coordination does not eliminate the groups and the various interests they represent, but the struggle to assert these interests now must frequently be carried out within the unity party itself (Senegal, Ivory Coast and other countries). Particularly the unions often constitute the left wing in this system of coordinated mass organizations. Also 2) that these unity parties seek to suppress any form of opposition. The suppression of the "United Party" in Ghana, where a social-revolutionary program was proclaimed under Nkrumah, is not the only example. The unity parties in such moderate and Western-oriented countries as the Ivory Coast or Senegal also repressed their opposition and former fellow freedom fighters and fellow ministers, all in order to secure the dominance of the unity party.

This raises the question whether the one-party systems in the underdeveloped countries are imitations of the Eastern model. The one-party regimes have indeed adopted forms and methods of the totalitarian regime of communism to solve developmental problems. The founding of politbureaus which determine government policies, the introduction of the system of democratic centralism, the coordination of unions and similar measures are instances of such imitation. However, what differentiates the one-party regimes in the developing countries from the communist one-party system is the lack of ideo-logical objective and of ideological conformity.

The first one-party systems of the kind that we encounter today in the developing countries were Sun Yat-sen's regime in China and Kemal Ataturk's dictatorship in Turkey. Both these regimes also adopted communist organizational forms and methods to solve de-velopmental problems, without however embracing communist ideol-ogy. Sun Yat-sen's program for the "National Renovation of China" of April 1924 envisioned a three-stage plan for China's development into a democratic state. After the first phase of a national-revolutionary dictatorship, which was to be established to unify China, the second phase of this plan intended to establish a "paternal, educational democ-racy" in which the "people, that were not yet of age" would be pre-pared for the third phase of parliamentary democracy, all of this to happen under the leadership of the unity party, the Kuomintang. Chiang Kai-shek, Sun Yat-sen's successor, ruled for a long time with the help of the Kuomintang within the framework of the second phase of Sun Yat-sen's plan. Kemal Ataturk also adopted communist organiza-tional and developmental forms without making any concessions to communist ideology. He too promised to adopt parliamentary democ-racy once the developmental tasks had been solved. Indeed, this promise was kept in Turkey. In China, however, due to particular cir-cumstances which merit special examination, the Kuomintang's one-party rule was succeeded by Mao Tse-tung's totalitarian regime.

Richard Löwenthal characterizes these one-party regimes in the underdeveloped countries as developmental dictatorships, as distinct from communist dictatorships, which he calls ideological dictator-ships.[108] We want to adopt this definition with but one qualification: countries where the leadership enters into pacts with the communists and makes them members of the unity parties are in the first stage of a transformation from developmental dictatorships to ideological dic-tatorships. Yet we could not possibly agree more with the conclusion to which Löwenthal comes with regard to the by far greater majority of the one-party regimes in the developing countries. He writes: "None of these regimes, not even the unqualified developmental dic-tatorships, are enslaved to dogma, but are ideologically open. They are open to new ideas and to influences from the outside world—in-cluding the old industrial countries of the West—since they do not consider themselves as being in an unresolvable conflict of principle with the rest of the world. Therefore they are open to a political evo-

[108] Richard Löwenthal, "Staatsfunktion und Staatsform in den Entwicklungs-ländern," from Die Demokratie im Wandel der Gesellschaft, Colloqium Verlag Berlin, no year, p. 189.

lution inasmuch as the solution of their immediate modernization problems evolves together with their political means." [109]

COMMUNIST STRATEGY TOWARD THE UNITY PARTIES

The one-party systems became problematical for communism as soon as Moscow was forced to recognize that several countries (such as Algeria under Ben Bella and the UAR under Nasser) were entering on a program which the communists had reserved for what they called the "State of National Democracy"; at the same time, however, communist parties in these countries frequently were prohibited.

For the communists it became impossible to continue to oppose governments that, although they prohibited communist parties, realized a program that the communists had to regard as a positive development. Since mid-1963 the Soviet bloc therefore began to change its attitude toward the unity parties which henceforth were divided into two groups: the first and supposedly progressive group consists of those unity parties which contain "patriotic forces," social revolutionary strata and the "Revolutionary Democratic Intelligentsia." Moscow now regards those elements as "Revolutionary Democrats" that execute a noncapitalist development in their countries. Algeria's and Ghana's unity parties were considered part of this group until recently. At present it consists of the UAR, Burma, Guinea, Mali and more recently also Congo (Brazzaville).

The other group of countries with unity parties is described in the following way: "By no means did truly national parties led by revolutionary democratic leaders come into power in every African country that achieved independence. In a number of countries the imperialists succeeded in eliminating the freedom fighters and in installing their own puppets who, supported by foreign monopolies, established dictatorial regimes in the young countries and repressed all patriotic forces and organizations. These puppets of imperialism, Ahidja in Cameroon and Tomblbaye in Chad, also sing the praises of the advantages of the one-party system for the progress of their nation; but in fact they are primarily interested in asserting their power, so as to please their imperialist masters, and not in allaying their nation's need." [110]

The Soviet theoreticians are opposed to this group of countries with Western-oriented unity parties. V. P. Werin, a Soviet expert on constitutional law, wrote a special article dealing with the theoreticians'

---

[109] *ibid.*, p. 191.
[110] *Probleme des Friedens und des Sozialismus* (East Berlin—Prague), No. 3/1963, pp. 157-8.

conflict with the unity parties in the African countries which, until recently, belonged to the *Union Africaine et Malgache.*

According to the Soviet theoreticians' new insight, the so-called revolutionary democrats play a leading and progressive role in the first group of countries with unity parties. The Soviets ascribe to these parties—whether they like it or not—the fulfillment of tasks in their countries which the communists themselves would have to fulfill if they came to power. The director of the Moscow Institute for World Economy and International Relations, A. A. Arsumanyan, states: "Essentially the revolutionary democrats have found original forms to realize historically necessary measures which the proletarian avant garde would have to fulfill if it were strong enough, well enough organized and sufficiently powerful to come to power. The revolutionary democrats eliminate all vestiges of the political rule of imperialism, seek to nationalize foreign undertakings, have a foreign policy that fights colonialism, support all suppressed peoples, refuse to enter into imperialist military pacts, actively support the fight for peace and enter into close and friendly relations with socialist countries. By convincing themselves that the old state forms are unsuitable for solving the new problems, the revolutionary democrats are in the process of destroying the earlier state machinery and of placing people from the lower strata into responsible positions. That is essentially nothing but the Program of the State of National Democracy." [111] When they established this Program of the State of National Democracy in 1960, the communists, as has been mentioned, still felt that one of the basic prerequisites of this program was the existence of political parties, by which they meant communist parties. Today they have rescinded this demand in the case of some countries and instead ask Party members to enter the "progressive unity parties."

Several communist authors have dealt with this strategy of communist infiltration of the unity parties in the UAR, Burma, Mali, Guinea, Congo (Brazzaville) and until recently Algeria and Ghana. Thus the African communist A. Pela writes: "In several African countries there is a possibility of transforming extant mass parties into parties of the socialist revolution. These are parties in which the influence of the working class must be strengthened and in which Marxism-Leninism must be accepted as the ideological basis. It could be very harmful for the communists were they to begin with the buildup of separate parties where these possibilities exist. Rather, the main emphasis ought to be placed on the examination of Marxist-Leninist ideas, on the buildup of a Marxist-Leninist nucleus and on the

---

[111] *Mirovaya ekonomika i mezhdunarodnie otnosheniya*, No. 12/1964, p. 95.

strengthening of the influence of the working class in these parties." [112]

Izvestia observer Kudrjavzev expresses himself even more pointedly: "Let us take the African states that have decided on a noncapitalist path to development, states with a poorly developed economy devoid of a proletariat and with a national bourgeoisie only in its first stages. What is the situation of a one-party system in such a country? If in fact these parties represent a united front of the patriotic workers, farmers and the intelligentsia, all striving to reach a new life on a noncapitalist road to development, why should the progressive elements not support such a party, why should they not work within such a party to isolate the rightist elements among the leadership that might be capable of a policy of collaboration with the former colonial rulers, why should they not gradually seize the leadership of such a party?" [113]

Arsumanyan also emphasizes the necessity of isolating the rightist elements, since, as he says, "this will enable the revolutionary wing, which is indivisibly allied to the people, to achieve the proletarian ideology and scientific socialism, achieve it by way of petty bourgeois socialism, utopian socialism and by way of different kinds of—as Lenin says—'transitional' socialisms." [114] And he adds: "The logic of development leads the honest political functionaries from the bourgeois intelligentsia to an understanding of the decisive role of the working class and to an adoption of its ideology." [115]

In his recent book *Africa—the Way Forward*, the communist Africa expert Jack Woddis, who regards the African unity parties as mass parties and national unity fronts, established the following rules for communist behavior toward these parties. The communists must support the existence of a single mass party as long as they can play an effective role in it. However, the communists have no choice but to work for the creation of their own party as soon as their activities within the unity party are restricted. Yet the Algerian communists have not attempted anything of the sort since they were eliminated from the FLN. Apparently they still hope to be able to return into the fold of the FLN.

The communists' reappraisal of the leading forces of the unity parties in several developing countries, of whom they say that they fulfill tasks the communists would have to fulfill themselves if they were in power, and the communist thesis that these leading forces will acquire communist ideology by the logic of the development—

---

[112] From the *International Workers' Movement*, No. 15/1963, p. 31.

[113] *Aus der internationalen Arbeiterbewegung* (East Berlin), No. 17/1963, p. 31.

[114] *Mezhdunarodnaya zhizn*, No. 11/1963, p. 65.

[115] *Mirovaya ekonomika i mezhdunarodnyie otnosheniya*, No. 12/1964, p. 95.

these two judgments constitute the theoretical basis of the communist tactic of the "Trojan horse," i.e., the policy of infiltrating certain unity parties in the developing countries. Part of this policy is that the communists are even supposed to accept the "religious prejudices" of the present leaders so as to be able to march one step forward.

COMMUNIST INFILTRATION OF THE UNITY PARTIES

Meantime, we have received the first reports about the "Trojan horse" policy toward the unity parties: after Nasser released the communists from the concentration camps they decided to join the "Arab Socialist Union of the UAR." The Algerian communists, who, when their party was prohibited, organized a protest in the entire communist world in 1963, became members of the FLN under Ben Bella. At that time the former First Secretary of the Central Committee of the Algerian Communist Party, Bachir Hadj Ali, made the following statement: "Joining this party [the FLN] is by no means a tactical move by the communists. They take this position on principle. The communists will be loyal and faithful within the FLN. They have no intention of forming a faction or direction within the party." (*Probleme des Friedens und des Sozialismus*, No. 1/1965, p. 46.) Bachir Hadj Ali had to make this declaration since the old FLN fighters are still mistrustful of the communists. For the Algerian Communist Party, in accordance with French Communist Party policy, opposed Algeria's separation from France for many years. When Bachir Hadj Ali subsequently had to criticize his party's position in public, he put it this way: "The Algerian Communist Party overestimated the chances of a proletarian revolution in France for a long time. This led us to believe that victory in Algeria would come by way of a proletarian victory in France." [116]

Bachir Hadj Ali's assertion that the communists have no intention of forming a faction within the FLN is illustrated by a gathering of Arab communists in December 1964. For the first time in the history of communism this conference was not proclaimed as a gathering of the "representatives of the communist parties" but, in order to disavow any factional activity, was designated a "meeting of the representatives of the communists of the Maghreb and the countries of the Arab East." [117]

Whether or not the communists constituted a faction within the FLN is immaterial today since they were relieved of their functions after Ben Bella's downfall. However, the Algerian case was instructive for the evaluation of communist tactics.

In his article, "Anti-imperialist Revolution in Africa," the South Af-

[116] *ibid.*, p. 52.
[117] *Pravda*, December 11, 1964.

rican communist, A. Leruma, states: "Understandably there can be no universal recipe for the solution of the complicated organizational problem [of communists joining the unity parties]. The Marxists will have to solve this problem in each country according to the obtaining concrete conditions." [118] What is meant is that the communists should certainly not join the unity parties in each and every country. Thus the communists in Iraq and Tunisia are opposed to the respective unity parties in their countries. The Syrian Communist Party also opposes the one-party system and it seems as if not even the coming into power of the "Baath-Chinese" has changed their attitude.

Mounir Ahmid, a member of the Central Committee of the Communist Party of Iraq, made the following declaration when the "Arab Socialist Union of Iraq" was founded: "The Communist Party of Iraq considers the introduction of a one-party system in our country as wrong as the monopolization of the right to political activity by one party." [119]

The general secretary of Syria's Communist Party, Chaled Bagdache, when asked how unity ought to be established, replied that unity could only be realized by means of a national-democratic front of all groups and directions within which the Party would have to retain its autonomy.[120] The general secretary of Tunisia's Communist Party, Mohammed Ennafaa, also opposed the creation of the unity party *Parti Socialiste Destourien*.[121] Another Tunisian communist, Mohammed Harmel, said: "After the prohibition of the Tunisian Communist Party in January 1963 the governing Neo-Destour Party, later renamed the Socialist Destour Party, was the only party left in the country. We feel that this unity party constitutes an obstacle and not an advantage in consolidating the alliances of all the forces . . . Unity front, but not unity party—that is our opinion." [122]

These few examples show that the communists in the Arab world employ widely different tactics and roles.

But now let us examine one of Asia's unity parties. In Burma, as we have mentioned, there exist three communist parties: the illegal communist party of the "Red Flag," which Moscow calls Trotskyite; a communist party of the "White Flag," which also has been prohibited for a long time and which practices guerrilla warfare and belonged in Moscow's camp before switching over to the Peking line; and third of

---

[118] *Probleme des Friedens und des Sozialismus* (East Berlin—Prague), No. 2/1966, p. 105.
[119] *ibid.*, No. 11-12/1964, p. 955.
[120] *Aus der internationalen Arbeiterbewegung* (East Berlin), No. 19/1964, p. 15.
[121] *ibid.*, No. 20/1964, pp. 23-24.
[122] *Probleme des Friedens und des Sozialismus* (East Berlin—Prague), No. 12/1965, p. 1024.

all, a Marxist-Leninist United Workers' Party which was founded with Moscow's support in 1962. After all parties were banned on 28 March 1964 this new communist party immediately joined the Party of the Burmese Socialist Program and has been active within it ever since. So much then for countries with one-party systems that also had communist parties or still have them.

It is characteristic of unity party countries, without communist parties, where Soviet bloc trained individual communists or functionaries are supposed to become active, that we are dealing with young and relatively inexperienced parties which have not, or hardly, been in conflict with the communists; and that these parties and countries have a dearth of trained specialists and experienced functionaries, which means that every trained activist plays a much greater role in these countries than in a developed country.

These two factors, which also hold true for the UAR to some extent, are advantageous for communist infiltration tactics. The Armenian development expert, Karen Brutenz, has good reason for remarking that the individual communists are tested, trained, tough and experienced organizers and propagandists.[123] He means to underscore the fact that even single communists in the young and relatively inexperienced unity parties can exert great influence, which is why the Soviet bloc seeks to place individual communist functionaries in these unity parties and countries into crucial positions in the schools, cadres, adult education programs, radio, TV, and press, in publishing and printing as well as in the training program for party and state functionaries. Although communist influence on the mass media in Africa and Asia deserves separate analysis, we want to cite a few examples from the mass of material that treats of this new communist endeavor. Though communist influence in Ghana now has been thwarted, we will use Ghana under Nkrumah as an example, since communist influence in Ghana was comparable to what is still happening in other countries where the communists work within a unity party. From 15 December 1962 until Nkrumah's fall, there appeared a weekly paper in Ghana called *The Spark*, which was officially published by the Bureau of African Affairs in Accra. It was founded with support of communist cadres and it reprinted material from East bloc journals. The Kwame Nkrumah Ideological Institute, as a party university of the Convention People's Party for the training of party and state functionaries in Winneba, was cited by the SED paper *Neues Deutschland* (SED = Socialist Unity Party of Germany) as a successful example of the effective use of a few East bloc-trained function-

---

[123] *Kommunist* (Moscow), No. 17/1964, p. 33.

aries. In mid-1964 230 students at this party university were attending lectures on political science, economics and constitutional law. "The DDR is not unknown in this party university," the SED article said, an understandable claim when one reads that the director of the school, Kodwo Addison, "majored in Marxist literature and went to Hungary in 1952 where he studied for three years at the institute for political science . . . Today Kodwo Addison is a member of the Central Committee of the Convention People's Party. Very recently he was appointed to the three-man presidential commission that, under special circumstances, assumes Doctor Nkrumah's responsibilities. He is one of the politicians in Ghana who is charged with solving major tasks and preparing a socialist order, and his party university in Winneba plays a not insignificant part in this."

The report about the instructors at this party university goes on to say: "Dr. J. N. Nsarkoh, the school's assistant director, recently returned from the DDR. There, at the Karl Marx University in Leipzig, he made an excellent and factual defense of his dissertation, 'The Local Organs of the Power of the State in Ghana'—the first comprehensive representation by a Ghanaian on this subject which is so important to the development of Ghana. Dr. Nsarkoh taught Government Theory and Constitutional Law at Winneba." [124]

The communist influence in Ghana has been broken. But the "Kwame Nkrumah School" set an example. Recently the Soviets presented Mali with a similar party university which has been established in Bamako, the capital. While the Soviets were constructing the school buildings in Bamako, fourteen leading functionaries of the *Union Soudanaise* were being trained at the CPSU party university in Moscow as teachers for the Bamako school.

Two other schools, the union school in Dalaba (Guinea) constructed with help of the communist WFTU, and the *Université Ouvrière Africaine* in Conakry, which is modeled on the FDGB University "Fritz Heckert" and whose buildings were constructed by the DDR, perform a similar function as cadre training centers within the framework of the new communist policy of infiltrating the unity parties. Similar attempts to train communist cadres have also been made in Kenya. Although the Soviets do not consider Kenya a country that is executing a program of noncapitalist development under the leadership of revolutionary democrats, the Kenya African National Union (KANU) represents a union of various political directions. Thus, this party has a left wing under the leadership of Oginga Odinga whom the Soviet bloc has supported for a long time. In the

[124] *Neues Deutschland,* (East Berlin), July 1, 1964.

case of such a unity party as KANU, which has a leftist-oriented wing, the new communist tactics consist of letting individual communists become active within this left wing. Odinga, the leader of the left wing of KANU, proposed an Afro-Asian university for the training of cadres at the third Afro-Asian People's Solidarity Conference in February 1963 in Moshi (Tanganyika).[125] His plan found little backing at the time. In the meantime, however, the Lumumba Institute for the schooling of party and government functionaries was inaugurated on 12 December 1964 in Nairobi. The left wing of KANU hopes that this party university will play a similar role to that of the "Kwame Nkrumah" school in Ghana. At the inauguration ceremonies of this training center, the administrative chairman, Bildad Kaggia, also a member of the KANU left wing, emphasized that this institute was constructed with help from African and Socialist states.[126] In fact, the Soviet Union donated the funds for the construction of the buildings. Several Soviet instructors were also supposed to teach at the Lumumba Institute, together with some leftists from KANU. The communist International Journalists Organization (IJO) also managed to play a part in the construction of the training center. The organization's general secretary, Jiri Meisner, acknowledged "that the IJO had helped with the construction of the Lumumba Institute" and "will also lend material support to the development of the young African press in Kenya." [127]

Yet the communists did not make much headway in Kenya either. Kenya's government took over the reigns of the Lumumba Institute and eliminated the left-wing men.

However, all these examples are very instructive since they help us answer the question: from where do the few communists that become active in several countries with unity parties take the necessary functionaries? They train them themselves at the unity parties' party universities.

Moreover, the Soviet bloc has come to realize that a mass deployment of functionaries is unnecessary in the underdeveloped countries, that a few individual activists can have a decisive influence in the development of these societies.

Thus a recent DDR publication states: "In view of the initial low level of general education and widespread illiteracy in most national states, the course of the societal development of these countries will

[125] *Third Afro-Asian People's Solidarity Conference,* Speech by Oginga Odinga, Leader of Kenya Delegation, no year, multigraphed, p. 6.
[126] *Pravda,* December 14, 1964.
[127] *Neues Deutschland,* (East Berlin), December 24, 1964.

be influenced to a particularly high degree by a few leaders. The leaders of these countries organize the realization of national policy and direct the activity of thousands and millions of people." [128]

A NEW SYSTEM OF INTERNATIONAL RELATIONS

Simultaneous with its infiltration of several unity parties in Africa and Asia the Soviet bloc seeks to establish a new system of international relations between the communist parties and the national unity parties. Ghana's and Guinea's unity parties were represented at the XII CPSU party congress in 1961 and afterward at several other party congresses of various Soviet bloc nations.

Firm accords existed between the CPSU and SED on the one hand and Nkrumah's Convention People's Party on the other about the exchange of mutual experiences. The SED and the Convention People's Party reached a new agreement as recently as March 1965.

During Sékou Touré's recent visit to Moscow the CPSU and the *Parti Démocratique de Guinea* agreed that: "The CPSU and the *Parti Démocratique de Guinea* (PDG) are of the opinion that development of relations between the two parties, improvement of party contacts, the exchange of information, each party's acquaintance with the other's experiences during their economic, governmental and cultural construction, and reciprocal study of the methods of party work will contribute to the strengthening of cooperation between the CPSU and the PDG." [129]

And during Modibo Keita's visit to Moscow it was agreed that "The CPSU and the party *Union Soudanaise* are of the opinion that the expansion of inter-party relations, the reciprocal acquaintance with each other's experiences in the building of the state, the reciprocal study of methods of party work and reciprocal exchange of information will serve to fortify cooperation between the two parties." [130]

The League of Yugoslav Communists and the Italian Communist Party have taken the initiative in improving relations with the unity parties headed by "revolutionary democrats." The Italian Communist Party gave as its reason that relations with the national unity parties were of particular importance during the prevailing situation of pluralistic communism.

It is a known fact that the Yugoslav and Italian communists had particularly close ties with the FLN during Ben Bella's time. However,

---

[128] *DDR-Wirtschaftshilfe contra Bonner Neokolonialismus*, East Berlin 1965, p. 127.
[129] *Pravda*, August 1, 1965.
[130] *Pravda*, October 12, 1965.

during that period the FLN had also established relations with the CPSU, the SED, the French Communist Party, the Chinese Communist Party, and particularly the Castro Party in Cuba.

The *Mouvement National Révolutionnaire* of Congo (Brazzaville) maintains relations with the Communist Party of China and the CPSU. The Arab Socialist Union of the UAR sent a delegation to the eighth party congress of the League of Yugoslav Communists in December 1964, and was invited by the Unity Party of the Cuban Socialist Revolution to attend the sixth anniversary of the Cuban revolution in Havana, which it did. Finally, in February 1965 a delegation of the politbureau of the Italian Communist Party and the Arab Socialist Union met in Cairo and reached a firm agreement about mutual cooperation.

These few examples suffice to show that international communism seeks to establish a new system of relations with the national unity parties.

THE TACTICS TOWARD THE WESTERN-ORIENTED UNITY PARTIES

I will only add a few comments about communist tactics vis-à-vis Western-oriented unity parties in Africa. The communists claim that these parties are unstable. They say: "These regimes, which flourish rapidly with the leaven of neocolonialism, disintegrate just as rapidly under the onslaught of the masses of the people unceasingly struggling for democracy and their rights. Thus, for example, the viceroy of French imperialism in Brazzaville, Abbé Youlou, who had believed that the dissatisfaction of the masses could be suppressed by eliminating all opposition through the forcible destruction of every party but the government party, was overthrown. This also was the fate of Hubert Maga, the dictator of Dahomey, whom the people overthrew in October 1963."

In the case of all Western-oriented unity parties the communists concentrate their efforts on infiltrating the unions, which are also coordinated with the unity parties in these countries, in order to gain influence and to supplant the Western-oriented government by way of the unions and other mass organizations.

A communist author claims that "unity parties in several countries of the African-Madagass Union were founded with Western blessing." He does not comprehend that these unity parties are the product of special conditions in Africa, conditions that prevail in the developing countries. However, the West itself so far seems to lack a concept for its relations to the unity parties and the unions attached to them that would be acceptable to the developing countries.

ROLE OF THE COMMUNIST PARTIES

As can be gathered from our preceding description, the new communist policies of infiltrating the extant unity parties while not building up or furthering an existing communist party is confined to a few countries. In Algeria and Ghana the communists have already suffered setbacks with this new policy. In by far the greater majority of the developing countries communism focusses on the existence of a communist party "as a special political party in contrast to the parties formed by the nationalists." These communist parties in the developing countries are confronted by very contradictory tasks by the consequences of the Soviet bloc's coexistence strategy.

On the one hand, these parties are charged with supporting all measures of their respective governments, which Moscow's foreign policy has labeled progressive (neutralism, expropriation of foreign concerns, friendly relations with the Soviet bloc, and the like). Thus, it was not by mere chance that Aziz el Hadsh defended Soviet foreign aid to his nation (Iraq) against the Chinese viewpoints, even though Kassem was even then suppressing the Communist Party of Iraq. On the other hand, the communist parties are given the task of organizing a national unity party of workers, peasants, national bourgeoisie, and the democratic intelligentsia in their respective lands, in order to end the national revolution through erection of a national democracy and thus move on to a "higher stage of development."

The communists of the developing countries can carry out this task only in opposition to the very government whose "progressive measures" they are to support. For it is evident that a great majority of Asian governments is far from ready to accede to a Popular Front and to prepare its own demise by way of national democracy (India, Iraq, and others).

These dualistic tactics of the communists in the underdeveloped nations have been the subject of several international conferences. Under the heading "Disintegration of the Colonial System of Imperialism after World War II," the editorial staffs of the Soviet periodical *Mezhdunarodnaya Zhizn* and the Chinese periodical *Shih-chieh Chih-shih* jointly organized a consultative meeting in Moscow in January 1959. In May 1959 the Institute of Universal History of Leipzig's *Karl Marx Universität* conducted an international discussion about "the role of the national bourgeoisie in the national freedom movement of Asia, Africa, and Latin America," in which participated communist delegates from Algeria, Argentina, Chile, Indonesia, Iran, Jordan, Lebanon, Morocco, Nigeria, Syria, and Tunisia, besides representatives from East Germany and the USSR. China abstained. In July

1960 a conference called by the Soviet Institute for World Economy and International Relations, and the *Mirovaya Ekonomika i Mezhdunarodnie Otnosheniya* periodical concerned itself with "The Current Phase of the National Freedom Movement in Latin America." [131] Several similar scientific meetings occurred during 1962 to 1964. A study of pertinent source material shows that the common subject at all these conferences was a discussion of Communist Party tactics *vis-à-vis* today's national leadership corps, and the individual communist party's approach to the creation of a Popular Front under the assurance of gradual Party domination.

Academy member A. A. Guber, at the January 1959 Moscow meeting, dealt with the most ticklish question of communist behavior toward their respective governments. Guber's guidelines remain valid to this day, even though some of his formulations—he spoke of "people's democracy," whereas today the proper phrase is "national democracy"—are no longer in use. They were specifically seconded at the Twenty-Second Party Congress by the representative of the banned communist parties of Iraq, the subsequently murdered Salem Adil, and by Syria's Chaled Bagdash. Guber put forth the following basic ideas:

1. The national independence of the underdeveloped nations is to be looked upon "solely as a stage and as a prerequisite for the social restructuring" in these countries, "as well as for the subsequent phase-over of the national-colonial into the socialist revolution." [132]

2. The communist struggle toward a "people's democracy" in the underdeveloped countries "not only does not preclude unconditional exploitation of those possibilities inherent in the national-bourgeois, anti-imperialistic movement, but, on the contrary, presupposes it." [133]

3. Guber emphasizes that the communist tactics in the underdeveloped areas must be very agile and at the same time strictly adhere to principles and to the guidance of one basic criterion: "In accordance with these Moscow directives, the communist parties in the underdeveloped countries" in their relations with the "parties and governments in power" must be guided by "to what degree their policies serve the best interests of assuring national political autonomy and to what extent these policies serve to weaken the economic strongholds of foreign monopolies." [134]

---

[131] Literature on these three conferences is found in: *Mezhdunarodnaya zhizn,* No. 3/1959; *Probleme des Friedens und des Sozialismus,* Nos. 8 and 9/1959; *Mirovaya ekonomika i mezhdunarodnie otnosheniya,* No. 9/1960.
[132] *Mezhdunarodnaya zhizn,* No. 3/1959, p. 95.
[133] *ibid.,* p. 97.
[134] *ibid.,* p. 98.

Guber writes: "The support rendered by the national bourgeoisie in power to all that, from a domestic and foreign policy point of view [i.e., Moscow's view] is objectively progressive and by way of strengthening independence, does not at all impede the struggle of the working class for hegemony but, on the contrary, creates the most favorable conditions for it. Proof of this lies above all in the numerical growth of the communist parties in those Eastern countries where this situation exists, but also in a stiffening of the alliance between working class and peasantry and the growing influence of the working class on the urban petite bourgeoisie, on the intelligentsia, and on the middle classes." [135]

As was pointed out, these tactics bore results only temporarily in Indonesia, and this only because of that country's internal condition. As regards the second task, that of organizing a Popular Front in the Afro-Asian countries, the communists have hardly advanced at all since 1959.

COMMUNIST PARTY STRENGTH

Membership of Communist Parties[136]

(in thousands)

	1928	1935	1939	1945	1957	1960	1963
Worldwide Membership	1680	3141	4202	20,000	33,000	36,000	42,800
of these outside Soviet bloc	433	785	1750	4800	4600	5300	6000
and in Asia	–	–	22	–	1700	2500	2500
Latin America	–	–	90	–	200	250	250
Africa	–	–	5	–	20	50	50

The 1961 Twenty-Second Party Congress put worldwide communist membership at 40 million in eighty-seven communist parties. In 1963 there are supposed to have been ninety communist parties with a total membership of 42.8 million. Of the 2.5 million party members on the Asian continent (a figure that remained unchanged between 1960 and 1963) 2 million members belonged to the Indonesian Communist Party (by 1965 that party's membership had risen to 2.5 million), which has since been destroyed. Communist Party membership in India in 1963 was given as 150,000. For 1964, in which India's Communist Party underwent a split, the Soviet-oriented Indian Communist Party cites a membership figure of 136,888 and the Peking-directed faction

---

[135] *ibid.*, p. 98.
[136] *Mirovaya ekonomika i mezhdunarodnie otnosheniya*, No. 5/1961, p. 37. *Probleme des Friedens und des Sozialismus* (East Berlin—Prague), No. 9/1964, p. 718.

a figure of 104,421—figures that cannot be checked for their accuracy. All other Asian communist parties are small cadre parties, some of which, like that in Ceylon, have split. Latin America's twenty-one listed communist parties contain a total of 250,000 members, of which Argentina claims 100,000; Brazil 25,000; Chile 20,000; Venezuela 35,000; and Uruguay 10,000.

The 50,000 members listed for Africa in 1963 are said to be distributed among nine Marxist-Leninist parties. These are the Communist Party of Lethos in Basutoland, which is legal and was only founded in November 1961; the Communist Party of Madagascar (legal); the Communist Party of Morocco (prohibited); the Socialist Workers and Farmers Party of Nigeria which was founded in 1963 (legal until now); the Communist Party of Reunion (legal); the *Parti Africain de l'Indépendance* of Senegal (prohibited); the Communist Party of Sudan (prohibited); the Communist Party of South Africa (prohibited); and the Communist Party of Tunisia (prohibited). No details of the individual parties' strength have been published so far.

Since the fall of 1959 *The African Communist* has been the central publication of the communist movement in Africa. Disguised as the organ of South Africa's Communist Party, the periodical is published in London.

Besides the African communist parties mentioned above, there also exist several parties the communists consider sympathetic to them and with which the CPSU, and especially the Communist Party of China, have relationships. These are the *Movimento Popular de Libertacao de Angola* (MPLA); the *Partido Africano do Independencia da Guine e do Cabo Verde* (PAIGC); the *Union des Populations du Cameroun* (UPC); the *Frente de Libertacao de Moçambique* (FRELIMO); the Sawaba Party of Niger, and the Afro-Shirazi Party of Zanzibar. The small Communist Party of Madagascar uses the *Antokon'ny Kongresin'ny Fahaleovantenan'i Madagasikara* (AKFAM) as a propagandistic and operational basis.

Senegal's illegal *Parti Africain de l'Indépendance* (PAI), in a salutatory letter to the Twenty-Second Party Congress, referred to itself as "one of the youngest of Marxist-Leninist parties." This party is to be sponsored by the French Communist Party. The *Union des Populations du Cameroun* (UPC) also collaborates with the French communists "in the spirit of proletarian internationalism."

THE IMPORTANCE OF THE ILLEGAL CADRE PARTIES

According to Ponomaryev, forty-eight of the world's total of eighty-seven communist parties in 1960 were active in the underdeveloped countries of Asia, Africa and Latin America. But the majority of these are banned and work illegally. But the role and importance of this large number of small and illegal communist parties, especially in Africa and Asia, are often misjudged. It would be wrong to compare them to their European counterparts, for here we deal with an elite of small, well-trained cadre parties that stand ready for instant commitment during periods of upheaval in countries with many unsolved problems.

In Cuba the small and illegal communist *Partido Socialista Popular* was initially taken by surprise and left in the lurch by the events of January 1959. But the party soon adapted to the new set of circumstances and gained mass influence. Before the army *coup d'état* of 1958 the Communist Party of Iraq counted barely a thousand members. The "Revolution of 14 July" was certainly not its doing. But immediately following the *coup,* its trained cadres started a mass propaganda campaign and founded trade unions and other organizations.

Guber's guidelines for banned communist parties working illegally were formulated in these words: "In a number of Eastern countries, the communist parties were dissolved or banned by government decree . . . But even in these cases, the communists determine their relations to the government in the first instance by applying the basic criterion of what role is played by the government in the struggle against imperialism. At the same time, they strive to gain a free hand in unfolding democratic activity . . ." [137]

Salem Adil, first secretary of Iraq's Communist Party (who was murdered), could still report to the Twenty-Second Party Congress in October 1961 that in his country "all party activity is strictly watched and, above all, the Communist Party is legally banned," and that extensive arrest campaigns had thrown several thousand communists in jail. Yet he nonetheless emphasizes: "Our party supports all government measures against imperialism, conspiracies, military alliances, and monopolistic oil companies."

---

[137] *Mezhdunarodnaya zhizn* (Moscow), No. 3/1959, pp. 98-99.

The Strategy of Mao Tse-tung

The views of Moscow and Peking are not in conflict when it comes to the revolutionary goal of transforming the independent Afro-Asian states into "lands of socialism." Yet, right away one must qualify: The "how" plays a decisive part in the Sino-Soviet polemics. According to Soviet planning, still obligatory for almost the entire Soviet bloc, the "transition to a higher developmental stage" within the young sovereign nations is generally postponed to some future date. In a veiled attack against the Chinese, Soviet academician J. Zhukov wrote: "Lenin foresaw the revolutionary transition from capitalism to socialism as marking *an entire historical epoch* in which the proletarian revolution [i.e., the Soviet bloc] unites with a whole series of democratic and revolutionary movements, among them the national-revolutionary freedom movements in the undeveloped, backward, and suppressed nations." [138] Soviet strategists see "broad, objective possibilities of achieving total and genuine national autonomy, as well as realistic prospects for a development toward people's democracies, in the Afro-Asian countries." They base their forecast on further exploitation of a still strong national-revolutionary fervor of the national leadership forces, and on a strengthening of the communist parties in the under-developed nations themselves. *Far greater weight*, however, is attached to a successful outcome of the Soviet coexistence policy and of Soviet futuristic plans whose goal is the political, military, and economic out-stripping of the West. It need hardly be pointed out that this Soviet design is tacitly linked with safeguarding for the industrial giant USSR

[138] *Pravda*, 26 August 1960.

the leading role, as much in the Soviet bloc as in the revolutionary process of transition at work in the underdeveloped areas.

On the subject of "how," the Chinese are of different opinion. For in questions of strategy; in the question of who is to lead the national freedom movement even in its present *phase;* in the relationship to the bourgeois-nationalistic leadership forces of the underdeveloped nations; in the question of transition from national to social revolution, and also in the question of who is entitled to the leadership role in Asia, Africa, and Latin America—Peking or Moscow—the Chinese have their own ideas.

Sum and substance of the current ideo-political controversy between Peking and Moscow centers on the basic question of communist doctrine, and on problems of domestic and foreign policy, such as the relationships of the bloc members and the communist parties to each other as well as among themselves. The scope of our survey precludes dealing with all of these matters and forces us to limit our review of the controversy to the extent the latter relates to our objective, namely, the study of the divergent strategy and policy of the two communist centers in regard to the underdeveloped areas.

THE ROOTS OF THE SINO-SOVIET CONTROVERSY

The roots of the Sino-Soviet controversy over what course to take in the national liberation movement go deeper than the dispute in the past several years has revealed. For a more detailed knowledge of this controversy, the entire history of the Chinese Revolution and Moscow's part in it must be analyzed.

Maoism and its doctrine of the political and military strategy and tactics to be applied in the underdeveloped countries, resulted largely from the fiasco of Moscow's and the Comintern's 1927 China policy. Also, the failure of Stalin's China policy in the decade following the 1927 defeat, in contrast to Mao's victories especially since 1937, served to launch Maoism. It was not by chance that the politburo of the Chinese Communist Party's Central Committee emphasizes, in the well-known article "Concerning the Historic Experiences of the Dictatorship of the Proletariat" of 5 April 1956, that it was Stalin's policy of directing the main effort in the civil war struggle during the years 1927 to 1936 against the intermediary powers that isolated and severely harmed China's Communist Party. Mao, adds the article, corrected the error.

Several facets of Russia's China policy during the period from the Sino-Soviet alliance of 1923 until Mao's take-over of communist leadership in China in 1935 deserve mention. The 1923 alliance, engineered by Joffe and Sun Yat-sen between Bolshevism and Chinese nationalism and of great benefit to the *Kuomintang* under Chiang Kai-shek after Sun's death, served the Soviet Union primarily to break out of its foreign political isolation and to create an anti-Japanese, anti-West Chinese government. Initially, China's Communist Party played a secondary role in this alliance. Similar to the current "alliance policy" in the underdeveloped countries, China's Communist Party, ensconced as a growing Trojan horse within the *Kuomintang*, was to be readied for the second phase of the Chinese Revolution. Chiang Kai-shek put the quietus on Moscow's plans with his April 1927 strike against the communists. China's Communist Party was the first to pay for the Comintern's defeat. Only a week before Chiang Kai-shek's bloody suppression of the Chinese communists with his Soviet-organized national forces on 12 April 1927, Stalin had stressed: "At the moment, we need the Right in China. It contains capable men who, besides, are in command of the army and lead it in the battle against imperialism." [139] Even after defeat, Stalin defended his China foreign policy concept in a dispute with Trotsky. In August 1927 he still claimed the support of the *Kuomintang* as the correct course, for the *Kuomintang's* attack "broke up the power of imperialism and, by weakening and degrading it, made easier the development of the USSR." [140] One might add: at the expense of the Chinese communists.

Certain parallels exist between Moscow's China policy of the 1920s and that, for example, toward India today. Here, USSR aid also is dictated by foreign policy considerations, in this case a strengthening of India's anti-imperialistic, neutral position. Yet, as the Chinese are pointing out today, the 1923 alliance between Soviet Bolshevism and Chinese nationalism, doomed to failure in 1927, had had the more auspicious beginning of the two, highlighted as it was by Chiang's victorious march northward, at his side the communist political commissar Chou-En-lai who thus achieved freedom of movement for China's Communist Party. In India, no similar situation obtains today, not even to mention Iraq in this connection. The 8 February 1963 *coup* in Iraq afforded the Chinese renewed certainty in their criticism of Soviet policy.

Another factor that gave Chinese communism its special imprint lies in the two courses pursued in China since the 1927 defeat. One was the Comintern's demand for establishing "the proletariat's leadership in the Chinese Revolution." This was to be accomplished through uprisings in the cities and by winning over the weak industrial centers.

---

[139] Quoted by W. W. Rostow in *Rot-China—Wirtschaft und Politik*, Cologne 1954, p. 54.

[140] Stalin, *Der Marxismus und die nationale und koloniale Frage*, Berlin 1955, p. 301.

Every one of the many Comintern-directed city uprisings failed; the party itself, and the trade unions it dominated, were banned and suppressed by Chiang; and Chinese communism was completely isolated from the feeble industrial labor force. Only in 1946—as Mao writes in his *Selected Works*—were the latter two reunited. But in the earlier days, communism in China was saved by an outsider who, in contrast to the Comintern course, saw the mainspring of China's Revolution in the peasantry. While it is true that Lenin before had looked upon the peasantry as the proletariat's natural ally, it was Mao who first built it into, and exploited it as, the "basic power behind the Revolution." During the period of the *Kuomintang* alliance Stalin, as Trotsky and Sinovyev exposed at the time, had slowed down China's agrarian revolt to avoid conflict with Chiang. In 1927 Mao reproached the First Secretary General of China's Communist Party, Chen Tu-shiu (1921-27), for not having assumed leadership over the peasant masses. But the latter pointed out: "With no firm standpoint of my own, I stuck loyally to the opportunistic politics of the Comintern and was nothing but a tool of the narrow-minded Stalinist faction." [141] The "resolution concerning several questions of the history of our party" of 20 April 1945 reveals that from 1927-35, "during the period of revolutionary agrarian warfare" (Mao), bitter strife raged in China between the various Comintern-appointed party stewardships and Mao disciples over the peasant question.[142]

Mao and his followers—the resolution reads—were accused by the official party leaders of "a specifically agrarian revolutionism" as representatives of "peasant capitalism," "big farm owners," and "kulaks." Comintern partisans in China "resorted in this 'internal party struggle' to measures appropriate only against criminals and enemies . . . Many of our best comrades were wrongly indicted and, though innocent, liquidated." [143] "Mao's rise," Rostow writes, "resulted from his approach to the problem of political power of Chinese communism via a detour: by organizing the peasantry. In all the years since 1927 this path proved more successful than that pursued by the men successively appointed and directed by the Comintern: Chu Chi-pin, Li Li-san, Wang Ming, Po Ku, and, in 1934, the latter's successor, Chang Wen-tien. Moscow and the Comintern adhered to Lenin's strict formula that saw in the urban proletariat the most important, if not the only, instrument of revolution, until events proved Mao right and left his tactics as the only alternative." [144]

---

[141] Quoted by Robert S. Elegant, *Chinas rote Herren*, Frankfurt/M. 1952, p. 56.
[142] Mao Tse-tung, *Ausgewählte Schriften*, East Berlin 1956, pp. 222-85.
[143] *ibid.*, pp. 269-70.
[144] W. W. Rostow, *Rot-China, op. cit.*, pp. 56-57.

The conclusion the Chinese must draw from their own historic past is: if events proved Mao right then, why should they not prove Mao right now? Also, the Chinese see themselves borne out by the post-1946 turn of events in China. Stalin at the time had recommended they forgo the uprising and, together with Chiang Kai-shek, search for a *modus vivendi*. They, however, unleashed the civil war and won.[145]

MAOISM AS SPECIAL SCHOOL OF COMMUNISM

Mao's doctrine concerning strategy and tactics in colonial and semicolonial countries is chiefly formulated in the following of his works: *Concerning the Classes of Chinese Society* (March 1926); *Why is Red China a Possibility?* (October 1928); *Strategic Problems of the Revolutionary War in China* (December 1936); *On Practicalism* (*Concerning the Interrelatedness of Cognition and Practice, of Knowledge and Action*) (July 1937); *On Contradiction* (August 1937); *Strategic Problems of Guerrilla Warfare against the Japanese Invaders* (May 1938); *The Chinese Revolution and the Communist Party* (December 1939); *Concerning the New Democracy* (January 1940); *Concerning the Coalition Government* (April 1945); and *On Democratic Dictatorship of the People* (July 1949).

It would be wrong, in light of this literature, to assume that Maoism as a special school in international communism came into being only after communist victory in China, after the establishment of the Chinese People's Democracy in October 1949. The roots of Peking as Moscow's co-doctrinal center plainly reach back to 1927 when Mao, in contrast to the Comintern, drew his own lessons from defeat. The birth certificates of Maoism, which in Chinese eyes raised it to doctrine generally applicable also to other Afro-Asian countries, were two documents, both dating back to 1945, four years before the take-over. One was the "Resolution concerning several questions of the history of our party" of 20 April 1945; the other, the May 1945 speech on the party statute by Chairman Liu Shao-chi.

In the resolution on party history we read: "In the struggle the Party brought forth its own leader in the person of Comrade Mao Tse-tung. As representative of the Chinese proletariat and the Chinese people as a whole, Comrade Mao Tse-tung creatively applied the highest achievements of human thought, the scientific theory of Marxism-Leninism, in such a vast, semi-feudal and colonial country as China, where the masses are made up of peasants and where the immediate task is the struggle against imperialism and feudalism; in a country, where the situation is extremely complex and the struggle

---

[145] See Klaus Mehnert, *Peking und Moskau*, Stuttgart 1962, pp. 310-11 and 409.

is carried on under immensely difficult circumstances; in a country of tremendous size and a population of untold millions. Comrade Mao Tse-tung has splendidly developed the Leninist doctrine on the revolutionary movement in the colonial and semi-colonial countries as well as on the Chinese Revolution." [146] To this, Liu Shao-chi added a month later (in May 1945) that Mao's doctrine constituted "a progressive development of Marxism in the national democratic revolution of a colonial, semi-colonial, and semi-feudalistic country." [147] At a time when Stalin's word was still law in international communism, Liu already claimed: "The Marxists in the rest of the world have never solved or even considered these problems." [147] Against the current Moscow practice of confronting the Chinese with Lenin quotes, the Chinese Communist Party has become all but immune, for as early as 1945 they claimed that Maoism "in the realm of theory had had the creative courage to dispense with certain Marxist principles and conclusions that were outdated and incompatible with the practical requirements of China." [147]

In a 1947 interview with Anna Louise Strong, Liu Shao-chi formulated once more: "Mao's great achievement is the changing of Marxism from a European into an Asiatic form. Marx and Lenin were Europeans . . . Mao Tse-tung is Chinese . . . Mao not only adapted Marxism to new circumstances, he advanced its development. He created a Chinese, or Asiatic, form of Marxism." [148] From this, it was but a logical deduction that the Communist Party of China "is in no way inferior to the proletarian party of any capitalist country," that "the proletarian program and party policy are different from those of any other party," and that the Chinese Communist Party "in its own right organized and carried out the neo-democratic revolution of the Chinese people." A few weeks after the communist victory in China, Liu Shao-chi once more underscored the validity of Maoism for all colonial countries. In the opening address of the trade union conference, held by the Asian and Pacific nations in Peking on 16 November 1949, Liu said: "The classic type of revolution in Imperialist countries is the [Russian] October Revolution. The classic type of revolution in colonial and semi-colonial countries is the Chinese Revolution, the experiences of which are of inestimable value to the peoples of these countries." And on another occasion he states: "The road which the Chinese people chose for victory over imperialism and its henchmen and which led to the erection of the Chinese People's

---

[146] Mao Tse-tung, *Ausgewählte Schriften*, Berlin 1956, Vol. 4, pp. 222-23.

[147] Liu Shao-chi, *Über die Partei*, Berlin 1954, pp. 18-19 and 29-36.

[148] Anna L. Strong, "The Thought of Mao Tse-tung," *Amerasia*, Vol. IX, New York 1947, No. 6, p. 161.

Republic, this is the road which the peoples of many colonial and semi-colonial lands must choose in their struggle for national independence and for the establishment of people's democracies . . . This road is the road of Comrade Mao Tse-tung." [149]

When the Soviet Asia specialist Zhukov at one of the high points in the Sino-Soviet controversy charged the Chinese "dogmatists and sectarians" with ignorance of the "laws underlying social evolution," claiming that "Lenin had thought it natural for the bourgeoisie to act as leader in any national uprising and had called for support of the revolutionary elements in the bourgeois-democratic national freedom movement," [150] Liu had already given his answer. In an article on the tenth anniversary of the Chinese People's Democracy, entitled *The Victory of Marxism-Leninism in China,* he pointed out that precisely the opportunists of the Right had taken a capitulatory attitude toward the bourgeoisie, "having considered the democratic revolution as primarily a bourgeois matter." These people "drew their chief support from the Popular Front with the bourgeoisie and merely concluded an alliance with the latter but did not carry on the fight against it." [151]

MAO TSE-TUNG'S CONCEPT

It is precisely on the role of the national bourgeoisie, of the leadership corps especially in India and Iraq, that the current Sino-Soviet controversy centers, a controversy in which the Chinese proclaim "the necessity of opposing the national bourgeoisie." Based on the teachings and writings of Mao Tse-tung, the Chinese strategy embraces four points of fundamental importance:

1. Chinese communists reject the Soviet contention that during the initial phase of the struggle for national independence, the national bourgeoisie, here still conceded a progressive function, may hold leadership. The Chinese claim *leadership for the Communist Party* from the very onset of the struggle for independence. In those countries where as yet no communist party exists, the leadership belongs to a militant-revolutionary vanguard, as for example to the UPC in Cameroon. In Chinese eyes, the national bourgeoisie is incapable of carrying out a consistently antifeudal and anti-imperialistic program. To leave leadership even temporarily in its hands would "seriously damage the image of the revolution." The Chinese view is: "The revolutionary movement as a whole, led by the Communist

---

[149] Chen Po-ta, *Mao Tse-tung's Idea—the Fusion of Marxism-Leninism with the Chinese Revolution* (Russ.), Peking 1951, p. 96.

[150] *Pravda,* 26 August 1960.

[151] Liu Shao-chi, *Der Sieg des Marxismus-Leninismus in China, Peking* 1959, p. 8.

Party, is a uniphase revolutionary movement, embracing both the democratic, as well as the socialistic, revolutionary stages." [152]

2. In contrast to the Soviet "phase theory" (first phase: national revolution under bourgeois-national leadership; second phase: socialist revolution under leadership of the working class) and the concept of "an entire historic epoch" of transition which—as was pointed out—coincides with Soviet futurism, the Chinese subscribe to the doctrine of "permanent revolution" under Communist Party leadership. In the words of Liu Shao-chi, the mission of the Communist Party is "through exploitation of every possibility during the democratic stage of the revolution to create the preconditions for the impending socialistic revolution, so that *immediately, without break,* and everywhere at once, the victorious democratic revolution will phase into the socialistic revolution." [153]

3. The Chinese see the *mainspring of colonial revolution* in the *peasants,* whom a militant-revolutionary Communist Party must organize and lead in the struggle against feudalistic conditions toward successful conclusion of the agrarian revolution, thereby awakening the peasantry to revolutionary consciousness.

4. The Soviet *Popular Front policy,* the policy of the "zone of peace," i.e., of alliance with the Afro-Asian nationalist and neutralist forces, is based on the "possibility of relatively peaceful development" in which communist victory in the underdeveloped areas will result largely from competition between East and West. The communist parties in the underdeveloped countries—whether legal or illegal— also for this reason gear their own attitude toward their governments to the latter's stand on neutrality. The Chinese, believing in the "permanent revolution" and seeing the national and the social revolution as a uniphase, continuous process under communist direction, consider the Soviet approach a gambling away of communist chances in the underdeveloped areas. This, they argue, might give a vacillatory bourgeoisie that tends toward anticommunism time to consolidate its power. Thus Mao's "neo-democratic revolution," which he advertises as a model to the peoples of Asia and Africa, is *not* identical with the newly-hatched "national democracy." Both are considered as transitional phases—within Lenin's meaning—from national to social revolution. Both are also based on a quadripartite alliance. But the Chinese see the "neo-democratic revolution" successful only through a quadripartite alliance of workers, peasants, urban petite bourgeoisie, and the national bourgeoisie, *with the Communist Party in the vanguard* in the struggle against feudalism, landowners, those in the pay of

---

[152] Mao Tse-tung, *Ausgewählte Schriften,* Vol. 3, p. 122.

[153] Liu Shao-chi, *op. cit.,* p. 5.

foreign capital, and imperialism. "National democracy," as was pointed out, is to be based initially on a quadripartite alliance of workers, peasants, the democratic intelligentsia, and the national bourgeoisie under leadership of "any democratic class."

Here we deal with fundamental differences on the question of leadership and the attitude toward the "national bourgeoisie." Under the Chinese concept, leadership is to be with the Communist Party from the very outset, this being a pre-condition for the establishment of the Popular Front and for the conduct of the "neo-democratic revolution." The national bourgeoisie, insofar as it submits to communist leadership and takes part in the struggle against feudalism and imperialism, may yet play a progressive role, may even be re-educated, according to the Chinese viewpoint. Thus, the transition to the "social revolution" in this concept requires no change in leadership, but may be executed fairly "peaceably" with a shift in revolutionary content under an already existing communist leadership. The Chinese deny that in a "national democracy," which may initially be led by "any democratic class," the Communist Party can peaceably acquire leadership through a burgeoning proletariat. They consider the transition from a bourgeois-nationalistic to a communist government without forcible destruction of the state machinery an impossibility. To the Chinese, the "neutralism" of the national governments smacks of camouflage. In Nehru's India, especially, they saw a representative of imperialist interests in Asia.

The Chinese concept is of political import, especially to those countries not as yet independent, as well as to underdeveloped nations with centers of unrest, and to those countries labeled by Markov "states where the national bourgeoisie is in undisputed possession of the commanding heights." The Chinese recommend and are eager to apply Mao's *Problems of Strategy in Guerrilla Warfare* to all countries that are embroiled in "revolutionary action" (e.g., Angola and Cameroon). But the Chinese main thrust is against those "states where the national bourgeoisie is in undisputed possession of the commanding heights," in particular against the national leadership corps of India. Nor do they see any hope in state capitalism freeing these countries from enslavement and exploitation. Thus, Soviet bloc aid to these countries is worse than futile, serving only to support capitalistic development and anticommunist trends.

Behind the Sino-Soviet quarrel over peaceful coexistence and the avoidability or inevitability of war, there looms the demand of the Peking doctrinal center as focal point of Chinese communism for coequality with the Soviet Union in socio-economic evolution. To Peking the USSR, as an economically more advanced industrial nation, has an overriding commitment to the needs of the backward countries of the Soviet bloc—such as China—and "should make its material achievements available to the latter." "He who holds this belief," says Liugo Longo, deputy secretary general of Italy's Communist Party, in a commentary on the Chinese stand, "cannot accept economic competition between the USSR and the U.S. and other capitalist countries. Nor can he agree to peaceful coexistence, or to Soviet foreign aid to underdeveloped countries. Such aid should be reserved for backward nations in the socialist camp." [154] As was pointed out in the chapter on *State Capitalism and Foreign Aid*, the Iraqi communist Aziz al Hadsh turned against the Chinese because of their opposition to Soviet foreign aid to bourgeois-nationalist powers that "suppress the democratic movement" and "turn against socialism."

There is a causal relationship between the quarrel over "peaceful coexistence" and the question of whether Soviet foreign aid may be given to the underdeveloped nations or whether such aid should be reserved primarily to strengthen backward Soviet bloc countries— such as China.

This fundamental opposition of the Chinese to Soviet economic aid to national bourgeois governments of underdeveloped countries, however, does not prevent the Chinese from granting economic aid of their own even to countries with strong ties to the West (Pakistan) if this fits into their foreign policy.

COEXISTENCE, CHINESE STYLE

It is doubtlessly untrue that Peking opposes coexistence as such, as the Soviets claim today. Many facts speak against it. While the Chinese oppose Soviet peaceful coexistence as world-revolutionary strategy in the atomic age, they themselves have often practiced coexistence as a tool of foreign policy. Sino-Soviet relationship, examined in the light of the dialectic law of "unity of opposites," shows instructive periods of unity between the two partners. Thus, after the October 1949 communist victory in China Moscow accepted the Chinese Revolution "as prototypal of revolution in colonial and semi-colonial countries." The Soviet bloc press at the time applied Liu Shao-chi's formulation. Mao's guerrilla strategy also was being applied in the young nation states whose independence Moscow at the time thought sham and bluff. The communist parties of Burma, Malaya, India, and Indonesia, as is known, during the late 1940s and early 1950s also practiced this strategy, a strategy Moscow did not abandon until after the Bandung Conference. It is entirely possible, too, that in those days Moscow and Peking even divided Asia among themselves into

---

[154] *L'Unità*, 23 December 1961.

spheres of interest. The former Soviet diplomat in Burma, e.g., Aleksander Kaznacheev, speaks of such agreement.[155]

The final phase of the Korean War also fell into a period of Sino-Soviet accord. At the time, the Chinese passed through their "Rightist stage" and resolutely applied coexistence as a means of foreign policy. On 20 April 1954 they concluded the so-called Tibet Pact with India which laid down the five principles of coexistence. The summer of 1954 saw them in Geneva, participating in the Indochina Conference. On 28 June 1954 Chou En-lai once more (in his negotiations with Nehru at New Delhi) reaffirmed the five coexistence principles. And at the Bandung Conference, to which the Chinese, in contrast to the Soviets, were invited, they lapped the USSR from the right, so to speak.

The Chinese set out to achieve victory in the economic arena as well. At the time, they saw the answer to the leadership question in Asia—China or India?—in terms of economic competition. Later they even spoke of attaining England's level of raw material production in fifteen years. In this economic race the Chinese counted quite understandably on Russia's help, for two reasons:

1. Khrushchev, before he made his 1955 trip to Belgrade to make peace with Tito, visited Peking in October 1954 to normalize Sino-Soviet relations. The Soviets were ready to contribute a large pump-priming sum to China's industrialization, provided for in that country's first Five-Year Plan of 1953-1957. A study of all Sino-Soviet agreements shows that Khrushchev, on 12 October 1954, made great concessions to the Chinese and roused their hopes. Thus, the last of the "lopsided pacts," forced on China by Stalin in 1950, were scrapped, the naval base of Port Arthur was returned to China, agreement was reached on the turnover of Soviet shares in four Sino-Soviet corporations, the increase in Soviet delivery to China of industrial machinery was fixed, a new credit of $130,000,000 was granted to China, and the construction of the Mongolian Railroad, as well as the rail linking Lanchow and Alma-Ata, were agreed upon.

2. In 1954 there was as yet no mention of Soviet aid to underdeveloped Afro-Asian or Latin American countries. A Soviet foreign aid policy for countries outside the Soviet bloc did not exist!

Even though Soviet-supplied economic aid to China should not be underrated, it must be emphasized that Peking, at the end of the first Five-Year Plan in 1957, was disappointed in the results. Some facts about Soviet aid to China:

During the three years 1950-52 the USSR delivered to China com-

---

[155] Aleksander Kaznacheev, *Inside a Soviet Embassy,* Philadelphia and New York 1962, p. 143.

plete industrial plants valued at $73,910,000. The amount was raised to $703,870,000 for the first Five-Year Plan period 1953-57, and peaked at $939,670,000 for the years 1950-60, delivered in complete industrial plants.[156]

Oddly enough, during the years 1958-60, when Sino-Soviet tension had already begun to mount, the USSR delivery of complete plants had a higher monetary value than that made in the entire period 1950-57. A Chinese economist has solved this apparent paradox by claiming that the materials delivered by the Soviets during 1958-60 were late shipments of commitments made by the USSR toward fulfillment of China's first Five-Year Plan (1953-57). The USSR, so the argument runs, carried out these commitments very reluctantly and with much procrastination. The fact that Soviet delivery of plant equipment dropped from $373,800,000 in 1960 to $78,900,000 in 1961 lends credence to this argument.

At the end of their first Five-Year Plan in 1957, the Chinese also lost all hope of further Soviet credit grants. After 1957 China had to make do without Soviet credits. The last credit installments that the Chinese People's Republic received from the USSR, the only creditor it had, were 117,400,000 *yuan* in 1956 and 23,300,000 *yuan* in 1957. It is not clear if China waived further Soviet credits since that time, or if the USSR was unable to extend further credits to its Chinese partner because of commitments to India, Indonesia, Egypt, and others. Chinese criticism of Soviet credit policy, and of Soviet "aid to the national bourgeoisie" of Asia and North Africa, points to the latter as the true reason. Early in 1958, Soviet credit aid to underdeveloped countries outside the Soviet bloc passed the one billion dollar mark, whereas China has been cut off from Soviet credit since 1957. Actually, the Chinese People's Republic has received a total of only $1,357,500,-000 in credits from the USSR.[157]

On 21 December 1964, Chou En-lai, in front of the National People's Congress, said that total Soviet economic aid including interest amounted to 1,406 million rubles ($1,562,000,000).

In late 1957 and early 1958 it became obvious that China's hope, with Soviet help, to reach England's level in raw material production would not materialize. Peking could no longer count on Soviet help to decide the question of Chinese or Indian hegemony. Even then, the Soviet concept of an economic race with the West was oriented toward building up Russia's economic strength and also included in-

---

[156] Vierteljahresberichte der Friedrich-Ebert-Stiftung (Hannover), No. 7/1962, p. 48.
[157] *Die wirtschaftliche Verflechtung der Volksrepublik China mit der Sowjetunion,* Frankfurt/M.—Berlin 1959, pp. 43-44.

creased foreign aid to the "national bourgeoisie" nations, among them India, the country China was most eager to outstrip. Following the 1958 publication of the outline of Russia's Seven-Year Plan, which couched the world-revolutionary objective in terms of outstripping the U. S. economically, Sino-Soviet relations were bound to worsen. Within the framework of such an objective, China as a backward land can only play a subordinate role. For Peking, coexistence at government level, and world revolution as the ultimate objective, are two aims to be rigorously kept apart. Chinese reaction to the Soviet foreign aid cutoff came as early as 1957. On 29 June of that year, Li Hsien-nien, China's Finance Minister, declared before the National People's Congress: "We can rely on our own accumulation of capital." [158] In a report *How China Finances Herself*, the financial self-sufficiency of China's economic buildup was proudly stressed.[159] Chou En-lai later declared: "Of all the social forces of production, man is the decisive factor, the most precious 'capital.'" [160] The slogan "go-it-alone" was revived in China, in an attempt to carry out the economic race. The setting up of the people's communes and the "great leap forward" campaign mark the leftist turn in China's domestic, as well as foreign, policy.

The "people's communes" did not only represent China's claim to its own "road to communism," coequal with and at the same tempo as the USSR. They were also to serve very real economic functions. Through the militaristically organized people's communes, it was hoped to tap an enormous, hitherto unproductive manpower reservoir that would enable China "under its own steam" to win out in its ambitious economic race, even without Soviet aid. Natural disasters and poor planning put an end to the undertaking. The way out was a policy of aggression.

THE SINO-INDIAN BORDER CONFLICT

China's undeclared border war with India can be really understood only against the problems discussed: the Chinese attitude to the "national bourgeoisie" in principle; the cutoff of Soviet aid to China, with a simultaneous increase of such aid to India; the domestic economic crisis in China; and the rejection in principle of the Soviet brand of coexistence. Peking engineered the border conflict under the old China-or-India formula for these reasons:

1. To strike a blow against Nehru's India as "imperialism's extended arm in Asia"; to demonstrate China's military superiority; and

---

[158] *Hsinhua*, 29 June 1957.
[159] *China Reconstructs*, No. 10/1957.
[160] Chou En-lai, *Das grosse Jahrzehnt*, Peking 1959, p. 31.

to raise Chinese prestige with the smaller Asian states or else overawe them.

2. In view of China's own domestic economic crisis, to create economic trouble for India, and impede her economic development. It is known that the Chinese border incursion forced India to sidetrack funds, allocated for industrial development, to the military sector.

3. To torpedo Russia's coexistence policy.

There is an apparent contradiction in China's relation with the great national states like India and Egypt on the one hand, and her attitude to the smaller nations like Burma, Nepal, and Cambodia on the other. In the latter countries, also, there are nationalist, even feudalistic governments in power. But it is part of Mao's strategy to divide his enemies and strike only against a few at a time.

It is with its neighbors, and with those nations that are in open conflict with the West or that offer bases of operation against the West, that China "coexists" and maintains friendship pacts and aid agreements. By its Indian border action, Peking increased the pressure on the tiny border states. To bolster its foreign policy, China concluded border treaties with Burma, Nepal, Pakistan, and even with Mongolia. This was to demonstrate that Peking can solve its border problems with all nations of good will; only with India a solution is impossible because of "opposition of the pro-imperialistic circles in India."

In granting credits and other economic aid to countries not counted among its chief foes (e.g., to Burma, Ceylon, Ghana, Guinea, Indonesia, Yemen, Cambodia, and Nepal among others), Peking poses as an economic power in the underdeveloped areas, thus seeking to enhance its political status and prestige. India, it may be pointed out, does not furnish like economic aid to other countries.

On the whole, China's relation with the underdeveloped countries reveals an application of the strategy which had been used in China itself: the main thrust is directed against the upper bourgeoisie and the agents of foreign capital, namely, against India; collaboration and coexistence with the petite bourgeoisie and the intermediary powers—with Burma, Nepal, Cambodia, and others; safeguarding the leadership of the Communist Party, represented by Communist China.

The difference in Sino-Soviet strategy, and the rivalry between the two bloc partners, lead on the one hand to an intensified activity by both sides in the field of political propaganda; to a mutual, active wooing for favor and influence among the peoples of the underdeveloped areas, and to an application of a variety of methods. On the other hand, their alienation leads both sides to compete for leadership in the communist parties of the underdeveloped countries, thus exerting a retarding influence on the communist parties of Asia and North Africa.

Focal Point Africa

"The African continent currently plays an avant-garde role in the struggle against the colonial system."[161] The Soviet bloc has recognized this fact since 1959, when it became obvious that many African nations would become independent in 1960.

Today, Soviet bloc strategists consider Africa south of the Sahara the weakest link in the chain of the one-time colonial system. It is this area that has become the focal point of Soviet bloc attention, and especially also of East Germany. Though in matters of Soviet bloc foreign aid the countries south of the Sahara run a poor second to Southeast Asia and the UAR, it is in these countries that the Soviet theoreticians *in general see possibilities for a noncapitalistic road to development. Especially in parts of Dark Africa do they see propitious conditions as objectively and subjectively maturing.* Chief proponent of this view is the Soviet African expert I. I. Potekhin, the Soviet bloc voice on African studies until June 1964.

It was in Africa that the somersault in Soviet foreign policy was greatest. As recent as 1954 Potekhin, in his standard work *Narody Afriki,* spoke about a national bourgeoisie forming as a class in Equatorial Africa. African society, he claimed, was split up in classes, with the working class the decisive social force. African developments converted Potekhin to other views.

Until a few years ago Soviet policy concerned itself primarily with North Africa, with only France's Communist Party scoring some temporary gains in Dark Africa between 1946 and 1950. Now, how-

---

[161] *Sovremenni vostok* (Moscow), No. 2/1961, p. 41.

98

ever, the main effort is to be applied in the countries south of the Sahara, which are then to be used as bases for communist penetration of the entire continent.

THE SOVIET CLASS ANALYSIS

We have already discussed the Soviet bloc's strategic focus on such countries as the UAR, Guinea, Mali and Congo (Brazzaville) as beachheads for the establishment of national democratic states. But in determining their strategic and tactical approach, as well as their methods and forms of activity toward the other African countries, the majority of whom are oriented toward the West, the Soviet theoreticians currently distinguish between the requirements of North Africa and those of countries south of the Sahara. Potekhin certainly is not making a new discovery when he states that "the lands of the Maghreb and Egypt are decidedly more advanced in all respects than the countries south of the Sahara." Here he finds capitalistic conditions prevailing on a relatively broad front and sees a national bourgeoisie being formed which, in league with diverse feudal and semifeudal groups, takes "the leading role in the struggle for national liberation."

In 1963, Potekhin added that only in the UAR and in Algeria had the national bourgeoisie not gotten a chance to establish capitalism. Since then it was said of Ben Bella and Nasser that they were executing a noncapitalist development program. Which road to development Algeria has taken since Ben Bella's downfall has not been investigated by the Soviet theoreticians so far. In North Africa—Potekhin goes on to say—the Moroccans, Algerians, Tunisians, and Egyptians had already formed national states in which even the labor movement had a certain tradition, and communist parties were active for some time.[162]

What Potekhin really wants to point out is that communist policy in North Africa must take into account conditions similar to those prevailing in India and other Asian countries. But south of the Sahara he sees entirely different requirements. "In the nations of Equatorial Africa," says Potekhin, "the class-forming process is not yet completed . . . With the exception of several regions in Nigeria and Uganda, there is no feudal class in contraposition to the peasantry . . . The formation of an African national bourgeoisie as a class in contraposition to the proletariat is a process far from completed." [163]

---

[162] *Problemy vostokovedeniya* (Moscow), No. 1/1960, p. 15.

[163] I. I. Potekhin, *Africa Looks Ahead* (Russ.), Moscow 1960, pp. 18-19. Under the same title an Eng. ed. also app. in Moscow in 1960. A Ger. ed. appeared in East Berlin 1961.

Potekhin returns to this theme of an as yet virgin political soil of class warfare in another publication: *"A different picture* [than in North Africa] *is seen in the colonies south of the Sahara. Here, the transition from colonial suppression to political sovereignty occurs under circumstances that allowed insufficient development to class differentiation among the African population. A national bourgeoisie is barely beginning to form and is economically still very weak. In the villages, patriarchal bonds prevail, with characteristic and as yet very strong remnants of tribal organization. In these countries the noncapitalistic road to development is a possibility."* [164]

On the one hand, Potekhin seems to realize there is something wrong with the standard Soviet version that characterizes Africa's leadership corps as a "national bourgeoisie." On the other, by saying that Africa has not as yet formed social classes, he fears to broach the ideas of a classless African society. "No," he hastens to emphasize in a more recent statement, "it would be entirely wrong to call today's African society a classless one." [165] And he adds: "Now, with independence, the national bourgeoisie is given several new chances for development. There is appearing a new type of indigenous middle class, which might be called the bureaucratic middle class. This is the civil servant body, grown affluent through high salaries." [166]

In Africa, Soviet theoreticians are increasingly faced with the fact that the young African national states are headed by leaders of a social background different from the communist class warfare version. The property interests of these leaders are weakly developed and they lean neither in the direction of liberal capitalism nor in that of communist doctrine. G. Mirsky, section head for socio-economic development in liberated countries at the Soviet Institute for World Economy and International Relations, sets out to correct Potekhin. "It would be a simplification," he stresses, "to assume that the national bourgeoisie will without doubt become the ruling class in all or the majority of the African states." [167] And he goes on to say: "So far, we have made no attempt to analyze those social elements in the societies of the underdeveloped countries that do not fit the term 'bourgeoisie.' I am thinking here of the intelligentsia and the armed forces. It is precisely from their ranks that revolutionary and national democrats appear." [168] But Mirsky, also, cannot escape

---

[164] *Problemy vostokovedeniya* (Moscow), No. 1/1960, p. 15. Italics are this writer's.

[165] *Mezhdunarodnaya zhizn* (Moscow), No. 1/1963, p. 103.

[166] *ibid.*, p. 103.

[167] *Mirovaya ekonomika i mezhdunarodnie otnosheniya* (Moscow), No. 2/1963, p. 65.

[168] *ibid.*

the pull of doctrine and he qualifies therefore: "These are not elements that exist outside or above the classes but express the interests of certain classes." [169] What classes, is not said, and since the term bourgeoisie "does not fit them," it is most difficult to make a guess. What is meant are the forces that govern in Guinea, Mali, and several other countries, as well as Egypt. The Soviet expert stresses: "The forces in power here can scarcely be called representatives of the bourgeoisie." Mirsky was the first to label them representatives of the "progressive intelligentsia," the "revolutionary democrats," and the "patriotic army circles" [UAR].

The direction in which these countries will develop depends on the political views of their leaders. If the latter should ally themselves with the masses and accept help from "the socialist camp," national-democratic revolution might be engendered in these lands.

According to Mirsky, it cannot be claimed that the "national bourgeoisie" is in power in those countries that are associated with the Common Market. Mirsky calls the ruling elements in these countries the "bureaucratic elite" and a "bourgeoisie of the new type: the civil service bourgeoisie." Allegedly, this type bourgeoisie, with "direct or indirect support of colonialism," became prominent especially in Senegal.[170] A "national bourgeoisie" in these countries is only in the making, it "has not as yet achieved power, and represents a potential revolutionary element." The inference here is that this rising national bourgeoisie in the EEC-associated countries, together with the workers and peasants, is destined eventually to relieve those in power today. Mirsky's theorizing only serves to point out the dilemma facing the Soviets in Africa today.

It seems odd that the question of "transition to socialism without passing through capitalism" should be raised in connection with those underdeveloped nations which have just become independent and which the Soviet theoreticians also count among the most backward of nations. An examination of the voluminous material on hand reveals that the Soviet bloc theoreticians are concentrating on *four factors*, uniquely applicable in Africa, which are to serve as theoretic backbone to stepped-up political activity:

1. The relative political, social, and economic weakness of the national leadership corps;

2. The peculiar circumstances under which the African labor movement began and developed;

3. The lack of a firmly established *African* capitalistic production climate and a socio-economic backwardness that, coupled with the

---

[169] *ibid.*

[170] *Probleme des Friedens und des Sozialismus*, No. 10/1962, p. 830.

first two factors, are expected to favor a noncapitalistic development; and

4. The deep-running current of Pan-Africanism to be applied as a means of influencing the entire continent.

The aforementioned "alliance policy" proceeded from the assumption that in Asia above all a citizenry with an ancient tradition must be taken into account, one that rose to a position of great influence in the national liberation movement and created organizations that—like India's National Congress—are also experienced in dealing with communism. Africa, on the other hand, is ruled by an assortment of social forces, by the "democratic intelligentsia" and "patriotic military circles" in some countries, and by a "bureaucratic elite" in others. Political parties as such appeared in Africa only after World War II, stemming in part from those trade unions that not only played an important role during the liberation, but, in several of these political parties, exert an active voice today.

The growth of a landowning class—so the argument runs—is impeded by tribal property customs which deny this class a power it enjoys in Asia. "Capital and labor in the African sense are not opposing elements."

In contrast to Asia, Soviet strategists see Africa's social and national evolution still to come. This evolution can be achieved only by forces that command the necessary organization and influence. But the communist theoreticians themselves are by no means sure how the transition from tribe to nation is to be achieved or the problem of national borders to be solved. Markov simply declares this to be something the African peoples must solve themselves. But Nigeria's Leipzig-trained Modilim Akhufusi states: "It is at any rate the task of the Nigerian working class to find a solution to the national question in conjunction with solving the social question." [171]

The absence of communist parties and the weakness and inexperience of the emerging national bourgeoisie caused the Soviet theoreticians, in violation of all Marxist doctrine, to see *that the labor unions south of the Sahara were ordained to play the leading role in the completion of the national revolution and in the solution of political problems*. To these theoreticians, class warfare is identical with the struggle for national freedom, which to them is a struggle of African labor against foreign capital. They also see the African proletariat as a child of foreign, not African, capitalistic parents.

S. Datlin, Soviet African expert, argues: "The capitalist system was introduced in Africa by West European capitalists. The latter

---

[171] *Geschichte und Geschichtsbild Afrikas*, p. 131.

opposed the evolution of an indigenous bourgeoisie but were of course unable to do without the proletariat as a labor source. In this manner an alien bourgeoisie became the exploiting class in Africa, but those exploited were the African wage earners." [172] From this, Dr. Walter Markov deduces: "Africa's industrial proletariat is a young, numerically as yet weak, class. In only a few countries is it therefore organized into a homogeneous revolutionary class party. There where it exists it exerts a direct influence on a militant vanguard of the workers and peasants. *On the other hand, the African proletariat has already formed strong, battle-tested labor unions that in the present phase serve as the most effective allies of the peasants in defending the interests of the wage earners.* Opposed to any kind of exploitation, the union-organized sons of the working class represent the best, most incorruptible, and most tireless patriots of their African homeland. Belonging to a class that is instrumental in developing Africa's productive capabilities, they have at the same time reached the highest degree of national consciousness through an insight into the social perspectives. There can never be a victorious freedom movement without them, even less against them. In this regard, Africa has already achieved some novel results: the conclusion of an alliance between organized labor and the farmers' association in Guinea, and the establishment of a solid labor union front in West Africa. 'Africa's hour' will become the world's hour if the African patriots succeed in militantly spreading this knowledge." [173]

THE "LEADING ROLE OF THE LABOR UNIONS"

The Communist Party's slogan, "leading role in the national freedom movement," was replaced in the African countries south of the Sahara by the slogan, "the leading role of the working class, with organized labor in the lead." Now the claim is: "It is known that under certain conditions the labor unions, led by men trained in theory, may assume the role of leadership over the working class and represent the latter in its relation with the broad masses." [174] As was pointed out earlier, south of the Sahara communist parties exist only in the Union of South Africa, Basutoland, Madagascar, Nigeria, Senegal and Reunion. The intent, without doubt, is to implant hard-core communist cadres, trained in special Soviet bloc trade union schools, within the African labor organizations. The African communist N. Numadé believes that an "immediate industrialization would bring about a rapid growth in Africa's proletariat . . . an intensification of class warfare

---

[172] S. Datlin, *Africa Throws Off Its Chains* (Russ.), Moscow 1960, p. 25.
[173] *Geschichte und Geschichtsbild Afrikas, op. cit.*, p. 131.
[174] *Problemy vostokovedeniya* (Moscow), No. 1/1960, p. 19.

. . . and the evolution of a powerful Marxist-Leninist movement." [175]
Only to a minor extent is the Soviet bloc's union activity, aimed at
securing political leadership for the labor unions in Africa, carried
out via unions that are members of the communist *Weltgewerkschaftsbund*. In 1961 only eight African labor unions belonged to this Communist World Federation of Trade Unions (WFTU), compared to
thirty-two that belonged to the "International Federation of Free
Trade Unions," and nineteen in 1960 that were members of the "International Federation of Christian Trade Unions." Since 1959, communist labor union policy has been tailored to fit the African independence movements and is primarily oriented toward penetration
of existing unions of all persuasions.

The new tactics were plainly in evidence at the Fifth World Congress of the WFTU, held 1-16 December 1961 in Moscow. In addition
to the aforementioned eight communist labor unions, the congress
was attended by observer delegations from twenty-one unions of
various political leanings from eighteen African countries (Aden,
Algeria, Angola, Basutoland, the Congo, Ghana, Kenya, Mali, Maure-
tania, Morocco, Niger, Nigeria, Northern Rhodesia, Portuguese Guinea,
Senegal, Somalia, Tanganyika, and Zanzibar). Most African trade
union headquarters, because of their politically neutral stand, often
send delegations to Moscow, as well as to Prague and East Berlin.
This "weakness" is exploited by the communist union strategists, who
in this follow Lenin's pointer: "One . . . must be ready for any sacrifice, even—if need be—for all sorts of ruses, tricks, illegal methods,
ready for dissimulation and hiding of the truth, only to get into the
labor unions, remain in them, and there at all cost advance the cause
of communism." [176]

In line with its new tactics, the communist WFTU skillfully established contact with the existing regional African trade union centers.
Several methods of collaborating with the "International Federation
of Arabic Trade Unions" were developed. Former functionaries of the
WFTU maintained contact with the *Union Générale des Travailleurs
d'Afrique Noire* (UGTAN) and its subdivisions. In order to penetrate
the All-African Trade Union Federation (AATUF, a Pan-African
trade union federation founded in Casablanca), the WFTU exploits
the differences existing between the AATUF, the African Trade Union
Confederation (ATUC, a Pan-African trade union federation founded
in Dakar), and the International Federation of Free Trade Unions

---

[175] "The African Communist," from *Aus der internationalen Arbeiterbewegung,*
(East Berlin), No. 13/1961.
[176] Lenin, *Samtliche Werke,* Vol. XXV, Berlin-Vienna 1930, p. 240.

(IFFTU). Even the latter, which stoutly opposes all Popular Front attempts of the WFTU, is not immune to the WFTU's tactics in Africa. For years the WFTU has worked at building up its contacts with and increasing its influence over the IFFTU-affiliated Moroccan Trade Union Federation and the Trade Union Federation of Algeria. Currently, the WFTU is making a concentrated effort at penetrating the trade unions of Tanganyika, the Congo, Somalia, and Kenya. Both the Moroccan as well as the Algerian federations have in the meantime resigned from the IFFTU, as has the trade union of Tanganyika.

At the same time, the infiltration methods became more diverse. The government machinery of the more important Soviet bloc countries is at the disposal of the WFTU and its affiliated Soviet bloc unions for the training of African union functionaries, for opening of trade union schools in Africa, the paying of African union functionaries, and the printing of trade union periodicals for Africa in Soviet bloc countries. It is well known that members with trade union experience are assigned to Soviet bloc trade delegations and missions. Their work and the union activities of the communist countries in Africa stand under the control of the Africa Section of the communist *Weltgewerkschaftsbund*.

At the sixth world union congress of the communist WFTU (8-22 October 1965 in Warsaw) the WFTU approved the All-African Trade Union Federation's action program which the AFTUF had adopted at its second congress (10-14 June 1964 in Bamako). The AFTUF was also represented at the sixth WFTU congress with a strong delegation.

This means that the communists support the following tasks for the African unions:

In the countries that are still colonies the African unions are supposed to organize masses of workers, raise the self-confidence of the national liberation movement and inject a revolutionary and social element into them;

in those countries that are taking the path of a radical social-economic reorganization, that is, in the UAR, Guinea, Mali, Congo (Brazzaville) and to some extent also in Tanganyika: work in the administration of the economy and further the constant improvement of production; strengthen the country's revolutionary orientation in close cooperation with the unity parties and the political apparatus; assist in the training of competent political, social and economic leaders, and work to increase the influence of the working class in the government, state, administration and economic apparatus;

in those countries "which are still ruled by neo colonialism and re-

actionaries," which means all other African countries, particularly those which are Western-oriented:

"To resist the subversive acts and the meddling of imperialism, and to use two main weapons in this endeavor: unity of the workers and independence of the unions from the counter-revolutionary regime which is an enemy of the people," that is, independence from the unity parties; raise the revolutionary consciousness of the masses; use all possible means in the fight against economic exploitation and falsification of the will of the masses and "unite all patriots and democrats of the country around the truly revolutionary political parties." [176a]

Congo (Brazzaville), where the state president and government chief Abbe Fulbert Youlou was overthrown on 15 August 1963 with the help of the unions and where a socialist-revolutionary regime was installed, is presented as a model to the unions in the last-named group of countries.

As we have mentioned, the different interest groups (unions, youth, women's and farmers' organizations) are also coordinated with the unity parties in the Western-oriented African countries. Conflicts and discussions that result from different interests therefore have to take place within the forum of the unity party. Tensions inevitably arise between the party leaders and the unions. They have become noticeable already in several countries and also during the overthrow of several African governments early in 1966. Moreover, unions constitute the left wing in almost all African unity parties.

As has been mentioned, various interest groups (unions, youth organizations, women's leagues, farmers' associations) in the African countries that lean toward the West are also made part of the unity parties. Struggles and discussions that arise out of conflicting interests therefore take place within the parties. Tensions between party and union leadership are inevitable, and have been in evidence in several countries, also during the overthrow of several African governments in the beginning of 1966. Moreover, the unions constitute the left wing of the unity parties in almost all African countries, a peculiarity taken into account by the Soviet bloc in dealing with Africa.

The Soviet bloc publication *Problems of Peace and Socialism* notes a "trend toward the formation of unitarian, national mass organizations" in Africa. The "struggle for democracy," i.e., for the "national-democratic state," it is further claimed, is far more diversified in Africa than in Asia. "In this regard, the trade unions carry a special responsibility." [177] These words indicate that the battle for the "na-

---

[176a] *Probleme des Friedens und des Sozialismus* (East Berlin—Prague), No. 2/1966, p. 151/152.

[177] *Probleme des Friedens und des Sozialismus* (East Berlin—Prague), No. 4/1962, p. 349.

tional-democratic state," is to be fought within the unity parties.

The Soviet bloc hopes to achieve its goals via the detour of winning over the labor unions, as well as the youth, students and women's organizations. A communist penetration of these organizations would remove the latter from the control of the political leadership and tear asunder the unity parties. With this, the subjective preconditions for the intermediate "national-democratic" communist goal would have been attained.

THE NONCAPITALIST ROAD TO DEVELOPMENT

The Soviet African expert, I. I. Potekhin, posed the question: "What is the situation in those parts of Tropical Africa, in which conditions for a noncapitalistic development prevail?" [178]

In his answer, Potekhin at first describes the special aspects we have sketched above. A national bourgeoisie in contraposition to the working class, he explains, has not as yet appeared in Africa south of the Sahara. Though there are capitalistic elements in agriculture, in the trades, and in business, the overall capital accumulation and the number of capitalistic enterprises are very low. "The chief factor is that they are few in number and economically extremely weak." On the other hand, he reports the number of workers in these countries as relatively high, putting the figure for all of Africa at 15 million wage earners. Potekhin describes another aspect that is to facilitate a noncapitalistic development: "The national industry in the countries of Tropical Africa is largely in government hands because private capital is as a rule too weak to assume the construction of factories and plants. In order to industrialize, the governments of these countries are forced to resort to a public-financed and controlled buildup of industry (there is no other way open to them). Many call this state capitalism. It is at any rate a public and not a private sector." A third factor is tied in with agrarian reform and development. Here the governments of Tropical Africa face the tremendous task of converting from the most primitive farming methods to modern agricultural techniques. Again using Ghana, Guinea, and the Republic of Mali as examples, Potekhin explains the process to be applied: "In states like Ghana, Guinea, and Mali the governments have begun to build up production cooperatives and to set up machine-tractor stations. This is the only way to a quick solution of the agrarian reconstruction problem. The collectivization of agriculture is simplified by the fact that the land is still chiefly communally owned." A fourth aspect of the noncapitalistic road Potekhin carefully formulates in one sentence: "Finally—and this may be the main-

---

[178] I. I. Potekhin, "Africa: Results and Prospects of the Anti-Imperialistic Revolution," in *Aziya i Afrika segodnya* (Moscow), No. 10/1961, p. 15.

spring behind Africa's forward march along the noncapitalistic road to development—socialism is a mighty force in the world today."

But Potekhin has become very cautious. He comments: "Soviet experts have often discussed in their writings the objective requirements for a noncapitalistic Africa. Yet, a still deeper and more exhaustive analysis of the problem is needed. Objectively, the preconditions for a noncapitalistic development do in fact exist in the majority of African states. But although the possibility for a transition to socialism while bypassing the capitalistic developmental stage exists in Africa, the transmuting of possibility into reality depends on many other factors, above all on the interrelation of the class dynamics within the African states." [179]

V. Tjagunenko, another Soviet writer, makes an even more detailed analysis of the conditions favoring a noncapitalistic road to development in Ghana, Guinea, and Mali. He sees in the socio-economic restructuring of industry, agriculture, and commerce, as well as in the activation of the masses, a step in the direction of the noncapitalistic road. Meanwhile, however, the Soviet experts seem to realize that in Africa anticapitalism and a state-controlled economy are not necessarily a vindication of the "national democracy" thesis, but simply characteristics of the "third way." Moans Tjagunenko: "A bitter and tenacious struggle between the forces of progress and the reactionary elements . . . is still ahead." [180] Subjectively—he goes on to say—future development hinges in the final analysis on the "interplay of class dynamics" and on the "attitude of the ruling powers." That is, further development is decisively dependent on the unity parties and their leadership. Attempts to create internal conditions favorable to the communist goals, however, must lead to friction.

PAN-AFRICANISM

In its efforts to gain a foothold in Africa, the Soviet bloc even looks favorably on an old African concept, Pan-Africanism. As was pointed out earlier, the theses of the Second Party Congress proclaimed the need for "fighting Pan-Islamism, the Pan-Asia movement, and similar trends." The International Trade Union Committee of Negro Workers of 1930 specifically fought against the Garvey Movement and Pan-Africanism. There was opposition also to the Pan-Arabic move toward unity, expressed by the Syrian communist leader Chaled Bagdash at the founding of the UAR. Bagdash was willing to accept the UAR only as "a loose confederacy" that would allow freedom of action

---

[179] *Narody Azii i Afriki* (Moscow), No. 1/1962, pp. 11-12.

[180] *Mirovaya ekonomika i mezhdunarodnie otnosheniya* (Moscow), No. 3/1963, pp. 29-33.

to the communists. With the United Arab Republic in mind, Khrushchev commented in 1959: "The federation of a group of states is a complicated matter. History teaches that nations, especially those only recently freed from foreign subjugation, very jealously guard their sovereign rights . . . The federation of states is of benefit to the people only if the requisite political and economic conditions have sufficiently matured, and if all peculiarities of the uniting partners are being considered . . . Wisdom and patience are needed to find solutions to these questions. Precipitousness is likely to lead to undesirable results." [181] In his *Africa Looks Ahead*, Potekhin decidedly wanted to see Khrushchev's counsel also applied to Pan-Africanism. Following his return from the First Conference of Independent African States, held in Accra, Ghana, December 1958, Potekhin wrote that Pan-Africanism contains much that is alien to world communism.[182]

In its reaction to Pan-Africanism, the Soviet bloc underwent a change similar to that of its revised attitude concerning neutralism. In both cases, an attempt is made to turn an existing situation to politico-tactical profit. The reasons behind the communist reversal in position lay in the difficulties encountered by the Pan-African movement.

Pan-Africanism was proclaimed in the United States as early as 1903. There it was part of the emancipation movement of the North American Negroes who, as descendants of African slaves, propagated the unity of all Negroes in a world movement for human rights, as well as the return of the Negroes to Africa. The organizational vehicles of this movement were the Pan-African Congresses of which five were held before World War II. A sixth convened in Manchester in 1945.

With the achievement of independence by many African states, the old idea of unity gained a new meaning. It became the concept of Africa itself, the goal being the independence and autonomy of all African countries, and the unification of the continent in preparation for the establishment of a so-called United States of Africa. Leadership of this movement now fell largely to the statesmen and functionaries of the first nations to achieve independence. Organizationally, the movement took the form of Conferences of Independent African States, principally that of the All-African People's Conference (AAPC). The first All-African People's Conference convened (8-13 December 1958) in Accra, capital of the new state of Ghana. The

---

[181] *Pravda*, 17 March 1959.
[182] *Mezhdunarodnaya zhizn*, (Moscow), No. 2/1959, p. 118.

second AAPC was held in Tunis 25-31 January 1960. The third AAPC took place in Cairo 25-30 March 1961, but a Fourth Conference could not be convened so far. Prudently, the Soviet bloc nations sent observer delegations to these conferences.

Pan-Africanism is deeply rooted in all of Africa. But its strongest influence fell in the pre-independence days, when it acted as a potent catalyst among the African peoples. This role all but disappeared with the appearance of numerous new nations, the victorious national movement with the emergence of a leadership caste in each country, and the associations of groups of states. Now that the old Pan-African concept is within the realm of possibility, a number of pretenders, motivated by the national interests of their own country, have come to the fore with leadership claims of their own, or at least opposing those of other national leaders. Prominent among claimants for leadership of All-African unity were such countries as Ghana (under President Kwame Nkrumah). Presently the idea of unity is supported by Guinea and Mali, joined by the UAR, Morocco, and Algeria. The countries associated with the Common Market have stayed away from the All-African People's Conferences. The latter were, however, conspicuously attended by political opponents and emigrants from these countries.

The Soviet bloc tries to profit by these developments. What matters to the communists is that the Pan-Africanists and the Casablanca group should remain in active opposition to other state groupings and movements. A deepening of the rift between the opposing factions, they feel, will benefit their own policy. Both the Pan-Africanists and the communists have come to see that in the Africa of today organization is of decisive importance. Thus, the leadership of the All-African People's Congress, aware that Pan-African unity would not be achieved by way of federation of independent states, began the buildup of mass organizations on an interstate basis to carry Pan-Africanism everywhere. The third AAPC, held March 1961 in Cairo, passed the following resolution:

> "The Third All-African People's Congress appeals to all trade unions and all youth, peasants, and women's organizations with the request to:
>
> 1. convene an African Trade Union Congress for the purpose of founding an All-African Trade Union Federation;
>
> 2. call an African Youth Conference and organize an African Youth Festival in order to create a homogeneous African youth movement;

3. call a conference of all women's clubs of Africa to found a uniform women's organization;

4. call a conference of all farmer associations and organizations to create a uniform All-African peasant movement.

The Congress requests the Steering Committee to take all necessary steps toward the establishment of an African press agency and an African information center." [183]

To penetrate these organizations, influence them, and win them over, is beyond doubt more important to the Soviet bloc today than African foreign aid. Here, Lenin's guideline applies: "It is necessary to learn to make any sacrifice, to surmount the greatest obstacles, in order patiently, systematically, tenaciously, and assiduously to conduct propaganda and agitation in precisely those societies, clubs, and unions to which the proletarian or semiproletarian masses belong." [184]

The All-African Trade Union Federation was called into being at an African Trade Union Congress, held in Casablanca May 1961. As has been noted, sharp differences exist between this organization and both the African Trade Union Confederation of Dakar, and the International Federation of Free Trade Unions. The communist World Federation of Trade Unions, which is not represented in the All-African Trade Union Federation, exploits the situation by tactically supporting the Pan-African union organization in order to penetrate it.

An All-African Youth Movement organization was founded 1 May 1962 at an All-African Youth Congress in Conakry, attended by representatives of twenty-five African youth organizations. This movement is headquartered in Conakry and maintains branch offices in Lagos and Cairo.

An All-African Farmer Union resulted from the first African Farmers' Conference, held in Accra in March 1962. Delegates from sixteen African countries participated in this conference.

An All-African Women's Conference, that is to meet every two years, was founded in the summer of 1962 at a conference in Dar-es-Salaam in which seventy-two delegates from the following countries took part: Ghana, Guinea, Ivory Coast, Kenya, Liberia, Mozambique, Mali, Niger, Portuguese-Guinea, Senegal, South Africa, Southwest Africa, Ethiopia, Tunisia, Tanganyika, Togo, Zanzibar, Northern Rho-

---

[183] *Troisième Session de la Conference des Peuples Africains,* Accra o.f., pp. 50-51; Vierteljahresberichte der Friedrich-Ebert-Stiftung (Hannover), No. 4/5/1961, p. 44.

[184] Lenin, *Der "Radikalismus", die Kinderkrankheit im Kommunismus,* Berlin 1945, p. 36.

desia, and Egypt. The communist International Democratic Federation of Women has already succeeded in establishing contact with this organization in several African countries.

An All-African Press Club was called into being at a conference of African journalists, held in Bamako, capital of Mali, 23 May 1961. A school of journalism and the establishment of an African news service followed. Working through the International Journalists Organization of Prague, the Soviet bloc exerts an influence on African journalists greater than that on any other group.

All above-listed organizations were called into being to become active not only in Ghana, Guinea, Mali, and the so-called Casablanca states, but to engage in political, propagandistic, and organizational work on behalf of Pan-Africanism in all of Africa.

Neither Western trade unions nor Western youth and women's groups maintain much contact with these Pan-African organizations. International communist front organizations, on the other hand, are all the more active in worming themselves into these organizations by means of every conceivable kind of aid and assistance. Should the Soviet bloc succeed in large-scale penetration of these organizations, it would gain control over decisive instruments in Africa.

From the communist side, the signing of the Africa Charter and the founding of a loose Organization of African Unity at the conference of heads of states and governments in Addis Ababa in May 1963 was hailed as a "positive event." This, however, does not signal a change in current Soviet bloc tactics. Rather, according to Soviet press comments, the belief seems to be that now "the struggle between the progressive and reactionary elements" within this organization will be forced into the open. For the same purpose, it is also desired to fit the aforementioned mass organizations into the new Organization of African Unity.

COMMUNISM AND AFRICAN SOCIALISM

Pan-Africanism—to repeat—is Janus-faced in the communist view. It is seen as positive, because the difficulties encountered in the attempt to achieve African unity can be tactically exploited. In principle, however, Pan-Africanism is rejected because it belongs to the African ideologies of the "third way." Potekhin says: "The struggle between the two basic ideologies of our time—that of dying capitalism and that of burgeoning socialism—is complicated on the African continent by heterogeneous ideological currents of local African character: Pan-Africanism, 'African Socialism,' and others. Pan-Africanism played and continues to play an important positive role, promoting, as it does, the unification of the peoples of Africa for the struggle against imperialism and colonialism. But it contains weaknesses, too, that become sources of extreme forms of nationalism and that may be exploited by the enemies of peaceful coexistence to set the black and white races against each other. Also, Pan-Africanism may be enlisted by the exploiter classes to cloak their own class dominance with an apparent unity of racial interests of the Negroid race. Similarly, one should not out of hand condemn 'African socialism.' It embodies the sincere efforts of progressive people to find a road to socialism that best suits the peculiar African situation. But at the same time, the theory of 'African socialism' is being used as a means of duping the working masses for the benefit of a capitalistic development." [185]

Potekhin in effect admits that his is a most difficult task of crossing swords not only with the West but with African ideologies as well. As an alternative to Marxism-Leninism, the African intelligentsia has evolved its own views: side-by-side with Pan-Africanism, the theory of "renunciation of resistance to force" (African Gandhism), the "idea of the African personality," and "African socialism," which denies the existence of classes in Africa and rejects the communist class warfare thesis.

"The struggle is becoming more and more of a 'conflict of ideas,' of a fight for the mastery of the science of social reconstruction—of scientific socialism versus 'African socialism'," writes the British communist Idris Cox. In order to intensify and exploit this conflict, Cox and the Soviet theoreticians also accept the vague concepts of Nkrumahism, his conscientism, and the "scientific socialism" of the leaders of Mali and Congo (Brazzaville).

The Soviets also seek to make propagandistic use of 'African socialism' by claiming that it is an expression of "the rejection of capitalism by the African peoples" and proof of "the strength of the idea of socialism throughout the world" as fostered by the Soviet model. Thus Cox says: "Although reactionary elements have misused the concept of 'African socialism,' it also has supporters who consider it to be *the* progressive program for Africa. With hatred of imperialism and neo-colonialism, with their striving for the unity of the African continent, and with their realization of the necessity of reconstructing the old colonial economy as their point of departure, they see something positive in the concept of African socialism . . . Future developments in the struggle for African unity and socialism undoubtably will show that there is no other course except scientific socialism . . . The concept of 'African socialism' would isolate Africa's struggle from the rest of the world and would be of advantage to the enemy." [186]

---

[185] *Narody Azii i Afriki* (Moscow), No. 1/1962, p. 15.
[186] *Probleme des Friedens und des Sozialismus* (East Berlin—Prague), No. 2/1966, p. 142.

Meanwhile, however, Soviet ideologists have come to see that "African socialism," from a propaganda angle, cannot be exploited as cheaply as Pan-Africanism.

In early December 1962 a colloquium met in Dakar for the purpose of coming to an understanding "about economic developmental policy and the various roads to socialism." Delegates from twenty African nations attended. At this colloquium only one Czech delegate, a student of the *Fédération des Etudiants d'Afrique en Noire France,* and an Italian leftist socialist confessed to Marxist-Leninist views. Said Léopold Sédar Senghor: "Obviously, our socialism can no longer be that of Marx and Engels. Their socialism evolved a century ago and was based on the scientific methods and conditions of the nineteenth century. Even Lenin, a European after all, found: 'To us, Marxist theory is not at all something final and sacrosanct. On the contrary, we are convinced it represents only the cornerstone of the very science, which socialists must continue to develop in every direction to remain abreast of life. We believe that it is especially necessary for the Russian socialists to work out their own application of Marxist theory.' Our socialism, the socialism of the Africans, will not so much evolve out of the independence of our thinking, as out of its creative *autonomy.* From the West—and other countries—we shall choose the most economical, most modern, and above all most effective methods, institutions, and technical know-how. But these will be effective only if tailored to our *African realities,* above all to our geography, our history, our culture, and our character.[187]

Communism's stand on "African socialism" was predetermined by Lenin, who wrote in March 1913: "Whoever, after the experiences of Europe as well as Asia, talks about a politics *not* class-oriented, and a socialism *not* class-oriented, deserves simply to be shut up in a cage and put on exhibition next to some Australian kangaroos." [188]

The new Communist Party program condemns "African socialism" as an "aberration of the petty bourgeois illusion about socialism" and a "theory for misleading the masses." Khrushchev personally took a stand on this modern phenomenon in a Sofia speech on 19 May 1962, when he said: "Numerous leaders of countries that have achieved independence try to follow some middle-of-the-road political philosophy which they call classless. They ignore the real class structure and class warfare existing in their own nations . . . Now the talk in several Afro-Asian countries, just rid of the yoke of colonialism, is about a buildup of socialism . . . But which socialism do they mean? What is their understanding of socialism?" Khrushchev does not

---

[187] Quoted from *Neues Afrika* (Munich), No. 1/1963, p. 24.
[188] Lenin, *Ausgewählte Werke,* (Russ.), Vol. I, Moscow 1946, p. 71.

answer these questions. But he proclaims that "victory is possible only in league with the working class as the most progressive and revolutionary social class, in alliance with the peasantry, and with the support of all forces of progress." To the proponents of "African socialism" he says: "Either they learn to understand this, or they will be replaced by people who are better acquainted with the demands of life." [189]

But the national leaders of Africa, who take a neutralist stand in the East-West quarrel, defend their "third way" policy against Soviet leadership claims. In the polemic between them and the Soviet-Bloc theoreticians, they defend their own road to economic development and their African ideologies. Western politicians must take this fact into consideration.

[189] *Pravda,* 20 May 1962.

The Latin American Center
of Communism

"Cuba represents a turning point in the national movement in Latin America"—that is one of communism's main theses about the subcontinent today. Yet by making this their thesis the communists indirectly admit that the Latin American communist parties, some of which have existed since 1918, with twenty parties by the end of World War II, have been unimportant and uninfluential groups and sects for generations. Despite the best possible social-economic preconditions, they were unable to gain a mass following. Until the 1960s the Latin American communist parties willingly and precisely followed the "general party line" laid down by their Moscow-trained leaders. But the fact is that Moscow had no real understanding of Latin American conditions and today is still seeking to comprehend the peculiarities of the subcontinent. For the Soviets did not recognize until 1960, that the Latin American countries should be considered developing countries. In 1964 one of the theoreticians of Latin American communism, Rodney Arismendi, who was trained in Moscow, acknowledged that the communists had regarded Latin America something like a "world village" in their strategy for world revolution. He writes: "Despite its extensive territory and its strategic importance Latin America was frequently regarded as a province at some remove from the actualities of the world revolution, that is, until the victory of the Cuban revolution. One could say that for many people socialism in Latin America was more a matter of the distant future than a pressing problem of the present. Yet the trumpet sounds of the Cuban revolution announced to the world: Latin America stands at the threshold of the decisive battles of the century." [190]

[190] *Probleme des Friedens und des Sozialismus* (East Berlin—Prague), No. 10/1964, p. 816.

116

Yet the trumpet sounds Arismendi mentions were not sounded by the communists but by petty bourgeois extremists.

THE PETTY BOURGEOIS REVOLUTION
AND THE COMMUNISTS

Whoever considers the Cuban Revolution under the leadership of the rebel Fidel Castro as Moscow-inspired and equates the Movement of 26 July with Cuba's communist *Partido Socialista Popular,* is hardly able to assess correctly the new turn in Cuban affairs. Cuban communists had relatively little to do with Castro's victory. They abided by the Party line, binding on all Latin America, according to which revolution can be successful only under "leadership of the working class, with the Communist Party in the vanguard." Both Castro's abortive uprising of 26 July 1956, which gave his movement the name, and his more successful venture of 2 December 1956, when at the head of forty-eight insurgents he landed in Oriente Province, were rejected by the communists as petty bourgeois putschism and adventurism. Castro's attempt to gain headway for his revolt by means of a "revolutionary general strike," called 9 April 1958, was sabotaged by the *Partido Socialista Popular.*[191] When in July 1958 Castro reached an agreement in Caracas on a common "Revolutionary Front" between his Movement of 26 July and other anti-Batista bourgeois groups, including the *Partido Autentico,* the communists again remained aloof. "Neither capitalism nor communism" was the watchword of the Revolutionary Front at the time.

Up to 1960, Soviet bloc comments on the Cuban Revolution charged the Movement of 26 July and its tactics of petty bourgeois adventurism with all past reverses, while the Cuban Communist Party was credited with allegedly having contributed to the 1959 victory. Recent history books create the impression that in all decisive Cuban events the *Partido Socialista Popular* set the example. The facts are otherwise. For the truth is that the Cuban events took the Soviet bloc by surprise. All sources agree that only since the beginning of 1960 did the Soviets become actively engaged in Cuba. After Castro's victory on 1 January 1959, the Soviet bloc journal *Problems of Peace and Socialism* made the following assessment of events in Cuba in August 1959: "The armed conflict was begun by representatives of the petite bourgeoisie. For a series of reasons, the proletarian forces were prevented from being the mainspring of the Revolution." The "series of reasons" given prove the isolation of the communist *Partido Socialista Popular* from the workers and labor movements. The strike

---

[191] *Cuba's Struggle for Freedom and Independence* (Russ.), Moscow 1959, pp. 54-64.

and anti-election slogans of the PSP "played only a subordinate role." It is reiterated: "The Revolution moved triumphantly from the villages to the cities, from the provinces to the capital. The political leadership of the conflict was in the hands of the petite bourgeoisie. The insurgent army consisted largely of poor peasants and agricultural laborers." [192]

It is thus admitted that events in Cuba refuted the communist "theory," which holds the petite bourgeoisie incapable of leadership in the struggle for national independence. In Cuba, the Party line was inoperable and for this reason the *Partido Socialista Popular,* in order to attain power after Castro's victory, was forced to take the detour of fusion with the leftist-radical wing of the petite bourgeoisie.

On 1 February 1961, at a time when Castro's change-over to communism had already been decided on, *L'Unità,* Italy's communist paper, published a self-critical Fidel Castro interview. Here Castro says: "In the beginning, the communists did not trust me or any of us insurgents. Theirs was a justified distrust and their attitude was absolutely right, both from the ideological and the political points of view. The communists had reason to distrust us because we, the leaders of the insurgents, the partisans, despite our having read some Marxist literature, were vacillating and full of the prejudices of the petite bourgeoisie." [193] Though the leaders of the Latin American communist parties hail the Cuban Revolution as of great import for the entire continent, stressing that the new Cuba has raised the revolutionary struggle for national freedom on a higher plane in all countries, they still carefully disassociate themselves from some petty bourgeois peculiarities that are part of the Cuban development. The First Secretary of Uruguay's Communist Party, Rodney Arismendi, for example, writes in the Soviet magazine *Communist* that Castroism, i.e., revolutionary leadership by the petite bourgeoisie, had been a uniquely Cuban affair. "It would be wrong to think that the bell tolls the same throughout the continent," says Arismendi. He is loath to leave any hope to the radical element of the petite bourgeoisie in any other Latin American country.[194]

In the transition of Castroism to communism, a variety of factors are of moment. Cuba's being dragged into the East-West quarrel and its alienation of the United States weakened the Movement of 26 July. Unity among this crazy-quilt movement of diverse bourgeois interests lasted only long enough to achieve its immediate objective.

---

[192] *Probleme des Friedens und des Sozialismus* (East Berlin—Prague), No. 8/1959, p. 18.
[193] Quoted from: *Pravda,* 2 February 1961; *L'Unità,* 1 February 1961.
[194] *Kommunist* (Moscow), No. 5/1961, p. 72.

With Batista removed, this unity disappeared in the ensuing squab-
bles over agrarian reforms and nationalization of foreign and domestic
firms and of capital interests. The moderate elements within the
"movement" were either sloughed off or expelled, its extreme leftist
wing radicalized. Success became a heady medicine. The *Partido
Socialista Popular*, having tried since January 1959 to put the "working class in the lead," i.e., to secure its membership in the government, at first applied a policy that, in the words of Blas Roca, was designed "by delicate handling and a flexible approach" to support the
leftist Fidel Castro Wing and to "drive forward the revolution." Since
Cuba's Communist Party, in contrast to the vacillating petite bourgeoisie Movement of 26 July, was the country's only tightly organized
party, the communists were successful in entrenching themselves in
the people's militia as well as in the administrative and economic
bureaucracy.

A further factor was the Soviet bloc's appearance on the Cuban
scene since 1960. At the Twenty-Second Party Congress in Moscow,
the Latin American communist speakers almost to a man claimed to
see in Cuba a vindication of the CPSU's politics. *In Cuba they saw
the first instance where Soviet bloc political, economic, and military
aid, made available at low commercial rates, reaped a political harvest.*
Blas Roca, in particular, emphasized that the rapid progress and outcome of the Cuban Revolution had been made possible only thanks
to the assistance of the socialist camp, with the Soviet Union in the
lead.

The aforementioned Rodney Arismendi sees in the Cuban Revolution proof positive that "the socialist camp and the Soviet Union are
the determining factors in international relations in our age." "Were
this not so," he continues, "Cuba, despite the heroic efforts of its
people, would be turned into a wasteland, drenched by rivers of
blood. It could never teach us this all-important lesson: *the economic
aid of the socialist camp and the support of the Soviet Union, together
with the steadfastness and unity of the people and the international
solidarity, can serve as a protective shield for the independence of
even the smallest of nations; they can force imperialism to abandon
its aggressive plans and counterrevolutionary local wars; and they
can promote the transition to more progressive forms of social liberty.*" [195] All these statements by Latin American communists show
that they sought to subordinate the Cuban Revolution to Moscow's
strategy from the very beginning, something which met with Fidel
Castro's resistance for years, and in particular that of Ché Guevera.
Castro did not switch to the Moscow line until 1965.

---

[195] *ibid.*, pp. 70-71.

STRATEGY AND TACTICS IN LATIN AMERICA

The victory of the revolution in Cuba, which resulted in the creation of extremist, petty bourgeois, fidelista groups in many Latin American countries, groups that even outdid the communists, compelled the communist theoreticians to re-examine their Latin American policy and find new guiding principles for their operations.

Many statements by Latin American communist leaders, as well as the works of Soviet theoreticians, indicate that the Soviet bloc is set to apply a strategy and tactics in Latin America which differ from that of Asia and Africa. All Soviet bloc theoreticians are agreed that because of Latin America's socio-economic structure, its social and political incongruities, and the international power constellation, the Western Hemisphere offers no permanent chance to national-bourgeois governments after the model of Asia (India and Indonesia), all the less if, as in the latter's case, a neutralist foreign policy course is followed. In Asia, reforms are feasible only under the aegis of the proletariat. There, where the petite bourgeoisie comes to power (Cuba), the revolution is seen to be in jeopardy and the danger of a return to the old conditions as acute, unless the road to a "higher phase of development" is taken immediately. Every statement on this subject stresses that Afro-Asian conditions must not be superimposed on Latin America, nor Afro-Asian methods and forms of political struggle applied there.

The following differences of approach to Asia and Africa on the one hand, and Latin America on the other, are highlighted:

1. Soviet proximity lent impetus to the national freedom movement in the Afro-Asian countries, and in Asia the existence of Communist China and other Asian members of the communist bloc (North Korea, North Vietnam, and Mongolia) exert an influence that is missing in Latin America. Only with Cuba did a "turning point in the national freedom movement of the peoples of Latin America occur." [196] "The revolution, that heretofore knew only Russian and Chinese, now begins to speak Spanish as well." [197]

2. While most Afro-Asian countries gained independence only since World War II, with some nations still struggling for freedom, the Latin American countries achieved formal political and national autonomy largely in the first half of the nineteenth century. This difference influences the attitude of the national bourgeoisie. In Asia and North Africa, the latter is still revolutionary, decisively active, willing to defend its own interests, and able initially to lead in the

---

[196] *The Labor Movement in Capitalist Countries* (Russ.), Moscow 1961, p. 228.
[197] *ibid.*, p. 249.

national struggle for freedom and take over the government in the newly sovereign nations. In Latin America, on the other hand, the bourgeoisie is vacillatory even in looking to its own interests, and its national-revolutionary potential is exhausted. For this reason, Latin America is considered as poor soil for "positive neutralism," and a Latin American "Bandung" seems most unlikely. "The example of Asia and Africa, where many countries, ruled by the bourgeoisie, found the way to the 'zone of peace,' has a positive influence on the national consciousness of the peoples of Latin America. But at the same time, an illusion, a fata morgana, is being nurtured, namely the belief that it would be easy, in collaboration with the broadest of social forces, to bring about a Latin American Bandung." [198]

3. Capitalistic development is far more advanced in Latin America than in Asia and Africa. "The nations of Latin America have their own special traits that set them off from the other underdeveloped countries of Asia and Africa. We particularly note that Latin America as a whole enjoys a higher level of industrialization than other underdeveloped nations. Nearly 45% of the entire industrial output of the underdeveloped countries, and more than half of their machine tools, are produced in Latin America." [199] But in contrast to Asia and Africa, this more advanced industrial development in Latin America is said to have led to a more pronounced differentiation within the bourgeois ranks.

4. The bourgeoisie in Latin America is seen as split. A progressive segment of industrial capital seeks economic independence from U. S. monopolists. Its members are drawn from the middle and lower-middle classes and this segment alone may be properly labeled "national" in the socio-political meaning of the word. The upper-middle class constitutes another bourgeois segment, whose interests run to banking, business enterprises, and large landholdings. This segment, however, is seen as again split into two wings: an anti-national corrupt sector in collusion with imperialism, and a compromise-prone sector opposed to imperialism. In the political arena, Latin American communists want to see a line drawn between these differences, emphasizing at the same time that it is important "not to fall victim to the illusion that the compromise-prone bourgeoisie could become an active force in the struggle against imperialism." But, in contrast to Asia's national middle class, the national bourgeoisie of Latin America is unfit for consequential leadership in the struggle for economic independence. It is "not interested in resolving the basic questions of national liberation but only in acquiring the rights of

---

[198] *Probleme des Friedens und des Sozialismus* (East Berlin—Prague), No. 6/1959, p. 30.

[199] *Mirovaya ekonomika i mezhdunarodnie otnosheniya*, No. 9/1960, p. 90.

personal exploitation of national resources and cheap labor." And it is in Latin America that "the main conflict between U. S. imperialism and the people coincides wiith most crass contrast between labor and capital." [200]

5. Potekhin propagated the "possibility of a noncapitalistic road to socialism" by means of a strong governmental role in economic affairs in those most backward of African nations that lack any sizeable accumulation of capital. In Latin America, with its relatively high degree of capitalism (compared to Asia), this possibility is ruled out by the Soviet theoreticians. Here, state capitalism is considered progressive only if brought about by control over and sequestration of foreign capital, and if it abets the friction between the local and foreign vested interests. "In Cuba, the government takeover of economic functions via the complete nationalization of foreign concerns and capital investment created the preconditions for the immediate transition to socialism." At the same time, in regard to the question of state capitalism in Latin America the Soviet bloc theoreticians in part accept almost "Chinese" views. Thus they claim: "The development of state capitalism in Latin American countries leads to a strengthening of the economic independence of these countries and intensifies the mobilization of the masses for the anti-imperialist struggle. However, the possibilities of state capitalism in Latin America must not be exaggerated. When the upper-middle class takes the initiative in the development of state capitalism, it does so to exploit the latter for selfish purposes, to gain favorable credit terms at the expense of the tax-paying workers, to set inflationary prices for goods produced in state-owned factories, and the like. Not all measures of state capitalism bear the imprint of anti-imperialism. Often, they turn out as weapons in the hands of U. S. monopolies, especially in those cases where the state capital is invested in so-called 'mixed' undertakings together with private (national and international) capital. In such case, state capitalism often only cloaks foreign interests." [201]

6. "No doubt," says the aforementioned Arismendi, "Latin America's past does not justify belief in the possibility of a 'decisive struggle' (if this is to mean a consequential revolutionary struggle) led by the bourgeoisie. It is also a fact that the bloody history of our countries shows many instances of the bourgeoisie collusion with the large landholders, feudal lords, and imperialists against the proletariat, the peasants, and the radical petite bourgeoisie." [202] "It should there-

---

[200] *The Labor Movement in Capitalist Countries, op. cit.,* p. 228.
[201] *Latin America Past and Present* (Russ.), Moscow 1960, pp. 45-47. See also G. A. Vartov, *The National Freedom Movement in Latin America* (Russ.), Moscow 1960.

fore be plainly understandable that the national bourgeoisie cannot furnish the leadership capable of advancing the cause of the peoples of Latin America for national independence to ultimate victory. This leadership, capable of directing the struggle for freedom, can only be supplied by the working class." [203] This, in Latin America, calls for popular-front tactics that embrace the working class, the peasantry, the student body, the patriotic intelligentsia, the politically active wing of the petite bourgeoisie, and the progressive elements of the national bourgeoisie, led by the Communist Party against U. S. imperialism, its local agents, and the upper-middle classes. This popular front is variously propagated as "national-democratic front," "unity front of leftist forces," "people's action front," and the like.

7. Finally, Moscow has also conceived of a "peaceful parliamentary way" for the Latin American parties to assume power. Particularly the communists of Chile, Uruguay, Brazil and Argentina have made this concept part of their program. "Under the present favorable international conditions . . ." it says in the program of Uruguay's Communist Party, "political power can be achieved by peaceful means and parliament can be transformed into an organ that will be the true executor of the peoples' will." [204]

Chile's Communist Party program also proclaims the "peaceful parliamentary way" to assume power, but it adds: "That depends on the extent to which the reactionary elements use force during one or another stage of the revolution. If this should happen, there is always the possibility that the revolutionary process will proceed in another, an unpeaceful way." [205]

In any case, the conception contains an escape clause. It hardly need be pointed out that the fidelistas and Peking never condoned the peaceful-parliamentary way, but some other countries, like Venezuela, did not accept it either.

In the meantime, however, the concept of a peaceful parliamentary way has placed the Latin America communists in a serious dilemma. For example, the Chilean communists' and socialists' attempt to organize the *Frente de Accion Popular* to elect the popular front candidate Allende during the September 1964 elections, did not succeed. Jose Manuel Fortuny, a member of the central committee of the Guatemala Party of Work (the name of Guatemala's communist

[202] *Probleme des Friedens und des Sozialismus* (East Berlin—Prague), No. 6/1959, p. 28.
[203] *Latin America Past and Present*, p. 20.
[204] *Program Documents of the Communist and Workers Parties in the Latin American Countries* (Russ.) Moscow 1962, p. 273.
[205] *ibid.*, p. 324.

organization) asked himself in August 1965: "Can the governments of Stroessner in Paraguay, Duvalier in Haiti, the brothers Somoza (who govern their country with their puppet Rene Schik) in Nicaragua allow a peaceful alternative? Is there a possibility of forming a government that would re-establish the national sovereignty in Panama in a peaceful way?" [206]

Furthermore, Fortuny disclaims any possibility of a peaceful parliamentary way in El Salvador after the *coup d'état* of 1961, in Ecuador after the fall of Arosemena's government, the fall of Ydigoras Fuentes' government in Guatemala, Villeda Morales' in Honduras, Juan Bosch's in the Dominican Republic in 1963, Goulart's in Brazil in 1964, as well as in the Dominican Republic after the American intervention. He reaches the conclusion that the majority of Latin American countries can only look forward to an armed struggle: "It seems to me that in the Latin American countries with few exceptions (of which Chile is the most obvious) there exists no possibility for the victory of the revolution in another, peaceful way at the present stage. The Chilean situation, which I consider an exceptional one, is due to a number of factors, among them the existence of a communist party which in every respect can be called a mass party." [207]

However, Fortuny believes that most Latin American countries lack the subjective prerequisites, mass influence of the communist parties, for an armed fight. And Arismendi warns against flirting with armed insurrections.

While Cuba is outgrowing its leftist-extremism, as is evidenced by the debarment of the guerrilla strategist Ché Guevera, it becomes clear that the communists in other Latin American countries are adopting his approach. Yet the chief obstacles that confront communism and leftist-extremism and their peaceful and nonpeaceful ways in Latin America result from a *waning of revolutionary fervor on the continent*.

THE WANING OF REVOLUTIONARY FERVOR

A wave of revolutionary fervor swept Latin America in the wake of Fidel Castro's 1959 victory. His example found a lively echo. Everywhere groups friendly to Castro sprung up and wanted to imitate his methods in their country. Bourgeois and social democratic parties and even governments professed solidarity with Castro and his movement. Groups friendly to Castro left democratic leftist parties, everywhere

---

[206] *Probleme des Friedens und des Sozialismus* (East Berlin—Prague), No. 8/1965, p. 657.
[207] *ibid.*, p. 656.

fidelistas sprang up and in some instances even reactivated several old communist parties.[208]

When we speak about the waning of the revolutionary impetus we do not, of course, mean that any fundamental problem has been solved; the *objective* conditions continue to be favorable to communism. What we mean is that Cuba has become less of a center of the revolution and as an imitable model and example has lost much of its dynamism.

Even the Latin American theoreticians have concluded that the "period of the revolutionary situation" (1959-1961) has been succeeded by a period of "gathering of strength." Fortuny asks: "Has the revolution in Latin America become more difficult?" Noting that it would be wrong to deny an element of prognostication in his statements, he answers his question by citing the American sociologist Irving Horowitz: "The price of revolution in Latin America has risen considerably, and only in exceptional cases can the leaders, the party or the people speak of a comprehensive revolution in Latin America (with the exception of Cuba)." [209]

Ernesto Guidici, a member of the Central Committee of the Argentine Communist Party, asks: "What tendency prevails in Latin America today—successes in the development of the people's liberation struggle, or a reactionary counteroffensive?" "The latter has evidently become more active," is his answer.[210]

The Latin American communist theoretician Rodney Arismendi soothes his comrades by writing: "Anyone who has believed that the revolution will develop unhindered in our continent as a triumphant march, might lose sight of the growing stubbornness and bitterness of the struggle. However, we believe we are in a state of transition toward great revolutionary fights." Elsewhere he amplifies this statement: "No matter whether we regard the transitional period Latin America is experiencing today as a new stage in the fight or not— it is obvious that we face difficult times." [211]

All these statements show that the communist leaders' hope to repeat the Cuban experiment has waned.

However, the communists only cite one reason for the regression of the revolutionary wave in Latin America: "The international bourgeoisie has also learned a lesson from the Cuban Revolution and has

---

[208] Comp. Robert J. Alexander, "Die Kommunisten in Lateinamerika," in: *Studien zur Aktivität des Ostblocks in den Enturcklingsländern,* Hannover 1963, pp. 103-121.

[209] *Probleme des Friedens und des Sozialismus* (East Berlin—Prague), No. 8/1965, p. 655.

[210] *ibid.,* No. 2/1965, p. 103.

[211] *ibid.,* No. 10/1964, p. 817 and 821.

become more watchful"; especially "American imperialism is doing everything in its power to prevent a second Cuba."

But one can list a number of other reasons for the waning of the revolutionary wave that emanated from Cuba:

1) Cuba's foreign political isolation from the subcontinent. This isolation came about because Cuba's example has lost its appeal in other countries. Presence of strong communist or fidelistic mass influence would probably have prevented the governments of some countries from breaking off relations with Cuba.

As the Latin America expert of the Friedrich-Ebert-Stiftung, Robert F. Lamberg, emphasizes, certain other factors, related to the first, are also responsible for the communists' and fidelistas' lack of success:

2) Castro's embracing of Marxism-Leninism in December 1961. This appalled certain petty-bourgeois social revolutionaries and thus weakened the fidelistas' front.

3) The missile crisis of the fall of 1962 and its effect on Cuba and Latin America. It revealed Cuba's dependence on Moscow and triggered a negative reaction among the masses who despise any form of dependence.

4) The defeat of guerilla tactics in Venezuela which was practiced together by the fidelistas and the Communist Party.

5) The failure of the peaceful-parliamentary way of assuming power with the help of popular front tactics during the Chilean elections in September 1964. The Soviet had hoped for an election victory in this country in order to have proof for their policy and to make Chile into a second Latin American center of communist activity.

6) Finally, the revolutionary impulses that Castro's victory unleashed in Latin America were stultified by the economic difficulties engendered by Cuba's hurried industrialization program after Soviet recipe.[212]

Therefore, it does not seem logical to regard every action of the democratic forces in Latin America (Dominican Republic) as part of Castro's or Cuba's machinations, at least not under present circumstances.

THE CUBAN BEACHHEAD

Two events—the "failure of the world revolution" to spread to the mainland and the difficult economic situation in which Cuba found itself as a result of following the Soviet formula for primary emphasis on the development of heavy industry—also had a sobering effect on the Cuban leadership. Immediately after Fidel Castro's first visit

---

[212] Compare Robert F. Lamberg, "Die gegenwärtige Lage des lateinamerikanischen Kommunismus," and "Kubas Einfluss auf Lateinamerika," in Vierteljohres berichte der Friedrich-Ebert-Stiftung, Hannover, No. 18/1964 and No. 20/1965.

to the Soviet union in 1963 Cuba broke with the "industrialization concept of the first stage of the revolution" and switched over to a development of those "industrial branches whose growth is favored by conditions obtaining among us . . . with the resources provided us by sugar and the foreign currency accumulated through the sale of sugar." [213] Even at that time Castro committed himself to economic cutbacks, began to depend on Soviet aid, sought to win Western trading partners and even made tentative overtures to Washington. Though Cuba took a neutral position in the Soviet-Chinese conflict at that time, one could already detect two differently-oriented groups in the Cuban leadership. This becomes evident from a comparison of Castro's speech on economics on the occasion of the fifth anniversary of the Cuban Revolution with an article by Ernesto Ché Guevera in *Cuba Socialista*, of September 1963.[214] Guevera was proposing daring guerilla actions in Latin America for which he had Peking's support.

Peking's claim that Cuba has begun to side with Moscow due to its dependence on Soviet economic aid, is undoubtably true. Cuba costs the Soviet Union 1 million rubles a day. As of 28 July 1965 Cuba owed a total of $1 billion to the entire Soviet bloc; $850 million to the USSR, $430 million to the CSSR, $250 million to Poland, $85 million to Rumania, $70 million to Hungary and $14 million to Bulgaria.[215] Debtors are obligated to their creditors also within the "socialist camp," and moreover, politically, too.

However, the quarrel between Havana and Peking was not first precipitated by the rice-sugar controversy which Castro publicized in January 1964. The curtailment of Chinese rice deliveries, which Castro called a "Chinese participation in the U. S. A.-imperialist blockade" and a criminal act of "economic aggression," was Peking's answer to Cuba's switch to the Soviet line in the Soviet-Chinese conflict. This switch had been made apparent by the participation of a Cuban delegation of the Party of the Cuban Socialist Revolution at the Moscow consultation meeting of the nineteenth communist and workers parties in March 1965.

Let us quote a Yugoslav comment on the Cuban adoption of the Soviet line: "Cuba too has made its contribution to the re-establishment of good relations with the Soviet Union. The first step in this direction was taken several months ago when a Cuban party delegation participated at the consultation meeting of the communist and workers

---

[213] Fidel Castro's speech on the fifth anniversary of the Cuban Revolution, 2 January 1964, *Aus der internationalen Arbeiterbewegung* (East Berlin), No. 2/1964 p. 12; also compare Castro's speech at the sixth anniversary of the Cuban Revolution, from *From the International Workers Movement*, No. 3/1965, p. 12.
[214] *Guerilla Warfare: A Means*, reprinted in *Peking Review*, No. 2/1964, p. 14.
[215] *Archiv der Gegenwart*, (Bonn—Vienna—Zurich), Sequence 30/1965, p. 11977.

parties in Moscow. At that time only a few people realized that Cuba's participation at the Moscow meeting signalled the onset of a new phase in Cuban policy, characterized by a renunciation of Peking's policies which exerted a negative influence on Cuban-Soviet relations.

"It has now become perfectly clear that the main supporter of the Chinese viewpoint was Ché Guevera who resigned before the consultation meeting of the nineteenth communist and workers parties in March 1965 in Moscow. Ché Guevera's disappearance from the Cuban political scene, as was noted in Moscow, was by no means easy to accomplish since this man was someone who had been of great service to the Cuban Revolution. According to Moscow, Guevera belonged to the ultra-leftist direction. His visits to China probably confirmed him in this direction. For, here in Peking he was esteemed as a man unafraid of war. However, such an attitude corresponds neither to Cuba's interests nor to the progressive calming down in the Caribbean area." [216]

N. Sanmugathsan, a member of the politbureau of the pro-Chinese Communist Party of Ceylon, regards the elimination of Ché Guevera, "the brain of Fidelism," as proof of "how far Cuba has diverged from the revolutionary road." However, Sanmugathsan is certainly being somewhat too farsighted about possible developments when he states that "Castro has been gradually won over to a peaceful coexistence with the U. S. A., in which policy is implicit that he will support no revolutionary movements in Latin America that are directed against the U. S. A. This agreement was reached by way of Moscow. It is not surprising therefore that we have heard of no recent attacks by Johnson on Cuba." [217]

We have no evidence that the agreement Sanmugathsan mentions exists. Yet a complete break between Cuba and China would undoubtably facilitate the re-establishment of contacts between Washington and Havana.

Cuba's shift to the Soviet line in the Chinese-Soviet conflict, however, does not mean that Cuba has become a Soviet satellite despite its economic dependence on the Soviet bloc. For communism is being created under special conditions on this island. It is known that in our age of pluralistic communism even the old communist leadership cadres in Europe, who have been schooled in Moscow, seek to accommodate communism in their countries (in Italy among others) to the special conditions obtaining there. In Cuba, however, the installation of a communist party is being directed even more strongly by the willful ideas of its leader, Fidel Castro.

---

[216] *Radio Zagreb* (Serbian) on 22 October 1965.
[217] *Peking Rundschau*, No. 19/1966, p. 19.

The buildup of the *Partido Unido de la Revolucion Socialista* (PURS—Unity Party of the Socialist Revolution) in Cuba began in 1961 with the establishment of the *Organizaciones Revolucionarios Integrados* (ORI—United Revolutionary Organizations). The ORI united Fidel Castro's petty bourgeois Movement of the 26th of July, the *Partido Socialista Popular* (PSP—Cuba's old Communist Party) and the *Revolutionary Directorate of March 13*, which—*Neues Deutschland* states, as recently as 24 July 1965—"considers individual terror, bombings, and armed attacks on public institutions as the most effective methods of the revolutionary struggle."

Between 1961 and 1962 the Cuban communists, experienced organizers and propagandists all, sought to fashion this crazy-quilt organization (ORI) into a Bolshevik party of a "new type," and undoubtedly they had Moscow's approval. Under the leadership of the communist organization secretary of the ORI, Anibal Escalante, the communists occupied the key positions in the new organization. Of the twenty-five leaders of ORI ten were former PSP men whose political effectiveness was bound to play a much greater role than the fidelistas who were inexperienced in the day-to-day work of politics and organizing. However, the communist plan failed. In March 1962 Castro launched a counter offensive. He asserted, "The communists have grabbed everything for themselves," and proceeded to cleanse the ORI of the "sectarians," that is, the old-time communists with Escalante in the lead. The former general secretary of the communist PSP, Blas Roca, was able to salvage his leading position by compromising. Moscow, too, was forced to approve the elimination of the old guard. *Pravda* wrote that "the right mixture of old [communist] cadres and young [fidelista] cadres provided one of the surest guarantees for the correct development of a Marxist-Leninist unity party in Cuba." [218] However, it should be noted that the "right mixture" of cadres is being determined solely by Fidel Castro.

For example, during the so-called Organization Year 1963 the *Partido Unido de la Revolucion Socialista* (PURS) was to be baptized during a party congress. But no such party congress ever took place. Rather, in 1963 Castro surprised everyone by publicly proclaiming that the unity party PURS now existed.

The "founding" of the Cuban Communist Party on 3 October 1965 was handled in a similar fashion. During a festive occasion Fidel Castro simply announced this as a *fait accompli*. But, as could be ascertained, the lower party organizations knew nothing of the creation of the party for several days afterward and continued to operate under the old name.

[218] *Pravda,* 11 April 1962.

"People disappear but the peoples remain; the leadership disappears but the revolution remains," Castro proclaimed on this occasion. He forgot to add that he himself remains. But one of the persons who disappeared or had to disappear from the highest leadership organ, the politbureau, was the leftist-extemist Ernesto Ché Guevera and the last old-time communist, Blas Roca. The politbureau of Cuba's new Communist Party has no old-time communists. Blas Roca is only a member of the party secretariat and the chairman of the constitutional commission. He was also relieved of his post as the editor-in-chief of the party paper. There is no telling which path the Cuban leadership will take, now that it has been cleansed of the Peking-oriented guerrilla strategists and old-time communists. Everything depends on whether the USSR continues to be willing to sacrifice a million rubles a day for Cuba and to what degree Washington's Cuba policy will be able to accommodate itself to the changes that have taken place on the island.

PART II

Within the Vortex
of Coexistence

Foreign Trade, Economic Aid, and

Training Assistance

Handbook for Action

The Party Program of the Twenty-Third CPSU Party Congress in March/April 1966 again emphasized the objective of peaceful competition between socialism and capitalism, although with perhaps less fanfare than before.

Though the new party leadership carefully avoids announcing any new deadlines when the USSR will surpass the "wealthiest and mightiest capitalist country, the U. S. A.," the competition is still regarded in the light of what Khrushchev said at the Twenty-First Party Congress in January 1959: "During the first phase of the competitive struggle with capitalism, beginning with the glorious socialist October Revolution, Lenin's famous formulation 'who whom?' [who conquers whom?] in our country was resolved in favor of socialism . . . Now we are entering upon a new phase of economic competition with capitalism." [1]

Often the question is asked what meaning there is behind the Soviets' avowed attempt to overtake the West in all areas. Khrushchev supplied the answer: now, he said, the time had come where the question "who whom?" has assumed global proportions! It should be remembered that in the Stalin era, Lenin's "who whom?" question was largely a domestic matter of "liquidating the remnants of capitalism," of "an all-out collectivization of agriculture," and of industrializing the country. Now, however, "peaceful coexistence" and economic competition were to create the conditions that will solve the "who whom?" question on a worldwide basis.

Our interpretation of Khrushchev's statement is borne out by the

[1] *Pravda,* 28 January 1959.

Soviet historians T. T. Timofeyev, A. B. Weber, K. G. Kholodkovskii, and K. L. Maidanik, whom we shall quote in some detail. They write: "The present is characterized by world socialism's fully deployed attack on all fronts against the capitalist system: in the field of *economic* competition, in the sphere of *political* and *ideological* struggle, and in the ever mounting superiority of the socialist over the imperialist camp in the *techno-scientific* and *military* areas . . . Today as never before, an ingrowing capitalist system is weakened and undermined not only by proletarian, socialistic revolutions, but also by the national liberation struggles and anti-imperialistic movements in the Afro-Asian and Latin American countries." [2] These words leave no doubt of the importance attached by the Soviet bloc to the underdeveloped countries in the "deployed attack." The authors state in another place that those young nations that adhere to neutralism, are "in this question (of the deployed attack!) the allies of the international proletariat."

The Soviet bloc's foreign trade, its credit offers, its economic and training aids furnished the underdeveloped nations, are all part and parcel of the militant spirit underlying the policy of "peaceful coexistence" and economic competition. Even the communists themselves barely bother to deny this. N. Patolichev, Soviet Minister of Foreign Trade, bluntly admits as much when he writes: "Our opponents often claim that the Soviet Union's foreign trade connections serve its foreign policy aims. We freely admit that the economic relations of the USSR with other countries are designed to safeguard peaceful coexistence, peace, and friendship among nations. The Soviet Union's foreign trade does in fact serve the noble foreign political aims of the socialist state." [3]

But foreign trade, credit offers and economic aid, the construction of industrial plants and works, furnishing of specialists, and the training of Afro-Asian engineers and technicians, are *only part* of the overall Soviet bloc plan and design. Vis-à-vis the challenging noises made at the Twenty-Second Party Congress, it behooves us to take a much closer look at Soviet bloc activity in the backward countries. The differentiated *strategy and tactics* that we have outlined *serve as a handbook for action*. They are guideposts that direct the activity of agencies, organizations, and institutions, routinely under Soviet bloc control, and are binding on the various aid measures in the underdeveloped countries. For the realization of its set goals, the Soviet bloc is currently committing the following in accordance with a grand design:

[2] *The Labor Movement in Capitalist Countries, op. cit.,* pp. 69-70.
[3] *Vneshnyaya Torgovlya* (Moscow), No. 11/1961, p. 4.

a. The government apparatus of every Soviet bloc nation, in particular the foreign and foreign-trade ministries with their Afro-Asian and Latin American sections, as well as the ministries of commerce and culture;

b. Such government-controlled organs, as the "State Committee for Foreign Economic Contacts at the Council of Ministers of the USSR," the "State Committee for Foreign Cultural Contacts at the Council of Ministers of the USSR," and similar Soviet bloc institutions;

c. The eighty-eight Communist Parties in the world with roughly 50 million members;

d. The institutes for the study of Afro-Asian and Latin American countries, such as the "Institute of the Asian Peoples at the USSR Academy of Sciences," with headquarters in Moscow and branches in Leningrad; Baku (Institute for Oriental Studies); Erivan (a Section for Oriental Studies at the academy, founded late 1958); Tiflis (Institute for Oriental Studies, founded July, 1960); Stalinabad, now Dyushanbe (a Department for Oriental Studies at the academy, founded April, 1958); Tashkent (Institute for Oriental Studies, founded 1952, and the National-Pedagogic Foreign Language Institute). Also in this category are Moscow's Africa Institute of the USSR, the Africa Institute of Leipzig, the Institute of Latin American Affairs at the Central Committee of the Chinese Communist Party (founded 1959); the Latin American Institute of the USSR (founded late 1961); the Prague Institute for Oriental Studies; the Moscow Institute for World Economics and International Relations of the Foreign Ministry; the Soviet Foreign Trade Ministry's Institute of Economic Research; and others;

e. The Afro-Asian Peoples' Solidarity Organization, with seat in Cairo and branches in the underdeveloped countries and the USSR, in China, Mongolia, North Korea, North Vietnam, and in other bloc countries;

f. The Solidarity organization of the Afro-Asian-Latin American peoples, founded in January 1966 and with headquarters in Havana, and the Organization of Latin American Solidarity, which also has its head office in Havana.

g. The Friendship Societies, such as the Society for Indo-Soviet Friendship or East Germany's German-Arabian Society, of which currently there are about a hundred in the Soviet bloc, though their counterparts in the underdeveloped countries are lacking;

h. The international front organizations, with their offices and departments for Asia, Africa and Latin America and their branches in the underdeveloped countries themselves. These include the World Federation of Trade Unions (WFTU), the World Peace Council, the

World League of Democratic Youth, the International Students League, the International Democratic Federation of Women, the International Organization of Journalists, the International Association of Democratic Jurists, the World Federation of Teachers, the International Radio and Television Organization, and many subdivisions.

The above-listed Soviet bloc organizations, agencies and institutions, all designed for penetration of underdeveloped areas, may serve as an outline in the evaluation of Soviet bloc activity in the countries of Asia, Africa and Latin America. The Soviet bloc differentiates between aid measures of governments and the activities of so-called "suprapartisan" organizations. The latter carry out the Party directives, and the strategy and tactics we have sketched are binding on them all. A comprehensive view of the sum total of Soviet bloc activity in the backward countries is possible only through a survey of the activity of each of the organizations listed. We shall begin with an examination of the activity of the governments and government agencies, continue with a study of foreign trade, of credit and economic aid, and conclude with an analysis of the training of engineers, technicians, scientists, and specialists from the Afro-Asian and Latin American countries.

Foreign Trade Ties With
Underdeveloped Nations

In November 1961, the Soviet Minister of Foreign Trade, N. Patolichev, declared, "Trade is a healthy basis for peaceful coexistence" and "Communist Party and the Government of the Soviet Union regard development of economic ties with those countries, whose people have thrown off the colonial yoke, as one of the most important foreign policy tasks." [4]

The Soviets put increased emphasis on trade with the underdeveloped countries as a matter of foreign policy only after the historic Bandung Conference of 1955. Until then, the Soviet bloc on the one hand lacked the politico-ideological background for an expansion of trade ties with the new nations; on the other, the material pre-conditions for such expansion were not adequate at the time. Although foreign trade had been a tool of foreign policy even under Stalin—the Soviet-German trade agreements following the Rapallo Treaty of 1922, and the 1939 Hitler-Stalin Pact are called to mind—such trade during Russia's "first industrial revolution" served primarily as a means of acquiring badly needed producer goods for the buildup of the home industry. Only with the advent of the second industrialization phase, with the appearance of a "socialist world market," and with the force-fed industrialization of European bloc members, at the expense of the agricultural structure in some countries, did certain raw materials of the backward nations become of interest to the Soviet bloc. Now, the latter also emerged as an exporter of producer goods. With this, the pre-conditions for today's battle cry of

---

[4] *ibid.*

136

"peaceful competition between socialism and capitalism" had been established for the underdeveloped areas. The Soviet bloc's propaganda phrase in Asia, Africa, and Latin America is today: "You are no longer dependent upon the capitalists in matters of machine tools and equipment but can procure these under better conditions in the socialist world market."

FOREIGN TRADE AGREEMENTS AND TRADE MISSIONS

Prior to the Bandung Conference, the USSR maintained trade relations with only eight underdeveloped nations: *Afghanistan* (Trade Agreement of 17 July 1950); *Iran* (Trade Agreement of 25 March 1940); *India* (Trade Agreement of 2 December 1953); *Lebanon* (Trade Agreement of 30 April 1954); *Turkey* (Trade Agreement of 8 October 1937); *Egypt* (Trade Agreement of 18 August 1953); *Argentina* (Trade Agreement of 5 August 1953); and *Uruguay* (Trade Agreement of 28 July 1954). In the wake of the 1955 reappraisal of its foreign policy in Asia, Africa, and Latin America, the USSR, in 1958, maintained trade relations on the basis of formal agreements with fifteen underdeveloped countries.[5]

In 1961 the Soviet Union was trading with more than eighty countries,[6] among them thirty-five Afro-Asian and Latin American states, with whom the Soviets concluded bilateral trade agreements.[7] In 1961, the USSR Ministry of Foreign Trade had listed only twenty-seven underdeveloped countries with whom bilateral trade agreements had been concluded. This figure is probably correct for that time.[8]

"At present the USSR has permanent economic relations with forty developing countries based on trade and payment agreements," reports the foreign trade ministry of the USSR for 1964.[9]

Just as the Soviet Union during the 1920s resorted to foreign trade agreements at government level to achieve political recognition, the Chinese People's Republic, and even more East Germany, put trade in the service of the same political goal today. The People's Republic of China has in fact succeeded, partly via trade contacts, to break out of its political isolation in the Afro-Asian area. Thus in 1964 Communist China maintained diplomatic relations with Afghanistan, Burma, Ceylon, India, Indonesia, Iraq, Yemen, Cambodia, Laos, Nepal, Pakistan, Syria, Burundi, Algeria, Egypt, Ghana, Guinea, Kenya, Mali,

[5] *Economic Collaboration and Mutual Aid in the Socialist Camp* (Russ.), Moscow 1959, p. 157.
[6] *Vneshnyaya torgovlya* (Moscow), No. 11/1961, p. 4.
[7] *Pravda*, 25 October 1961.
[8] *Vneshnyaya torgovlya* (Moscow), No. 11/1962, p. 25.

USSR Trade Agreements with Underdeveloped Nations[9]

Nation	Type of Agreement	Date Signed
ASIA		
Afghanistan	Trade and payment agreement	17 July 1950
Burma	Trade agreement	1 July 1955
Cambodia	Trade and payment agreement	31 May 1957
	Prolongation of the trade agreement	12 September 1960
Ceylon	Trade and payment agreement	8 February 1958
	Agreement on bilateral delivery of goods 1962-64	22 February 1962
	Agreement on bilateral delivery of goods 1965-67	1 October 1964
India	First trade agreement	12 August 1953
	Second trade agreement	16 November 1958
	Third trade agreement	10 June 1963
	Fourth trade agreement for 1964-68	7 January 1966
Indonesia	Trade agreement	12 August 1956
	Trade agreement for 1961-63	9 July 1960
Iran	Trade and maritime treaty	25 March 1940
	Trade agreement for 1964-67	20 June 1964
	Payment agreement for one year	20 June 1964
Iraq	Trade agreement	11 October 1958
Laos	Trade agreement	1 December 1962
	Payment agreement	1 December 1962
Lebanon	Trade and payment agreement	30 April 1954
Pakistan	Trade agreement for 1965-67	7 April 1965
Syria	Trade and payment agreement	16 November 1955
	Trade agreement for 1966-68	4 November 1965
Turkey	Trade and maritime treaty	8 October 1937
	Trade and payment agreement	8 October 1937
	Exchange agreement	7 December 1965
Yemen	Trade agreement	8 March 1956
AFRICA		
Egypt (UAR)	Payment agreement	18 August 1953
	Trade agreement	27 March 1954
	Long-term trade and payment agreement	23 June 1962
	Trade agreement of 1965-70	30 December 1965

Nation	Type of Agreement	Date Signed
ASIA		
Ethiopia	Trade agreement	11 July 1959
Ghana	First trade agreement	4 August 1960
	Second trade agreement and long-term payment agreement	4 November 1961
Guinea	Trade and payment agreement	8 September 1960
Cameroon	Trade agreement	24 September 1962
Mali	Trade agreement	18 March 1961
Kenya	Trade agreement for three years	29 April 1964
Dahomey	Trade agreement	10 July 1963
Algeria	Trade agreement for three years	4 November 1963
	Payment agreement for three years	4 November 1963
Congo (Brazzaville)	Trade agreement	28 May 1964
Madagascar	Trade agreement	23 October 1964
Morocco	Trade agreement	19 April 1958
	Trade agreement for 1966-68	30 November 1965
Nigeria	First trade agreement	25 April 1962
	Trade agreement for three years	2 July 1963
Senegal	Trade agreement	14 June 1962
Sierra Leone	Trade agreement	25 April 1965
Somalia	Trade and payment agreement	2 June 1962
Sudan	Trade agreement	16 March 1959
	Long-term trade agreement	1 November 1961
Tanzania	Trade agreement	14 August 1963
Togo	Trade agreement	12 June 1961
Tunisia	Long-term trade and payment agreement	14 March 1962
Uganda	Trade agreement	8 May 1964
LATIN AMERICA		
Argentina	Trade and payment agreement	5 August 1953
Brazil	Trade and payment agreement	19 December 1959
	Trade and payment agreement	20 April 1963
Uruguay	Payment and goods agreement	28 July 1954

---

[9] *ibid.*, No. 11/1965, p. 9.

Morocco, Zanzibar, Somalia, the Sudan, Tanganyika, Tunisia and Uganda.

Communist China, in late 1952, maintained normal trade relations with only one underdeveloped nation, Ceylon. At the time of the Bandung Conference, this had increased to four countries: Ceylon, Indonesia, Burma, and India (which did not renew the Trade Agreement in 1962). By mid-1959 China had concluded trade agreements at government level with twelve underdeveloped countries, a total that had increased to twenty-five in 1962 and included Afghanistan, Burma, Ceylon, India (not renewed), Indonesia, Iraq, Yemen, Cambodia, Lebanon, Nepal, Syria,[10] Egypt, Algeria, Ghana, Mali, Morocco, Nigeria, Somalia, the Sudan, Tanganyika, Tunisia, and Cuba.

According to a report by *China's Foreign Trade*, Peking was trading with sixty Asian and African countries in 1965.

In 1961 East Germany maintained trade relations with eleven Asiatic countries (Burma, Ceylon, India, Indonesia, Iraq, Iran, Yemen, Lebanon, Pakistan, Saudi Arabia, and Syria), ten African underdeveloped nations (Ethiopia, Ghana, Guinea, Congo, Libya, Morocco, Nigeria, Sudan, Tunisia, and Egypt), and ten Latin American republics (Argentina, Bolivia, Brazil, Chile, Colombia, Cuba, Mexico, Peru, Uruguay, and Venezuela).[11] For the moment, we shall not concern ourselves with the low trade exchange volume between East Germany and the thirty-one underdeveloped countries listed. For East Germany, the overriding consideration was the establishment of contacts *per se*. For comparative purposes it may be mentioned that the Federal German Republic, in 1962, traded with thirty-nine African, forty Asian, and twenty Latin American nations and territories.[12] It should also be mentioned that the trade contacts listed for East Germany are general in nature. The number of official government trade agreements is lower than total contacts shown.

In March 1961, Gerhard Weiss, East German Deputy Minister of Foreign and Intra-German Trade, wrote in *Der Aussenhandel* that the East zone at the time maintained trade relations, on the basis of government, bank, or chamber of commerce agreements, with thirty-three countries (including the underdeveloped nations) from the capitalist camp. This figure meanwhile has risen to thirty-six. East Germany maintains official trade missions in the following underdeveloped countries on the basis of government-level trade agree-

---

[10] The Sino-Syrian Trade and Payment Agreement of 30 November 1955, which assumed new importance when Syria left the UAR.
[11] *Statistiches Jahrbuch der DDR*, East Berlin 1959, 1960, and 1961.
[12] *Statistisches Jahrbuch der Bundesrepublik*, 1960, pp. 316-17; 1961, pp. 328-29.

ments: in Algeria, with seat in Algiers; in Burma, with seat in Rangoon (Consulate General); in India, with seat in New Delhi and branches in Bombay, Calcutta and Madras; in Indonesia, with seat in Djakarta (Consulate General); in Iraq, with seat in Baghdad (Consulate General); in Yemen, with seat in Sana (Consulate General); in Lebanon, with seat in Beirut; in Syria, with seat in Damascus (Consulate General) and a branch office in Aleppo;[13] in Ceylon, with seat in Colombo (Consulate General); in Cambodia, with seat in Phnom Penh (Consulate General); in Egypt, with seat in Cairo (Consulate General) and a branch office in Alexandria; in Guinea, with seat in Conakry; until now in Ghana, with seat in Accra; in the Sudan, with seat in Khartoum; in Morocco, with seat in Rabat; in Tunisia, with seat in Tunis; in Mali, with seat in Bamako; in Tanzania with a Consulate General in Dar-es-Salaam and Consulate in Zanzibar. To these must be added the missions, opened on the basis of bank-consortium agreement, in Brazil, with seat in Rio de Janeiro; Colombia, with seat in Bogotá; and Uruguay, with seat in Montevideo. In Cairo, East Germany additionally maintains an Office of the German Democratic Republic's Government Plenipotentiary for the Arab States, headed by "Ambassador" Dr. Ernst Scholz.

The purposeful enlargement of trade contacts and the opening of trade missions of course serves not only to raise the volume of trade as a concomitant of coexistence and a bond between the Soviet bloc and the underdeveloped countries. For the East German Government in particular, the conclusion of government agreements and opening of trade missions are viewed as "*de facto* recognition of the German Democratic Republic." A large staff of co-workers at the trade missions maintains contacts with business circles and labor unions, collects pertinent information about the partner nation, and serves public relations purposes.

In contrast to the large number of trade missions maintained by the Soviet bloc in the underdeveloped areas and the many government-level trade agreements concluded, only few countries play a meaningful role in actual goods exchanged. In Africa, Egypt has so far served the Soviet bloc as its foreign trade bridgehead. In countries south of the Sahara, trade operations are still in the buildup stage. Most trade agreements here were concluded only during 1960-62 (Ghana, Guinea, Cameroon, Laos, Mali, Niger, Senegal, Somalia, Togo, Tunisia, and lately also with Dahomey). In Latin America, Cuba became the Soviet bloc trading post in 1960. In this connection

---

[13] An East German press service report, claiming the consulate was changed back into a trade mission, was not verified.

it should be mentioned that the USSR maintains trade relations with only six Latin American Republics (Argentina, Brazil, Cuba, Mexico, Uruguay and, since 1961, Peru). In Asia, India ranks first in Soviet bloc foreign trade, followed by Indonesia, Iraq, Syria, Malaya, and Ceylon.

The Development of Foreign Trade

As sources we now have two comprehensive reports which are the result of thorough investigations by Soviet market researchers. One of them deals with "The Foreign Trade of the West European Countries with the Developing Countries," [14] the other with the "Development of the Foreign Trade of the European Socialist Countries during the Years of the Rule of the People." [15]

Though the first report is written in such a way as to "buttress" the communist propaganda thesis of the "neocolonialist permeation of the developing countries," it nonetheless offers revealing data that proves the great superiority of Western economic aid over that granted by the East bloc. A comparison of the sources for both reports confirms what was revealed by the final document of the UN Conference in Geneva for trade and development, namely, that of all trade with the developing countries, the West accounted for 90% and the East bloc for barely 10%.

The Soviet market researches set a value of 22.1 billion DM (roughly $5.5 billion) for the Federal Republic of Germany's trade with "Third World" countries in 1964. The USSR's total foreign trade with the developing countries during the same year amounted to only 1,430 million rubles (roughly $1,589 million) and the Soviet authors report that the total value of the foreign trade of Bulgaria, Hungary, the DDR, Poland, Rumania and the CSSR, and Yugoslavia with the "Third World" was approximately 1,540 million rubles ($1,711 million); that

---

[14] *Bjulleten inostrannoy kommercheskoj informacii* (BIKI), supplement 21/1965.
[15] BIKI, supplement 22/1965.

is, COMECON trade (plus Yugoslavia) with the developing countries in 1964 totalled $3,300 million.

Thus West Germany's $5.5 billion foreign trade with the "Third World" compares with the eight mentioned socialist countries' $3.3 billion trade turnover. The foreign trade of the East bloc countries is also still underdeveloped when regarded from the point of view of the developing countries' share in the East bloc's total foreign trade.

Share of "Third World" Countries in the Total Foreign Trade Turnover
of the Western and Eastern Countries in 1964[16]

		%		%
Federal Republic of Germany		17.9	Yugoslavia	14.6
England (1963)	Import	32.0	USSR	10.3
	Export	28.0	CSSR	9.0
France	Import	29.2		
	Export	26.9	Poland	7.7
Italy	Import	25.0	Hungary (1963)	6.4
	Export	17.5	Bulgaria	5.0
Holland		14.1	Rumania	5.0
Belgium		12.0	DDR	3.8

The share of the Eastern and Western world in the foreign trade of the developing countries is shown in the following UN survey.

The Distribution of Foreign Trade in the Developing Countries[17]

(in millions of U. S. $)

		1955	1960	1963	1963 share in %
The developing countries' total turnover	Export	23,679	27,340	31,220	100
	Import	22,430	28,530	31,000	100
	Turnover	46,100	55,870	62,220	100
Capitalist World Market share					
	Export	17,080	19,770	22,760	72.9
	Import	16,050	21,230	22,330	72.0
	Turnover	33,130	41,000	54,090	72.5
Socialist World Market share					
	Export	575	1215	1570	5.1
	Import	625	1260	2195	7.1
	Turnover	1200	2475	3765	6.1

---

[16] Data according to BIKI, supplements 21 and 22/1965; USSR calculated according to *Vneshnaya torgovlya SSSR za 1964 god;* DDR share in total trade includes trade with West Germany.

[17] *UN Monthly Bulletin,* New York, June 1963/June 1964.

In 1963, therefore, the developing countries conducted 72.5% of their foreign trade with capitalist countries, 21.4% with each other and 6.1% with East bloc countries.

The comparatively small volume of trade of the "socialist world market" can only be effective with respect to a few developing countries. For, as in its economic aid, the Soviet bloc concentrates its foreign trade on crucial areas (particularly on India and the UAR). Thus the DDR's foreign trade expert, Dr. G. Scharschmidt had to admit: "The concentration of trade on a few countries up until now has become particularly evident, for example, in Asia where in 1961 roughly 74% of the export and 85% of the import trade of the socialist states (i.e., to and from the ESCAFE countries) was *with six countries* . . . " [18]

At the UN conference in Geneva March/June 1964 several Soviet bloc delegations announced that they would double their trade with the developing countries by 1970.

The *Soviet delegation* declared that its total trade volume would *more than quadruple* between 1963 and 1980, during which period *its trade with the developing countries is supposed to grow to eight times its 1963 volume.* The trade turnover of the USSR with the developing countries in 1962, 1963 and 1964 amounted to roughly 1,400 million rubles per year. By 1970 therefore it is supposed to be 3,300 million rubles and 10,000 million rubles by 1980. The *Czech delegation* announced it would roughly double its foreign trade with the developing countries by 1970. The turnover is supposed to have a value of $900 million by that time. The *Polish delegation* only said that Poland would increase its import from the developing countries from $125 million (1963) to $300 million by 1970. *Hungary* intends to increase its turnover from $160 million (1963) to $310 million by 1970.

These announcements will stir a certain amount of hope in the developing countries. Yet even if one uses the Soviet figures for one's calculations, and even if the Soviet plan succeeds, the Soviets will not substantially increase their share of the developing countries' foreign trade relative to the West's share. Soviet economists claim that the West can only count on a yearly increase of 4% or 5% in its trade with the "Third World," while the Soviet bloc will be doubling its trade with the developing countries by 1970. Using the data in the final document of the aforementioned UN conference about East and West trade with the developing countries in 1963, this would mean that by 1970, 88.3% of this trade would still be with the West and only roughly 11.7% with the East bloc.

---

[18] *Aussenhandel,* East Berlin, No. 3/1965, p. 40.

Moreover, Soviet bloc statistics show that the Soviet bloc has not substantially increased its trade with the developing countries in the past three years. This holds particularly true for the USSR.

SOVIET TRADE WITH THE DEVELOPING COUNTRIES

1964, for which we have the Soviet foreign trade statistics, saw no improvement over 1963 in Soviet trade with the developing countries. The developing countries' share in the 1964 Soviet trade turnover was smaller than in the two previous years—and this despite the Soviet's professed aim to double their trade with the developing countries by 1970.

Developing Countries' Share in Total Foreign Trade Turnover of the USSR[19]

(in millions of rubles)

	1958	1959	1960	1961	1962	1963	1964
Total turnover	7782	9463	10,071	10,643	12,137	12,898	13,876
Developing countries' share	805	825	783	1033	1415	1405	1430
Developing countries' percentage	10.3	8.7	7.7	9.7	11.6	10.8	10.3

The developing countries continue to receive a smaller share of the increase in USSR foreign trade than any other group of countries.

As this table shows, the USSR in 1964 increased its imports from all groups of countries with but one exception: the developing countries. Despite its announcement at the world trade conference, the USSR imports from the "Third World" countries diminished in 1964. In 1963 they amounted to 583.8 million rubles, in 1964 to only 563.5 million rubles. If the USSR were to realize its professed objective of increasing its trade with the developing countries to 3,300 million rubles per year by 1970, it would have to increase its trade by roughly 270 million rubles or 180% each year. However, in 1964 the USSR upped its trade with the developing countries by only 25.5 million rubles or by only 1.8%. Of the thirty-nine trading partners listed in the 1964 USSR statistics (seventeen Asian, seventeen African and five Latin American countries) the USSR was only able to show an increase in its trading volume with twenty-two countries, and only with a few countries did the volume increase according to the rate proposed at the world trade conference. In comparison with 1963, 1964 Soviet trade regressed with seventeen countries. Among these

---

[19] For the years up to 1963, according to the corrected statistics in *Vneshnaya torgovlia SSR za 1959-1963 god; 1964—Vneshnaya torgovlya SSSR za 1964 god.*
[20] *Vneshnaya torgovlya SSR za 1964 god.*

USSR Foreign Trade Turnover According to Groups of Countries, and Its Increase[20]

(in millions of rubles)

Total turnover		1963	1964	share 1964 in %	1964;1963 1963-100
	Export	6545.2	6913.2		
	Import	6352.9	6963.0		
	Turnover	12,898.1	13,876.2	100	107.6
East bloc share					
	Export	4589.5	4865.7		
	Import	4487.8	4812.2		
	Turnover	9077.3	9677.9	69.7	106.6
COMECON share					
	Export	3849.6	4175.1		
	Import	3778.7	4057.1		
	Turnover	7628.3	8232.2		
Capitalist countries' share					
	Export	1955.7	2047.5		
	Import	1865.1	2150.8		
	Turnover	3820.8	4198.3	30.3	109.8
Industrial countries' share					
	Export	1135.0	1180.8		
	Import	1381.3	1587.3		
	Turnover	2416.3	2768.1	20.0	114.5
Developing countries' share					
	Export	820.7	866.7		
	Import	583.8	563.6		
	Turnover	1404.5	1430.2	10.3	101.8

seventeen countries are Indonesia, Iraq, Yemen, Cambodia, Malaysia, Pakistan, Thailand, Cyprus, Guinea, Morocco, Senegal, Sudan, Tunisia, Zambia, Brazil, Mexico and Uruguay. The USSR was able to increase its trade with several other developing countries only at the expense of the aforementioned seventeen.

Only 1,226.8 million rubles of the 1,430.2 million rubles total Soviet trade with the developing countries in 1964 is identified. Asia's share was 757.0 million rubles, or 61.7%, Africa's 387.0 million rubles or 31.6% and Latin America's was 82.8 million rubles or 6.7%.

ASIA

Of the seventeen countries that appear on the USSR foreign trade list, trade with only twelve of them exceeded 10 million rubles in 1964. These twelve countries are listed in the following table.

The Development of Soviet Foreign Trade with Several Asian Countries

(in millions of rubles)

		1963	1964	1964;1963 1963 - 100
India	Export	199.7	208.6	
	Import	85.3	140.3	
	Turnover	285.0	348.9	122.2
Malaysia	Export	3.9	3.0	
	Import	120.4	63.8	
	Turnover	124.3	66.8	53.7
Indonesia	Export	44.9	42.0	
	Import	26.8	23.2	
	Turnover	71.7	65.2	90.9
Afghanistan	Export	40.4	42.7	
	Import	17.6	20.4	
	Turnover	58.0	63.1	108.8
Ceylon	Export	17.3	22.2	
	Import	6.6	20.6	
	Turnover	23.9	42.8	179.1
Iran	Export	21.4	19.6	
	Import	16.0	18.9	
	Turnover	37.4	38.5	102.7
Iraq	Export	39.1	28.2	
	Import	4.7	2.2	
	Turnover	43.8	30.4	69.4
Syria	Export	11.8	11.0	
	Import	12.8	16.0	
	Turnover	24.6	17.0	109.8
Burma	Export	6.0	5.9	
	Import	12.4	18.3	
	Turnover	18.4	24.2	131.5
Turkey	Export	7.8	8.9	
	Import	6.4	8.3	
	Turnover	14.2	17.2	121.1
Pakistan	Export	5.6	9.9	
	Import	8.7	2.4	
	Turnover	14.3	12.3	86.0
Lebanon	Export	4.1	5.4	
	Import	1.0	4.8	
	Turnover	5.1	10.2	200.0

As can be gleaned from this table, the USSR was unable to increase its trade volume in accordance with the increase proposed at the world trade conference except for five countries. These are Lebanon, Ceylon, Burma, India and Turkey. The main emphasis of Soviet-Asian trade and its trade with the developing countries as such, is India. India's share of the USSR's total trade volume with the developing countries in Asia was roughly 46% (40% in 1963). It is characteristic of Soviet-Indian trade that the balance for all years shows a Soviet surplus.

The Balance of Soviet-Indian Foreign Trade

(in millions of rubles)

	1955	1956	1957	1958	1959	1960	1961	1962	1963	1964
USSR export	6.6	36.4	76.2	117.0	61.2	42.4	85.9	112.3	199.7	208.6
USSR import	4.0	16.5	37.8	45.8	54.5	61.6	60.2	64.5	85.3	140.3
Turnover	10.6	52.9	114.0	162.8	115.7	104.0	146.1	176.8	285.0	348.9
Balance	+ 2.6	+19.9	+38.4	+71.2	+ 6.7	-19.2	+25.7	+47.8	+114.4	+68.3

USSR exports in the preceding table include goods deliveries made as part of Soviet credit grants. The credits the USSR granted to India between 1955 and March 1965 total 917 million rubles ($1,018.5 million), but not all of this credit has been used so far.

The above table shows a 375.8 million rubles Soviet surplus in its trade with India during the ten listed years. There is no way of ascertaining the size of India's debt to the USSR from this table. The Soviets publish no statistics about their balance of payments. The statistics list equipment and material shipments but not weapon deliveries. Nor do the Soviet reports allow one to ascertain the cost of Soviet research, surveying and planning work, service work, technical aid rendered by specialists sent abroad, and so forth. However, we are confirmed in our assumption, which has also been voiced by the press, that India is unable to repay its credits through a surplus in its trade with the USSR.

AFRICA

Only with nine of the seventeen African countries with which the USSR conducts foreign trade did the 1964 turnover exceed 5 million rubles. Here then is a list of these nine countries in the order of their relative importance.

The Development of USSR Trade with Several African Countries

(in millions of rubles)

		1963	1964	1964;1963 1063=100
UAR	Export	121.7	140.1	
	Import	111.2	111.2	
	Turnover	232.9	251.3	107.9
Ghana	Export	15.0	17.6	
	Import	19.4	18.7	
	Turnover	34.4	36.3	105.5
Algeria	Export	4.6	14.1	
	Import	0.6	3.4	
	Turnover	5.2	17.5	336.6
Mali	Export	11.0	11.9	
	Import	2.7	3.3	
	Turnover	13.7	15.2	111.0
Morocco	Export	8.8	7.3	
	Import	9.1	5.9	
	Turnover	17.9	13.2	73.3
Sudan	Export	12.2	5.9	
	Import	15.5	4.5	
	Turnover	27.7	10.4	37.5
Guinea	Export	12.7	8.3	
	Import	2.1	2.0	
	Turnover	14.8	10.3	69.6
Somalia	Export	6.1	7.7	
	Import	0.2	0.0	
	Turnover	6.3	7.7	122.2
Ethiopia	Export	1.0	3.0	
	Import	1.8	2.1	
	Turnover	2.8	5.1	182.1

Soviet foreign trade with Algeria is only in its beginning stages. Except for the UAR and Ghana, USSR foreign trade with African countries remained underdeveloped in 1964. It regressed in the case of Sudan, Guinea and Morocco; and amounted to less than 5 million rubles for Tunisia, Tanzania, Senegal, Nigeria, Libya, and Zambia. In 1964 the USSR conducted 64.9% of its Africa trade with the UAR (1963 = 61%).

The Development of Soviet Trade with the UAR*

(in millions of rubles)

	1955	1956	1957	1958	1959	1960	1961	1962	1963	1964
USSR export	9.9	34.6	74.0	78.9	79.2	62.8	97.8	93.0	121.7	140.1
USSR import	13.8	45.3	99.8	96.4	83.4	1C9.2	86.6	65.7	111.2	111.2
Turnover	23.7	79.9	173.8	175.3	162.6	172.0	184.4	158.7	232.9	251.3
Balance	-3.9	-10.7	-25.8	-17.5	-4.2	-46.4	+11.2	+27.3	+10.5	+28.9

This table shows that the USSR was willing to accept an unfavorable balance of trade with the UAR until 1961—(until 1960, Soviet imports from the UAR consisted 98% of cotton)—in order to get a foothold in this country. The UAR exemplifies a tendency that holds true for almost all developing countries that receive Soviet credits and economic aid: the balance of trade begins to favor the USSR when the USSR makes good on its economic aid commitment (the UAR received its first USSR credits in 1958) and delivers machinery and equipment, especially for complete plants.

The Share of Machinery and Equipment in the USSR Export to the UAR

(in millions of rubles)

	1955	1956	1957	1958	1959	1960	1961	1962	1963	1964
Total USSR Export	9.9	34.6	74.0	78.9	79.2	62.8	97.8	93.0	121.7	140.1
Machines and equipment	--	4.4	13.8	13.4	19.1	21.0	39.7	53.3	75.5	96.4
Complete plants	--	--	0.4	1.1	14.1	14.3	31.7	37.4	43.3	55.7

LATIN AMERICA

Latin America continues to be a bottleneck in the Soviet trade. Since 1955 the Soviet Union has had trade relations with only five or six of the countries on the continent. In order to gain an opening in the

* exclusive of Syria in each instance.

Latin American market, the Soviets are willing to accept an unfavorable balance of trade, relatively small volume of Soviet export versus a high Soviet import volume from a few countries. In 1964, Soviet trade with its Latin American partners receded in every case except that of Argentina.

USSR Foreign Trade with the Latin American Countries

(in millions of rubles)

	1960	1961	1962	1963	1964
Brazil					
Soviet export	14.2	16.5	27.1	26.5	21.6
Soviet import	8.4	21.6	32.2	39.9	33.4
Turnover	22.6	38.1	59.3	65.6	55.0
Argentina					
Soviet export	12.6	9.5	7.2	0.8	4.0
Soviet import	19.5	17.9	8.8	16.8	17.9
Turnover	32.1	27.4	16.0	17.4	21.9
Mexico					
Soviet export	0.7	0.1	0.1	0.1	0.3
Soviet import	3.0	0.3	6.6	7.4	1.9
Turnover	3.7	0.4	6.7	7.5	2.2
Uruguay					
Soviet export	1.2	0.5	0.2	0.2	0.2
Soviet import	1.2	3.7	13.8	4.7	0.9
Turnover	3.4	4.2	14.0	4.9	1.1
Peru					
Soviet export	--	--	--	--	--
Soviet import	--	2.2	5.2	0.2	--
Turnover	--	2.2	5.2	0.2	--

Summarizing Soviet trade with the developing countries in 1964 we can say: USSR imports from the "Third World" did not increase in 1964; as a matter of fact they were less than in 1963. The USSR trade with the developing countries did not grow at a faster rate in 1964 than did its total volume of trade. Compared with 1963 the total 1964 USSR trade volume with all countries in the East and West rose by 7.6%, whereas Soviet trade volume with the developing countries grew by only 1.8%.

Of the thirty-nine trading partners listed in the USSR statistics, the USSR was able to achieve an increase corresponding to the announcements by its economic expert with only eight countries. In part this increase came about at the expense of regression of trade volume with other trade partners in the developing countries. The result of USSR trade with the developing countries in 1964 is that the Soviet promises, assertions and declarations at the UN conference for trade and development have little but paper value up until now.

CSSR TRADE WITH THE DEVELOPING COUNTRIES

CSSR trade with the developing countries is supposed to constitute more than 33% of its trade with nonsocialist countries. The developing countries accounted for roughly 9% of the CSSR's total trade volume in 1964.

CSSR Foreign Trade According to Groups of Countries

(in millions of kcs)[21]

		1953	1958	1960	1963	1964
Total Turnover	Export	7153	10,895	13,892	17,723	18,545
	Import	6330	9772	13,072	15,554	17,488
	Turnover	13,483	20,667	26,964	33,277	36,033
East bloc share:						
	Export	5587		10,041	13,382	13,691
	Import	4992		9316	11,437	12,693
	Turnover	10,579		19,357	24,819	26,384
Capitalist Industrial countries:						
	Export	1062	1847	2316	2712	3058
	Import	943	1903	2477	2669	3374
	Turnover	2005	3750	4793	5381	6432
Developing countries:						
	Export	504	1367	1535	1629	1796
	Import	395	976	1279	1448	1421
	Turnover	899	2343	2814	3077	3217

Of the CSSR's 3,217 million Kcs total trade volume with "Third World" countries in 1964, 1,677 million Kcs or 52.1% was with Asian countries, 1,049 million Kcs or 32.6% with countries in Africa, and 491 million Kcs accounted for by CSSR-Latin American trade.

Machinery and equipment are supposed to account for 66% of Czech export to the developing countries at this time. This would come to roughly 1,185 million Kcs, or $165.6 million in 1964. In com-

[21] 1 Kcs = 0.1398 U. S. $; 100 Kcs = 12.50 rubles—according to the New York and Moscow rate respectively.
Sources: BIKI, supplement 22/1965, p. 167, 173, 185 & 183; *Handbook of Czech Foreign Trade 1965; Statistická ročenka CSSR 1962.*

parison let us note that Holland exported machinery and equipment valued at $177.3 million to the "Third World" in 1964, that is, 27.7% of its total "Third World" trade of $640 million. The source is the same as that for the Czech figures.[22]

CSSR Foreign Trade with the Individual Developing Countries

(in millions of kcs)

	1948	1953	1958	1960	1963	1964
Total for Asia	777	445	1091	1408	1548	1677
Burma	1	2	81	24	49	54
India	--	72	147	227	479	616
Indonesia	19	28	12	95	125	92
Iran	61	36	--	104	64	101
Cambodia	1	--	5	35	73	54
Pakistan	--	15	41	53	38	36
Turkey	225	160	206	210	148	110
Ceylon	3	7	18	32	46	44
Total for Africa	355	246	742	746	1016	1049
Ghana	--	--	13	17	88	120
Morocco	9	16	--	42	124	103
Nigeria	--	--	--	37	52	73
UAR	213	148	432	303	440	424
Tunisia	2	2	8	18	31	33
Total for Latin America	389	208	510	660	513	491
Argentina	192	46	154	182	94	69
Brazil	145	106	219	259	166	173
Mexico	16	12	--	21	55	37
Uruguay	24	7	33	15	34	42

POLAND'S TRADE WITH THE "THIRD WORLD"

In 1964 the People's Republic of Poland conducted 63.7% of its foreign trade with East bloc countries and 36.3% with capitalist and developing countries. The developing countries' share in Poland's total trade volume that year was 7.7% of Poland's trade with noncommunist countries in 1964, 78.5% was with the capitalist industrial nations and 21.5% with the developing countries.

---

[22] *Handbook of Czech Foreign Trade 1965.* BIKI, supplement 22/1965, pp. 184, 196/97.

Polish Foreign Trade According to Groups of Countries

(in millions of zlotys)[23]

		1960	1963	1964
Total turnover				
	Export	5300.0	7080.0	8380.0
	Import	5988.0	7920.0	8290.0
	Turnover	11,280.0	15,000.0	16,670.0
Capitalist industrial countries	Export	1517.0	2029.0	2308.0
	Import	1773.0	2106.0	2423.0
	Turnover	3290.0	4135.0	4731.0
Developing countries				
	Export	388.8	529.2	660.1
	Import	406.7	501.1	637.5
	Turnover	795.5	1030.3	1297.6

Of Poland's total foreign trade with the developing countries in 1964 (1297.6 million zlotys = $325.7 million), 682.5 million zlotys (52.5%) was conducted with Asian countries, 373.3 million zlotys (28.8%) with African countries and 241.9 million zlotys (18.6%) with the Latin American countries. The following table tells something about Polish foreign trade with the Asian, African and Latin American countries.

Polish Foreign Trade with Asia, Africa and Latin America[24]

(in millions of zlotys)

	1948	1951	1954	1957	1960	1963	1964
Asia							
Export	17.4	35.8	78.8	107.2	190.0	283.3	430.6
Import	2.6	94.0	74.9	99.2	127.2	226.5	251.9
Turnover	20.0	129.8	153.7	206.4	317.2	509.8	682.5
Africa							
Export	3.7	13.2	22.6	40.4	67.5	174.3	174.9
Import	19.6	16.3	23.6	70.2	84.0	126.5	198.4
Turnover	23.3	29.5	46.2	110.6	151.5	300.8	373.3
Latin America							
Export	12.7	28.0	86.6	71.3	131.4	71.6	54.6
Import	85.8	48.1	110.5	90.1	195.5	148.1	187.2
Turnover	98.5	76.1	197.1	161.4	326.9	219.7	241.8

[23] 1 zloty = 0.2510 U. S. $; 100 zloty = 22.50 rubles—according to New York and Moscow rates respectively.
Sources: BIKI, supplement 22/1965, p. 126 & 128; *Statistics of Foreign Trade, 1964*, Warsaw, May 1965; *Handel Zagraniczny*, No. 7/1964.
[24] Source: BIKI, supplement 22/1965, p. 126; *Statistics of the Foreign Trade 1964*, Warsaw, May 1965; *Handel Zagraniczny*, No. 7/1964.

In 1964 Poland traded with thirty-eight developing countries on the basis of inter-governmental agreements. Yet Poland was able to reach long-term accords of from three to five years only with Brazil, Burma, India, the UAR, Ghana, Guinea, Nigeria, Tunisia and Afghanistan.

In 1963, machinery and equipment is supposed to have represented 32.2% of Polish export to the developing countries. That would mean that Poland delivered machinery and equipment in the value of 170.4 million zlotys ($42.8 million) to the developing countries that year.

The authors of the aforementioned Soviet market research report complain that Poland was forced to acquire part of its raw material imports (especially of zinc concentrates and copper) from the developing countries by way of third countries in the West. In 1963 this import by way of third countries is supposed to have represented one quarter of the Polish imports from the developing countries.

HUNGARY'S TRADE WITH THE YOUNG NATIONAL STATES

Hungary's trade with the developing countries is supposed to have increased 3.9 times from 1950 to 1963 and is supposed to have accounted for 1.9 billion forints ($164.4 million) in 1963.

In 1964 the developing countries accounted for 6.4% of Hungary's total volume of foreign trade and 21.3% of Hungary's trade with the noncommunist countries.

Hungary's Foreign Trade According to Groups of Countries

(Export & Import)[25]

(in millions of forints)

	1950	1955	1960	1963
Total turnover	7563.4	13421.9	21715.2	29482.2
East block share	4643.1	8198.3	15401.8	20536.1
Cap. Ind. states	2428.2	3955.8	5098.6	7036.6
Developing countries	429.1	1267.8	1214.8	1909.5

Hungary's trade with the developing countries is unstable and particularly its trade with the Latin American countries is beset by constant fluctuations. Almost half of Hungary's trade with the "Third World" is with Asia, with its chief trading partners being India, the UAR, Argentina, Iran, Turkey, and Brazil. In 1964 these countries ac-

---

[25] 1 forint = 0.0865 U. S. $; 100 forints = 7.67 rubles—according to the New York and Moscow rate respectively.

counted for roughly three fifths of Hungary's trade with the developing countries and roughly 4% of its total foreign trade volume.

Hungary's Foreign Trade with the Developing Countries[26]

(in millions of forints)

	1950	1955	1960	1963	1964
Total	492.1	1267.8	1214.8	1909.5	---
Asian total:	186.4	549.3	554.2	922.9	---
India	2.6	8.1	158.4	388.2	461.8
Indonesia	0.1	169.2	13.5	33.2	74.4
Iraq	11.4	26.8	40.4	42.1	34.8
Iran	0.5	---	79.7	64.2	130.9
Turkey	116.2	262.8	153.9	130.3	122.8
African total:	92.3	303.1	292.7	590.0	---
Ghana	---	---	2.6	78.3	105.5
UAR	82.0	178.5	187.4	293.6	255.4
Sudan	---	16.5	36.3	32.5	35.0
Tunisia	---	---	5.7	6.2	6.2
Latin American total:	213.3	415.4	367.9	396.6	---
Argentina	204.4	169.2	218.4	185.9	199.1
Brazil	1.1	172.0	96.2	134.0	107.4
Columbia	---	---	22.9	15.3	---
Uruguay	2.7	23.5	10.6	13.8	---

Almost half of Hungary's export to the developing countries is supposed to consist of machinery, equipment and products of the precision tool industry. Hungary has supplied the complete equipment
for power plants, for an electricity meter plant and for a foundry;
Indonesia received the equipment for a chemical plant in Sumatra;
Hungary is equipping a telephone exchange in Syria. Hungary delivered mill and power plant equipment to the UAR.

BULGARIA'S TRADE WITH THE "THIRD WORLD"

At present, Bulgaria trades with more than fifty developing countries, and has been able to establish trade missions in thirty of them.
Bulgaria has reached one-year agreements with eight developing na-

Source: BIKI, supplement 22/1965, pp. 47, 52, 65 & 63; *Statistikai Evkönyv*, 1949-
1955, 1962, 1963; *Külkereskedelem*, No. 4/1965.
[26] Source: BIKI, supplement, 22/1965, p. 63; *Statistikai Evkönyv*, 1949-1955,
1962, 1963; *Külkereskedelem*, No. 4/1965.

tions and long-term accords with the UAR, Tunisia, Guinea, Ghana and India.

Bulgaria's trade with the developing countries is supposed to have grown more rapidly than its trade with the industrial countries of the West. In 1964, "Third World" countries accounted for 5% of Bulgaria's total volume of trade and 25% of its trade with noncommunist states.

Bulgaria's Foreign Trade According to Groups of Countries[27]

(in millions of levas)[28]

		1950	1955	1960	1963	1964
Total Turnover	Export	137.0	276.4	668.6	975.8	1146.2
	Import	155.0	292.4	740.1	1091.9	1243.0
	Turnover	292.0	568.8	1408.7	2067.7	2389.2
East bloc share	Export	125.9	247.9	561.7	801.4	913.5
	Import	133.1	261.2	621.0	899.7	940.1
	Turnover	259.0	509.1	1182.7	1701.1	1853.6
Cap. Ind. states	Export	9.8	23.0	83.5	126.1	173.0
	Import	20.2	27.1	101.6	162.4	247.3
	Turnover	30.0	50.1	185.1	288.5	420.3
Developing countries	Export	1.3	5.5	23.4	48.3	59.7
	Import	1.7	4.1	17.5	29.8	55.6
	Turnover	3.0	9.6	40.9	78.1	115.3

Of the developing countries only seven are listed as having a significant trade with Bulgaria. They account for more than half of Bulgaria's trade with the developing nations.

Bulgaria's Foreign Trade with Several Developing Countries

(in millions of levas)

	1950	1955	1960	1963	1964
Algeria	--	--	0.3	5.2	6.9
Ghana	--	--	--	1.2	6.6
India	--	0.2	1.4	18.1	19.4
Indonesia	--	--	2.9	0.5	5.7
Iraq	--	--	3.0	5.0	4.8
Syria	0.3	0.5	3.4	2.8	7.8
UAR	0.1	0.8	12.3	11.1	13.9

---

[27] Source: BIKI, supplement 22/1965, pp. 17, 22, 36, 34 & 33; *Vunsna Turgovia na NRB*, Statistical Omnibus volume, Sophia 1965.

[28] 1 lev = 0.86 U. S. $; 100 levas = 76.92 rubles—according to the New York and Moscow rate respectively.

The aforementioned Soviet market research report states: "It has been noticed that Bulgaria's trade with the developing countries has been marked by new forms and methods which have an advantageous effect on its foreign trade relations. The Bulgarian foreign trade undertakings establish direct contacts to the national firms in their partner countries, found mixed trade and production corporations and bureaus for technical services. For example, a mixed Bulgarian-Ethiopian company has been operating for more than a year in Ethiopia. Seventy per cent of its founding capital was provided by the Bulgarian state undertaking, *Rodopa*, while the other 30% was raised through the sale of stock to Ethiopian citizens. This company built a large slaughter house in Ethiopia and a fish cannery. It has three freighters, two of them refrigeration ships. This company is supposed to increase the export of fish and meat to Bulgaria and increase the exchange of goods. A Bulgarian architect's bureau, founded by the foreign trade undertaking, *Technoexportstroy*, is operating successfully in Ethiopia.[29]

RUMANIA'S TRADING ACTIVITY IN THE "THIRD WORLD"

In 1964 Rumania was conducting foreign trade with more than sixty developing countries; however, with only twenty countries on the basis of trade or economic agreements and only with India, Indonesia, the UAR, Ghana, Iran and Brazil on the basis of long-term agreements.

Of Rumania's total volume of trade of 13,009 million lei ($2,168.6 million) 68.4% was accounted for by its trade with the East bloc, 26.6% with the capitalist industrial nations and 5% with the developing countries.

The Soviet economist Prochorov gives a figure of $82.2 million for Rumania's foreign trade with "Third World" countries in 1961 and $98.9 million for 1962.[30] The figure for 1964 is estimated to be $105 million.

---

[29] BIKI, supplement 22, p. 34.
[30] G. M. Prochorov, *The Two World Systems and the Liberated Countries* (Russ.), Moscow 1965, p. 140.

Rumania's Foreign Trade Turnover with Its 10 Principal Partners in the
"Third World"[31]

(in millions of lei)[32]

	1958	1960	1961	1963	1964
UAR	131.8	102.8	177.8	112.6	150.7
Syria	15.1	15.8	35.1	100.5	95.6
India	15.8	89.7	52.1	64.3	76.4
Indonesia	--	5.2	20.6	35.4	75.0
Lebanon	11.1	39.6	54.4	67.2	68.0
Brazil	0.9	24.7	21.9	43.6	42.3
Sudan	---	14.2	10.4	41.4	27.8
Argentina	55.1	22.7	27.2	18.2	23.9
Iraq	0.3	8.3	4.6	15.2	15.3
Ceylon	1.5	15.4	11.3	38.9	12.5

The Soviet market researches emphasize that roughly half of Rumania's trade with the developing countries can be accounted for by its trade with the six countries with whom it has negotiated long-term agreements. In 1960 Rumania reached accords about the creation of binational commissions for economic and scientific-technical cooperation with the UAR and Indonesia.

Equipment for the oil industry plays an important part in Rumania's export to the developing countries. One of Rumania's main selling points is its ability to help in the construction and improvement of a developing country's oil industry.

Beside machinery and equipment the SRR also delivers many raw materials, particularly oil products, woods, cement and other building materials to the interested Asian, African and Latin American countries. Traditional buyers of these products are the UAR and other Near East states. For the time being the export of soda products, medicines, and other products of the chemical industry continues to grow, as does the export of textiles, shoes, glassware, sugar, vegetable fats.

An increasing amount of the developing countries' traditional export is in turn imported into Rumania as part of the bartering arrangements and as payment for economic aid. The delivery of rubber from Indonesia and Ceylon, of cotton from the UAR and Syria, and unfinished leather from Argentina cover Rumania's major import needs of these commodities. The developing countries also pro-

---

[31] Source: BIKI, supplement 22/1965, p. 154; *Anuarul statistic al R.P.R. 1965.*
[32] 1 lei = 0.1667 U. S. $; 100 lei = 15 rubles—according to the New York and Moscow rate respectively.

vide Rumania with large amounts of jute fibres, natural tanning materials, shellac, sisal and other raw materials. On the basis of an accord that Rumania reached with India at the end of 1960, iron ore
deliveries from India to Rumania are to be increased from 0.2 million
tons per year in 1961 to 1 million tons per year by 1966. In 1961, Rumania signed a three-year agreement with Brazil which stipulates an
increase of Brazilian iron ore shipments from 0.15 million tons to 0.30
million tons. In 1963 alone roughly 0.6 million tons of iron ore were
imported from the developing countries, which amount covers more
than one quarter of the SRR's yearly import needs. Beside industrial
raw materials, Rumania also buys most of its coffee, cocoa, peanuts,
and tropical fruits from the Asian, African and Latin American countries. The import of these commodities makes for an improvement in
the population's standard of living.

DDR TRADE WITH THE "THIRD WORLD"

The DDR has not published any exact data about its trade with the
Asian, African and Latin American countries since 1962. In the last
four years the DDR's statistical yearbooks have only published reports about DDR trade with several "selected" "Third World" countries. The Soviet market researches also omitted a thorough representation of DDR trade with the developing countries. All that can be
gleaned from their report is that the DDR's total trade volume in 1964
amounted to 4,966 million rubles, of which the developing countries
accounted for 190 million rubles ($211 million), that is 3.8% of the
total turnover. The DDR therefore is one of the most underdeveloped countries with respect to trading with the "Third World." We
offer a survey of the distribution of the DDR foreign trade, based on
a variety of sources and documents.

DDR Trade According to Groups of Countries[33]

(in millions of rubles)[34]

	1960	1961	1962	1963	1964
Total turnover					
Export	1971.5	2035.3	2124.8	2422.9	2622.0
Import	1952.8	1994.6	2135.8	2066.5	2344.0
Turnover	3924.3	4029.9	4260.6	4489.4	4966.0
East bloc share					
Export	1491.3	1520.3	1670.4	1912.9	2034.0
Import	1443.5	1510.3	1696.9	1614.4	1763.0
Turnover	2934.8	3030.6	3367.3	3527.3	3797.0
Capitalist countries					
Export	480.2	515.0	454.4	510.0	588.0
Import	509.3	484.3	438.9	452.1	581.0
Turnover	989.5	999.3	893.3	962.1	1169.0
West Germany					
Export	216.4	196.9	189.1	218.0	237.1
Import	185.7	176.8	172.7	172.8	226.9
Turnover	402.1	373.7	361.8	390.8	464.0
Developing countries					
Export	81.2	88.4	85.3	96.9	99.8
Import	85.8	68.4	86.6	82.7	89.9
Turnover	167.0	156.8	171.9	179.6	189.7

As becomes evident from the above table, *in all the years it has traded with the developing countries the DDR trade volume has barely reached half of its small volume of trade with West Germany.* Moreover, DDR trade with the young national states is quite unstable. Of the thirty-five trading partners in the "Third World" listed in the DDR 1961 statistics, only twenty are still listed in the 1963 and

---

[33] *Total trade turnover* and *East bloc trade* according to BIKI, supplement 22/1965, pp. 82 and 86; *trade with the capitalist countries* through calculation; *trade with West Germany* according to *Statistisches Jahrbuch der DDR 1964* recalculated in rubles; *trade with the developing countries* for 1960 and 1961 according to *Statistisches Jahrbuch der DDR 1961*, for 1962 and 1963 calculated according to the share (4%) in the total trade turnover (W. I. Solotarjev, *The Foreign Trade of the Socialist Countries* (Russ.), Moscow, 1964, p. 298), for 1964 = 3.8% share according to BIKI, supplement 22/1965, pp. 82 and 96.

[34] The official Moscow rate for 100 marks of the Deutsche Notenbank (MDN) is 40.50 rubles; the Deutsche Notenbank in East Berlin has set a course of $1 = 2.22 MDN. The conversion of MDN into rubles and of rubles into MDN in the DDR trade statistics is handled (as becomes evident from a comparison of the ruble figures in the *Statistisches Jahrbuch der DDR 1963* with the MDN figures in the *Statistisches Jahrbuch der DDR 1964*) by way of the clearing-U. S. $. This conversion course is: 1 clearing-U. S. $ (0.90 ruble) = 4.20 MDN; 1 clearing-ruble = 4.67 MDN, 100 clearing-MDN = 21.41 rubles.

1964 *Statistical Yearbooks*. The other fifteen were omitted, probably because the trade volume was minimal. Among these fifteen are *Algeria*, Ethiopia, *Burma*, Bolivia, Chile, *Yemen*, *Cambodia*, *Congo* (Brazzaville), Libya, *Mali*, Mexico, Pakistan, Saudi Arabia, *Tanzania*, and Venezuela. (Italicized are those countries where the DDR has trade missions.)

Yet of the twenty countries listed in the trade statistics for 1964 only three—India, the UAR and Brazil—account for 96.5 million rubles of the DDR's total trade volume of 190 million rubles with the developing countries. And this despite the fact that DDR trade with the UAR had been regressing for years and recently also with India. Here then, a survey of DDR's foreign trade with countries in which it has or had (Ghana) trade missions until 1964.

DDR Trade with Its Principal Partners in the "Third World"[35]

(in thousands of rubles)[36]

Asia		1961	1962	1963	1964
India	Export	17,269	22,285	22,686	19,376
	Import	11,770	18,709	21,856	21,324
	Turnover	29,039	40,994	44,542	40,700
Turkey	Export	4992	4368	5186	7129
	Import	4919	1350	4460	4218
	Turnover	9911	5718	9646	11,347
Indonesia	Export	1479	864	303	4988
	Import	687	749	35	578
	Turnover	2166	1613	338	5566
Ceylon	Export	113	1303	1378	2441
	Import	958	1622	444	2654
	Turnover	1071	2925	1822	5095
Lebanon	Export	2397	1233	1378	2226
	Import	1254	903	906	1306
	Turnover	3642	2136	2284	3532
Iraq	Export	2382	1493	2094	3425
	Import	434	206	510	43
	Turnover	2816	1699	2604	3468
Syria	Export	1729	1465	1093	1199
	Import	1102	1124	1539	942
	Turnover	2831	2589	2632	2141
Africa UAR	Export	23,617	21,707	17,249	13,874
	Import	16,324	15,025	13,754	16,999
	Turnover	39,941	36,732	31,003	30,873
Ghana	Export	1955	2336	4254	3682
	Import	3064	2016	3607	3276
	Turnover	5019	4352	7861	6958

---

[35] *Statistisches Jahrbuch der DDR*, 1962, 1963 & 1964.
[36] Compare footnote 34.

		1961	1962	1963	1964
Sudan	Export	1416	858	1081	1220
	Import	469	3365	2833	2699
	Turnover	1885	4223	3914	3919
	Turnover	7558	3763	3403	3725
Morocco	Export	936	1133	1607	1541
	Import	809	1114	1309	2184
	Turnover	1745	2247	2916	3725
Tunisia	Export	322	181	469	514
	Import	302	175	211	385
	Turnover	624	356	680	899

Latin America

		1961	1962	1963	1964
Brazil	Export	14,517	7648	5295	11,390
	Import	13,453	7982	10,385	13,352
	Turnover	27,970	15,630	15,680	24,942
Colombia	Export	1835	2242	2866	5095
	Import	3089	3518	2935	4689
	Turnover	4924	5760	5801	9784
Uruguay	Export	343	384	221	299
	Import	798	1644	463	3875
	Turnover	1141	1992	684	4174

DDR propaganda places special emphasis on the three crucially important trading partners: India, the UAR and Brazil. The DDR reached its first long-term agreement with India in 1954. This was replaced by the five-year trade agreement of December 1959. A new trade agreement between India and the DDR was signed in September 1964 and is valid for the three-year period 1965-67.

The Soviet market research report has the following to say on the subject of India: "Approximately two-thirds of the DDR export to India consists of products of the metal industry. The DDR also exports chemical products and mass consumption items to India and imports industrial raw materials, wood, cotton, jute fibres, tea, vegetable fats, cotton and silk textiles and other goods . . .

"The DDR assists India in the development of its national industry, it provides India with licenses for the manufacture of machine tool machinery, motor scooters, typewriters, photo apparatuses, cable products; it acquainted Indian specialists with the operation of blast furnaces, gave technical assistance to the great Indian steel company, 'Iron and Steel Co.,' and helped India with surveying the soft coal regions in Madras, with the construction of steel works and machine tool plants." [37]

---

[37] BIKI, supplement 22/1965, pp. 96-97.

Noteworthy for the trade relations between the DDR and the UAR is that the regression of the foreign trade volume between these two countries can be accounted for primarily by a decrease of DDR exports (compare with the preceding table). In 1958, with a 44.8 million-ruble volume, the trade between the two countries was higher than during any year in the 1961-64 period listed in the statistics.

Nonetheless, all DDR publications continue to speak about an increase in the DDR-UAR trade. A 40% increase was proposed for 1965, but there is no telling yet whether this goal was met.

The Soviet market researches have this to say about UAR-DDR trade relations: "DDR trade with the UAR in 1964 was conducted according to the accord of 16 December 1963 for the years 1963-1965. Metal products represented an important part of the DDR export to the UAR, particularly tool manufacturing machines, diesel motors, automobiles, optical products, office machines, and scientific apparatus. Complete plants also play an important role in DDR deliveries to the UAR. During the 1955-1961 period the DDR delivered several complete plants to the UAR, specifically complete cotton and worsted plants, spinning mills, a power plant with a 30,000-kw capacity, transformer substations, grain mills, and two printing plants. The DDR also exports chemical products such as chemical fertilizer, insecticides, pharmaceutical products, and also paper and articles for mass consumption.

Cotton and cotton thread account for roughly nine-tenths of DDR imports from the UAR. The DDR also imports fruits and vegetables.

At the International Leipzig Fair in the autumn of 1965 the DDR and UAR reached a long-term trade and payment agreement for the years 1966-1970. The agreement foresees an important increase in trade between the two countries. For example, the agreement plans on a 40% increase in 1966 over the 1965 trade volume between the two countries." [38]

The DDR's third principal partner is Brazil. The Soviets have this to say: "Trade between the DDR and Brazil expanded significantly between 1953 and 1964. The DDR exported machine tools, agricultural machinery, office and printing machinery, equipment for the textile industry. DDR imports from Brazil primarily consist of coffee, tobacco, wood. Trade relations between the two countries were furthered by a $40 million credit which the DDR granted Brazil in 1961." [39]

---

[38] BIKI, supplement 22/1965, p. 97.
[39] ibid., p. 97.

YUGOSLAVIA'S TRADE WITH THE "THIRD WORLD"

"The foreign trade of the Federal People's Republic of Yugoslavia with the developing countries of Asia, Africa, and Latin America rose from $144 million in 1961 to roughly $300 million in 1963; that is, it more than doubled. In 1963 the developing countries accounted for more than 16% of Yugoslavia's total trade volume." [40] Thus says a Soviet source.

That would mean that Yugoslavia's trade with the developing countries far exceeded that of the DDR. The per-country volume of the DDR trade with the developing countries in 1963 amounted to roughly $10.5 million, Yugoslavia's to $15.8 million.

The large share the developing countries have in Yugoslavia's foreign trade also becomes evident when one compares Yugoslavia's trade with the "Third World" to its trade with the seven European COMECON countries. According to Soviet sources Yugoslav trade with the "Third World" amounted to $300 million in 1963, and to $452 million with the seven COMECON countries. [41]

Yugoslavia's Foreign Trade According to Groups of Countries [42]					
(in billions of dinars) [43]					
Total Turnover	1960	1961	1962	1963	1964
Export	170.0	170.7	207.1	237.1	268.0
Import	247.9	273.1	266.3	317.0	397.0
Turnover	417.9	443.8	473.4	554.1	665.0
East bloc share					
Export	55.1	54.1	50.4	64.3	92.0
Import	62.9	51.4	58.2	72.4	118.1
Turnover	118.0	105.5	108.6	136.7	210.1
Capitalist countries[30] share					
Export	88.8	89.6	107.7	129.5	131.0
Import	152.4	205.4	175.0	196.7	215.0
Turnover	241.2	295.0	282.7	326.2	346.0
Developing countries					
Export	24.7	24.6	47.3	39.0	42.9
Import	30.1	22.5	32.8	47.4	54.4
Turnover	54.8	47.1	80.1	86.4	97.3

---

[40] *Ekonomika stran sotsialisma,* Moscow 1964, p. 237.

[41] *ibid.,* p. 238.

[42] BIKI, supplement 22/1965, p. 195, 201, 208, & 214; adding the group figures results in small differences which are also contained in the source.

[43] The statistical yearbook of the FPRJ 1964 (page 42) cites a rate of 300 dinar = 1 U. S. $ as used for foreign trade purposes until and including 1964.

Of Yugoslavia's trade with the "Third World" in 1964, Asian countries accounted for 50.5%, African countries for 30.8% and Latin American countries for 18.7% of this trade.

Yugoslavia's Trade with the Developing Countries According to Continents[45]

(in billions of dinars)[43]

		1960	1962	1963	1964
Asia	Export	12.0	24.0	19.6	24.9
	Import	11.0	212.1	25.0	24.2
	Turnover	23.0	45.1	44.6	49.1
Africa	Export	9.9	17.0	15.5	12.6
	Import	14.4	7.2	13.6	17.4
	Turnover	24.3	24.2	29.1	30.0
Latin America					
	Export	2.8	6.3	3.9	5.4
	Import	4.7	4.5	8.8	12.8
	Turnover	7.5	10.8	12.7	18.2

[44] The import figures include the goods delivered as part of American aid.
[45] BIKI, supplement 22/1965, p. 214.

CHINA'S FOREIGN TRADE WITH THE "THIRD WORLD"

As we know, Peking has not published any statistics about its foreign trade for years. The available Western data therefore cannot be compared with Chinese figures. Western sources generally over-estimate the part of Chinese trade that is calculated in rubles. Their considerations do not take account of the unfavorable price and conversion relation in Chinese-East bloc trade.[46]

The following data may serve to give a general picture of the total trade volume of China and its East bloc trade.

The People's Republic of China's Foreign Trade Turnover According to Groups of Countries[47]

(in millions of $ U. S.)

		1959	1962	1963	1964
Total Turnover					
	Export	2230	1510	1525	1670
	Import	2065	1160	1190	1335
	Turnover	4295	2670	2715	3005
East bloc share					
	Export	1651	925	800	700
	Import	1370	500	410	355
	Turnover	2985	1425	1210	1055
Other countries					
	Export	615	585	725	970
	Import	695	660	780	980
	Turnover	1310	1245	1505	1950

---

[46] Compare Kurt Müller & D. E. Gross, *Die wirtschafliche Verflechtung der Volksrepublik China mit der Sovietunion,* Frankfurt a/M-Berlin 1959, p. 29.

[47] Wolfgang Bartke, *Die Volksrepublik China,* Monthly Report, Hamburg, May 1965; appropriate for 1964.

According to Chinese information, China's 1961 trade with the underdeveloped countries amounted to roughly 18% of its total foreign trade.[48] A Western survey for 1960 shows China's foreign trade breakdown as 65.2% with Soviet bloc countries, 17.7% with Afro-Asian countries, and 17.1% with other countries.[49] The survey lists China's trade with the underdeveloped countries of Asia and Africa as follows:

China's Trade with Afro-Asian Nations [49]

(in millions of $ U.S.)

	1955	1957	1958	1959	1960
Asia					
Export	280	233	311	350	388
Import	176	173	219	259	294
Volume	456	506	530	609	682
Africa					
Export	1	23	28	34	50
Import	26	54	46	49	65
Volume	27	77	74	83	115
Total Volume	483	583	604	692	797

Without doubt, these figures are padded. Very likely, the exaggerated figures in the above table result from the inclusion, under "Asia," of China's Hongkong trade, averaging a third of the Chinese Asian trade.

One can estimate that China's 1963 trade with African and Asian countries (excluding the Hong Kong trade) amounted to roughly $485 million.

For our evaluation it is important that we keep in mind that:

1. In 1962, China's trade volume reached its lowest level since 1953.

2. The volume of trade began to increase again in 1963 and there was a noticeable reorientation toward Western countries.

3. Even during the critical years, Peking always sought to keep up its trade relations with the Asian and African countries, and even to improve them in some cases. Peking's trade with Latin America was never highly developed except for its grain imports from Argentina.

---

[48] Radio Peking, 3 February 1962.
[49] *Neue Zürcher Zeitung*, 31 January 1962.

The Policy of the Unfavorable Balance of Trade and the East Bloc's Importation of the Developing Countries' Traditional Export Commodities

Western publications tend to corroborate the assumption that the "socialist world market" follows a policy of the unfavorable balance of trade; that is, that it buys more in several countries than it sells to them so as to help the young national states that are short of foreign currency and have few markets for their products. Statistics show that several Soviet bloc countries and especially Communist China accepted an unfavorable balance of trade during the period 1955-1959/60. However, in most cases the purpose was to establish initial trade relations in order to obtain a foothold in these countries. In 1963 and 1964 Soviet Russia showed an unfavorable balance of trade in its trade relations with Zambia, Kenya, Nigeria, Senegal, Tanzania, Argentina, Brazil, Mexico, Uruguay, Jamaica and Peru. All these are countries with which the USSR has not had stable and lasting trade relations until now.

Generally, the balance of trade begins to favor the East bloc as soon as the relations to the developing country have been cemented and the trade relationship has been augmented through credit grants and economic aid. Since 1961 the Soviet Union has been able to register a trade surplus with those countries whom it has granted credits and who have begun to make use of these grants. (Afghanistan, Ceylon, India, Indonesia, Iraq, the UAR, Ethiopia, Ghana, Guinea, Mali among others.)

The assumption is not borne out that "East bloc trade furnishes India with an increasing flow of currency that it can use to cover the long-term developmental credits from the East bloc." [50]

---

[50] *Neue Zurcher Zeitung*, March 25, 1961.

The East bloc, however, accepts an unfavorable balance of trade with a few countries from whom it needs to obtain badly needed raw materials and consumer goods. Due to their accelerated industrialization, the tightening of their own agricultural structure and due to economic difficulties, several European East bloc states have become especially dependent on such imports. For example, its unfavorable balance of trade with Malaysia is acceptable to the USSR since it obtains large amounts of strategically important rubber from that country.[51]

USSR RUBBER PURCHASES IN MALAYSIA

USSR Rubber Purchases in Malaysia [51]

	1960	1961	1962	1963	1964
USSR-export in million rubles	1.9	1.8	2.0	3.9	3.0
USSR-import in million rubles	100.4	152.6	144.9	120.4	63.8
Rubber import in million rubles	100.3	152.4	144.8	118.9	56.8
Rubber import in 1000 tons	132.2	267.7	280.2	240.6	124.8

It has also been suggested that Soviet import surpluses are the result of its trade with countries that receive USSR military aid, and that such surpluses should be regarded as repayment for such aid. This may hold true for the UAR until 1960 and for Syria for the years 1962-1964. It certainly does not hold true for other countries that have received Soviet military assistance. Even China—as Peking has announced—had to pay for its Soviet military help with gold and hard currency.

In recent years the East bloc has purchased more and more of the developing countries' traditional export commodities. At the UN conference for trade and development in 1964 in Geneva the Soviet, Czech, Polish, and Hungarian delegations declared that they wanted to more than double their imports from the "Third World" by 1970.

It is a known fact that more than 60% of all Egyptian cotton exports go to the East bloc, and that cotton constitutes the major share of Soviet imports from the UAR.

---

[51] *Vneshnaya torgovlya SSSR za 1959-1963 god*, Moscow 1965, p. 398 & *Vneshnaya torgovlya SSSR za 1964 god*, Moscow 1965, p. 243.

USSR Cotton Imports From the UAR[52]

	1960	1961	1962	1963	1964
USSR-export in million rubles	62.8	97.8	93.0	121.7	140.1
USSR-import in million rubles	109.2	86.6	65.7	111.2	111.2
Cotton-import share in million rubles	108.7	84.9	57.5	81.8	65.0
in 1000 tons	111.0	91.8	67.5	99.5	75.3

Roughly 25% of Burma's rice export for the past several years has gone to the USSR, with another 20% to the remaining Soviet bloc countries. After some initial difficulties, several Soviet bloc members (USSR, China, East Germany, Poland, and Hungary) in 1961 declared themselves ready to absorb Ghana's chief export product of cacao beans. Cacao beans are the only article on the export lists of Ghana, Cameroon, and the Ivory Coast to the USSR. The following table of the UN Economic Commission for Europe (ECE) shows that as early as 1958 the Soviet bloc imported its tropical products largely from the underdeveloped areas:

1958 Soviet and East European Imports of Tropical Products

Product and Import Area	in 1000 Tons	% of Total Imports		
		From East Bloc Trade Area	From Western Industrial Nations	From Less Industrial Nations
Coffee Beans				
Soviet Union	4	5	54	41
East Europe	24	-	-	100
Cacao Beans				
Soviet Union	10	-	1	99
East Europe	29	-	42	58
Tea				
Soviet Union	26	2	52	46
East Europe	7	100	-	-
Citrus Fruits, Bananas, Dates				
Soviet Union	149	-	-	60
East Europe	108	-	89	11

Source: "Economic Survey of Europe," United Nations, Geneva 1961, Chap. V., p.17

---

[52] *Vneshnaya torgovlya SSSR za 1959-1963 god,* Moscow 1965, pp. 443 and 449, and *Vneshnaya torgovlya SSSR za 1964,* Moscow 1965, pp. 271 and 275.

[53] *Vneshnaya torgovlya SSSR za 1959-1963 god,* Moscow 1965, pp. 443 and 449; and *Vneshnaya torgovlya za 1964 god,* Moscow 1965, pp. 271 and 275.

Another ECE table, unfortunately not including a breakdown of export areas, shows the planned step-up in Soviet bloc purchases of tropical products until 1965 (end of the Soviet Seven-Year Plan) and until 1980 (end of the Twenty-Year Plan).

1965 and 1980 Tropical Fruit Import Forecast for USSR and East Europe

Product and Import Area	in 1000 Tons	Import 1965 Increase in % (Basis 1958)	Import Forecast 1980 in 1000 Tons	Value of Imports in Million Dollars Prices of 1958 Forecast 1958	1965	1980
Coffee beans						
Soviet Union	70	1650	1440	26	128	1230
East Europe	68	180				
Cacao beans						
Soviet Union	25	130	820	33	84	690
East Europe	75	160				
Tea						
Soviet Union	-	-100	..	39	21	..
East Europe	18	150				
Citrus Fruits Bananas, Dates						
Soviet Union	330	135	9124	32	75	1030
East Europe	250	130				

Source: "Economic Survey of Europe," United Nations, Geneva 1961, Chap. V., p. 17

The Soviet Union inserted the following survey about its planned import increases from the developing countries into the final document of the UN Conference on Trade and Development (UNCTAD):

USSR Imports of Tropical Goods from the Developing Countries

		1963	1970	1980
Cocoa beans	in 1000 tons	54.0	120.0	350.0
Coffee	in 1000 tons	29.1	60.0	120.0
Citrus fruits	in 1000 tons	60.2	180.0	750.0
Coconut oil, palm oil and other fats	in 1000 tons	212.0	300.0	1000.0

The document goes on to say that the USSR also intends to increase its imports of the following goods from the developing countries: cotton fibre, wool, tea, bananas, pineapples, spices, as well as some products of the mining industry and raw materials for the chemical industry. It also intends to increase its purchase of manufactured goods and half-finished goods from the developing countries, and it intends to do so on the basis of trade agreements which include reimbursement for credits the USSR has granted these countries.

CSSR, Hungary, and Poland inserted similar estimates about their import increases into the closing document of the above-named conference.

However, the Soviet Union, speaking for all Soviet bloc delegations, felt it was necessary to state the following precondition at the conference: "That the Socialist countries' import increase from the developing countries must be accompanied by an increase in developing country purchases as well as by a general normalization of world trade." That means that the East bloc is unwilling to increase its imports from the "Third World" unless the developing countries adjust their trade to East bloc demands.

The sale of their chief export crops to the Soviet bloc strengthens the ties of the underdeveloped countries with this bloc. But in quite a few cases goods so purchased were resold by the bloc members on the "capitalist world market" in order to obtain foreign exchange for the purchase of badly needed production goods. Examples of the re-export of Egyptian cotton and Burmese rice are well known. This re-export, sometimes at dumping prices, narrows the free market access for the underdeveloped states. The Soviet-Egyptian Payment Agreement of 18 August 1953 expressly banned re-export. But the USSR managed to include a clause in the agreement to the effect that "re-export of Egyptian goods by the USSR may be freely made to Poland, Czechoslovakia, Rumania, Bulgaria, Hungary, and East Germany." These countries became the USSR channels for Egyptian cotton to the West.

Export of Machine Tools and
Plant Equipment to Backward
Nations

Soviet statisticians, in line with and in support of Soviet bloc propaganda about the industrialization of the backward nations, endeavor to put the spotlight on the export of machine tools and equipment. Adam Kruczkowski, editor-in-chief of the Polish periodical *Spravy Miedzynarodove,* claims that 40% of Poland's exports to the new national states are in the form of machine tools and entire plants. This would indicate that 50.8 million of a total of 129.3 million dollars of Poland's 1961 exports consisted of machine tools and equipment. Czechoslovakia claims to supply a third of the machine tool exports of the European COMECON members to the underdeveloped countries. Allegedly, 55% of Czechoslovakia's total export to these countries is in this form. However, Czechosolavakia does not submit absolute figures about the size of this export. K. H. Domdey claims that "in the past several years more than 66%" of East Germany's export to the backward nations was in the form of machine tools and basic industrial goods. Yet, he lists East German machine tool delivery to India as only 39.3% and to Egypt as only 35.9% of total exports to these countries.[54] It must be remembered, too, that East Germany's total exports to the underdeveloped nations amounted to only 90 million dollars. Thus, even 66% does not amount to much.

From Soviet statistics it becomes evident that of the total Soviet exports to the "Third World" in the amount of 866.7 million rubles in 1964, roughly 47.7% or 413.1 million rubles went for the export of machinery and equipment. The USSR has considerably increased its

---

[54] K. H. Domdey, *Neo-Kolonismus oder sozialistische Wirtschaftshilfe,* East Berlin 1962, p. 62.

export of machinery and equipment to the developing countries since 1960.

USScR Machine Tool and Equipment Export

(in millions of rubles)

	1955	1958	1960	1964
Total export of machinery and equipment	539.1	715.3	1027.1	1449.7
East bloc share	521.7	536.0	899.9	1012.8
COMECON share	298.8	244.6	407.4	764.6
Capitalist countries	17.4	152.3	127.2	436.9
Industrial countries	12.8	9.0	15.5	23.8
Developing countries	4.6	143.3	111.7	413.1

Let us look at Soviet machine and equipment exports to the individual "Third World" countries.

Soviet Machine Tool Deliveries to "Third World" Countries

(in thousands of rubles)

Asia	1960	1961	1962	1963	1964
Afghanistan	18,432	21,087	20,288	24,874	28,228
Burma	123	135	600	3166	2588
Ceylon	34	12	873	2628	6507
India	22,742	48,524	69,925	107,886	160,990
Indonesia	8913	19,102	42,023	37,159	33,345
Iraq	11,032	22,137	34,733	36,472	21,214
Iran	2083	1559	920	1251	1579
Yemen	2066	420	134	336	594
Cambodia	469	513	482	359	710
Lebanon	178	210	242	240	981
Pakistan	72	262	3251	3992	7550
Syria	2654	8774	2297	7829	5811
Thailand	2	8	45	1	87
Turkey	4836	2231	1457	1155	807
Africa					
Algeria	-	-	-	532	8310
Egypt (UAR)	20,969	39,666	53,281	75,496	96,379
Ethiopia	51	34	37	41	2087
Ghana	3446	12,073	3811	6840	8730
Guinea	1240	20,073	8653	8332	5502
Libya	-	-	45	111	547
Mali	-	6620	5081	5460	8625

	1960	1961	1962	1963	1964
Morocco	42	20	17	18	47
Somalia	-	18	94	4103	6398
Sudan	335	120	161	2735	3568
Togo	-	2	100	16	3
Tunisia	168	58	7	678	129
Latin Amercia					
Argentina	10,908	7453	5790	44	172
Brazil	-	-	44	97	211
Mexico	475	18	3	45	177
Uruguay	4	18	21	59	77

The above table lists the monetary value of all types of equipment including machine tools, tractors, trucks, passenger cars, electrical installations, and many other categories of equipment. Complete industrial plants—including steel foundries and shoe factories—are also part of the items listed. In a sense, the export of entire plants is a measure of the aid promised by the Soviet bloc, for the whole scheme of industrializing the backward nations hinges on the availability of precisely such plants. The aforementioned Adam Kruczkowski comments on this subject: "Of especial importance is the export of complete industrial plants, for this is the most profitable form of export. The importing nations, also, benefit most from the delivery of investment goods since these are the very building blocks of industrial development."[55]

Poland specializes in the export of shipyard equipment, small power plants, furniture factories, charcoal and cement factories, and the like. East Germany concentrates on the export of entire printing plants, cellulose factories, and plants for the production of film, optical instruments, and measuring devices. Half of Czechoslovakia's export of complete installations is said to be in the electrical field. It is openly admitted that the exports of Poland, Czechoslovakia, East Germany, Rumania, Bulgaria, and Hungary are largely limited to small and medium plants that do not require high capital investment. "Poland maintains an export stockpile of small plants in the price range of 50,000 to 100,000 rubles."[56]

Because of the COMECON-imposed industrial restriction—called "socialist division of labor"—none of the European bloc members would even be able single-handedly to construct complex major

---

[55] *Die Presse der Sowjetunion* (East Berlin), No. 45/1963, p. 978.
[56] *Mirovaya ekonomika i mezhdunarodnie otnosheniya* (Russ.), No. 11/1962, p. 125.

works. This only the USSR is able to do, since it alone within COMECON may engage in untrammeled economic development.

In 1964 the Soviet Union exported complete industrial plants in the value of 266.2 million dollars to the underdeveloped nations. This is roughly 64.4% of the machine tool and equipment export and 30.7% of the entire Soviet export to the backward nations for that year. It should be remembered that these figures do not reveal an exact picture, for some countries receive a lion's share of plant deliveries. Of its thirty-nine trading partners, the USSR supplies only twenty with entire plants. The export table of complete plants is revealing, for it indicates to what degree and in which countries the USSR is living up to its aid commitments.

USSR Export of Complete Industrial Plants

(in millions of rubles)

	1955	1958	1960	1964
Total export of complete plants	249.1	395.9	511.7	542.0
East bloc share	248.1	204.8	449.9	275.4
COMECON share	119.2	51.6	109.5	190.5
Capitalist countries	1.0	101.1	61.8	266.6
Industrial countries	0	0	0	0.4
Developing countries	1.0	101.1	61.8	266.2

As we have stated, in 1964 only twenty countries received complete Soviet plants. These are:

USSR Export of Complete Industrial Plants to the Developing Countries

Asia	1960	1961	1962	1963	1964
Afghanistan	15,684	16,730	17,377	21,526	25,078
Burma	-	-	-	853	1991
Ceylon	-	-	835	2583	6507
India	16,343	35,648	58,262	73,230	116,696
Indonesia	4520	8128	6669	8733	16,337
Iraq	3841	14,347	26,776	23,335	16,486
Yemen	1902	417	108	45	239
Cambodia	-	-	-	-	520
Pakistan	-	218	3152	3881	2688
Syria	1806	7746	1953	1546	933
Turkey	3330	1250	202	116	6

Africa

Algeria	-	-	-	532	1788
Egypt (UAR)	14,266	31,684	37,377	43,309	55,746
Guinea	92	8198	6662	6616	3520
Mali	-	520	2403	3028	3690
Somalia	-	-	43	2465	4796
Sudan	-	-	73	2303	3382
Tunisia	-	-	-	600	4
Ethiopia	-	-	-	-	1966
Ghana	-	70	2365	4131	4062

The export of complete industrial plants is part of the machine tool and equipment export. Figures shown are therefore included in the previous table.

The above table is the *pièce de résistance* of Soviet foreign trade statistics, revealing as it does trends in foreign aid that lie outside the field of foreign trade. Thus the following may be noted:

1. Most profitable of all exports is that of complete plants, for this export is linked with several other factors that do not show up in the trade statistics. It is coupled with research and design work, as well as other technical services, the cost of which would appear only on the (unpublished) balance-of-payment sheet.

2. Of the 1964 total of $266.2 million worth of completely equipped plants to the twenty countries on the preceding list, a little more than 80% ($214 million) was shipped to four countries: 43.7% to India, 20.8% to the UAR, 9.4% to Afghanistan and 7% to Iraq. These four countries have been the principal recipients of Soviet foreign aid for some time. As background material to the Soviet-Chinese conflict we should mention that neutral India received a greater number of complete plants in 1964 (116,696,000 rubles worth) than North Vietnam (16,-253,000 rubles worth), than Communist China (11,074,000 rubles worth), North Korea (16,865,000 rubles worth), Mongolia (30,408,000 rubles worth) and Cuba (33,612,000 rubles worth) combined.

It should be noted that the USSR had made the following commitments: to supply fourteen developing countries with complete plants by 1959, twenty countries by the end of 1960; twenty-two countries according to the reports of the twelfth Moscow Party Congress in October 1961; and, according to 1965 data, to supply twenty-two national states with complete plants.

3. The table is thus also seen to mirror Soviet aid delivered, in comparison to aid promised. More will be said on this subject later.

In this short survey of Soviet bloc foreign trade we have already touched on the subject of foreign aid. This was quite inevitable, for part of this aid, as laid down in credit agreements and in "agreements on economic and technical collaboration," and as exemplified by delivery of complete plants and credit amortization via the counter-delivery of finished goods, flows through normal trade channels.

The Indian Example

Soviet bloc trade with India serves as an illustrative example. Ten Soviet bloc nations (the Soviet Union, Czechoslovakia, East Germany, Poland, Hungary, Rumania, Bulgaria, Mongolia, Albania, and North Korea) maintain foreign trade relations with India largely on the basis of government-level trade agreements. Of these nations, the USSR, Czechosolvakia, East Germany, Hungary, Poland, and Rumania are suppliers of investment goods. The Sino-Indian Trade Agreement of 14 October 1954, not renewed since, has been the only form of economic cooperation between India and Communist China. There never has been a formal foreign aid agreement between these two countries.

The Soviet bloc share of India's foreign trade was roughly 6% in 1959 and only 5% in 1960. According to Indian statistics, of which more later, 8.4% of India's 1959 exports and 4.2% of its imports were with the Soviet bloc. For 1960 these figures were 3% for exports and 8.1% for imports. Indian sources list the Soviet bloc share in India's foreign trade for the years shown as follows:

Soviet Bloc Share in India's Foreign Trade[57]

(in millions of $ U. S.)

Indian Exports	1956	1957	1958	1959	1960
Total	1657.0	2154.3	1814.8	1863.5	2138.1
Soviet bloc	69.8	85.7	79.6	77.3	64.5
in %	4.2	4.0	4.4	4.2	3.0
Total	1227.5	1339.3	1198.2	1293.1	1342.2
Soviet bloc	43.1	50.3	70.3	108.3	109.0
in %	3.5	3.8	5.9	8.4	8.1

---

[57] *Monthly Statistics of Foreign Trade of India,* December 1956, 1957, 1958, 1959, and 1960. Rupee conversion at the rate of 1 rupee = .2114 dollars.

181

Based on the Indian statistics, a Soviet bloc source lists the share of individual countries in the Indian trade in 1959-1960 as follows:

Share of Soviet Bloc Nations in India's Export and Import[58]

(in %)

	Export	Import	Export	Import
	1959		1960	
USSR	4.9	1.9	4.8	1.3
Czechoslovakia	.7	.4	1.0	.7
China	1.2	.5	.9	.3
East Germany	.4	.3	.6	.3
Poland	.6	.4	.5	.3
Rumania	.3	.2	.2	.4
Hungary	.1	.3	.2	.2
Bulgaria	.03	.03	.03	.04

India's entire 1960 export to the Soviet bloc breaks down as follows: USSR 58%; China 10.8% Czechoslovakia 11.6%; Poland 6.5%; East Germany 7.7%; Hungary 2.1%; Rumania 2.8% and Bulgaria .3%. India's imports from Soviet bloc countries for the same year were: USSR 37.2%; China 9.1%; Czechoslovakia 20.1%; Poland 8.4% East Germany 7.4%; Hungary 6.0%; Rumania 10.7%; and Bulgaria 1.0%.[59]

All above data, however, is based on Indian statistics. There are material differences between the official Soviet and official Indian trade figures, in particular in those concerning Soviet exports to India. The Soviet export data includes goods delivered against credit extended. Such exports do not show up in Indian statistics. A comparison of the two statistics is highly revealing:

A Comparison of Indo-Soviet Statistics[60]

(in millions of $ U.S.)

	1956	1957	1958	1959	1960	1961	1956-61 Inclusive
USSR Export to India							
Soviet data	40.4	84.6	130.0	68.0	47.1	95.4	465.5
Indian data	31.3	47.6	45.6	35.0	29.6	51.0	240.1
						difference:	225.4
USSR Import from India							
Soviet data	18.3	42.0	50.9	60.5	68.4	66.9	307.0
Indian data	25.9	36.7	49.0	63.7	66.9	50.0	292.2
						difference:	14.8

[58] *Economic Conditions in Asia in 1960* (Russ.), Moscow 1961, p. 35.
[59] *Economic Conditions in Asia and Africa in 1960* (Russ.), Moscow 1962, p. 106; after *Commerce,* 1 and 15 April 1961.
[60] *Monthly Statistics of Foreign Trade of India* and official USSR Foreign Ministry foreign trade statistics.

It was not to be expected that India's trade exchange statistical data should tally exactly with that of the USSR. It is usual for small differences to crop up in a comparison of the trade statistics of two countries. In our dollar conversion, also, some minor discrepancies were unavoidable because of inherent ruble-versus-rupee disparities. Yet, the above table shows the six-year total of *USSR imports* from India as nearly identical in both statistics. Thus, the Soviet statistics for the period 1956-61 show an import from India higher by 14.8 million dollars than the Indian statistics of export to the Soviet Union reveal. But the *Soviet exports* to India (Indian imports from Russia) for the same six-year period show a difference of 225.4 million dollars. The cause lies in the higher export figures used by the Soviets.

Indian statistics for the six-year period show a 52.1 million dollar trade balance in favor of India (Indian export of 292.2 million dollars versus an import total of 240.1 million).

But the Soviet statistics show a Soviet trade balance surplus for the same six years of 158.5 million dollars (Soviet exports of 465.5 million dollars versus an import total of 307.0 million). The Soviets simply included deliveries on credit in their export data.

The belief that India is able to amortize its USSR loans by means of a regular favorable trade balance with the Soviet Union is not borne out. The foreign trade statistics do not reveal India's total commitments to the USSR. While the Soviet statistics show deliveries of machine tools and equipment as well as complete plants, they do not list those "invisible assets" that are concomitants of plant deliveries and services rendered, such as payments for the remunerative Soviet-conducted research and development work, or for technical assistance including the service of specialists and the training of future technicians and engineers.

Also questionable is the Soviet bloc propaganda claim that the backward nations, by paying for Soviet bloc goods with their own traditional monocultural products, may husband their limited foreign exchange reserves. A look at several trade agreements with India shows otherwise. An Indo-Soviet agreement of 13 December 1955 fixed the sale by the USSR to India of ingot steel and equipment against USSR purchases from India of raw materials and manufactured goods. India at the time "expressed the hope [!] that the overall value of these [Soviet] purchases, including the sums required for the maintenance of official Soviet aid organizations in India, would equal in amount India's purchases in the USSR." [61] In March 1956

---

[61] Bulganin and Khrushchev, *Reden während des Besuches in Indien, Birma, und Afghanistan,* East Berlin 1956, pp. 298-99.

"Mikoyan (in New Delhi) once more confirmed the intent of the USSR to expand its Indian purchases to the point where Soviet imports from India would equal its exports to that country." [62] The Soviet foreign trade statistics prove this hope to have been in vain.

The first Indo-Soviet Trade Agreement of 2 December 1953, which remained in force until 31 December 1958, had provided for payments, including those for technical assistance, in Indian rupees. Yet, the actual agreement reads verbatim: "Any one of the rupee accounts, maintained by the USSR State Bank with India's Reserve Bank or with commercial institutions authorized to engage in currency operations, is convertible on demand in pound sterling at the customary rate of pound sterling exchange as fixed from time to time by the Indian Association of Monetary Institutes." [63] A change was made only with the Indo-Soviet Trade Agreement of 16 November 1958, effective 1 January 1959 for a period of five years. Concerning this agreement, *Pravda* reported the Indian rupee as the monetary unit for clearing purposes. Such clearing operations are "to be effected without conversion of the Indian rupee into pound sterling." It was particularly agreed that "trading will be on a balanced basis without recourse to foreign exchange." In the new agreement, the USSR further promises to apply "any payments received in amortization of Soviet credits to the purchase of Indian goods." [64] In 1959, Poland, East Germany, and Czechoslovakia joined the new accounting methods of the Soviets. Yet *Pravda's* point that the new agreement provides for "trading on a balanced basis without recourse to foreign exchange" proves that this was not the case before. Even today it is not true in every case that underdeveloped nations are able to conduct their Soviet bloc trade without recourse to foreign exchange. Whereas the Soviet-Guinea Agreement of 8 September 1960 provides for payment of any ensuing debts by means of goods shipments, that with Afghanistan furnishes several examples to the contrary. Article 6 of the Afghan-Soviet Trade and Payment Agreement of 17 July 1950, still in force at this writing, states: "The USSR State Bank or, respectively, the State Bank of Afghanistan, may at any time demand a settlement of any account mentioned in Article 5. In such case, the debtor bank is obliged to pay the balance either in gold, dollar remittance, or any other curency agreed on between the banks, into a bank of the credi-

---

[62] *USSR Foreign Trade with Asia, Africa, and Latin America* (Russ.), Moscow 1958, p. 36.
[63] *Sbornik deystvyiyshtsikh dogovorov* . . . Vyp. XV, pp. 51-60.
[64] *Pravda*, 17 November 1958.

tor bank's designation." [65]

But the aforementioned propaganda claim concerning the savings in foreign exchange deserves to be treated in the larger context of the ideology and the reality of Soviet bloc foreign trade.

---

[65] *Sbornik torgovikh dogovorov i soglasheniy SSSR s inostranami gosudarstvamy,* Moscow 1961, p. 58.

Ideology and Reality of
Soviet Bloc Foreign Trade

Konrad Illgen has formulated the salient points of Soviet bloc propaganda in the backward areas about the "advantages" of trading with the bloc members in these words: "The trade treaties (of the Soviet bloc) are based on the *mutual exchange of goods of equivalent sum total value*. They enable the weakly developed nations *to obtain advantageous prices* for the surpluses resulting from their monoculture, as well as for the products of their young industry. At the same time, they enable these nations to procure the installations, equipment, and other items required in the national buildup. The *conclusion of these treaties on the basis of the weakly developed nations' currencies* represents *a marked saving in foreign exchange*, which anyway, because of the nonequivalent nature of trade with the imperialist states, would hardly be sufficient to finance projects on a national scale. Additionally, the *price-structuring* of their economic interrelations with the socialist states often guarantees the weakly developed nations a *higher export income*, which serves by way of important capital accumulation for the national economy. This price structure is entirely different in nature from that of the crisis-prone capitalistic market in which *the prices of raw materials and of manufactured goods become increasingly disproportionate*." [66]

First, concerning the "marked saving in foreign exchange." As the example of India until late 1958 shows, trade agreements on the basis of the underdeveloped nation's currency are no guarantee for the

[66] Konrad Illgen, *Freundschaft in Aktion*, East Berlin 1961, p. 160. Italics added.

186

saving of foreign exchange when, as is here the case, debts in local currency must be converted and paid in a foreign currency. Also, a review of twenty-four trade or payment agreements between the USSR and underdeveloped nations reveals that only four provide for clearing in the local currency.

The Soviet-Lebanese Trade and Payment Agreement provides for settling of accounts in either rubles or Lebanese pounds; that with Morocco calls for contracts in either Moroccan francs or the currency of a third country (namely Swiss francs, British pounds sterling or U. S. dollars). A high number of trade agreements between the USSR and underdeveloped countries provide for settlement of accounts in pounds sterling or U. S. dollars.[67] The Soviet-Senegalese Trade Agreement of 14 June 1962 simply states: "Payments resulting from the goods exchanged under this Agreement shall be in a freely convertible currency." The same stipulation is found in agreements with other countries, e.g., Togo and Ethiopia. The Economic Aid Agreement of the USSR with Tunisia of 30 August 1961, while containing the provision that accounts received in amortization of loans are to be applied to the purchase of Tunisian goods, goes on to say: "In the event the Soviet agencies are unable to procure appropriate goods under the conditions of this Agreement, these accounts may be paid in pounds sterling, U. S. dollars, or other currencies agreed upon between the State Bank of the USSR and the Central Bank of Tunisia." Whether or not "appropriate goods" are available for procurement is left to the political discretion of the Soviet agencies. And such "may be" phraseology that leaves open several courses of action depending on political opportuneness is found in most Soviet bloc trade, payment, and credit agreements with the underdeveloped nations.

Nor does Illgen's claim apply to East Germany except in isolated instances. The Payment Agreement of 29 August 1960 between East Germany and Cambodia provides for a pounds sterling settling of accounts. An account payable in excess of 100,000 pounds sterling must be settled by the terms of this agreement in mutually agreed-upon goods shipments. "If at the expiration of six months the debtor side is unable to deliver the agreed-upon goods, and if the account payable remains in excess of 100,000 pounds sterling, the amount in

---

[67] The first trade agreement between the USSR and Ghana of 4 August 1960 provided: "Contracts that provide for payments in accordance with this Agreement are to be in terms of the Ghanaian pound or in the convertible currency of third countries (in particular: Swiss francs, pounds sterling, or US dollars), with payment in Ghanaian pounds or a convertible currency. "Only with the new Payment Agreement of 4 November 1961 was it agreed that payments would be "as a rule in Ghanaian pounds," though "permission for making payments in a convertible currency may be granted."

excess of the credit maximum must on demand of the creditor side be immediately paid by the debtor side in any other currency, acceptable to the creditor side." [68] The Payment Agreement of 8 August 1960 between East Germany and Morocco provides for the settling of accounts receivable in U. S. dollars. "If no agreement is reached between the two partners, or if after a lapse of six months an imbalance continues to exist, the latter shall be settled in a convertible currency or in any other currency, agreed on by both partners." [69] Today, with East Germany eager to establish trade connections at all cost, such elastic provisions may be meaningless. But at a future date the East Germans have the choice of coming to an agreement or of demanding payment in a hard currency.

Even more problematic than the foreign exchange question is the *price structuring* that is to assure the underdeveloped countries a *higher* export income. True, at first, in order to gain a foothold in the trade with the backward nations or to cut out Western competition, the Soviet bloc countries offered more favorable price terms. Such prices, however, are only *more favorable in relation to world market prices;* they do not in any way provide a fundamental solution to the price squeeze between finished goods and raw materials. All Soviet bloc agreements with the underdeveloped countries stipulate that "prices for goods to be delivered shall be fixed on the basis of world market prices." This, as some trade agreements put it, "is the basic market price for corresponding goods." G. Prochorov, Soviet economics specialist, laments: "The problem of equivalence in the exchange of goods is one of the most complicated questions in the theory and practice of foreign trade relations. But, at the moment, the economically weakly developed nations are conducting their foreign trading largely within the framework of the capitalist world market. For this reason, the socialist camp, in its relation with the underdeveloped nations, must consider the price level of goods on the world market." [70] Does this economist perhaps mean that the backward nations must join the "socialist world market" to obtain more favorable price terms and achieve "equivalence" in the exchange of goods? But "the socialist world market" has not even achieved its own price structuring within the Soviet Bloc itself. Here as well, "capitalist world market prices" serve as the basis for foreign trade. Soviet finance experts even claim: "The new ruble rate was fixed on the basis of the actual purchasing power of both ruble and dollar in accordance with cor-

---

[68] *Dokumente zur Aussenpolitik der DDR,* Vol. VIII, East Berlin 1961, pp. 372-75.
[69] *ibid.,* pp. 401-04.
[70] *Voprosy ekonomiki* (Moscow), No. 11/1962, pp. 78-80.

responding USSR and U. S. A. prices." [71] Here, also, we find conformity with Western pricing methods.

The price tag put by the Soviet bloc on the export goods of the underdeveloped nations, as well as its so-called *long-term purchasing commitments* for these goods, are dependent on what is politically opportune. For, while it is true that the Soviet bloc usually concludes five-year agreements with the underdeveloped countries, price and delivery terms are only generally outlined in these agreements. In annual protocols, prices and delivery dates are separately negotiated for each year. It is hardly necessary to point to recurring difficulties, encountered in the negotiations of such protocols between the USSR and Egypt, to prove that price fixing and delivery agreements depend on the political climate of the time. The Soviet bloc itself furnishes apt examples of how shortsighted may be the hope of long-term purchases, as well as of deliveries, of goods. Yugoslavia and Albania are cases in point. The Sino-Soviet trade relations also are instructive in this regard.

There can be no question of a "mutual exchange of goods of equivalent sum total value" between the Soviet bloc and the underdeveloped nations. Because world market conditions prevail in Soviet bloc trade with the underdeveloped nations, the price structure of this market benefits particularly the industrially more advanced Soviet bloc nations. Soviet economists find: "In 1955-57 it was generally possible to buy 50% more raw material from the sale of one ton of finished export goods than in 1948, and 250% more than in 1928 . . . This margin has increased even more during the years 1958-61." [72] The "socialist world market," which allegedly favors trade with the backward nations, has not solved this problem nor eliminated the margin.

A. A. Arsumanyan, the late director of the Soviet Institute for World Economics and International Relations, attempted to prove that the West's trade with the backward nations is not "equivalent." But about the Soviet bloc trade he remained silent. Arsumanyan wrote: "First of all, the gap that exists between the per capita production in the industrialized capitalist states and that of the economically more retarded nations of Asia, Africa and Latin America has not closed but increased. According to available estimates, this rate in America is ten times, in England six times, that of India. England's rate is twenty times that of its African colonies. Insofar as this gap in productivity

---

[71] *Voprosy ekonomiki* (Moscow), No. 2/1962, p. 75.
[72] *Mirovaya ekonomika i mezhdunarodnie otnoshenya* (Moscow), No. 2/1962, pp. 30-31.

level remains, there also remains the basis for a nonequivalent trade exchange." [73]

Khruschev, on the other hand, used to claim that the USSR had already surpassed several Western industrial states in labor productivity and would surely catch up with and overtake the U. S. This of course means that the gap in labor productivity is widening between the USSR and the underdeveloped countries and, following Arsumanyan's argumentation, an "equivalent" exchange of goods between the Soviet bloc and the nations of Asia, Africa, and Latin America is out of the question.

On the basis of the differences in labor productivity that also obtain in the Soviet bloc, Yugoslavia's Minister of Foreign Trade Milentye Popovich, a Marxist who applied in general the same doctrine Arsumanyan had reserved only for the West, stated in 1950 that nonequivalent trading occurs even within the Soviet bloc, that the "principle" of "business is business and friendship, friendship" held sway, and that "modern conditions justifiably grant the more advanced socialistic states the capitalistic right of exploiting other nations." [74]

We can only add that the propaganda of the Soviet bloc is contradicted by its foreign trade practices, a fact unfortunately not yet well known in the underdeveloped countries. The actual advantages enjoyed by the backward nations in their trade with the Soviet bloc are temporary in nature. They are:

1. An initial willingness of the Soviet bloc to accept an unfavorable trade balance in its trade with several underdeveloped nations, a condition impossible to maintain indefinitely.

2. Soviet bloc purchase of goods not easily sold on the world market (Egyptian cotton, Burmese rice), which, because of re-exporting, proves to be a two-edged sword.

3. Conditional long-term purchase agreements for the products of the underdeveloped countries which, though assuring these countries of a market for long periods of time, also serve to supply the Soviet bloc with important raw materials.

4. A temporarily advantageous price structure for the purpose of cementing existing trade relations.

5. Facilitation of commercial transactions between the governmental and semigovernmental foreign trade organizations of the underdeveloped nations on the one hand, and the Soviet bloc nations on the other.

---

[73] *Mirovaya ekonomika i mezhdunarodnie otnosheniya* (Moscow), No. 12/1961, p. 12.

[74] M. Popovich, *Über die wirtschaftlichen Bezichungen zwischen sozialistischen Staaten*, Mainz 1950, pp. 19, 30 ff.

Despite its rate of increase, the Soviet bloc share in the foreign trade of the backward nations is as yet small. The Soviet bloc foreign aid program is also still largely written in the stars. Whether the Soviet bloc will always be ready to accept the traditional export articles as compensation for its industrial machinery will not be clear until loan repayment becomes an acute problem for a larger number of under-developed nations. As has been mentioned, a large number of Soviet bloc trade agreements cannot serve to reassure the backward nations in this respect.

The Foreign Aid Program
of the Soviet Bloc

Khrushchev, at the Twenty-Second Party Congress, hailed the alliance with the young nation states as the pillar of international politics for countries within the orbit of communist power. Foreign aid is to be one of the underpinnings of this alliance. To the Soviet bloc, however, the concept of foreign aid as a form of collaboration carries a far broader meaning than in the West. The East, which counts all kinds of cultural as well as economic relations as foreign aid, includes in its foreign aid program:

1. Foreign trade as "foremost in economic collaboration" and "a form of aid." [75]

2. Credits and nonrepayable aid.

3. Techno-scientific collaboration (building of plants and installations, research and planning, technical services and furnishing of specialists).

4. Cultural collaboration and training aid.

As shown, a major portion of the East's credit aid and technical collaboration falls within the field of foreign trade, e.g., delivery of equipment, or loan amortization and interest payment through counter-delivery of goods. Soviet bloc experts consider foreign trade the most important form of foreign aid because, as a concomitant of "competition with capitalism," it sets the stage for the penetration of the backward nations' economies and the domination of their markets.

Soviet loans come with strings attached, for they are to pay for equipment and materials purchased in the Soviet bloc. It is indicative that several Soviet economists in recent times have singled out these

---

[75] *Mezhdunarodnaya zhizn* (Moscow), No. 2/1962, pp. 50-59.

192

loans as pump primers of foreign trade and a modern form of export subsidy. A Soviet article on backward nations states: "Quite aside from their great importance, foreign loans and technical assistance actually serve only the ancillary function of raising the economy of the backward countries. The latter can be most effectively assisted through establishment of mutually profitable trade relations." [76] The Soviet bloc viewpoint is expressed even more succinctly by Soviet expert A. Kodachenko, who stresses: "Foreign trade is one of the most important, and one of the most promising, forms of economic collaboration between the underdeveloped countries of Asia, Africa, and Latin America, and the USSR and other socialist states." [77] And he adds: "The credits granted by the Soviet Union under the terms of its trade and aid agreements with the underdeveloped nations serve as a potent stimulus for Soviet exports to these states. Not only do these credits, as noted in the UN World Economy survey of 1958, create conditions favorable for continuous exchange of raw materials against manufactured goods supplied by countries operating under a centrally planned economy, but they may have an important effect on future exports to these underdeveloped nations." [78]

Professor A. M. Smirnov frankly declared: "To the USSR, granting credits and other aid to the backward nations is not a charitable undertaking but assistance on a commercial basis." [79]

---

[76] *The Underdeveloped Countries in the Capitalistic Economy* (Russ.), *op. cit.*, p. 473.

[77] *Mezhdunarodnaya zhizn* (Moscow), No. 2/1962, p. 50.

[78] *Mezhdunarodnaya zhizn* (Moscow), No. 2/1962, p. 55.

[79] A. M. Smirnov, *USSR International Currency and Credit Relations* (Russ.), Moscow 1960, p. 275.

Comments on Some Propaganda Claims
about Backward Nations

In the Soviet Union, the material as well as politico-ideological preconditions for loan grants to backward nations did not exist until ten years after World War II. After 1946 only Soviet bloc members enjoyed the benefit of Soviet loans. Not counting the 30 million dollars loaned by the USSR to Argentina for purchase of Soviet machine tools and equipment under the Trade and Payment Agreement of 5 August 1953, the Soviet Union first appeared as creditor to an underdeveloped nation outside the Soviet bloc with a 3.5-million-dollar loan to Afghanistan on 27 January 1954. Communist China had applied the more liberal practice of outright monetary gifts since 1953 in the Soviet bloc part of Asia, and since 1956 also in the underdeveloped nations of Asia.

Obviously, the foreign aid program which the West initiated soon after World War II also served as impetus to the East to extend credit. Yet, current Soviet bloc propaganda in the underdeveloped countries claims that the USSR long before World War II had begun to extend credit and other economic aid to the backward nations; and that "roughly forty years ago" the USSR had been "in a similar plight as the backward nations today, but had transformed itself into a mighty industrial nation without having called on foreign aid."

The statement that the USSR was in a similar situation to that of today's underdeveloped countries is a calculated misrepresentation. A look into Lenin's *Evolution of Capitalism in Russia* of 1899 (subtitled *The Process of Creating a Domestic Market for Heavy Industry*) should convince the Soviet theoreticians that the process of a dynamic industrial evolution, nowhere near at hand in the under-

194

developed nations of today, had already set in in Russia even at that time.

Other, similar, statements contradict the facts, facts that are admitted in only a few publications of Soviet scholarly literature. Thus, the USSR Handbook for Foreign Trade recognizes that: "The postwar growth of the USSR as a major economic power, and the rise in production in all branches of industry and agriculture, enabled the USSR to extend economic aid to foreign states also in the form of loans. In this regard the USSR changed from a *debtor nation*, which it was until the end of World War II, into a significant *creditor nation* . . . Until World War II, the USSR was primarily a *debtor nation* which applied the credits advanced by whatever country to a speed-up of reconstruction and the socialistic industrialization of the national economy." [80] Such words, however, are hardly ever heard in the backward nations. But several recent Soviet writers are all the more eager to "prove" that the USSR has rights of primogenture in the field of economic and credit assistance. Thus L. A. Fitulin and V. D. Shchetinin write: "The bourgeois economists try to convince world public opinion that the USSR and other socialist nations [!] appeared only recently on the foreign aid scene and only for commercial and political reasons. Contrary to these statements the history of meaningful aid furnished the economically weak countries dates back to 1917, to the Great Socialist October Revolution." [81] The authors go on to cite as economic aid the Soviet renunciation of Czarist privileges, demands, and concessions in Iran, Turkey, and Afghanistan during 1921-22, as well as the so-called "Boxer indemnity," which was forgiven China in 1924. These "renunciations" are simply declared as aid to the countries listed. An example of this type of "economic aid" as cited by the authors runs as follows: "In Iran, the Soviet Government renounced its rights and handed over into the custody of the Iranian people the monies and assets of the Discount and Credit Bank, as well as all fixed and movable property of this bank throughout the country. Iran thus acquired the equivalence of 64 million rubles in gold. Another 67.5 million rubles resulted from the Soviet Government's renunciation of a Czarist loan to Iran, as well as of the loan's repayment guaranty." [82] The same source assesses the return of the Czarist colonial concessions to Iran at 582 million gold rubles, those to Turkey at 103.7 million, and the Boxer indemnity to China at

---

[80] *Spravochnik po vneshney torgovley SSSR*, Moscow 1958, pp. 104-05. Italics added.

[81] *Problems Concerning Aid for Economically Weak Countries* (Russ.), Moscow 1961, p. 65.

[82] *ibid.*, pp. 67-68.

around 100 million rubles, all of which is credited as "Soviet aid." Also allegedly demonstrating the "good will of the Soviet Union and its readiness to aid the Chinese people" was the Sino-Soviet Agreement of 31 May 1924 regarding the Eastern China Railroad.[83] The facts are that the USSR in the cited agreement reasserted the old Czarist claims to the railroad and, despite Chinese protest on 23 March 1935 sold the Eastern China Railroad to the Japanese puppet state of Manchukuo. In 1945 the USSR managed to repossess the already-sold railroad. Only on 31 December 1953 was the railroad turned over to Mao Tse-tung's government without compensation.

These examples of this peculiar type of "economic aid" should suffice. Western renunciations of similar character are designated by communist propaganda as "reparation for injustice committed." Reparations for the Czarist colonial policy are redubbed "Soviet aid."

The meager Soviet aid program of those days, as cited by Fitulin and Shchetinin, consisted of: for *Turkey*, the equipping of two textile combines by the Soviets on the basis of an 8-million-dollar, non-interest-bearing loan; in *Afghanistan*, the installation of a telecommunications network from Herat to Kandahar during 1924-27, and the construction of several cotton mills in 1927-28 and 1930. In *Iran* the Soviet Union, in 1925, assisted in the construction of six silk processing and cotton ginning plants. Finally, in 1938-39, the USSR made three loans to the *Chinese government* of Chiang Kai-shek totaling 250 million dollars at 3% interest. The third of these loans, made in 1939, was to be amortized within fourteen years through shipment of merchandise.[84] These few Soviet aid measures, taken for reasons of foreign policy, can hardly be compared to the modern foreign aid program that the awakening of the peoples of Asia, Africa and Latin America has brought about. Yet, several recent Soviet publications have prominently featured the aforementioned renunciations and restitutions as "foreign aid," at the same time enlarging on such pre-World War II economic assistance as we have described.[85] Obviously, material is being assembled for spreading the word in the underdeveloped countries that the "USSR has always unselfishly made economic aid available." The *Handbook for Foreign Trade* must also be revised, for the statement that the USSR, until the end of the World War II, used foreign credits to industrialize itself no longer

[83] *ibid.*, p. 69.

[84] *ibid.*, p. 73.

[85] L. Stepanov, *Soviet Aid and its 'Critics,'* in *Mezhdunarodnaya zhizn*, No. 6/1960; *The USSR and the Eastern Countries' Economic and Cultural Collaboration* (Russ.), Moscow 1961; M. V. Lavrichenko, *USSR Economic Collaboration with the Countries of Asia, Africa, and Latin America* (Russ.), Moscow 1961, pp. 5-7.

serves USSR propaganda purposes in Asia, Africa and Latin America. Thus Khrushchev, in contrast to the views laid down in the *Handbook*, applied the current propaganda formula for the underdeveloped countries in his 15 February 1960 speech in Bhilai, where he said: "As you know, the USSR did without foreign aid and was able to overcome all obstacles without assistance. This was not because we did not want foreign help, but because there was no one to help us." [86]

This propaganda is to make plausible the "superiority of the Soviet system" to the peoples of the backward nations. Actually, the fact is that the West's role in the industrializing of the USSR is largely unknown in Asia and Africa and not at all well understood in Western countries. If the Soviet concept of economic aid, which embraces not only foreign trade and loan extension, but technical assistance such as patent rights, plans for entire works projects, and furnishing of specialists, is applied to the USSR itself, Western aid to the latter was not inconsiderable. Thus in June 1956, the London publication *World Today* wrote that "in the buildup phase following the 1917 October Revolution half of all machinery installed in Soviet factories came from the West, and in the two decades before World War II, non-communist countries supplied the USSR with production goods in the amount of 8 billion dollars." [87]

Zotchev states: "The first Five-Year Plan and the beginning of Soviet industrialization fell into the period of the Great Depression during the 1930s. Therefore, the Soviet requirements, especially for metal, metal products, machinery, and equipment in general, were a godsend for all industrial nations not only in the dwindling export trade, but for the market as a whole. Which explains why in 1932 nearly a third of the world export in machine tools and equipment went to the Soviet Union . . . Thus the USSR in 1931, the year of Germany's maximum export to the Soviet Union, absorbed 31.5% of the total German machine tool export, 30.4% of Germany's export of rolling mill equipment, 24% of the export of electrical machinery, 24% of the export of other machinery, and so on. During 1931 and 1932 no less than 60% of total Soviet imports consisted of machine tools and equipment, an indication of the immediate role played by the West's industrial nations in the buildup of Soviet industry." [88]

The Soviets, however, take exception to this and say it cannot be

[86] *Happiness and Peace to all the Peoples!* (Russ.), Moscow 1960, p. 69.

[87] Quoted from *Ostprobleme*, No. 32, 10 August 1956, p. 1091 Cf: E. S. Gorfinkel, *The USSR in the World Economic System* (Russ.), Moscow 1929, p. 180; *Foreign Trade of the USSR* (Russ.) ed. A. M. Smirnov and N. N. Lyubimov, Moscow 1954.

[88] Quoted from W. Joost and H. H. Führing, *Wie stark ist die Sowjetunion*, Bonn 1958, pp. 96-97.

considered aid, since the machines and arms the West delivered to the Soviet Union during those years of famine and crisis had to be paid for with grain and goods shipments. The term foreign aid is of course open to interpretation. The Soviets interpret it now as it was practiced by the West toward the Soviet Union prior to World War II. The underdeveloped countries also have to pay for Soviet machinery and arms with foodstuffs and raw material, and during 1960-62, their years of famine and crisis, the Chinese also had to compensate the Soviets for their industrial aid with grain and foodstuffs.

Production goods to the tune of 8 billion dollars were, as noted, delivered to the USSR by the West. This, even leaving aside the higher purchasing power of the dollar at the time, is more than fivefold the current annual export of machine tools and equipment of the highly industrialized Soviet Union. In 1960 the USSR exported machine tools and equipment (including complete plants) in the amount of 1.14 billion dollars, in 1964, 1.6 billion dollars worth. Communist China, until 1960 prime customer of Soviet investment goods, received from the USSR in the eleven years from 1950-60 a total of roughly only 3 billion dollars worth of machine tools and equipment. Total credits granted by the USSR to members of the Soviet bloc during the sixteen years 1946-61 are, at 8.9 billion dollars, only slightly higher than the West's prewar shipment of production goods to the USSR.

No inclusive data is available on the total number of foreign technicians and specialists who took part in the Soviet industrial buildup. It has been reported that during the years of industrialization more than 5000 engineers and technicians from the U. S. alone, which extended no credits to the Soviet Union until World War II, were employed in the USSR.[89] The number of German specialists and technicians was doubtless even considerably higher. In comparison it is mentioned that Mukhitdinov, at the Twenty-Second Party Congress, put the figure of Soviet specialists employed in Asia, Africa, and Latin America at 5000.

The Soviet Union has never published figures of credits received for its industrialization. Only certain hints may be gleaned from some special reports. A text for institutes and faculties dealing with finance management, entitled *Money Circulation and Credit in the USSR*, reports that from 1922 the USSR has made use of short-term foreign credits. Since 1926, European countries have employed the state-guaranteed form of credit in their dealings with the Soviet Union. As first examples of credit financing, the text lists a German credit in 1926 and an English one in 1929. In the end, the USSR also gained

---

[89] Report by Prof. Ellsworth Raymond at the International Conference of the Friedrich-Ebert-Foundation in Bergneustadt, 27 March 1962.

access to direct bank credits.[90] "During the first Five-Year Plan, the USSR made wide use of all aforementioned credit forms. In consequence, the nation's foreign debt at the end of 1931 stood at 1.4 billion old rubles, which is 4.88 billion new rubles (1.22 billion dollars) at the current rate of exchange." [90] Professor A. Smirnov listed a Czech credit to the USSR in 1935 in the amount of 250 million korunas and an English credit in 1936 of 10 million pounds. Other USSR credits were: from Germany, 200 million Reichsmarks in 1939; from Sweden, 100 million kronas in 1940. Because of the war, neither of the latter two loans were fully utilized.[91]

"Of the USSR wartime loans, the 100 million pound sterling credit granted by England in the Agreement of 16 August 1941 (at 3%, repayable at the average of five years) played a special role." [92] This credit was later increased several times, its interest rate lowered to ½%, and its amortization extended to 15 years (Agreement of 27 December 1947).

After the Lend-Lease Act of 1941, the USSR received from the U. S. goods valued at 9.8 billion dollars.[93] With the expiration of Lend-Lease the U. S., on 15 October 1945, granted the USSR a thirty-year loan at 2.375%. The loan was to be for 244 million dollars and was to cover payment of industrial equipment, ordered by the USSR after Lend-Lease. It was never fully used.[94]

Several sources report that since World War II the only loan granted the USSR came from Sweden. The amount was 1 billion Swedish kronas at 2.375%, to be used within five and repaid within fifteen years.[95] Only 50% of this credit was actually used.

Even if we cannot list all loans the USSR received from the West, it may be stated that, contrary to current Soviet bloc propaganda in the underdeveloped countries, the nations of the West even at that time made available to the USSR all currently known forms of foreign aid. Even the interest rates were no higher than those generally charged the underdeveloped nations by the USSR today.

An important source of capital for the post-World War II reconstruction of Russia's economy, as well as for its expansion, came from restitutions, reparations, dismantling of industrial plants, and deliveries from the current production of Eastern European countries as well as of Germany. All these factors served to no small degree to

---

[90] *Denezhnoe obrashchenie i kredit SSSR*, Moscow, 1957, pp. 292-93.
[91] *Vneshnaya torgovlya* (Moscow), No. 4/1958, p. 47.
[92] *op. cit.*, p. 47.
[93] *Malaya Sovetskaya Entsiklopediya*, Vol. V, p. 451.
[94] *Vneshnaya torgovlya* (Moscow), No. 4/1958, p. 47.
[95] *Spravochnik po vneshney torgovley SSSR*, p. 105.

create the very conditions that make possible the USSR foreign aid of today. "To an even greater degree, this probably applies to the wartime booty of patents, formulas, processes, construction plans, blueprints, new designs, and the like, all of which constituted invaluable material that enabled the Soviet Union to speed its industrial reconstruction on the basis of readily available methods and techniques, thus saving decades of research." [96]

[96] Zotchev, quoted in *Wie stark ist die Sowjetunion*, p. 98.

Principles of the Foreign Aid Policy

Active Soviet bloc participation in the field of foreign aid came only with Khrushchev's go-ahead signal at the 1956 Twentieth Party Congress. "For the buildup of their independent national economy, as for the improvement of their people's standard of living, these [underdeveloped] nations may draw on the successes of the socialist world system, even though they are not members," Khrushchev said. He went on: "Today, they no longer need plead with their former oppressors for modern industrial equipment. Such equipment is available to them in the socialist countries, with no political or military strings attached." [97] Politically, foreign aid is dressed up as "an expression of that peaceful economic competition which marks the current epoch of international relations." [98]

To be sure, even the Soviet bloc foreign aid experts themselves are aware that they cannot win such a competition in the underdeveloped countries by giving greater amounts of aid than the West. Therefore, to make the most political capital out of every penny loaned, economic competition is expressed in terms of a political confrontation of the socialist idea with that of the West. Soviet foreign aid expert Iskandarov underscores: "However meaningful Soviet aid measures may be, by themselves they tell little of the role this aid plays in the buildup of the national economy in the underdeveloped nations or in the latter's struggle against imperialism." [99]

Obviously, the relatively minor Soviet bloc loans are to be politically inflated. In the communist double talk used toward the underde-

[97] *Protokoll des XX Parteitages der KPdSU*, Düsseldorf 1956, p. 21.
[98] *Freundschaft in Aktion, op. cit.*, p. 160.
[99] R. B. Iskandarov, *Concerning Foreign Aid for Backward Nations* (Russ.), Moscow 1960, p. 17.

veloped countries, the East's massive penetration by means of the construction of huge industrial combines and installations is painted as real aid, whereas Western loans are slurringly labeled neocolonialism. Soviet bloc literature on the subject claims that the West offers free gifts and nonrepayable aid to the underdeveloped nations only to maintain its position and influence in these countries. Also, private Western investments are said to be nothing but the old form of capital export, and the credits extended by the Western governments, because of their high interest rates, are claimed to serve only the purpose of keeping the backward nations in debt and dependency.

Industrialization is the big catchword in the backward nations, and in many of these countries a variety of forms of a government-directed economy and centralized economic planning are being applied. For this reason the Soviet bloc points to the following differences between the foreign aid programs of West and East:

1. Whereas the West's concept of industrializing the backward nations envisages a gradual organic evolution through many stages that will take many years and cause these nations to remain backward for decades, the Soviet bloc's ready-made formula will achieve industrialization immediately.

2. Whereas the East's foreign aid program serves to strengthen the government's position in the national economy, the West only sponsors the development of private capitalism; and those cases where loans are granted to governments are only tactical maneuvers.

V. G. Solodovnikov presents the main argument against the West when he writes: "In one form or other, every bourgeois theory seeks to prove 1) that the backward nations are obliged to retread the same road in the mid-twentieth century which the more advanced capitalist countries traveled in the nineteenth; 2) that profound social restructuring is not at all required in the underdeveloped countries, nor a speed-up of industrialization necessary; 3) that the backward nations are unable to cope with the economic and social problems without recourse to Western private capital; 4) that the backward nations cannot travel the same road in overcoming their economic retardation and in solving their social problems as did the Soviet Union; 5) that it is necessary with the means at hand to keep the backward nations within the capitalist system and to force the people of these countries to come to terms with capitalism and await a 'natural' ripening of their own economy. This roughly outlines the field of inquiry with which the theoretical investigations of the modern bourgeois political economy is concerned." [100]

---

[100] V. G. Solodovnikov, *Bourgeois Theories and the Problems of Economic Development in Underdeveloped Countries* (Russ.), Moscow 1961, p. 31.

These arguments are components of the Soviet bloc's foreign aid propaganda in the backward nations, and are aimed at an intelligentsia which, in most cases, seeks to travel its own way to a better life. In painting its own foreign aid program, however, the Soviet bloc plays up to the hopes, wishes, and expectations of the backward nations. Here the key words are speedy industrialization and construction of industrial works after the model of highly industrialized nations. The main point of Soviet bloc aid—so the argument runs—is: "First of all, concentration on the development of key branches of the national economy in the backward nations (of which Bhilai and Aswan are the most outstanding examples), and above all the strengthening of government influence as the lasting base of true independence. Secondly, under the influence of the socialist states' foreign aid to the backward nations, a certain change is occurring in the international economic relations within the capitalist world economic system. Under the duress of 'forced competition,' the capitalist states in several instances are making concessions to the backward nations by granting them acceptable trade and credit terms. This is an indirect service of the socialist states to the underdeveloped nations." [101] The last argument in particular is currently stressed as a token of success of the "competition" policy, one aim being to exploit the vacillating of several national leaders between East and West.

Three features characterize the USSR policy of industrialization through the buildup of a heavy industry in the underdeveloped nation after the prototype of Soviet bloc industrial enterprises:

1. Some Soviet economists indirectly admit that the construction of large, state-owned enterprises is at first economically unprofitable.[102] But this "bookkeeping profitability" takes second place to political profitableness. Such enterprises are seen as symbols of the future greatness and coequality of the backward nations. The latter's hopes for the future are to be aroused, with profits in prestige accruing for the East bloc. Of the Aswan High Dam, for example, it is claimed that this project has aroused hopes for the future in people previously devoid of hope. Hundreds of thousands of *fellahin*, it is said, will live in these hopes for the coming years, hopes that will come to pass with the help of the Soviet Union.

2. Several Soviet bloc publications plainly state that an all-embracing industrialization is a precondition for separating the backward nations from the capitalist economic orbit.

3. The Party program openly proclaims that industrialization will bring forth new social classes and conditions in the backward nations;

---

[101] *Mirovaya ekonomika i mezhdunarodnie otnosheniya* (Moscow), No. 11/1961, p. 26.
[102] *Voprosy ekonomiki* (Moscow), No. 7/1961, p. 108.

above all, a modern industrial labor force destined to lead the class warfare struggle in these countries after replacing the current leadership.

The aforementioned Konrad Illgen comments: "An important aspect of industrialization is the strengthening of the working class. The latter, led by its revolutionary party and imbued with a deep knowledge of the laws of social evolution, is particularly fit to accomplish the aims of the struggle for freedom and to safeguard the fruits of the democratic revolution." [103]

But in Tropical Africa the industrialization concept of the Soviet foreign aid experts ran into a serious dilemma. Here, because of special conditions, they had to fall back, in a certain sense, on the very phase theory of the bourgeois national economy they criticized. They came to realize that the Soviet bloc formula for industrialization does not suit most African states south of the Sahara. Potekhin had already said: "For the time being, the conditions for the buildup of an industry that produces work benches and machine tools do not exist [in the African states]." [104]

In a publication of the USSR Africa Institute entitled *Africa 1956-1961*, we read: "It is no secret that many complicated problems, defying immediate solution, confront the African nations in their quest for freedom. There, where solutions were found (e.g., Egypt and Ghana), the governments of the independent nations have created a national industry including steel mills, machine tool manufacturing, and other branches of the capital goods industry. For the smaller countries, recently become independent, this procedure is practically impossible for the time being nor, in several cases, even desirable. Of fifty African territories, only eight have a population of more than 10 million. It is self-evident that not all branches of industry can, or should, be developed in countries of limited population. Natural resources must also be considered. Many African nations concentrate therefore on those branches of the economy that offer favorable conditions or that require little capital investment. In the main, mining enterprises are started, as well as processing plants (among them plants for the manufacture of mass consumer goods or the processing of export raw material). Also, agricultural production is increased. Obviously, the basic problems of independence cannot be solved by such orientation of economic development. Nevertheless, the conditions for a solution are created. A growing national industry, even if only a processing industry, enhances the value of exports, reduces

---

[103] *Freundschaft in Aktion*, p. 152.
[104] I. I. Potekhin, *Africa Looks Ahead* (Russ.), Moscow 1960, p. 42; also in German, Berlin 1961, p. 59.

the import of mass consumer goods, creates a market for the purchase of required machines and equipment, and boosts the national income of the African states. All of which facilitates their industrialization." [105]

To resolve this dilemma, the Soviet experts propagate the formation of an "African Common Market" and a division of labor among the nations after the Soviet bloc model. This, it is claimed, makes possible industrialization through concentration on large-scale industrial centers.

The Chinese, however, who have had unfortunate experiences with the Soviet conception of the pre-eminent importance of developing heavy industry, now advise the underdeveloped countries to distribute their investments sensibly and to pay heed to economic results. Thus the chairman of the China Committee for the Development of International Trade, Non Han-tchen, voiced almost Western views at the Afro-Asian economic seminar in Algiers on 23 February 1965: "One has to pay careful attention to the distribution of investments and their economic results. In principle it is preferable to make larger investments in profitable than in nonprofitable undertakings . . . The economic results of the investments are inevitably lowered if the objective conditions are disregarded and the main emphasis is put on large-scale modern undertakings and the planning of self-contained complexes."

The strengthening of state capitalism is considered one of the essentials in the "transition of these nations to a higher plane of development." This does not mean, however, that state capitalism, as well as economic planning and land reform, as such, constitute an absolute option for the East. Initially, they should be considered merely as peculiarities of the underdeveloped countries. Soviet bloc literature emphasizes that the state capitalism, economic planning, and agrarian reform of the backward nations differ fundamentally from the corresponding forms and measures of the Soviet bloc.[106] Everything, it is said, hinges on whose interest is served by this state sector and who is in power. State capitalism may play a decisively progressive role only in connection with social factors and the spreading of class warfare. This would be especially true in a national democracy. The Soviet bloc experts here indirectly admit that the state sector could and does serve the forces of the "third way" as well.

A novel twist in its foreign aid propaganda is the Soviet bloc's attempt to paint so-called Western "concessions" as "indirect aid of the socialist camp." Such "concessions" include the steel mills in India, built with, in addition to USSR aid, German and British assistance as

---

[105] *Africa 1956-1961* (Russ.), Moscow 1961, p. 221.
[106] *Freundschaft in Aktion,* p. 153.

well; the construction, with U.S. aid, of a power dam on the Volta River near the site of a similar Soviet project; and the increased emphasis placed on the underdeveloped nations by the U. S. foreign aid program, as well as the shift in this program from military to economic aid. "Under pressure of the aid from the socialist states" the West, it is claimed, has been forced to make credit concessions, increase the period of amortization, lower the interest rates, and permit repayment in local currency or through shipment of traditional export goods.[107] The following example, cited by Illgen, is typical of the attention paid Western measures and of their Soviet bloc exploitation: "Latest project for capital export under government aegis is the U. S.-guided International Development Association, which now copies features from the socialist aid program and grants loans under extended amortization terms and at a heretofore unusual interest rate of 2-3%. In the interest of the less-developed regions on earth, the socialist states welcome such attempts at imitation." [108]

Designed to influence the youth and intelligentsia of the backward nations, the Soviet bloc's comparative analysis is clothed in the political formula: "All of these concessions to the peoples of the former colonies, as well as the very economic and technical 'aid' of the imperialists themselves, must be seen as conquests of the underdeveloped countries under the terms of the economic competition between the two world systems." [109] Obviously, Soviet bloc propaganda seeks to exploit Western foreign aid as stemming from Eastern policies. Thus, much politico-psychological hay may be made with little personal investment.

Though the Soviet bloc continues to insist that Western foreign aid serves neocolonial purposes, it also wishes those recipients of Western aid who are led by "revolutionary democrats" to make full use of this aid. For example, 'Izvestia's' Africa expert, V. Kudryavyev, makes the following point: "Foreign aid received by these countries [meaning the UAR, Guinea, Mali, Congo (Brazzaville)] from capitalist nations can be used in the development of Africa, but only under the express condition that they be utilized under strict control of the individual states and in accordance with the dictates of a planned economy. If the foundations for an independent economy have been laid, capitalist help and its possible consequences are not

---

[107] *Role of the Socialist Orbit States in Economic Development of the Young National States* (Russ.), in Ychenie zapiski, IMO, Moscow 1961, *Vyp*, 6, *Seriia ekonomicheskaia*, p. 17.
[108] *Freundschaft in Aktion*, pp. 161-62.
[109] *The Underdeveloped Countries in the Capitalistic Economy* (Russ.), *op. cit.,* p. 431.

as pregnant with danger as is the case in countries that lack a national economic sector. For example, let us take the UAR, which has been rid of the influence of foreign monopolies and of indigenous capitalists, both medium and large, and in which the state sector predominates. Here the help the capitalist states render in the form of credits or loans can no longer disrupt the development of the states' preordained course. The situation is an entirely different one where no such foundation exists."

Forms and Terms
of Soviet Bloc Loans

Essentially, the Soviet bloc aid program includes two types of loans: medium and long-term credits for specific projects, and credits in a freely convertible currency. The latter type the USSR has so far granted only a few Soviet bloc countries (Poland, Czechoslovakia, and above all East Germany) to carry out their obligations toward the West. The former is the more usual type of Soviet bloc loan to lesser-developed countries of Asia, Africa and Latin America. Aid in the form of nonrepayable loans has thus far been applied chiefly only in North Korea, North Vietnam, and in Hungary in 1956. Only Communist China in several instances has made this type aid available to the underdeveloped countries. Though the USSR has "gift" agreements with several countries, she applies this type aid only supplementarily where it concern projects of political import, especially in the training field.

Loans granted by the Soviet bloc are negotiated with the country concerned and included in "Agreements for Economic and Technical Collaboration." Loans as part of trade and payment agreements or separate loan agreements are the rare exception.

Soviet bloc propaganda extols the highly favorable terms of communist loans to the backward nations. It is claimed that the loans are in no way tied to economic privileges or involve rights of co-ownership, that the usual amortization period is twelve years, and that the interest rate in most cases is 2.5%. Repayment starts one year following completion of the appropriate individual project, and is either in the local currency or in form of the products of the debtor nation, which thus saves foreign exchange.

Two of the above claims, that of the low interest rate of 2.5% and the repayment in local currency or traditional export goods, need particular examination. The question is whether the low interest rate is not or could not be compensated for by manipulating the prices of the goods which (a) the Soviet bloc sends the underdeveloped countries and (b) the latter send the Soviet bloc in exchange, or perhaps by a less productive but more profitable utilization of credits.

First, it should be noted that none of the Soviet bloc "Agreements for Economic and Technical Collaboration" with the underdeveloped countries contains a firm, long-term price determination. They are merely skeleton agreements that leave prices to be fixed "on the basis of world market prices." These agreements are later fleshed out with codicils, and these in turn with contracts and protocols, which at long last fix concrete prices. These subsequent price-fixing instruments are not only negotiated separately for each and every single project concerned, but additionally for every single aid category (e.g., delivery contracts, contracts for technical assistance, protocols for supplying specialists and for the training of indigenous technicians).

Ghana may exemplify this practice. On 4 August 1960 the USSR negotiated an "Agreement for Economic and Technical Collaboration" (skeleton agreement) with Ghana. A codicil was added on 23 December 1960, which fixed the individual projects to be collaborated on by Soviet and Ghanaian organizations, but which fixed no prices as yet. Price fixing is done subsequently in each specific case in separate contracts on the basis of the following codicillary stipulation: "These contracts shall determine the volume, prices, delivery dates, and other conditions for the delivery of equipment and materials and for the services that are required by the terms of the Agreement here in question." [110]

This detailed price-fixing scheme enables the Soviet bloc to adjust prices from case to case to world market conditions, to the political situation, or to the particular straits of the backward nation in question. Besides, it is most difficult for the latter to obtain competitive bids from Western countries once a skeletal agreement with a Soviet bloc nation is concluded.

The shipment of traditional export products in lieu of interest and amortization payments by the underdeveloped nations offers the Soviet bloc even better prospects of price manipulation to offset the

---

[110] *Vedomosty Verkhovnogo Soveta SSSR* (Moscow), No. 51/1960, p. 1171.

low interest rate. Prices of these products are negotiated annually. A look at the Second General Agreement of Economic and Technical Collaboration between the USSR and Indonesia, one of a host of such agreements, serves to illustrate the point. This agreement provides for amortization and interest payment on Indonesia's part through goods exported. It reads in part: "Three months prior to the end of each successive year of interest and amortization payment, the partners will mutually determine categories and prices of goods to be shipped, as well as their amounts and delivery dates." [111]

A number of agreements provide also that such shipments and their prices shall be arrived at in annual protocols and shall be executed under the terms of the existing trade agreement. This price-regulating mechanism accomplishes the following:

1. Much negotiation is required to fix prices, and this enables the Soviet bloc partners to make constant political and economic adjustments.

2. Skeletal agreements and codicils, though not fixing any prices, bind the underdeveloped nation to its Soviet bloc partner and make release from the contractual conditions difficult. Objection to price concessions demanded by the Soviet bloc partner might put the whole aid agreement with the underdeveloped nation in jeopardy and dash the aroused hopes of its population. Also, being a debtor, the underdeveloped nation is at a disadvantage because, should no price agreement be reached for the traditional export product that is to pay for interest and amortization, the Soviet bloc partner may under the terms of almost every existing agreement demand payment in foreign exchange.

Soviet bloc loans are not only scheduled for payment of machine tools and equipment, but also to pay for various types of technical assistance. Western usage provides this technical assistance mostly as component of the delivery contract without charge. This technical assistance (such as geological surveying; research and development; production planning, analysis, and control; data processing; selection of building sites; various training courses for specialists, and supply of professional training personnel and other specialists) in many Agreements for Economic and Technical Collaboration ranks very high in relation to the supply of machine goods and equipment. These profitable activities are elastic and depend largely on what the Soviet organizations consider necessary in the nature of planning, research, and analysis. Besides, as a look at the fine print of the USSR aid agreements reveals, not all of these profitable subsidiary activities can be

---

[111] *Izvestia*, 1 March 1960.

paid for out of the loan extended. Especially those agreements that concern larger projects—India, Iraq, Indonesia, Ceylon, Egypt, and other countries—stipulate that only the *travel expenses of the Soviet specialists* may be paid from the loan money, while all other expenses that the Soviet organizations incur during their indeterminate period of stay must be paid for by the host countries out of their own pockets.

Typical of a multitude of Soviet bloc aid agreements is the Agreement for Economic and Technical Collaboration between the USSR and the Republic of Iraq of 16 March 1959. Article 9 of this agreement states: "Except for travel expenses, the Iraqi Government will refund the Soviet partner all expenses accruing the Soviet organizations in connection with the construction works detailed in Annex 1 of this Agreement. These costs, agreed to in separate contracts, shall be deposited in Iraqi dinars to a special account to be opened by the Central Bank of the Iraqi Republic in the name of the USSR State Bank in favor of the Soviet organizations. The sums so deposited may be applied against current expenses of the Soviet organizations in Iraq. Any remainder may be converted into a foreign currency agreed on between the USSR State Bank and the Iraqi Central Bank." It should be noted that the special account mentioned in Article 9 is not identical with the credit clearing accounts, but is a direct debit against the underdeveloped countries. These extra costs, chargeable to the aided nations, are considerable, since Soviet specialists on projects in underdeveloped countries work in accordance with Soviet customs and usages. And it is a known fact that, in contrast to the West's economical and efficient use of technical skill, the number of technical personnel on a Soviet construction project is in comparison extraordinarily high even in the USSR itself. The same applies to USSR projects in the backward areas. An illustrative example is the Bhilai Works in India, on which between 600 and 1000 specialists were at times engaged. A similar British project at Durgapore required only 200 British specialists. England also far outstrips the Soviet Union in the use of indigenous labor per head of foreign skilled labor.

In some cases the training of indigenous skilled labor is also charged to the developing countries themselves. The Second General Agreement for Economic and Technical Collaboration between the USSR and the Indonesian Republic of 28 February 1960 may serve as example. This agreement stipulates: "Expenses accruing to the Soviet partner through the sending of specialists and skilled workers to the Indonesian Republic, or through USSR enrollment of Indonesian citizens for training in production methods and techniques, shall be put by the Indonesian Government in Indonesian rupiahs into a special account, which the USSR State Bank opens with the Bank of Indonesia in favor of those Soviet organizations supplying the services." This technical assistance is therefore not only most profitable but affords excellent chances to boost the 2.5% interest rate.

The Chinese have detected the Achilles' heel in the technical assistance part of the Soviet foreign aid program. In their competition with Big Brother in the underdeveloped countries, they therefore—in contrast to the USSR—not only granted several countries nonrepayable loans (Ceylon, Cambodia, Nepal) and non-interest-bearing credits (Guinea, Ghana, Yemen, Burma, among others), but in agreements with several underdeveloped countries concurred that China defray the travel expenses of the Chinese specialists. Several of the more recent agreements stipulate that the living standard of Chinese specialists sent to backward nations may not exceed that of their counterparts in these nations. This regulation, too, is aimed at the Soviet specialists who, as a rule, enjoy a very high living standard, and whose cost sometimes exceeds the loans granted.

In February 1964 the Chinese announced their "Eight Principles of Development Policy," intended as an answer to Soviet development policies. In this announcement it says: "The Chinese government makes economic aid available in the form of interest-free credits or credits with a low interest rate, and, if need be, will extend the payment deadline of these credits so as to ease the burden of the recipient states as best it can." Undoubtedly taking their own precarious financial condition and their own unfortunate experiences with the overly hurried buildup of a heavy industry into account, the Peking principles emphasize that "The Chinese government tries to do its best to help the recipient states to develop such projects that demand low investments but go more quickly into effect, thereby enabling the respective governments to increase their incomes and accumulate capital." About the matter of sending specialists the announcement says: "The specialists which the Chinese government sends to help with the construction in the recipient states will enjoy the same living standard as the corresponding specialists in the recipient country. The Chinese specialists are not allowed to express special wishes or to lay claim to any special privileges." [111a]

Finally, the Soviet allegation that credit amortization is possible in the local currency or through shipment of traditional export products is only conditionally true. In many instances, the stipulation contained in the Agreement for Economic and Technical Collaboration between the USSR and Ceylon of 25 February 1958 applies. This reads: "Interest and amortization payments shall be entered on a pound sterling account, to be opened at the Central Bank of Ceylon in favor of the USSR State Bank. Sums, deposited to this account, may be applied by the Soviet organizations toward purchases of Ceylonese goods in accordance with the existing Soviet-Ceylonese Trade and Payment Agreement, and/or may be converted into pound sterling or any other convertible currency agreed on between the USSR State Bank or the Central Bank of Ceylon." [112]

Again, a "may be" condition which Soviet negotiators may apply coercively in the annual price conferences on goods to be shipped against credit amortization. Such a "may be" condition is also included in those agreements that actually provide for the accounts to be kept in the local currency. Thus, at one time the monies kept in Egyptian pounds at the Central Bank of Egypt for the USSR State Bank could be applied by the Soviets for Egyptian purchases "and/or converted into pounds sterling or any other freely convertible currency agreed on between the two partners." [113] Meanwhile, the Payment Agreement of 23 June 1962 between the USSR and Egypt has changed these Egyptian pound accounts into pound sterling accounts. And despite all propaganda claims about the saving of scarce foreign exchange, correspondence exchanged regarding the Agreement of 23 June 1962 stipulated: "In connection with today's signing of the long-term trade and payment agreement between Egypt and the USSR, I am pleased to confirm that the goods quotas, contained in List 'A' of the Annex to the Long-Term Trade Agreement, also include the amounts or sum totals of those goods that may be shipped by Egypt to the USSR for credit amortization and interest payment in accordance with the appropriate agreements. *This agreement does not release the Egyptian Government from the obligation, on Soviet demand, to convert interest and amortization charge for the credits mentioned into pounds sterling or other freely convertible currency.*"

The texts of the agreements contradict the propaganda claims of the Soviet bloc. The saving of foreign exchange is a weasel-worded stipulation, contingent on the good will of the Soviet bloc partner. The pricing mechanism for goods shipped and bought and technical services rendered allows the Soviet bloc much leeway for compensating the low interest rate.

[111a] "China Reconstructs," No. 4. April 1964, p. 3.
[112] *Vedomosty Verkhovnogo Soveta SSSR* (Moscow), No. 11/1958, pp. 564-65.
[113] *Vedomosty Verkhovnogo Soveta SSSR* (Moscow), No. 8/1959, p. 181.

East Bloc Loans and

Nonrepayable Aid

According to American sources, total East bloc aid to the "Third World" between 1954 and mid-1964 amounted to more than $6 billion. The 1964 OECD report gives a figure of $5,393 million for the total aid granted by the communist countries from 1954 until the end of 1963. This report also tabulates the yearly rate at which the recipient countries availed themselves of these loans.

Soviet and Chinese Aid to the Developing Countries[114]

(in millions of $ U.S.)

Year	Grant	Payment
1954	11	1
1955	149	3
1956	608	107
1957	227	87
1958	556	205
1959	894	161
1960	1,165	186
1961	957	294
1962	507	391
1963	319	425
Total	5,393	1,860

[114] *The Flow of Financial Resources to Less-Developed Countries 1954-1963*, OECD, Paris 1964, p. 56.

According to this table, the East bloc had fulfilled 34.5% of its credit obligations by the end of 1963. Other Western sources only mention a fulfilment rate of 30%. East bloc literature on this subject, however, gives no figures that would allow us to confirm the Western estimates.

All Soviet reports cite a far smaller total sum for East bloc aid to the "Third World" than do Western sources. Since the East bloc has no central organization (such as the OECD and other organizations in the West), it does not tabulate the grants of the individual communist countries on a uniform basis, and the various reports that these countries publish are contradictory. Even K. H. Domdey, the DDR economic theoretician, has to admit that Western figures about East bloc loans to underdeveloped countries are often higher than those the East bloc itself publishes.[115] In February 1965, the authoritative Soviet journal of economics gave a figure of 4 billion rubles ($4,444.4 million) for the loans the Soviet Union and China had extended by the end of 1964.[116] G. M. Prochorov, the Soviet expert on developing countries, mentions the same figure in his newest book, which covers the same period.[117]

The Soviet Institute for World Economy and International Relations, in 1966, cited a figure in excess of 5 billion rubles ($5,555.5 million) for the total grants which the Soviet bloc and China had extended to forty Asian, African and Latin American countries during the last ten years. Of this sum, the Soviet Union "granted" more than 70% to twenty-eight developing countries.[118] In the same year (1966) the total amount of credits extended by the USSR is given as 4 billion rubles ($4,444.4 million).[119]

Our examination of the texts of the agreements and of other official documents confirms that the USSR has granted at least 4 billion rubles to the developing countries. However, we arrive at a higher figure than the Soviet authors do for the total grants that the Soviet bloc and China have made to countries of the "Third World," namely at the sum of 6.3 billion rubles (roughly $7 billion). This contradiction becomes comprehensible in view of the fact that the USSR experts have been quoting smaller figures for grants made by their partner countries than is actually the case. The grants made by the individual East bloc countries will be listed shortly.

---

[115] K. H. Domdey, *Neokolonialismus oder Sozialistische Wirtschaftshilfe*, East Berlin 1962, p. 72.
[116] *Voprosy ekonomiki*, No. 2/1965, p. 72.
[117] G. M. Prochorov, *The Two World Systems and the Liberated Countries* (Russ), Moscow 1965, p. 110.
[118] *Mirovaya ekonomika i mezdunarodnie otnoseniya* (Moscow) No. 4/1966, p. 117.
[119] *Voprosy istorii KPSS*, No. 4/1966, p. 20.

Total East bloc credit aid is very modest in comparison with Western aid. Already between 1959 and 1961, economic aid by Western industrial states (government programs, credits and loans by the World Bank and other international organizations, plus private loans and investments) reached a yearly average of $6.9 billion. A genuine comparison between Western and Eastern credit aid is hardly possible since all finances in the East bloc are state-controlled and there exists nothing comparable to private investments and loans. Such a comparison would also have to take into account that the USSR and the People's Republic of China did not only grant loans to countries of the "Third World" but also to developing countries within the East bloc itself. Once this is taken into account the sum total of the loans the East bloc has extended rises to at least $13 billion for the years 1946 to 1966. The Soviet Union alone granted at least 9 billion rubles ($10 billion) to countries within the East block, China more than $1 billion.[120]

The following is characteristic of East bloc foreign loan programs:

1. Only since the Bandung Conference (1955) has the East bloc, more accurately the USSR, appeared on the scene with sizeable credit grants to the backward nations. As it was, the total amount remained low until 1956 when the European bloc members and China joined the loan program.

2. The East bloc made its main credit thrust in 1959. Only in 1961 did a larger number of African countries receive loans, first from the USSR but then also from the other bloc members. Concurrent with a slump in the annual grants after 1959, there occurred a shift within the East bloc of the pro rata share that each member granted. The USSR share of the total credits extended between 1954-59 was 75.8%. This rose to 84.0% in 1959, fell to 63.1% in 1960 and 32.7% in 1961. For the years 1954-1965 the USSR share in the total credits pledges was 63%, versus 37% for all other bloc members.

3. The Soviet bloc's largess to the African nations (Egypt, Ethiopia, and Ghana excepted) was more frugal. Compared to India, Indonesia, Afghanistan, and Iraq, only small loans went to Guinea, Mali, Nigeria, Somalia, Sudan, and Tunisia. This is partly because of the smallness of these states, partly because the Soviet bloc program for them does not as yet include the buildup of heavy industry. A look at the agreements of the USSR with these countries shows that here the emphasis is on training. All of the more recent USSR-African nation agreements provide for the opening of teaching and training facilities.

4. All loan grants are promissory in nature. There is scant Soviet

---

[120] *Neue Zürcher Zeitung*, 1 December 1961.

bloc information on whether or not the loan commitments are met. In general, it may be stated that the Soviet bloc has fully met only a small portion of its commitments, and generally only for appropriations made in 1957 and 1959. The statistics on delivery of complete plants, cited in the foreign trade section above, furnish information on the extent of credit utilization.

USSR Loans to the Countries
of the "Third World"

It becomes evident from the available agreement texts, official communiqués when accords were reached, and from official announcements, that the USSR granted at least $4,660 million to "Third World" countries between 1953 and 1966. In several cases the size of the grants was not published and it was impossible to ascertain it from other sources.

In the previous table we included all twenty-eight developing countries that have enjoyed the benefit of Soviet credits. On the basis of this table we can conclude that 23.6% of all Soviet grants between 1953 and 1966 were made to India, that the UAR's share was 19.2%, Afghanistan's 11.3%, Indonesia's 9.%, Algeria's 5.3% and Syria's 5.2%, and that half of the credits the USSR granted to African countries was designated for the UAR. After India 40.7% of all Soviet grants were made to Asian countries. The countries listed here are the ones that have been of crucial importance to the Soviet aid and economic assistance program. Size, purpose and date of USSR credits to "Third World" countries can be found in the following list. Again we have relied solely on official agreement texts and official documentation.

Soviet Loans to the "Third World" from 1953 to 1966

(in millions of $ U.S.)

	1953	1954	1955	1956	1957	1958	1959	1960	1961	1962	1963	1964	1965	1966 First Quarter	1953–66 Total
ASIA															
Afghanistan	—	5.6	—	100.0	15.0	—	80.0	22.4	196.7	—	39.1	29.4	—	unkn.	488.2
Burma	—	—	—	—	39.3	—	—	—	—	6.5	—	—	—	—	45.8
Ceylon	—	—	—	—	—	30.0	—	—	—	—	—	—	—	—	30.0
India	—	—	137.5	—	125.0	—	420.0	—	125.0	—	—	—	211.0	—	1,018.5
Indonesia	—	—	—	100.0	6.7	—	17.5	250.0	—	—	—	—	—	—	374.2
Iraq	—	—	—	—	—	—	135.5	45.0	—	—	—	—	—	—	180.5
Iran	—	—	—	—	—	—	—	—	—	—	38.9	—	—	—	38.9
Yemen	—	—	—	15.0	—	—	—	—	25.0	—	unkn.	unkn.	—	unkn.	40.0
Cambodia	—	—	—	—	6.0	—	—	—	—	—	—	—	—	—	6.0
Laos	—	—	—	—	—	—	—	—	—	3.6	—	—	—	—	3.6
Pakistan	—	—	—	—	—	—	—	—	30.0	—	—	11.0	31.5	—	72.5
Syria	—	—	—	—	87.5	—	—	—	—	—	—	—	—	138.0	225.5
Nepal	—	—	—	—	—	—	—	—	—	11.1	—	—	—	—	11.1
AFRICA															
Egypt (UAR)	—	—	—	—	—	275.0	—	225.0	—	—	44.5	280.0	—	—	824.5
Algeria	—	—	—	—	—	—	—	—	—	—	100.0	128.0	—	—	228.0
Ethiopia	—	—	—	—	—	—	100.0	—	—	—	—	—	—	—	100.0
Ghana	—	—	—	—	—	—	—	40.0	40.2	—	22.2	—	—	—	102.4
Guinea	—	—	—	—	—	—	35.0	21.5	—	11.5	—	—	—	—	68.0
Kenya	—	—	—	—	—	—	—	—	—	—	—	42.0	—	—	42.0
Congo (Bra-zzaville)	—	—	—	—	—	—	—	—	22.2	—	—	—	—	—	22.2
Mali	—	—	—	—	—	—	—	—	—	—	—	12.2	—	—	12.2
Nigeria	—	—	—	—	—	—	7.5	—	44.5	3.6	—	—	—	—	55.6
Somalia	—	—	—	—	—	—	—	—	44.5	—	—	—	—	—	44.5
Sudan	—	—	—	—	—	—	—	—	52.2	—	—	—	—	—	52.2
Tanzania	—	—	—	—	—	—	—	—	—	—	—	42.2	—	—	42.2
Tunisia	—	—	—	—	—	—	—	—	27.8	—	—	—	—	—	27.8
Uganda	—	—	—	—	—	—	—	—	—	—	—	15.6	—	—	15.6
LATIN AMERICA															
Argentina	30.0	—	—	—	—	100.0	—	—	—	—	—	—	—	—	130.0
Total:	30.0	5.6	137.5	215.0	279.5	405.0	795.5	603.9	608.1	36.3	244.7	560.4	242.5	138.0	4,302.0

Recipients of Soviet Loans

Country	Purpose	Amount in Millions of Dollars
ASIA		
Afghanistan		
January 27, 1954	For two grain elevators, an electric grist mill, and a large mechanized bakery—3% loan, good for a period of eight years, five-year amortization period beginning in 1957	3.5
October 5, 1954	For road building equipment; an asphalt-concrete plant, paving of Kabul streets—2% loan good for a period of eight years, amortization as of 1957 over a period of five years	2.1
January 28, 1956	Granting of a 2% loan with a twenty-two year amortization period beginning eight years after the last part of the loan had been used. According to the agreement about the economic and technical aid of the USSR in the fulfillment of the first Afghan Five-Year Plan (1956-1961) of March 3, 1956, the loan is to be used for research and geodetic surveys and for the construction of fourteen facilities, among them: one hydroelectric plant each at Naglu and Pul-i-Khomri, one automobile repair plant in Djangalak, the construction of airports in Kabul and Bahram, the construction of the Salang Pass highway from Kysil-Kala along the Amu Darja by way of Pul-i-Khomri and Kabul to Torkham, construc-	

	tion of the Kjelabalad-irrigation canal, the construction of a transshipment port in Kysil-Kala	100.0
July 30, 1957	Granting of an interest-free loan for making areas with natural oil discoveries accessible—for a period of fifty years, repayable within a period of twenty-five years subsequent to the use of each part of the loan	15.0
May 28, 1959	Construction of a highway of roughly 425 miles from Kushka (the Soviet border) by way of Herat, Farah to Kandahar. The Soviet Union obligated itself to do the planning, the technical supervision, the delivery of road construction equipment at a cost of 80 million dollars. Afghanistan will supply and pay for the work force and the construction materials it can obtain	80.0
January 18, 1960	For the construction of Djelebad irrigation network and the irrigation of 40,000 hectare of land—grant of an additional loan	22.4
October 16, 1961	For Soviet aid toward the Second Afghan Five-Year Plan (1962-67), particularly the construction of plants for the oil industry, the chemical and the food industry, as well as the building of colleges and high schools—loans totalling	196.7
September 5, 1963	For cooperating in the field of using atomic energy for peaceful purposes and the construction of the appropriate facilities in Afghanistan—2% loan	0.167
October 17, 1963	For obtaining natural gas in North-Afghanistan and the construction of a natural gas pipeline	

	to the Soviet border for natural gas export to the USSR—2.5% loan	38.9
July 13, 1964	For the construction of and paving of streets in North Afghanistan—loan	29.4
July 28, 1965	Agreement about additional Soviet help. Granting of a further loan	unknown

Burma

January 17, 1957	For construction of a technological institute, a hospital, athletic facilities, etc.	29.8
December 2, 1957	For construction of two irrigation projects	6.3
December 2, 1957	For construction of an agricultural equipment factory	3.2
August 30, 1962	For the construction of irrigation facilities in the region of Chémoltaou	6.5

Ceylon

February 28, 1958	For research, geodetic surveys, construction of irrigation facilities, soil reclamation, construction of an iron foundry and other plants and facilities	30.0

India

February 2, 1955	For construction of Bhilai steelworks—2.5% loan	137.5
November 9, 1957	For the construction of five industrial plants: one plant for heavy equipment; one plant for mining equipment; one thermoelectric power plant; one optical glass plant; coal processing facilities—2.5% loan	125.0
May 29, 1959	For construction of plants for production of drugs, medicines, and surgical instruments—2.5% loan	20.0

September 12, 1959	For Soviet aid in buildup of industrial works as part of India's Third Five-Year Plan (1961-66)—2.5% loan	375.0
September 28, 1959	For construction of an oil refinery in Barauni—2.5% loan	25.0
February 21, 1961	For the construction of a hydroelectric plant in Bhakra, an oil refinery in the state of Gudsharat, a coal-processing plant in Karhara, a plant for fire-resistant materials, and for oil prospecting and drilling—2.5% loan	125.0
January 25, 1965	For the construction of a second steel works in Bokaro—2.5% loan	211.0

Indonesia

September 15, 1956	First major agreement for aiding in the construction of industrial plants and facilities and the training of specialists	100.0
February 20, 1957	For Soviet trucks to be delivered at a later date	6.7
July 28, 1959	For the construction of a technological institute in Ambon, a stadium in Djakarta, and the training of specialists	17.5
February 28, 1960	Second major agreement for the construction of steel works, chemical and textile plants, agricultural facilities and a plant for the peaceful use of atomic energy	250.0

Iraq

March 16, 1959	For construction of thirty-five industrial and agricultural facilities—2.5% loan	137.5
August 18, 1960	For construction of and equipment for Baghdad-Basra railroad including roundhouses—2.5% loan	45.0

Iran

July 27, 1963   For the construction of a dam at the River Arax, construction of eleven grain elevators, improvement of the port in Bandar Pahlevi at the Caspian Sea and for a fish breeding program 38.9

January 13, 1966   For the construction of three large plants: one steel works in Isfahan with a yearly capacity of 500,000 to 600,000 tons; one machine tool plant with a capacity of 25,000 to 30,000 tons of machine material, and a trans-Iranian natural gas pipeline with a length of 630 miles for the export of natural gas to the USSR—2.5% loan (260 million rubles) 288.9

Yemen

July 11, 1956   For the construction of two cement factories, one thermo-electric plant in Sana, agricultural facilities and a deep-sea port near Hodeida—2.5% loan 15.0

June 4, 1961   For operating port near Hodeida, for buildup of port administration, also for enlargement of Ras Ketib harbor, road construction, irrigation facilities, improvement of the towns of Hodeida and Sochna and the service of Soviet specialists and training of local technicians 25.0

Cambodia

May 31, 1957   Donation toward the construction of a hospital in Phnom Penh 6.0

April 15, 1963   For the construction of a hydro-electric plant ....   unknown

Laos

December 1, 1962   For the construction of a hydroelectric plant at the Nam-Nien
river with transmission lines and
transformer stations—2.5% loan   3.9

Nepal

April 24, 1959   For the construction of a hydroelectric plant, of a hospital, of a
cigarette and a sugar factory—
donation 7.5

February 6, 1962   A loan of 2.5 million rubles and
a gift of .7 million rubles for ob-
ject mentioned above and fur-
ther assistance 3.56

Pakistan

March 4, 1961   For oil prospecting activities, delivery of drilling equipment and
construction materials, and the
sending of Soviet specialists—loan   30.0

June 15, 1964   For agricultural machinery—3%
loan 11.0

April 7, 1965   Construction loan at 2.5% 31.5

Syria

October 28, 1957   For damn and power plant on
the Euphrates, irrigation facili-
ties, construction of chemical fertilizer plant, two rail lines, and
more—2.5% loan 87.5

                   Total for Asia: 2,826.0

AFRICA

Egypt (UAR)

January 29, 1958   Construction and improvement of
ninety industrial plants, among
them four iron mines, six oil refineries, two steel works, six machine tool factories, six chemical
and pharmaceutical plants, eight

	factories for food production and consumer goods, fifteen educational facilities—2.5% loan	175.0
December 27, 1958	For construction of section one of Aswan High Dam—2.5% loan	100.0
August 27, 1960	For completion of Aswan High Dam—2.5% loan	225.0
June 18, 1963	For the construction and improvement of industrial plants—2.5% loan	44.5
September 22, 1964	For the construction and improvement of thirteen facilities, building of training centers and training of specialists	280.0

Algeria

| December 27, 1963 | For the development of agriculture, building of dams, construction of several industrial plants, educational aid and construction of educational facilities—2.5% loan . . . . | 100.0 |
| July 3, 1964 | For the construction of a steel plant with a capacity of between 300,000 and 350,000 tons per year —2.5% loan . . . . | 128.0 |

Ethiopia

| July 11, 1959 | For the construction of an oil refinery in Assab, a caustic soda plant in Massana, a gold extraction facility, a small steel mill, and for geological research—2.5% loan . . . . | 100.0 |

*Ghana**

| August 4, 1960 | For power plant at the Black Volta, high tension lines, geologi- | |

---

* We have been unable to ascertain so far to what extent the USSR made good on its aid agreements before the downfall of Nkrumah. The question of whether the USSR will continue to provide Ghana with economic assistance has not yet been settled either.

	cal studies, construction of facilities for the fish industry, state rice and corn farms, apartment blocks in Accra and Tema, and the like—2.5% loan	40.0
November 4, 1961	For construction of plants for reinforced concrete parts and building material, cotton and paper mills, instructional facilities— loan of 2.5%	42.2
March 4, 1963	Additional loan for the construction of facilities designated in the earlier agreements	22.2

Guinea

August 24, 1959	For the construction of a cement factory, a railroad-tie manufacturing plant, a leather and shoe manufacturing combine, a fruit and vegetable canning plant, a refrigeration plant, the construction of a polytechnical institute for 1500 students, and a stadium seating 25,000 in Conakry	35.0
September 8, 1960	Shipment of equipment for gold and diamond extraction, sending of specialists	21.5
February 26, 1962	For the construction of an airplane hangar, for repair shops and two fuel depots for the care of IL18 and IL14 planes, for the shipment of railroad tracks for the thirty-mile-long line between Conakry and Mamou, and the like	11.5

Kenya

May 11, 1964	For the construction of agricultural facilities, of a textile factory, a fruit processing plant, a fish canning plant, a sugar refinery and a saw mill	44.5

Congo (Brazzaville)

December 14, 1964   For the construction of a drinking water supply system, of a hydro-electric plant with a capacity of 1500 to 2000 kw, for geological prospecting, and the construction of a hotel in Brazzaville—2.5% loan 12.2

Mali

March 18, 1961   For geological surveys, improvement of Niger shipping, construction of a 25,000-seat stadium in Bamako, construction of a railroad line (Mali-Guinea), a cement factory, and equipment of an instructional center for 300 students— 2.5% loan 44.5

October 10, 1962   For improvement of the state undertaking, "Office du Niger"— 2.5% loan 11.1

Nigeria

June 9, 1961   For the construction of agricultural facilities, processing plants and instructional centers—2.5% loan 44.5

Somalia

June 2, 1961   For a national grain farm, vegetable oil plant and cotton growing, construction of port facilities in Berber, a dairy, a meat combine, among other projects—40 million-ruble loan at 2.5%, plus 7 million rubles worth of goods the proceeds from which are to be applied to the construction of the plants 52.2

Sudan

November 21, 1961   For the construction of four canneries, an asbestos-cement plant, selectivity stations for geological research, and training centers for specialists 22.2

Tanzania

August 23, 1964   For the construction of industrial plants, of two hospitals, of one high school, among others 42.2

Tunisia

August 30, 1961   For construction of hydrotechnical facilities and the building and equipping of a National Technical Institute at Tunis University 27.8

Uganda

November 30, 1964   For seven development projects— loan 15.6

Total for Africa: 1,642.0

LATIN AMERICA

Argentina

August 5, 1953   For industrial equipment 30.0

October 27, 1958   For equipment for the oil industry, for electro-technical purposes, power and construction equipment, earth-moving machines, tool manufacturing equipment, and more of the like 100.0

Total for Latin America: 130.0

Total USSR loans: 4,660.5

USSR Gifts

In addition to the above loans for specific projects, Soviet aid in special cases also took the form of gifts. Here, the "gift of the Soviet people" to *Burma* of 17 January 1957 stands in first place as a shining example. The present: a technological institute for 1000 ordinary and 100 auditing students; a 200-bed hospital with polyclinic; a 1800-seat theater; a cultural-athletic center with stadium and swimming pool; an industrial exhibition hall with a conference room for 1000 people; and a hotel. All these facilities were put into operation on 15 July 1961. Actually, the "gift" was a barter deal, for, in consonance with the text of the "gift" agreement, we are informed: "In return for the Soviet people's gift of friendship the Burmese Government has agreed to deliver to the USSR in the form of a present a corresponding amount of rice and goods of Burmese manufacture. These goods shall be delivered to the USSR within twenty years after completion of construction [of the above facilities]." [121]

In Phnom-Phen, capital of *Cambodia,* a 500-bed hospital with polyclinic was ceremoniously presented as a Soviet gift on 29 August 1960. This hospital, whose staff is henceforth to include twenty Soviet doctors, was erected under the terms of a 31 May 1957 agreement. Also on a gift basis, the USSR committed itself to erect an engineering college for a 1000 students and four to five faculties in Cambodia. At this college some twenty to twenty-five Soviet professors and instructors are to teach, supported by five translators.

---

[121] *Friendly Aid and Mutually Profitable Collaboration* (Russ.), Moscow 1959, p. 42.

Already in operation in *India* is the Bombay Technological Institute, built with a $2.5 million-USSR-aid contribution to the UN and furnished with $750,000 worth of free Soviet equipment. For the time being fifteen Soviet professors instruct the 1200 regular and 600 auditing students. In the agreement of 12 December 1958, the USSR promised to train fifty Indian engineers "at Soviet expense," assuming also the cost of translating Soviet textbooks into English for use at Indian universities. Also among Soviet presents to India is a state farm of nearly 30,000 tillable acres in Suratgarh. Equipment and other inventory for this farm in the amount of 1.25 million dollars was supplied by the Soviet Union gratis. In Dehradun, seat of the Indian Oil and Natural Gas Directorate, the USSR erected an oil laboratory free of charge.

In January 1959 *Egypt* received from the USSR free of charge the complete equipment for a machine-tractor station at a state farm.

In 1958 the USSR donated to *Syria* the entire apparatus of a 200-bed eye clinic.

On the occasion of his visit to *Indonesia* early in 1960, Khrushchev also presented this country with a 200-bed hospital.

Cuba has been promised the gift of a 400-bed hospital.

Late in 1955 *Afghanistan* received the present of a 110-bed USSR hospital. In an agreement of 28 May 1959, the USSR committed itself to extend the Kushka-Herat motor highway to Kandahar. The USSR, to whom this road is of strategic importance, assumed the costs, evaluated at 80 million dollars, of planning, technical supervision, and supply of construction equipment. The Afghans are to supply labor and available materials.

Ethiopia is to get a USSR gift hospital. In Bahar-Dar the USSR built a technical school for 1200 students, which opened 11 July 1963.

In *Algeria* the USSR constructed an oil and natural gas institute with a technical school for 2000 students and donated it to the country.

In *Kenya* the Soviets have promised to construct free of charge a 200-bed hospital, a radio station, and a technical university for 1000 students.

In Conakry, *Guinea*'s capital, the USSR built free of charge the radio station called "Voice of the Revolution," which began broadcasting 28 September 1961. In addition, the USSR will present Guinea with the equipment and other inventory for a 1700-acre state rice farm. Guinea, too, received a 500-bed gift hospital.

Mali received a high school from the USSR free of charge, and recently the equipment for an administrative university for the unity party, *Union Soudanaise*.

In *Ceylon* the USSR has promised to construct a steel plate factory free of charge.

In March 1964 the Soviets promised *Yemen* to construct a hospital and polyclinic and three primary schools, all free of charge.

Laos, too, is supposed to receive a free hospital and a radio station from the USSR.

The USSR wants to construct the "East-West" highway in Nepal gratis, in competition with Peking.

African *Somalia* shall be our last example of Soviet largess. The communiqué on the 2 June 1961 aid agreement between the USSR and Somalia reads: "Motivated by its kind, friendly feelings for the Republic of Somalia, the USSR Government resolved to assist the Somalian Government free of charge in the construction of two hospitals, a high school, a printing plant, and a radio station. The USSR will further send at its own expense a group of Soviet doctors and teachers to work at appropriate Somalian installations. The USSR will also assist in the training of Somalian medical personnel in the Soviet Union." [122]

Besides the above, there are numerous small USSR gifts. Heads of state of the young nations receive airplanes, peace prizes are awarded, and libraries are offered to universities. The free outfitting of hospitals and schools is a favorite gift gesture because of its propagandistic-psychological effect. The placement of Soviet specialists within the various institutions make the latter into important USSR toeholds in the developing countries.

---

[122] *Pravda,* 3 June 1961.

China's Financial Aid

By the end of 1965, six communist and twenty "Third World" countries were on China's list for receiving financial aid. The total sum which Peking had granted to communist and noncommunist countries up to that point was $2,003.6 million, of which 1,161.6 million went to East bloc countries and 842.0 million to countries of the "Third World." However, due to setbacks in its foreign policy Peking had to discontinue its aid program to Indonesia, Ghana, and the Central African Republic.

However, it is noteworthy that Chinese aid matches the size of Soviet economic aid to China. The Soviet Union made loans to Peking only until 1957, and the size of these loans was put at 1,816 million rubles ($2,017.6 million) by Suslov before the Central Committee of the CPSU on 14 February 1964.[123] Chou En-lai, at the meeting of the National People's Congress on 21 December 1964, cited a figure of 1,406 million rubles ($1,562 million) for the total Soviet loans, including interest.[124] At the Afro-Asian economic seminar in Algiers the chairman of the Chinese delegation emphasized that "as everyone knows, during the past ten years the Chinese people, by husbanding their funds, have made money and materials available for the support of socialist and national-independent countries whose total amount exceeds China's debt plus interest on this debt to the Soviet Union, which have already been paid in full." [125]

[123] *Pravda* 3 April 1964.
[124] *Hsinhua* 30 December 1964.
[125] *Peking Rundschau*, No. 10/1965, p. 24.

Of the $842 million that Communist China granted the "Third World" countries between 1956 and 1966, $627.5 million, or 74.5%, were interest-free loans, $139.8 million, or 16.6%, were donations, and $74.7 million or 8.9%, bear a 2.0-2.5% interest charge. This credit policy of granting interest-free loans and making donations—as has been illustrated already—is unequivocally directed against the Soviets and their practice of credits to the developing countries.

Let us see what the Soviets have to say on this subject. "As in previous years, the People's Republic of China seeks to win prestige by granting economic aid to weakly developed Asian and African countries. While doing so, the Chinese leaders use every possible means to discredit the aid given these countries by other socialist states. With the aforementioned policy in mind, the People's Republic of China activated its relationship with Algeria. On 28 October 1963 the two countries signed an accord on scientific and technical cooperation and China granted Algeria an interest-free loan of $51 million. From 31 August to 28 September a Chinese exhibition of economic construction was held in Algeria and a part of the exhibit (tool making machinery, trucks, tractors, agricultural and medical equipment) was subsequently donated to the Algerian government . . . Earlier and recent Chinese grants have only paper value. The press of the respective recipient countries has mentioned this fact on several occasions." [126]

It is true that Chinese grants generally remain unfulfilled for a longer time than those from the Soviet Union. On several occasions China was unable to meet its obligations in Nepal and Burma and had to substitute less demanding projects for the ones it had intended to construct.

China's Loans and Nonrepayable Aid to Other Countries

Between 1953-61[127]

Country	Date Granted	Type and Purpose	Amount	In Millions of Dollars
Albania	20 Oct. 54	Gift for tenth anniversary of Albanian Republic	10 mill. rubles	2.5
	3 Dec. 54	Loan at .5% for 1955 to 1960	50 mill. rubles	12.5
	16 Jan. 59	Loan for 1961-65	55 mill. rubles	13.75
	2 Feb. 61	Loan for payment of investment goods and services	110 mill. rubles	122.2
	8 June 65	Loan for delivery of investment goods and technical assistance for the period 1966-1970	unknown	unknown

---

[126] *1964 Yearbook of the Great Soviet-Encyclopedia*, Moscow 1964, p. 285.

Country	Date Granted	Type and Purpose	Amount	In Millions of Dollars
Hungary	6 Nov. 59	Nonrepayable aid in goods	30 mill. rubles	7.5
	13 May 57	Loan at 2%, half in foreign exchange, freely convertible	200 mill. rubles	50.0
North Korea	23 Nov. 53	Turnover as gift of all goods and monies which China granted Korea between 25 July 1950 and 31 Dec. 1953	280 mill. yuan	56.9
	23 Nov. 53	Nonrepayable aid in goods for the period 1954-57	800 mill. yuan	162.5
	27 Sept. 58	Non-interest-bearing loan for a hydroelectric plant	40 mill. rubles	10.0
	27 Sept. 58	Loan at 1% for three plants	170 mill. rubles	42.5
	13 Oct. 60	Loan for 1961-64	420 mill. rubles	105.0
North Vietnam	7 July 55	Nonrepayable aid in equipment and goods	800 mill. yuan	162.0
	18 Feb. 59	Nonrepayable aid	100 mill. yuan	20.3
	18 Feb. 59	Loan at 1% for construction and expansion of forty-nine projects, linked with above 100 million yuans	300 mill. yuan	60.9
	30 Jan. 61	Loans for 1961-67	630 mill. rubles	157.5
Mongolia	29 Aug. 56	Nonrepayable aid for 1956-59	160 mill. rubles	40.0
	29 Dec. 58	Loan for 1959-61 for various construction projects	100 mill. rubles	25.0
	31 May 60	Loan for 1961-65 for industrial plants, roads, community projects	200 mill. rubles	40.0
Cuba	30 Nov. 60	Interest-free loan for the period 1961-65 for industrial facilities and technical assistance	240 mill. rubles	60.0
		East Bloc Total:		1,161.55
Afghanistan	24 Mar. 65	Interest-free loan	27.5 mill. $ U.S.	27.5
Burma	8 Jan. 58	2.5% loan	20.0 mill. kyat	4.2
	9 Jan. 61	Interest-free loan	30.0 mill. pd. st.	84.0
Ceylon	19 Sept. 57	Donation	75.0 mill. C. rp.	15.8

Country	Date Granted	Type and Purpose	Amount	In Millions of Dollars
	17 Sept. 58	Interest-bearing loan which changed to an interest-free loan on June 15, 1964, retro- actively valid	50.0 mill. C. rp.	10.5
	3 Oct. 62	Donation	50.0 mill. C. rp.	10.5
	21 Oct. 64	Interest-free loan	20.0 mill. C. rp.	4.2
Indonesia*	3 Nov. 56	Moratorium loan, 2.5%	15.0 mill. $ U.S.	15.0
	17 Apr. 58	2.5% interest-bearing loan	48.0 mill. S. fr.	11.5
	8 Oct. 58	Additional 2.5% loan	13.5 mill. $ U.S.	13.5
	11 Oct. 61	2% interest bearing loan	129.6 mill. S. fr.	30.0
	25 Jan. 65	Interest-free loan	50.0 mill. $ U.S.	50.0
Yemen	12 Jan. 58	Interest-free loan	70.0 mill. S. fr.	16.4
	24 Nov. 62	Interest-free loan	4.8 mill. $ U.S.	4.8
	9 June 64	Interest-free loan	10.0 mill. pd. st.	28.0
Cambodia	21 June 56	Donation	800.0 mill. riel	22.4
	24 Aug. 58	Donation	5.6 mill. $ U.S.	5.6
	19 Dec. 60	Donation	400.0 mill. riel	11.4
Laos	13 Jan. 62	Donation	4.0 mill. $ U.S.	4.0
Nepal	7 Oct. 56	Donation	60.0 mill. Ind. rp.	12.7
	21 Mar. 60	Donation	100.0 mill. Ind. rp.	21.2
	15 Oct. 61	Donation	3.5 mill. pd. st.	9.8
Pakistan	18 Feb. 65	Interest-free loan	60.0 mill. $ U.S.	60.0
Syria	21 Feb. 63	Interest-free loan	70.0 mill. S. fr.	16.4
		Total for Asia:		489.4
AFRICA				
Egypt (UAR)	10 Nov. 56	Donation	20.0 mill. S. fr.	4.7
	21 Dec. 64	Interest-free loan	80.0 mill. $ U.S.	80.0
Algeria	Nov. 58	Donation	4.7 mill. $ U.S.	4.7
	28 Oct. 63	Interest-free loan	250.0 mill. nf	51.0

Country	Date Granted	Type and Purpose	Amount	In Millions of Dollars
Ghana*	18 Aug. 61	Interest-free loan	7.0 mill. Gh. pd.	19.6
	15 July 64	Interest-free loan	8.0 mill. Gh. pd.	22.4
Guinea	13 Sept. 60	Interest-free loan	100.0 mill. rubles	25.0
Kenya	10 May 64	Donation	1.1 mill. pd. st.	3.1
	10 May 64	Interest-free loan	6.0 mill. pd. st.	16.8
Congo (Brazz- aville)	11 July 64	Interest-free loan, 50% in cash	5.0 mill. $ U.S.	5.0
	2 Oct. 64	Interest-free loan	100.0 mill. nf.	20.4
Mali	22 Sept. 61	Interest-free loan	4800.0 mill. Mali fr.	19.4
	22 Sept. 61	Donation	50.0 mill. Mali fr.	0.2
	3 Nov. 64	Donation	2000.0 mill. Mali fr.	7.9
Somalia	9 Aug. 63	Interest-free loan	2.0 mill. $ U.S.	2.0
	9 Aug. 63	Donation	3.0 mill. $ U.S.	3.0
Tanzania	21 Feb. 64	2.5% interest bearing loan to Zanzibar	0.175 mill. pd. st.	0.5
	8 June 64	Interest-free loan to Zanzibar	5.0 mill. pd. st.	14.0
	8 June 64	Donation to Zanzibar	1.0 mill. pd. st.	2.8
	16 June 64	Interest-free loan to Zanzibar/Tanganyika, 50% in freely convertible currency	10.0 mill. pd. st.	28.0
Central African Republic	14 Jan. 65	Interest-free loan	1000.0 mill. DFA-fr	4.1

Total for Africa: 352.6

Total to the "Third World": 842.0

[127] *Hsinhua News Agency; China Reconstructs; Foreign Trade of the People's Republic of China; Novaya Koreya; People's Vietnam; Sovremenaya Mongoliya; Economic Cooperation of the PR China with the Countries in the Socialist Camp* (Russ.), Moscow 1960; Anderson Shih, "Communist China's Asia Policy," presentation at the international conference of the Friedrich-Ebert Foundation 27 March 1962; *Communist China as a Developmental Model for Underdeveloped Countries, Research Institute on the Sino-Soviet Bloc Studies,* Monograph Series No. 1, Washington, D. C.

** Chinese economic aid to Indonesia and Ghana and the Central African Republic has been stopped in the meantime. It was impossible to ascertain to what extent these countries availed themselves of the loans that had been granted to them.

Some explanation is in order about China's nonrepayable aid to North Korea and North Vietnam. So far, there has been no agreement on the yuan rate of exchange. Partly, it has been assumed that the yuan rate normally used in clearing of trade transactions between the USSR and China (.975 yuan = one old ruble) was also applicable in the conversion of Chinese grants to North Korea and North Vietnam. Anderson Shih, on the other hand, applied the official rate of exchange (2.34 yuan = one U. S. dollar) at the aforementioned Bergneustadt Conference. Several publications, however, have pointed out that the most telling China yuan grants to North Korea and North Vietnam were "based on domestic wholesale prices in China." [128] It is known, too, that Vietnam's dong has been yoked to China's yuan until now and that trade between the two countries is cleared in yuan at Chinese wholesale prices.[129] A singular case in East bloc trade annuals! It may be assumed, therefore, that China's aid to North Korea and North Vietnam must be evaluated as domestic credits. East bloc government make such domestic loans available to plants and *kolkhozy* in the local currency and in relation to wholesale prices within the individual countries. Foreign loans, however, are loans where the local currency is brought into an artificial relation to the dollar, and goods shipped are costed at world market prices.

Our assumption that the loans just discussed were in fact domestic credits is confirmed by the Chinese economist Teh Chi-ta, who writes that China's nonrepayable aid to North Korea and North Vietnam for the period 1953-55 was calculated on the basis of an internal conversion rate. Teh Chi-ta applies the same conversion rate method to the Sino-Cambodian aid agreement of 21 June 1956. In this, Cambodia was to receive "merchandise and payments in kind in the amount of 800 million rials, which equals 8 million pounds sterling" (thus verbatim in the communiqué). Teh evaluates these 8 million pounds sterling at 110,280,000 "domestic" yuan,[130] which is at the rate of one pound sterling = 13.785 yuan (official Peking rate: one pound sterling = 6.85 yuan), or one yuan = .20312 dollars. Based on this rate (the least favorable of any conversion rates heretofore used), we recal-

---

[128] *Economic Development in the Countries of Asia's People's Democracies* (Russ.), Moscow 1957, p. 310; *Economic Development in the Countries of People's Democracies* (Russ.), Moscow 1958, pp. 167-69.
[129] See report of head of trade-finance section in the chancellory of Vietnam's Prime Minister, published in *The Socialist World Economic System* (Russ.), Moscow 1958, p. 518.
[130] Teh Chi-ta, *China's Budget During the Transition Period* (Russ., from the Chinese), Moscow 1958, p. 201.

culated the dollar equivalent of all Chinese nonrepayable aid and loans listed in yuan.

Loans by the People's Republic of China to the Developing Countries from 1956 to 1965

(in millions of $ U.S.)

	1956	1957	1958	1959	1960	1961	1962	1963	1964	1965	1956-65 total
ASIA											
Afghanistan	--	--	--	--	--	--	--	--	--	27.5	27.5
Burma	--	--	4.2	--	--	84.0	--	--	--	--	88.2
Ceylon	--	15.8	10.5	--	--	--	10.5	--	4.2	--	41.0
Indonesia	15.0	--	25.0	--	--	30.0	--	--	--	50.0	120.0
Yemen	--	--	16.4	--	--	--	4.8	--	28.0	--	49.2
Cambodia	22.4	--	5.6	--	11.4	--	--	--	--	--	39.4
Laos	--	--	--	--	--	--	4.0	--	--	--	4.0
Nepal	12.7	--	--	--	21.2	9.8	--	--	--	--	43.7
Pakistan	--	--	--	--	--	--	--	--	--	60.0	60.0
Syria	--	--	--	--	--	--	--	16.4	--	--	16.4
AFRICA											
Egypt (UAR)	4.7	--	--	--	--	--	--	--	80.0	--	84.7
Algeria	--	--	4.7	--	--	--	--	51.0	--	--	55.7
Ghana	--	--	--	--	--	19.6	--	--	22.4	--	42.0
Guinea	--	--	--	--	25.0	--	--	--	--	--	25.0
Kenya	--	--	--	--	--	--	--	--	19.9	--	19.9
Congo (Brz)	--	--	--	--	--	--	--	--	25.4	--	25.4
Mali	--	--	--	--	--	19.6	--	--	7.9	--	27.5
Somalia	--	--	--	--	--	--	--	23.0	--	--	23.0
Tanzania	--	--	--	--	--	--	--	--	45.3	--	45.3
Central Afr. Republic	--	--	--	--	--	--	--	--	--	4.1	4.1
Total:	54.8	15.8	66.4	--	57.6	163.0	19.3	90.4	233.1	141.6	842.0

Loans Made by European
Soviet Bloc Nations

Since 1956 (1954 in Czechoslovakia's case) the European members of the Soviet bloc have begun to extend loans to the developing nations. With the exception of Czechoslovakia, the volume of these credits can hardly match that of China. Even though united under the Council for Initial Economic Assistance (Comecon),* these communist European states do not boast a multilateral aid program. In capital-poor Poland and Hungary, voices are being heard demanding a common Soviet bloc fund of investment loans for the developing nations. The present charter and character of Comecon hardly favors such an idea. China is not a member of Comecon and only the USSR is permitted untrammeled economic development and expansion. Other members are compelled, in consequence of the principle of labor division, to limit their production to certain branches of industry. This is also reflected in foreign aid. In other words, Comecon's collaboration on foreign aid can never mean more than a supplementing of Soviet endeavor. Just how this works is made plain in the· 29 January 1958 Agreement on Economic and Technical Collaboration between the USSR and Egypt. The communiqué on this agreement reads in part: "The Agreement also provides that the Soviet organizations may call on corresponding organizations of the People's Democracies, with their consent, for preliminary planning and the supply of equipment, machines, and material." [131] A like proviso is contained in the 28 September 1959 Indo-Soviet agreement on the

* COMECON: USSR, CSSR, Poland, East Germany, Hungary, Rumania, Bulgaria.
[131] *Pravda*, 30 January 1958.

240

construction of an oil refinery at Barauni in the state of Bihar. Here, we read: "The Soviet partner is at liberty to cooperate with appropriate foreign organizations in the execution of assumed obligations concerning planning, equipment delivery, and other types of technical collaboration. The Soviet organizations will obtain prior clearance from Indian authorities in the event specialists from third countries are to be sent to India." There is thus far no knowledge of any agreement whereby Czechoslovakia or other Soviet bloc countries may also subcontract to Soviet organizations.

The European bloc members (except the USSR), on the other hand, because of the present form of labor division and production restrictions within Comecon, in order to carry out even minor projects in the underdeveloped countries are often at each others mercy. This situation determines the form that collaboration takes in countries whose production scope is limited. A more direct Comecon involvement in the developmental program would also mean a dimming of the USSR image in the countries of Asia, Africa and Latin America, which is contrary to the Party line.

For these reasons, only two commissions of the Soviet-dominated Comecon concern themselves with questions pertaining to the developing countries: the Commission on Economic Problems and the Foreign Trade Commission, both with seats in Moscow. These commissions essentially serve only as coordinators for pricing and delivery terms, selection of aid concentration points, and the dovetailing of bloc partners into the developmental projects of the USSR. It is illuminating that not a single article of the Soviet bloc's extensive literature on foreign aid problems mentions Comecon in any way. Comecon does not exist for the backward nations. Reports about foreign aid and loan extensions, issued routinely in the West by OECD and other agencies, do not exist in the Soviet bloc. Comecon thus far lacks all prerequisites for this type of report service. Polish and Hungarian economists are hopeful that this task might be carried out by the "Bank of Socialist Countries," whose founding was decided on at the Seventeenth Comecon Meeting in Bucharest in December 1962.

It is exceedingly difficult to present an accurate picture of the loans granted the backward nations by Czechoslovakia, Poland, Rumania, East Germany, Hungary, and Bulgaria. On the one hand, the Soviet bloc nations endeavor to inflate their loan grants, often adding short- and medium-term commercial credits to the category of foreign aid loans. On the other hand, in contrast to the USSR and China, these countries rarely publish the texts of agreements with backward nations, thus shutting out this source of control over figures presented.

DDR LOANS TO THE "THIRD WORLD"

It is extremely difficult to collect precise data about DDR credit grants since the DDR publishes no agreement texts but uses its loans as a propaganda means in the underdeveloped countries whenever it can. Even if its loan offers are not accepted, the DDR is supposed to appear as the willing and generous lender in these countries. In the following tabulation I sought to list the loan offers as well as the actual credit agreements into which the DDR entered. However, I only cite actual figures for those loans which I was able to ascertain had indeed been granted.

		In Millions of $U.S.
AFRICA		
UAR (Egypt)		
29 August 1958	Agreement about economic and technical cooperation—a long-term loan of 7.5 Egyptian pounds at 2.5%—constructed were one power plant in Damanhour, one cement factory in El Mex, one galvanizing plant, one overhead cable line 220 miles long, one cigarette factory, two coal-loading bridges in Alexandria, one cotton spinning plant in Alexandria, refrigeration plants and textile refinement facilities. Still under construction are one fibre plant in Damiette and a government printing press in Cairo.	21.5
27 November 1958	Additional investment loan for equipping the completed cotton spinning plant in Shibin el Kom with 100,000 spindles.	8.6
8 March 1961	Additional 2.5% loan for equipment and machinery for the completion of projects from the agreement of 29 August 1958—2.0 million Egyptian pounds.	5.7

1 March 1965	New agreement about economic and technical cooperation: two loans: a) short-term loan for a period of seven years for delivery of goods in the value of 11 million pounds sterling at 2.5%; b) long-term loan for construction purposes in the value of 25 million pounds sterling at 2.5%, for a period of twelve years.	30.8
		70.0

Ghana

8 July 1961	Agreement about economic co-operation and a loan at 2.5% interest. Building program: one building material plant, factory for radios, one government printing press in Tema which was completed in September 1964, one glass factory, one fish meal factory whose product was to be exported to the DDR.	4.0
24 July 1965	A 7.2 million pounds sterling loan for constructing and equipping a cellulose-paper combine and of a wood finishing facility. The agreement was not executed after Nkrumah's downfall.	20.2

Guinea

18 January 1960	A 2.5% loan for a period of five years. Construction program: a broadcasting station in Conakry, a large printing plant in Conakry, a building material plant, an experimental agricultural farm, a counselling center for the training of agricultural specialists. Almost all these projects have been completed. The DDR's FDGB (Free	7.0

German Trade Union League)
made a gift of and constructed
the buildings for the *Université
Ouvrière Africaine* in Conakry.

Sudan

10 June 1955	Agreement about scientific and technical cooperation. DDR agreed to undertake the preliminary studies for the construction of water conservation facilities. On 11 November 1964 the new Sudanese government was offered a loan of $12.5 million. No agreement has become known so far.	Unknown

Tunisia

16 March 1965	Agreement about economic cooperation. Building program: one sewing machine factory, equipment for a second sewing machine factory, chemical combine worth $1.5 million, calcium-carbonate plant, sending of DDR specialists.	0.3

Tanzania

16 May 1961	After gifts to Zanzibar for the construction of a clinic, the construction of apartment blocks, and payment for the work of DDR construction experts, planning experts and other experts, the DDR and Zanzibar reached an agreement about economic aid on 16 May 1961. The DDR granted a long-term loan about whose size we have no documents so far.	Unknown

ASIA

Burma

15 July 1958	Agreement about the construction of a cement factory in Thayatmyo, which began production in July 1962, of five rice-bran extraction facilities, one textile factory and one cotton mill. DDR loans to Burma which have been cited by Western sources cannot be verified with Eastern documents.	Unknown

Ceylon

22 February 1965	Economic assistance agreement for the construction of a textile combine and several chemical plants with a total value of 550 million C. Rp. The DDR obligated itself to accept the entire cost, in foreign as well as in the national currency. First DDR loan of 200 million C. Rp. at 2.5% per year. The national currency is supposed to be raised through the sale of DDR products in Ceylon.	42.2

India

16 July 1957	A $2.5 million loan at 2.5% for equipment for the textile industry.	2.5

Indonesia

3 February 1955	Agreement about DDR assistance in the construction of a sugar factory, a cement factory and a textile factory; loan at 2.5% per year. The DDR's new loan offer of May 1965 will probably not lead to an agreement due to the events of 30 September 1965.	8.6

Iraq

26 1960 October	Agreement about DDR assistance during the construction of a hosiery factory, a textile factory and construction of a large printing plant. In January 1965 the DDR proposed a loan which, however, seems not to have been accepted.	Unknown

Yemen

11 December 1962	Agreement about economic and technical cooperation between Yemen and the DDR. The DDR granted a loan whose size and conditions are unknown to us so far.	Unknown
29 April 1965	New agreement about economic cooperation; 2.5% interest loan.	5.0

Cambodia

2 February 1964	The DDR and Cambodia announced (in Phnom-Penh) a DDR loan repayable in goods. It is supposed to be a loan of $30.5 million. But an actual agreement to confirm this announcement has not become known to us so far.	Unknown

Lebanon

3 March 1965	Negotiations were held about an agreement about economic-technical and scientific-technical cooperation. However, documentation of such agreements are not yet available.	Unknown

Syria

17 October 1965	After the DDR had already constructed a cement factory in Aleppo and a shoe manufacturing plant in Homs, in accordance with its August 1958 agreement with	25.0

the UAR, Syria and the DDR, after several DDR loan offers, reached an agreement on 17 October 1965 in Damascus. This agreement about economic and technical cooperation stipulated that the DDR would grant a loan with a foreign exchange value of $25 million at 2.5% for a period of twelve years.

Total DDR loans that we have recorded: 265.4

Our presentation left out a $40 million loan to Brazil, which both Eastern and Western sources mention, since this was purely a credit allowance for the purchase of goods.

YUGOSLAV CREDITS TO THE DEVELOPING COUNTRIES

At the Eighth Party Congress of the League of the Communists of Yugoslavia (BDKJ) in December 1964, Tito emphasized that Yugoslavia had granted the underdeveloped countries of Asia, Africa and Latin America *investment credits in the amount of roughly $361 million*, of which $230 million had already been used. On 19 January 1965 *Tass* reported (probably on the basis of Yugoslavian UN documents): "The total amount of the export loans which Yugoslavia has granted since 1957 is $361 million, of which roughly $230 million have been used by these countries so far. As a rule, these loans were granted for periods from seven to ten years and at an interest rate of 3%." At the same time Yugoslavia granted the developing countries important technological assistance. More than 800 Yugoslav specialists were sent to these countries, particularly to Africa. Roughly 900 specialists from these developing countries are undergoing training in Yugoslavia; 1000 students from these countries are studying at Yugoslav universities.

The claim that $230 million has been used (63% of the loans granted) appears questionable in the case of a country like Yugoslavia, which is in a developing stage itself and is dependent on American loans. This figure comprises investments as well as export loans which are negotiated in special loan agreements about scientific and technical cooperation but also in trade agreements. In several cases they also serve to finance the delivery of machines and equipment for the construction of industrial facilities. Nor are they coupled to Yugoslav technical assistance in every case. Thus, for example, in April 1961 Yugoslavia granted Brazil a credit of $120 million, which was to be used for the following purposes: delivery of ships—65 million dollars; capital goods —20 million dollars; agricultural machinery—30 million dollars; and other equipment—5 million dollars. In the case of loans to other countries it is quite difficult to ascertain to what extent they only serve to help Yugoslav export by means of delivering equipment, and what part of them is used for the construction of facilities with Yugoslav assistance. In any case, we gather from *Yugoslavensky Pregled* No. 7/1963 that $94.1 million worth of equipment and machinery was delivered between 1957 and 1963, and that simultaneously Yugoslavia fulfilled its credit obligations to the extent of $21.8 million (a total of $115.9). The purposes and the peculiarities of the Yugoslav grants that we have named should be kept in mind in evaluating the following tabulation of Yugoslav credits.

Yugoslav Investment Loan Grants to the Developing Countries from 1957 to March 1965

Country	date	In Millions of $ U.S.
ASIA		
Afghanistan	January 1961	8.0
Ceylon	May 1959 (5.5 million pounds sterling)	15.4
India	January 1960	40.0
Indonesia	September 1959	10.0
"	April 1962	15.0
Yemen	February 1963	2.0
Cambodia	April 1963	6.0
"	October 1964	2.0
Pakistan	January 1961	10.0
"	March 1962	20.0
"	February 1964	15.0
	Total for Asia	143.4
AFRICA		
Egypt (UAR)	June 1958	10.0
"	June 1964	35.0
"	January 1965	17.5
Algeria	July 1963	10.0
Ethiopia	June 1959	10.0
Ghana	October 1961 (3.6 million Ghanian pounds)	10.1

Country	Date	In Millions of $ U.S.
Guinea	October 1960	5.0
Guinea	December 1961	2.0
Cameroon	December 1963	2.0
Kenya	December 1963	10.0
Mali	October 1961	10.0
Morocco	September 1961	5.0
Sudan	July 1959 (5.5 million pounds sterling)	15.4
Tanzania	December 1962	10.0
Tunisia	September 1960	5.0
Tunisia	February 1962	5.0

Total for Africa--162.0

LATIN AMERICA

Bolivia	October 1963	5.0
Brazil	April 1961	120.0

Total for Latin America--125.0

Grand Total: 430.4

The Yugoslav Foreign Trade Bank controls the funds for these loans. But they are made available through a special fund that absorbs the foreign exchange from the tourist trade, the money sent by Yugoslavs working in other countries and other income from "noncommercial" accounts. As of 3 June 1964 all Yugoslav undertakings and factories that are active in export, fulfill obligations in the developing countries and lend technical assistance in the construction of projects, must contribute from their own resources 5% toward the loan for the respective deliveries and labor.

FINANCIAL ASSISTANCE GRANTED BY THE CSSR, POLAND, HUNGARY, RUMANIA AND BULGARIA

At the UN conference for trade and development in the summer of 1964 in Geneva, the CSSR representative declared that Czechoslovakia had granted a total of $500 million to the African, Asian and Latin American countries. *Rude Pravo* of 25 May 1965 estimates the total financial assistance that the CSSR has granted "Third World" countries to be 400 million rubles ($444.4 million). This total is also cited by Soviet sources.

Thus, even the CSSR itself has no clear idea of the exact amount of

aid it has given to the developing nations. Since agreement texts are
hardly ever published in the CSSR a precise calculation of CSSR
assistance is almost impossible. What we attempt is to give a general
survey of CSSR aid based on Czech, Soviet and other East bloc sources.

Czechoslovak Financial Assistance to the Developing Countries

Country	Purpose	Amount in Millions of $ U.S.
ASIA		
Afghanistan		
August 1954	For equipping two cement factories, one cotton mill, one leather factory and the like, 3% loan for a period of eight years.	5.0
until March 1959	Increase of the grants for construction purposes to $12.32 million.	7.32
August 1960	Donation for educational and training purposes.	0.28
Ceylon		
End of 1957	For construction of a sugar refinery, a cement factory and the like.	10.0
January 1958	For construction of and equipment for one sugar and one shoe factory.	3.4
June 1964	For construction of a hydro-electric plant.	9.0
India		
Beginning of 1956	For construction of a cement factory.	2.1
July 1956	For construction of a sugar factory.	1.9
November 1959	For construction of three sugar refineries, two cement factories, two thermal-electric plants, one iron foundry and blacksmith shop in Rantchi, and other plants, a loan of 231 million rupees at 2.5%.	48.5
July 1961	Increase of the previous loan to 400 million rupees for the construction of a foundry and blacksmith shop, a heavy machine factory, a plant for electrical machinery and a plant for the production of high pressure boilers.	35.5
May 1964	For construction projects that are part of the fourth Indian Five-Year Plan (1966-70) a loan of 400 million rupees.	84.0
Indonesia		
May 1956	For construction of a rubber products factory, 4% loan.	1.6
January 1958	For the construction of a hydro-electric plant and the delivery of diesel locomotives and tractors.	20.8
November 1959	For the construction of cement factories and the like.	14.0
May 1960	For the construction of power plants, a highway, and the delivery of machines, equipment and rolling stock, a 12 million pounds sterling loan.	33.6

Country	Purpose	Amount in Millions of $ U.S.
Iraq		
October 1960	For construction of an oil refinery, hydro-electric plants, and the development of the chemical industry, a loan of 12 million pounds sterling.	33.6
Iran		
until July 1959	For construction of power plants and a sugar and ice factory.	6.0
Pakistan		
November 1964	For construction of cement and sugar factories and other plants, a 2.5% loan for a period of eight years.	14.0
Syria		
Until 1957	For construction of a sugar and a gasoline factory.	1.0
March 1957	For construction of an oil refinery, a cement and a sugar factory.	15.0
December 1960	For machines and equipment, a loan of 1 million pounds sterling at 3.75%	2.8
	Total for Asia	249.4
AFRICA		
Egypt (UAR)		
March 1956	For a cement factory.	4.0
March 1958	For various development projects.	56.0
June 1960	For construction of a refinery as well as machine and equipment deliveries.	15.5
May 1962	For machines and equipment, a loan of 20 million Egyptian pounds.	57.4
March 1965	Loan assistance for the second Five-Year Plan of the UAR, 25 million Egyptian pounds.	71.8
Algeria		
July 1964	Construction loan at 2.5% for a ten-year period, 100 million kcs.	13.9
Ethiopia		
1959	For construction of a hospital and for technical assistance.	2.0
January 1960	For improvement of mines, industrial plants, transportation system and agriculture, a loan of 24.5 million Egyptian pounds.	9.8
Ghana		
May 1961	For projects of primary importance and equipment, loan of 5 million Ghanian pounds.	14.0

Country	Purpose	Amount in Millions of $ U.S.
Guinea		
July 1959	For investment and assistance.	5.5
May 1961	Increase of the loan to $10 million.	4.5
Mali		
November 1960	According to an economic aid agreement.	10.0
June 1961	For improvement of airline service and airplane deliveries.	2.5
Morocco		
May 1961	In accord with an agreement about economic and technological cooperation, especially for training purposes.	0.4
Somalia		
June 1961	For agricultural, industrial and transportation purposes, 30 million Somali shillings.	4.2
Tunisia		
October 1961	For scientific and technological aid and delivery of investment goods, a loan at 2.5%	10.0
	Total for Africa	281.5
LATIN AMERICA		
Argentina		
1958	Loan for the construction of a power plant at 6%	2.0
Bolivia		
January 1962	For construction of an antimony preparation facility, a 5% loan for eight years	1.9
	Total for Latin America:	3.9
	Grand total:	634.8

The loans just listed should be regarded in the light of what we have said about Yugoslav credits. Frequently only a part of the funds pledged by the CSSR are designated for construction purposes, the other part being granted for the purchase of Czech equipment. Since the agreement texts are not published we are unable to separate the two precisely. Even so, we did not include a number of trade and purchase credits that were clearly in the nature of export loans. Among these are a loan to India, made in January 1958, in the amount of $34 million; a 1955 loan to Argentina in the amount of $15 million for the financing of coal mine equipment purchases; a loan to Colombia, made in May 1960, for the purchase of automobile parts in the amount of $35 million; a loan to Paraguay (1955) of $15 million for the purchase of plant installations. Several CSSR and Soviet sources also cite a 1961 loan of $60 million to Brazil. Evidently this is an export loan also and we did not include it in our list, particularly since it has not been used by 1964.

Finally, we are adding a survey of the loan grants made by other Comecon countries: Poland, Hungary, Rumania and Bulgaria.

Financial Aid of Several European Comecon Countries to the "Third World"

(in millions of $ U.S.)

	POLAND	HUNGARY	RUMANIA	BULGARIA
Ceylon	24.9	--	--	--
India	89.6	16.8	12.1	--
Indonesia	93.1	29.8	50.0	10.6
Iran	22.0	10.0	--	--
Pakistan	14.0	--	--	--
Syria	15.0	16.5	--	15.0
Egypt (UAR)	20.0	38.6	--	--
Ghana	14.0	14.0	10.0	7.6
Guinea	10.0	2.5	--	2.0
Mali	7.0	--	--	2.0
Morocco	9.6	--	--	--
Tunisia	10.0	--	--	--
Argentinia	5.0	--	--	--
TOTAL:	334.2	128.2	72.1	37.2

Several Western sources list far higher credit grants for these four Soviet bloc countries. These sources not only include the grants to Cuba but also large grants supposedly made to Brazil: Poland $70 million, Hungary $60 million, Rumania $50 million. Yet evidently all these grants are export loans since none of the sources can offer any information about the construction of projects or facilities by any of the above-mentioned countries.

According to *Zycie Gospodarcze* of 10 June 1962, the Polish $70 million-loan is good for eight years and is to be applied to the purchase of fifty Polish fishing vessels. The Rumanian journal *Probleme economie* No. 7 of July 1961 points out that the $50 million-loan to Brazil by Rumanian foreign trade undertakings was made as part of the trade and payment agreement of 5 May 1961 and of the agreement about scientific and technical cooperation.

Summing up, we arrive at the following breakdown of the loan grants which we have ascertained the Soviet bloc and China made.

Total Grants and the Share of Each Soviet Bloc Country and of China in

Supplying Them

(in millions of $ U. S.)

	Amount	in %
TOTAL	7 036.3	100.0
of which:		
USSR	4 306.3	61.5
PR China	842.0	12.0
CSSR	634.8	9.0
Yugoslavia	430.4	6.0
Poland	334.2	4.7
DDR	251.1	3.5
Hungary	128.2	1.8
Rumania	72.1	1.0
Bulgaria	37.2	0.5

Industrialization Aid

What purpose does the aid the East bloc countries supply to the developing countries serve? The communist development experts' answer reads something like this: the loans and donations of the communist states serve primarily to industrialize and develop the productiveness of the "Third World," whereas loans by Western industrial states essentially provide only foodstuffs and "luxury articles," which are quickly consumed and have no economically useful effect, or at best are designed to develop the infra-structure. Industrialization is the Soviet bloc's great slogan. Each industrial plant constructed with Soviet bloc help will be used as part of the propaganda campaign in the developing countries. The Soviet bloc publishes high figures about future projects in the "Third World"—something which must inevitably evoke hopes and illusions in the developing countries.

According to official figures, at the beginning of 1966 the construction of *1800* industrial facilities, power plants, agricultural undertakings and other projects in *forty developing countries* stood on the Soviet bloc's and China's buildings program.[132] This averages out to forty-five projects per country. We are also informed that the USSR alone will construct 600 of these projects in twenty-eight of the forty developing countries in the total aid programs,[133] that is, 20.7 projects per country. We have no documentation for 1966 of how the remaining

---

[132] *Mirovaya ekonomika i mezdunarodnie otnoseniya* (Moscow), No. 4/1966, p. 117.
[133] *Vneshnaya torgovlya* (Moscow), No. 4/1966, p. 25.

255

share of the 1800 projects is divided up among the other communist countries.

In 1964 the communist countries had a total of 1300 projects on their construction program. Of these the USSR was responsible for 500, the CSSR for 250, Yugoslavia for 105, China—according to Soviet sources—for 100 (125 according to Chinese data), and the DDR for fifty-two. The remaining 293 projects thus would be parcelled out among Poland, Hungary, Rumania and Bulgaria. The 1800 industrial facilities and other projects which the whole East bloc will construct as of 1966 include:[134]

East Bloc Industrial Facilities Scheduled for 1966

Steel plants, metallurgy plants, and coal mining plants......60

Machine building and metal finishing plant.................150

Facilities for the chemical industry and oil refineries.....100

Facilities for the production of foodstuffs, textile plants,

and light industry..300

Instructional facilities and study centers.................100

total   710

This data includes the plants and facilities that the USSR wants to construct. The 600 projects that the USSR wants to construct for the young national states include the following:[135]

USSR Projects for Young National States

Plants and sections of plants for the steel industry and metal-

lurgy industry...30

Machine building and metal finishing plants................45

Plants for the production of building materials.............16

Chemical plants and oil refineries.........................26

Hydro-electric plants......................................30

Plants for light industry and foodstuff production 80

Agricultural projects......................................100

Instructional facilities...................................90

total   417

---

[134] *Mirovaya ekonomika i mezdunarodnie otnoseniya* (Moscow), No. 4/1966, p. 117.
[135] *Vneshnaya torgovlya* (Moscow), No. 4/1966, p. 25; *Azija i Afrika segodnya* (Moscow), No. 11/1965, p. 6.

Heavy industrial projects supposedly constitute roughly 50% of the items on the USSR's building program.[136] Of the East bloc as a whole it is said that: "Approximately two-thirds of the aid granted the young industrial states by the socialist countries serve the development of their national industries. Many of the plants that have been or will be built represent the nucleus of their industry, are the foundation for their fight for economic independence." [137]

However, when evaluating these figures and judging the plant construction by the individual communist countries, we have to keep in mind what G. M. Prochorov[138] has said on this subject: "Every socialist country provides aid in the construction of plants in those branches of industry where it itself is most highly developed." Since only the USSR can develop every branch of its industry within the framework of division of labor and specialization practiced by Comecon, whereas the other members have to confine themselves to a particular industrial branch and specialize in it, it is only logical that only the USSR is able to erect large projects in the developing countries. For example, the average cost of the plants constructed by Poland is between fifty and 100 thousand U. S. dollars.[139]

A comparison of the credits granted by the East bloc with the number of projects on its building program shows the difference between the capacity of the USSR and that of other bloc partners. However, it also proves that the USSR generally is not able to construct anything but smaller or medium sized plants, and that large industrial plants are the exception within the 600-project Soviet program. According to the standing of April 1966, the comparison looks like this:

USSR vs. East Bloc Credits

	East bloc total	USSR alone
Credits pledged in mill. $ U.S.	7,036	4,306
Number of projects on building program	1,800	600
Size of credit per project average in mill. $ U.S.	3.2	7.2

---

[136] *Izvestia*, July 11, 1964.

[137] *Mirovaya ekonomika i mezhdunardnia otnosentya* (Moscow), No. 4/1966, p. 118.

[138] G. M. Prochorov, *The Two World Systems and the Liberated Countries, op. cit.,* p. 142.

[139] *Mirovaya ekonomika i mezhdunardnia otnosentya* (Moscow), No. 11/1962, p. 125.

G. M. Prochorov claims that the completion of the 1800 projects on the East bloc building program will enable the developing countries to "produce more than 6 million tons of steel, refine 16 million tons of crude oil, produce more than 30 billion kwh of electricity and produce millions of yards of textiles." [140] This would mean that the realization of the present building program will establish plants that will have six times the capacity of the first building phase of the Bhilai steel works in India (1 million tons per year), eight times the capacity of the oil refinery in Barauni in India (2 million tons per year) and roughly three times the capacity of the hydroelectric plant at the Aswan Dam, whose capacity it is estimated will be 2.1 million kw with an energy production of roughly 10 billion kwh. Prochorov also emphasizes "that every billion rubles permits the young national states to build plants that produce more than 1.2 million tons of steel a year, more than 6 billion kwh of electric energy and facilitates the irrigation of 200,000 hectare of land." [141]

Even if the USSR had applied its total grants solely for the construction of steel plants, hydroelectric plants and the construction of irrigation facilities, which is not the case, she was hardly in a position (according to Soviet figures for the period 1954-1966) to establish higher production capacities in the young national states than those specifically mentioned above; for, of its total credit assistance (4 billion rubles = $4,660 million) the USSR—as we have mentioned—has only fulfilled roughly 30%.

The available documentation does not allow us to determine the exact number of objects that the individual communist countries have constructed in the "Third World" so far. The Soviets claim that the People's Republic of China had completed only five industrial plants, three hospitals and several other projects of the 100 projects on its program by 1964. [142]

Up to this point the USSR has completed roughly 36% of its building program. Sixty-four per cent are only on paper or are only projected for the future. On the basis of periodically published Soviet figures about their building program, we juxtapose these figures with those of projects which, it has been announced, have begun production.

[140] Mirovaya ekonomika i mezhdunarodnie otnosheniya, No. 4/1966, p. 118.
[141] ibid., (Moscow), No. 4/1966, p. 120.
[142] Izvestia, 11 July 1964.

USSR Projects in the Developing Countries and Their Completion [143]

Number of Projects	Increase (additional promises)	of which completed	
Mid 1959--210	--		
End 1959--250	+ 40	20	8.0 %
Mid 1960--300	+ 50	-	
End 1960--350	+ 50	40	11.4 %
End 1961--380	+ 30	--	
Mid 1962--480	+100	100	20.8 %
Beg.1963--480	--	120	25.0 %
Mid 1964--500	+ 20	150	30.0 %
Mid 1965--600	+100	170	28.3 %

The Soviet publications continue to list a figure of 600 for the end of 1965 and the beginning of 1966 as being on the USSR building program.[144] Of the majority of the 170 projects completed by mid-1965 it cannot be a matter of a larger number of steel works, hydroelectric plants and irrigation facilities,[145] for—as we have stated—an average of only 7.7 million rubles worth of credit assistance is available for the construction of each plant.

For the completion of its projects and the start of production of the completed plants and facilities, the Soviets sent a total of 6510 engineers and technicians into the developing countries in 1960; in 1961 the number was 8500, and in 1962 it was 9620.[146] In the beginning of 1965 the number of specialists and experts sent by Comecon states to "Third World" countries was given as 29,000.[147] However, we have no way of checking this figure.

It is known that the USSR has available a pool of 25,000 experts with experience in foreign countries. Between 1950 and 1959 10,800 Soviet engineers and technicians were active in Communist China.[148] So far the Soviet authors have not mentioned a figure higher than the

[143] Based on statements in *Vneshnaya torgoulya, Aziya i Afrika segodnja, Voprosy ekonomiki, Mirovaya ekonomika i mezhdunanardnie otnoseniya, Pravda,* and *Ekonomiceskaja gazeta,* for the period 1959-1966.
[144] *Vneshnaya torgoulya* (Moscow), No. 4/1966, p. 25.
[145] Compare figures with source mentioned in footnote 141.
[146] Janos Horvath in *Hinter dem Eisernen Vorhang* (Munich), No. 1/1964, p. 11.
[147] *Politicheskoe samoobrazovanie,* No. 4/1965, p. 105.
[148] Chou En-lai, *Das grosse Jahrzehut,* Peking 1959, p. 31.

12,000 economic experts who have been sent to assist the developing countries during any one year. During 1964 approximately 10,000 Soviet specialists were supposed to have been active in the "Third World."[149] A more recent Soviet source informs us that "From 1957 to 1964 41,500 Soviet specialists and scientists, engineers, technicians and qualified workers were sent to the developing countries."[150] This sum total undoubtedly comprises all Soviet specialists who were active in the "Third World" during that period, be it for a shorter or a longer time. This would average out to 6000 specialists and other qualified personnel per year.

In 1963 the CSSR acknowledged that it had sent 1200 Czech specialists to the developing countries in 1963.

At the Eighth Party Congress of the BDKJ in December 1964, Tito, as we have mentioned, stated that "more than 800 Yugoslav specialists from a variety of fields were active as instructors or consultants in the production of the developing countries." Bulgaria reports a figure of 850 experts who were sent in 1963. According to Polish statements 350 specialists were in the developing countries during 1963. The number of specialists the DDR had sent to these countries by 1963 was given as 150.[151]

Recently the Soviet bloc has sought to make the consultants and experts even more specialized in their respective fields. The intention is to train special expert groups:

1) for planning in the developing countries;

2) for geological and other research work: geologists, hydrologists, oil and mining experts for drilling and survey work;

3) for education and health;

4) for the construction and initial operation of plants and facilities; the export undertakings are supposed to supply special engineers and technicians for this purpose.

Finally, we shall list several examples of the kind of industrial projects that the Soviet bloc and China are constructing in the developing countries:

STEEL INDUSTRY

India's Bhilai steelworks takes first place among the steel and non-ferrous metal plants which the USSR has projected for the developing nations. This project was pledged in the Indo-Soviet Agreement of 2 February 1955 and was put into operation in 1960. The capacity

[149] Vneshnaya torgovlya (Moscow), No. 8/1965, p. 4.

[150] Voprosy istorii KPSS (Moscow), No. 4/1966, p. 21.

[151] Wolfgang Spröte, Gerhard Hahn, DDR Wirtschaftshilfe contra Bonner Neokolonialismus, East Berlin 1965, p. 140.

of this steelworks, which in addition to ingot steel and iron also produces rolled steel, coke, sulfuric acid, tar, and chemical fertilizer, was initially set at a million tons of steel annually. In an agreement of 12 February 1960 the Soviets contracted to increase this capacity to 2.5 million tons annually as part of India's third Five-Year Plan (1961-66).

According to an agreement of 25 January 1965, the USSR promised to construct a second large steel factory in India (in Bokaro) a project that had been rejected by the United States. Initially this factory is to produce 2.5 million tons of steel per year, which capacity is to be increased to 4 million later on.

Under the terms of a loan granted in November 1959, Czechoslovakia is constructing a foundry and drop forge in Ranchi. This plant is to have six sections: a steel foundry, a cast iron section, a nonferrous metal foundry, a drop forge, a steel rolling equipment section, and a surface finishing section.

Poland, under the terms of a 143 million-rupee loan to India, is to build an ironworks of 30,000-ton capacity in Agra. Also to be erected by Poland are facilities for copper and zinc processing.

Indonesia is to get two ironworks built with Soviet help. Ground was broken in May 1962 on the western tip of Java for one of these works, which is to produce 100,000 tons of steel annually. Components of this plant are to be a steel smeltery, a rolling mill, a thermoelectric power plant, and repair shops. A second ironworks of 250,000-tons capacity is to be built on Borneo under the terms of the Soviet-Indonesian Agreement of 24 February 1961.

In Egypt, the USSR will build or enlarge, twenty-one steelworks. Most prominent of these is the expansion of the steelworks at Heluan, initially constructed by the two West German firms of Krupp and Demag. This works, which is said to have a current annual capacity of 265,000 tons, is to be expanded to 1.5 million tons and is to have a rolling mill and slag processing plant added. The USSR contracted to deliver for installation at Heluan rolling equipment in the value of 36 million dollars. A cement plant, furnished by the USSR, is to process the slag produced in the steel making operation. Planned also for Heluan is a 300,000-ton capacity USSR cokery, as well as a coke-chemical plant.

The second steel combine for the UAR on the USSR building program is to produce 1 million tons of steel per year. This combine will consist of one blast furnace plant, one agglomeration factory, one coke-chemical plant, one steel foundry and one rolling mill.

Under the terms of the Soviet-Iraqi Agreement of 16 March 1959, the USSR is building a steelworks near Baghdad with an annual capacity of 60,000 tons of medium-to-excellent rolled steel. Part of this works is to be a cast iron pipe foundry of 5000 tons capacity and a die casting plant also of 5000 tons annual capacity.

Ceylon is getting a 90,000-ton capacity USSR steel foundry under the terms of the 25 February 1958 Soviet-Ceylonese Agreement. This project is planned in three stages. At first the plant is to produce wire and wire mesh from imported ore. Stage two provides for steel production from pig iron and scrap. Only upon plant completion is the steel to be made from local ore.

On 3 July 1964, a steel factory in Algeria with a yearly capacity of 350,000 tons of rolled steel was placed on the Soviet building program.

According to the agreement of 13 January 1966, the USSR wants to construct a steel combine in Isfahan (Iran) with a yearly capacity of 500,000 to 600,000 tons.

In Ghana, Soviet specialists were exploring the practicability of a steel mill and/or a ferromanganese plant.

Even Ethiopia, which received a USSR credit grant of 100 million dollars, is to get a small steel mill from the Soviet Union. Agreement for its construction is contained in the Protocol of 25 March 1960.

And finally, China will build a small ironworks in Cambodia on the basis of a nonrepayable grant of 5.6 million dollars. No details have thus far been published.

The following other nonferrous metal plants the Soviets are building should be mentioned: an aluminum plant in Indonesia, to be erected as part of the Asahan complex with a capacity of 70,000 tons bauxite, 18,000 tons aluminum and 12,000 tons of rolled aluminum; a metal refining plant planned for Ghana; a gold extraction plant in Ethiopia. Also, the USSR is participating in the extraction of gold and diamonds in Guinea.

MACHINE TOOL MANUFACTURE

Since the agreement of November 1957, the USSR building program for India has included the construction of a heavy-duty machine tool plant and a plant for mining machinery. Agreement reached in New Delhi in February 1960 calls for the machine tool plant to be built at Ranchi and the mining machinery plant at Durgapore. Each is to have a capacity of 140,000 tons of finished products annually, and their construction is to be within the framework of India's third Five-Year Plan. The Soviet organization, Prommach Export, and India's Heavy-duty Machine Tool Corporation agreed in March 1960 to an initial Soviet delivery of equipment valued at 128 million rupees for the plant. This was to bring plant capacity up to 45,000 tons in the first construction phase. Soviet contribution to the mining machinery plant for the first phase of construction is to be a 75 million-rupees equipment shipment, expected to result in an annual production rate of 30,000 tons of machinery. With this, a USSR credit that had been pledged India two years before was first called upon for the delivery of equipment.

The heavy machine factory in Ranchi was inaugurated on 15 December 1963, and the first section of the plant has started production. The USSR wants to build a precision tool factory in Kotah (Rjastan), and a second plant of this kind is to be constructed in the state of Kerala, also with Soviet help.

In May 1962 the Leningrad institutes put on the drawing boards a machine tool manufacturing project for the construction of heavy-duty power installations. This plant, to be built near Hardwar, Uttar Pradesh State, will produce steam and water turbines with generators up to 200,000 kw for a total annual capacity of 1.5 million kw.

The USSR is planning other machine tool manufacturing plants in India. They will be financed within the framework of the $375 million USSR loan grant to India for the latter's third Five-Year Plan.

Czechoslovakia is also building a plant for the manufacture of heavy-duty machine tools in India and another for heavy-duty power installations. The money comes from the 231 million rupees CSSR loan grant to India of November 1959. Equipment deliveries have been estimated at 35 million rupees for the first plant and 75 million for the second. A tractor manufacturing plant is to be erected with CSSR help in Baroda.

According to the agreement of January 1958, the USSR will assist in the construction of six machine tool manufacturing plants and of a shipyard in Egypt. One machine tool factory, in Heluan, with a capacity of 725 machine tool machines per year, is supposed to have started production. A plant for cutting tools in Cairo and a file factory in Meadi, with a yearly capacity of 400 pieces, have also been completed. A textile factory in Bilbeis is still under construction. The Soviets also intend to construct a large heavy machine construction plant in the UAR. The shipyard and dry dock in Alexandria have been completed. East Germany will build several freight car plants in Egypt and Poland a small shipyard in Alexandria.

Included on the USSR list of machine tool plants for the under-developed countries are three automobile repair shops in Afghanistan, one of which is in operation in Djangalak, a repair works for automobile and airplane engines in Kabul, and a factory for textile machinery, also in Kabul.

A factory producing agricultural machinery is to be built in Burma by the USSR, which is building a similar factory in Iraq, capable of an annual production of 12,000 tons or 30,000 items, as well as a factory producing electromotors, a freight car plant, a shipyard, and repair shops for diesel locomotives and passenger and freight cars. The USSR obligated itself to construct a machine building plant with a capacity of 25,000 to 30,000 tons of machine material in Iran.

Ghana is exploring the feasibility of a tractor assembly plant, with parts shipped in from the Soviet Union.

POWER STATIONS

In May 1962 Afghanistan put into operation the 90,000 kw hydro-electric power station at Pul-i-Khomri, three years abuilding with Soviet assistance. Soviet specialists are also supervising the construction of a 67,000 kw hydroelectric plant at Naglu on the upper Amu-Darya. This station is to supply the Uzbek Soviet Socialist Republic with current. The Soviets are erecting other hydroelectric plants at Sarobi (22,000 kw) and at the Djelalabad Dam (11,000 kw).

In India, in addition to several smaller power works, the Soviets are erecting a thermoelectric power station at Neyveli (Madras State). Its initial output of 250,000 kw is to be stepped up to 600,000 kw upon completion of the project. The first turbogenerator at this station was put into operation in May 1962. Under the terms of the 21 February 1961 agreement, the Soviets also contracted for construction of a hydroelectric plant on the right bank of the Bhakra. Total output, produced by four separate hydroelectric units, is to be 480,000 kw. Altogether, the USSR obligated itself to construct thirteen power plants in India with a total capacity of 2.7 million kw and a production of more than 8 billion kwh.

A diesel power station, built by Czechoslovakia in Gaziabad, was opened in the summer of 1962. Hungary also participates in India's power generating program.

At Egypt's Aswan High Dam the Soviets are building a 2.1 million kw capacity hydroelectric complex that is to produce 10-16 billion kwh of electrical power. Two 400,000-500,000 volt high-tension lines, each over 500 miles long, are to bring the power from Aswan to Cairo. Also planned is a 132,000-220,000 volt high-tension transmission line of over 600 miles in length.

According to the agreement of 22 September 1964 the USSR obligated itself to build another power plant in the UAR, in El Mex, with a capacity of 200,000 kw, also transmission lines and sub-stations in Maghagha and Kus. Also in Egypt, in Damanhur, East Germany is building a thermoelectric plant as well as a 220-mile-long high-tension transmission line with twenty-seven transformers and twenty-one relay stations. Hungary plans to build a 45,000 kw thermoelectric plant in el-Tabini. Czechoslovakia also has a power station of two turbines, each of 12,000 kw capacity, on its building program in Egypt.

Russia's Syrian electrification projects, planned since October 1957, are still largely on paper. Planned are a hydroelectric power generating project on the Euphrates with an initial capacity of 100,000 kw, to be raised ultimately to 750,000 kw and to include high-tension lines to Aleppo; two small hydroelectric plants on Lake Homs and in the Yarmug Basin; power plants at dams to be built at Rastan and Mharda to a total 10,000 kw; and one thermoelectric plant at Damascus and another at Aleppo of 10,000 kw each.

As part of Iraq's Tigris-Euphrates irrigation project the Soviets have contracted to build several power stations, among them a 345,000 kw-capacity hydroelectric plant at Chaditcha.

In Indonesia, the Soviet hydroelectric project on the Asahan River, with an initial capacity of 120,000 kw, deserves mentioning. East Germany also is building a small thermoelectric plant in this country. Czechoslovakia built the Timur power station in Indonesia.

The USSR is building a hydroelectric plant in Iran (the region of Nachitchewan) with a capacity of 40,000 to 60,000 kw. On 1 December 1962 the USSR promised to construct a hydroelectric plant at the Nam-Nien River in Laos with a turbine capacity of 8000 kw, also the construction of transmission lines. Cambodia is to receive a hydroelectric plant with a 50 kw capacity. On 14 December 1964 the USSR obligated itself to construct a hydroelectric plant in the Congo (Brazzaville) with a capacity of 1500 to 2000 kw.

Ceylon is to get two Soviet power plants, one on the Malvatu-Oya River, the other in the Kalu-Ganga Basin. Also built by the Soviets is a thermoelectric plant in Sana, Yemen. Nepal is to get a USSR power station, including transmission lines. In Guinea, as part of an industrial complex, the USSR plans to erect a hydroelectric plant on the Konkouré River seventy-five miles from Conakry. Annual output of this plant is to be 3 billion kwh of electrical power. On the Soviet foreign aid building schedule for Ghana is a hydroelectric plant on the Volta River with a 200,000 kw capacity and a transmission line of 150 miles. Hungary is making preliminary surveys for a hydroelectric plant on the Pra River.

CRUDE OIL INDUSTRY

Since 1957 Soviet and Rumanian experts have been oil prospecting in India. The USSR has shipped oil drilling rigs and special geophysical research equipment to India. Mention has already been made of the oil laboratory equipment, presented as a gift by the USSR to the city of Dehra, seat of India's Oil and Natural Gas Directorate. Drilling for oil and gas has been successful in Javalamukhi, Hoshiapur (Punjab), Cambay (Bombay), and Gauhati (Assam). In September 1959 the Soviets granted India a 25 million-dollar loan for an oil refinery at Barauni (Bihar) with a 2 million-ton crude oil capacity. In planning also as part of India's third Five-Year Plan is a refinery near Cambay. On the basis of the 21 February 1961 agreement the USSR is committed to build an oil refinery, together with an electric power station, in the state of Gudsharat. The refinery is to have a 2 million-ton crude oil annual capacity. In Cambay and Anklesvar Soviet specialists are prospecting for oil, together with India's Oil and Natural Gas Directorate.

Rumania, in 1958, granted India a 52.4 million-rupee loan for the construction of the first state-owned crude oil refinery. The refinery, located in Gauhati (Assam) and of an initial 750,000-ton capacity, was near completion in 1961. The original loan was allegedly stepped up.

In northern Syria Soviet oil specialists are conducting test borings. Oil refineries are planned in Kameshly and Karachuk.

Under the provisions of a 104.8 million-koruna loan Czechoslovakia has shipped to Syria the equipment for a 1 million-ton capacity oil refinery, located at Homs. Poland is constructing oil reservoirs in Egypt and Syria. Already completed are twenty reservoirs of a 52,-800,000-gallon total capacity.

Afghanistan, with USSR help, has built liquid fuel dumps at Kabul, Herat, Mazar-i-Sharif, Kysyl-Kala, Kelif, Pul-i-Khomri, and Pul-i-Metan. Further, the USSR is constructing an oil refinery with a yearly capacity of 50,000 to 60,000 tons. The agreement of 17 October 1963 stipulates that the USSR would help with the extraction of natural gas in the northern region of Afghanistan to the extent of 2 billion cubic meters per year. The USSR has constructed a natural gas pipeline to its border and the USSR will receive 1.5 billion cubic meters of natural gas from Afghanistan per year.

In Iraq the USSR is assisting in the expansion of the state-owned Iraqi Petroleum Company. Soviet specialists conduct geological and seismologic oil probings in a 150-square-mile area of the Dzariya Pik, Kirkuk, and Chanikin regions. When a British group of about 150 technicians was recalled from the state-owned oil refinery at Dauna, near Basra, in 1959, the USSR committed twenty-four Soviet oil specialists at this refinery.

Rumania is planning a refinery in Ceylon. In Egypt the Soviets are planning to build six oil refineries. The USSR is conducting borings at Kosseir, Safaga, Ras Gharib, and in the Abu Senina region. Refineries are being built near Alexandria, Suez, and Rahmi.

With Ethiopia the USSR concluded a protocol in March 1960 for the construction of a 500,000-ton capacity oil refinery, to be located either in Fort Assab or in Massana. Meanwhile, Soviet specialists are conducting geological surveys in Ethiopia.

In Iran the USSR is building a trans-Iranian natural gas pipeline of more than 650 miles for the delivery of at least 10 billion cubic meters of natural gas to the USSR per year.

Rumania is shipping oil equipment to Indonesia and Iraq, Russia is doing the same to Argentina in the amount of a 100 million-dollar loan. East Germany is outfitting an oil cracking installation near Rangoon in Burma.

CHEMICAL INDUSTRY

Afghanistan: USSR plans call for a Chemical Research Institute in Kabul.

Burma: Czechoslovakia is building a bicycle tire and tube factory.

Ceylon: a tire plant, using indigenous rubber, is being built with Soviet assistance near Colombo. An initial capacity of 250,000 tires and tubes annually is to be boosted to 360,000 upon plant completion.

India: here the Soviets are concentrating on the development of chemical centers in Bombay, Hyderabad, and Durgapore. Further Soviet undertakings in India include a synthetic rubber plant in Hyderabad; an antibiotics plant in Rishikesh; and a plant to produce drugs for treatment of endocrine glands. Development of the natural gas industry at Durgapore is planned for India's third Five-Year Plan. Czechoslovakia has supplied India with the equipment for outfitting a technical rubber goods plant. Hungary has licensed the production of chemical equipment. No facts are as yet available on a Soviet-planned large-scale chemical complex near Madras.

Indonesia: the USSR is building a superphosphate plant of a 100,-000-ton annual capacity in Southern Java. As early as 1956, concurrent with its 100 million-dollar loan grant to Indonesia, the USSR contracted the building of a treatment plant at a sulfur mine as well as the prospecting for sulfur and phosphate deposits. On the basis of a 30 million-dollar loan, Czechoslovakia is building a tire factory at Djakarta and is completely outfitting twelve chemical works. East Germany is supplying the equipment for a tire plant.

Iraq: Soviet bloc activity is concentrated on the buildup of chemical centers at Kirkuk, Samarra, and Basra. Among Soviet projects are a chemical works in Kirkuk which is to produce an annual 110,000 tons of sulfuric acid and 65,000 tons sulfur from the natural gas deposits of Northern Iraq; a nitrogen fertilizer plant at Basra with a 60,-000-ton annual output of ammonia and the production of ammonium sulfate and ammonium nitrate; and an antibiotics and pharmaceuticals plant for the production of penicillin, streptomycin, biomycin, tinctures, salves, pills, and the like. With Polish assistance, a synthetic plate factory is being built in Baghdad.

Syria: a chemical fertilizer plant in Homs and a caustic soda works in Latakia are on the Soviet list. East Germany is exporting the equipment for a synthetic silk factory in Aleppo.

Egypt: planned by the Soviets are a cokery, a caustic soda plant in el-Tabir, and a calcium works in Aswan. Czechoslovakia is building a galoshes factory in the el-Tahir Province. Hungary is offering the patents for forty medicines, and assists in the construction of a pharmaceutical works.

Ethiopia: a caustic soda plant is to be built in Massana with Soviet assistance.

ATOMIC ENERGY

With the intent of symbolizing the coequality of the backward nations, the USSR is erecting installations for the peaceful uses of atomic energy in Egypt, Indonesia, Iraq, Afghanistan, and Ghana. This is not only to add luster to Soviet prestige, but this type of aid agreement also enables the USSR to join in the prospecting for uranium, beryllium, and other elements important in atomic energy production. In Indonesia, for example, Soviet specialists explored a uranium deposit in Borneo and a beryllium find in Sumatra. The beryllium deposits in East Pakistan are also being exploited by Soviet technicians. The Soviets have thus far had little competition from the West in this field of endeavor; and more than in the industrial sector the USSR is in control of the atomic program, including atomic research and development and the training of indigenous nuclear physicists in the backward areas.

As early as 12 July 1956 the USSR concluded an agreement with Egypt on peaceful uses of atomic energy. Under the terms of this agreement the Soviets are building a nuclear physics laboratory, electrostatic generators, experimental reactors, and geological research stations. Soviet atomic experts and professors are sent to Egypt, and Egyptian personnel are being trained in the USSR. The first reactor of 2000 kw capacity was put into operation in Inchas on 29 July 1961.

With Indonesia the USSR concluded an atomic energy aid program on 1 July 1960. Indonesian specialists in nuclear physics, radiochemistry, and the application of radioactive isotopes in biology and agriculture are being trained in the Soviet Union. Indonesia already boasts atomic study centers at Bogar, Bandung, Djakarta, and Jogjakarta. An agreement of 13 May 1961 provides for a Soviet-run nuclear physics faculty at Djakarta University.

On 17 August 1959 an agreement with Iraq was signed in Moscow which provides for Soviet assistance in the construction of an atomic reactor, isotope labs, atomic research station, and for the training of Iraqi nuclear physicists.

According to an agreement of 28 February 1961, the Soviet wanted to construct a 2000-kw atomic reactor in Ghana. Soviet atomic experts were to assist in site selection, data collection, programming, reactor construction, and in putting the reactor into operation.

With India, the Soviet Union allegedly concluded an agreement on peaceful uses of atomic energy on 6 October 1961 in Vienna, seat of the International Atomic Energy Agency.

In an agreement of 5 September 1963, the USSR also reached an accord with Afghanistan on the cooperation in the peaceful use of atomic energy.

LICENSE SALES AND MIXED ENTERPRISES

Mention should be made of two new forms of collaboration with the underdeveloped nations, practiced at the moment by several Soviet bloc members. These are the sale of production licenses and the establishment of mixed enterprises.

All USSR aid agreements examined by us include the gratuitous offer to the backward nations of *copyrights, production techniques, technical data, and details of technological processes.* The only charge is the cost of preparing the source material. But some Soviet bloc members, especially Poland and East Germany, make a lucrative business out of the sale of licenses and pertinent technical data. East Germany even created a foreign trade agency called *Limex* for exploiting this type of "collaboration." In Poland, *Polservice,* an offshoot of the Bureau for Technical Services (CEKOP), handles the license sales. So far, nothing has been published on conditions and prices of the sale of licenses and technical data. But the fact that special agencies like *Limex* were created for these sales indicates their remunerativeness. At the Leipzig Fair, *Limex* is constantly engaged in concluding agreements for the copying of East German products on a license-fee basis. Thus East Germany sold to India the licenses for the erection of two machine tool factories, one motorcycle factory, one typewriter plant, and a film manufacturing plant. "The UAR obtained licenses for the manufacture of fireproof Jena glass; Guinea, for the production of radio parts; Cuba, for the manufacture of porcelain and radio parts." [151a]

[151a] K. H. Domdey, *Neokolonialismus oder sozialistische Wirtschaftshilfe,* East Berlin 1962, p. 82.

The second form of collaboration, engaged in by East Germany, Poland, and Rumania, consists of setting up mixed plants on the basis of so-called cooperation agreements. These plants, though located in underdeveloped countries, serve as much to supply the Soviet bloc partners as they play a role in the economy of the developing nations. The loans granted are considered as capital shares in these undertakings and Soviet bloc engineers are on the management staff.

Of this type of cooperative production, which calls to mind the Soviet-Mongolian Joint Stock Companies and similar enterprises, it is said: "A few, so far rather limited, examples of a direct cooperative system of production between the industry of a socialist country and a backward nation presage in our opinion a new form of collaboration of great promise. In one form of cooperation, the socialist country supplies technical assistance to the state, often also to a private firm, for the *mutual manufacture of products*. Assembling is done in the developing country, which also receives such component parts as cannot be produced locally from other socialist countries. In this system of cooperative production, the limits of purchases and deliveries are not dependent on market conditions, but are fixed at the cooperative plant on the basis of a mutually developed plan of production goals. Without doubt, the number of works and whole branches of industry that may be developed under this system of cooperative production will increase in proportion to the industrialization of the backward nations and their progressively more complicated economic structure. A promising aspect of this cooperation also is *the supply of assemblies to the socialist states from plants that were built with their help in the underdeveloped countries*." [152]

A few examples will show that these mixed enterprises are in fact feeder works for the production expansion of the Soviet bloc nation. Thus, e.g., a 100,000-spindle cotton spinning mill, erected in Egypt in Shibin el-Kom with East German help as a "mixed enterprise" is to supply textile mills in East Germany for five years with 3000 tons of yarn annually. Ghana built a fish meal plant with East German assistance. Its production is to go to East Germany. On the basis of cooperation agreements Rumania is supplying Indonesia with several mining and ore-processing plants, production of which is slated for Rumania, allegedly as compensation for the plants. Held up as model for this type of cooperation is an agreement between East Germany's DIA Chemical Equipment concern and India's Walchandnagar Industries, Ltd. This agreement concerns the construction of works in

---

[152] *Mirovaya ekonomika i mezhdunarodnie otnosheniya* (Moscow), No. 11/1962, p. 127. Italics added.

the oil cracking and oil mill industries. Section two of the agreement provides that during phase one—as it is called—DIA signs responsibility for India's share in the construction, as well as for all technological installations and the training of the technical personnel. DIA is also fully responsible for the sale of the works and the execution of sales contracts with Indian buyers. "During phase two these tasks are taken over by the Indian Cooperator. From now on, East Germany's engineers serve primarily as technical advisors."

Negotiations for this agreement are said to have been on the following basic principles: "East Germany furnishes the Indian Cooperator technical assistance by supplying engineer cadres and technical data; India's share in the construction will be stepped up at certain planned intervals in accordance with the capabilities of the Indian producer; the Indian government agrees to a continuous issue of import licenses for East Germany's share of installed equipment. The government also agrees to issue the Indian Cooperator a manufacturing license; East Germany's technical assistance is compensated for by payments due; cooperation is to be in two phases. Phase one: the DIA is contract partner of the ultimate Indian owner, including all commercial and technical commitments. Phase two: the Indian Cooperator becomes contract partner of the ultimate Indian owner." [153]

This cooperative production scheme is exhibited as a type of aid. What is not mentioned is that this system is also a type of aid for the economy of East Germany, Poland, and Rumania. The products manufactured in the mixed plants with the cheap labor and the raw materials of the underdeveloped nations serve to some extent to supply the economy of the countries named.

---

[153] Domdey, *Neo-Kolonialismus*, p. 81.

The Soviet Bloc and the
UN Foreign Aid Program

"During the past decade, aid to economically weak countries on an international scale within the framework of the United Nations has assumed ever-increasing importance."[154] This the Soviet bloc came to see only after 1954. Since 1 July 1950 the UN has furnished technical assistance to the backward nations through its Expanded Program of Technical Assistance under the guidance of the Technical Assistance Board (TAB). In January 1949 the UN Special Fund also was called into being as an international agency for technico-economical assistance. Only in June 1953 did the USSR decide on joining the UN technical assistance program, making its first financial contributions, all being voluntary, in 1954. The other Soviet bloc members, who also belong to the UN, later joined the Expanded Assistance Program.

By no means are all UN agencies that deal with technical and economic aid supported by the Soviet bloc. The International Bank for Reconstruction and Development, the International Monetary Fund, and the International Finance Corporation are villified as "tools of American imperialism," called into being in aid of private capitalism in the underdeveloped countries. Poland (since 1957) is the Soviet bloc's only member belonging to the Food and Agriculture Organization of the United Nations (FAO). The USSR refused, in 1945, to sign the statutes of this organization. It should be noted that the FAO disposes of over 30% of the Expanded Program of Technical Assistance

---

[154] *Friendly Assistance and Mutually Profitable Collaboration* (Russ.), Moscow 1959, p. 61.

funds, and that this organization sends more than 700 agricultural specialists to underdeveloped countries annually.

The USSR did not join UNESCO, which had been established in November 1945, until April 1954. Today, the following Soviet bloc members have also joined the organization: Albania, the Byelorussian SSR, Bulgaria, Poland, Rumania, Cuba, Mongolia, Yugoslavia, Hungary, the Ukrainian SSR, and Czechoslovakia. In most of these countries, commissions in support of UNESCO exist. Membership dues make up UNESCO's budget, though as part of the Expanded Program of Technical Assistance it also receives funds for its educational, scientific, and cultural aid programs from the Technical Assistance Board. UNESCO conferences and seminars provide Soviet bloc scientists and educators with ready-made contacts to the backward peoples. Contrariwise, the Soviet bloc also calls trade union, cooperative, and educational seminars for Afro-Asian and Latin American functionaries, with UNESCO representatives invited to lend an air of neutrality. A case in point was the Tashkent Trade Union Seminar of April 1961 in which Afro-Asian union representatives of all persuasions took part, and which at the same time served as a seminar for UNESCO and the World Federation of Trade Unions. Through UNESCO, the Soviet bloc dispatches experts to the backward peoples, and UNESCO scholarships pay for the tuition of Afro-Asian students at Soviet bloc universities.

The UN economic aid program is largely shaped by the Economic and Social Council (ECOSOC), created in October 1946, assisted by its regional commissions, the Economic Commission for Asia and the Far East (ECAFE), established in March 1947, the Economic Commission for Latin America (ECLA), established in June 1948, and the Economic Commission for Africa (ECA), established in April 1958. The council, of which the USSR is a standing member, and ECAFE are exploited by the Soviet bloc in the underdeveloped areas and in touting its own foreign aid concept as "the stage on which the two systems compete."

The USSR is excluded from membership in both ECLA and ECA but has advisory rights as an observer in meetings of the latter commission. "As of 1953, the USSR contributes to the UN's Expanded Program of Technical Assistance, and as of 1959 to the UN Special Fund. Voluntary contributions of the USSR (including the Ukrainian and Byelorussian Soviet Socialist Republics) to the Expanded Program of Technical Assistance and the Special Fund up to 1961 [i.e., from 1953 to end of 1960] amounted to 9.4 million rubles [around $10.5 million].

Another source states: "Total contributions to the UN Fund under the purview of the Expanded Program of Technical Assistance for the period 1950 to 1959 amounted to $235 million, of which the USSR, Byelorussian SSR, and Ukrainian SSR (all three as UN members share in the fund) provided more than $8 million (32.2 million rubles)." This means the Soviet Union contributed 3.4% of the total fund up to 1959. The same source goes on to say: "In the past two to three years total contributions of all members was between $30-32 million, of which the USSR total was 4.7 million rubles ($1.2 million)." [155] Again, a USSR ratio of 3.7-4%.

At the time the UN Special Fund was established, the Soviet delegation agreed to contribute annually the same amount to this fund as to the Expanded Program of Technical Assistance, i.e., the USSR $1 million, the Ukrainian SSR $125,000, and the Byelorussian SSR $50,-000.[156] But only 25% of the pledged amounts is supplied the UN by the Soviet Republics in freely convertible currency! [157] This means that the Soviet share in the UN aid program can be spent only in the ruble bloc, for the 25% in convertible currency is required to defray the expenses of Soviet experts engaged in administering the aid program. Soviet publications emphasize that 74% of the funds expended under the UN technical assistance program is for the upkeep of experts, 16% for scholarships, and 9% for the supply of equipment and materials.[158] Thus, the Soviet projects within the purview of the UN aid program in all likelihood must themselves be financed by the convertible contribution of other members. The Soviet press criticizes the insufficient interest the UN aid program shows in the Soviet bloc.

On this point, some figures: In 1957 the Expanded Program of Technical Assistance provided 2061 scholarships for students from underdeveloped countries. Of these, 246 went to the U. S., 246 to England, 199 to France, 135 to Holland, 128 to Italy, 173 to Denmark, 193 to West Germany, 95 to the USSR, 3 to Poland, and 3 to Czechoslovakia.[159] The USSR share, it turns out, is 4.6% in comparison to that country's financial contribution of 3.7-4%, of which 75% is in nonconvertible rubles!

The Soviet Union admittedly fares less well where it concerns the prorating of experts, sent to backward nations. (It must be remembered, though, that this item requires larger sums of foreign ex-

---

[155] *Friendly Collaboration and Mutually Profitable Aid* (Russ.), pp. 60-61.
[156] *ibid.*, p. 63.
[157] *International Economic Organizations and Agreements* (Russ.), Moscow 1961, p. 35.
[158] *Problems Concerning Aid for Economically Weak Countries* (Russ.), p. 213.
[159] *ibid.*, p. 214.

change.) Of a total of 2200 experts sent under the UN aid program to underdeveloped countries in 1959, the West supplied 1400, the USSR forty, and the rest of the Soviet bloc twelve. For the USSR this figure was 47 in 1960.[160] East Germany's political pundit, Domdey, claims: "It is striking how West Germany's contributions to the UN aid program certainly increased but, since the program offers only limited means of exploitation and expansion, they never became of any importance." [161]

The truth of the matter is that West Germany, according to official UN sources, in the period 1952-62 contributed a total of $9,650,700 to the UN expanded aid program, while East Germany's share has been nil. The "never of any importance" contribution of West Germany still is larger in 1961 and 1962 than that of the USSR. While the latter remitted $2 million to the UN fund for each of the two years, West Germany gave $2.12 million in 1961, and $2.62 million in 1962. Even the annual contributions of individual underdeveloped nations to the fund are larger than those of some Soviet bloc members. Brazil, for example, gave $687,400 in 1961, whereas Czechoslovakia's total offer for the period 1954-62 only came to $659,200. India's contribution for 1962 ($820,000) exceeds that of the 1956-62 contribution of Albania, Bulgaria, Rumania, and Hungary together ($515,000). Even a Soviet source admits the relatively large contributions to the fund by the backward nations: "It must be stated that not only the industrial nations, but the underdeveloped countries as well contribute to the UN aid fund . . . Thus as early as 1957 Brazil had contributed $832,000, India $525,000, Argentina $360,000, the UAR $130,000, Mexico $114,-000 and Indonesia $36,000." [162]

The following table compares the UN Fund contributions of Soviet bloc members with those of underdeveloped nations. Figures are from the UN reports.

---

[160] *Mezhdunarodnaya zhizn* (Moscow), No. 9/1961, p. 109.
[161] *Neo-Kolonialismus, op. cit.,* p. 165.
[162] *Problems Concerning Aid for Economically Weak Countries* (Russ.), pp. 211-12.

Contributions of Soviet Bloc and Selected Backward
Nations to UN Expanded Program of Technical Assistance[163]

Country	Period	Dollars	Country	Period	Dollars
Albania	1957-62	12,000	Afghanistan	1950-62	131,000
Bulgaria	1956-62	98,000	Burma	1950-62	279,500
Belorussia	1954-62	550,000	Ceylon	1950-62	226,000
Czechoslovakia	1954-62	659,000	Ghana	1957-62	349,800
Poland	1953-62	800,000	India	1950-62	5,820,000
Rumania	1956-62	116,000	Indonesia	1950-62	716,700
USSR	1953-62	12,000,000	Mexico	1952-62	785,500
Ukr. SSR	1954-62	1,375,000	Sudan	1956-62	624,600
Hungary	1956-62	289,900	UAR *	1950-62	1,255,100

"Up to 1960 Soviet contributions included 20.1 million rubles ($5.025 million) for India; 1.2 million rubles ($300,000) for Afghanistan; 1 million rubles ($250,000) for Burma; 1 million rubles ($250,000) for Pakistan; 1 million rubles ($250,000) for UAR; 600,000 rubles ($150,000) for Ceylon, and 600,000 rubles ($150,000) for Chile." [164] In India, the USSR, as part of its collaboration in the UN aid program, has contracted for construction of a technological institute in Bombay; the equipping of the Statistical Institute in Calcutta, especially with computers; the establishment of tuberculosis aid stations, and the opening of trade schools. In Pakistan the Soviet will supply drill rigs for irrigation projects; in Afghanistan, the equipment for two hospitals and a physics faculty in Kabul; in Chile, equipment for a university; in Syria, the outfittings for laboratories at Damascus University; in Ceylon, equipment for hospitals; and in Mexico, geophysical and meteorological equipment. "During 1955-56 alone, Soviet economic agencies conducted five seminars for eighty-two specialists from eighteen developing nations within the purview of the UN technical aid program." [165]

---

[163] *Technical Assistance Newsletter,* Vol. II, No. 8 New York, August/September 1962, cutoff date, 1 June 1962.
* Egypt: 1959-62 incl. Syria.
[164] *Mezhdunarodnaya zhizn* (Moscow), No. 9/1961, p. 109.
[165] *International Economic Organizations* (Russ.), Moscow 1960, p. 118.

The Training of Functionaries
and Development of a National Elite

A review of Soviet bloc politics in the backward areas, where communist parties are few and far between and of no great help, calls to mind a 1919 cartoon appearing in a Soviet youth magazine. The cartoon shows Lenin and Clemenceau, who is asking: "And where do you think you'll get the troops?" Lenin's answer: "I plan on taking yours!" As early as 1902 Lenin, in his *What Shall We Do?*, hammered out the guidelines for this taking of "troops." With certain modifications they still apply in the entire Soviet bloc. Vis-à-vis the old, backward, peasant-ridden and illiterate Russia, Lenin came to the conclusion that "Social consciousness must be brought to the inchoate masses from the outside." This he held to be the task of a selected elite of trained professional revolutionaries, such as characterized the Bolshevik party, directed from abroad, in Czarist Russia. Parallels? Fritz Schatten writes about the backward nations that, here too "subversive and disruptive ideas entered from outside as intellectual contraband." [166] In addition, a national leadership, by means of politburos, central committees, unity parties, steered or autochthonous democracy, and drawing on experiences gathered in colonial days at Western universities in humanism and liberalism but also on lessons learned from communism, in many backward nations endeavors today to awaken a national consciousness among the illiterate, "still immature people." Here indeed is still virgin terrain for Soviet bloc political maneuvering or for competitive action, as signalized by the controversy between Daniel Sohod and Sekou Touré in Guinea.

---

[166] Fritz Schatten, *Afrika schwarz oder rot?*, Munich 1961, p. 346.

A history of the communist cadres is yet to be written. It is known that Lenin's professional revolutionaries were liquidated during the Great Purges of 1936-38, to be replaced by Stalin with the Party cadres who "decide everything." To the technicians of power, "cadre" connotes a carefully groomed young elite that may be committed on all sectors of the social front. But the cadres in the Soviet Union underwent and were made to undergo several metamorphoses. For the first industrialization phase, beginning in 1928, the Party cadres still called on aid from abroad, and Stalin's *Problems of Leninism* was their only "spiritual armory." But even in the 1930s, Stalin was obliged to include in the cadres the scientists, engineers, and technicians that the Party apparatus bore down on and had often decimated. Under the thesis of competition with capitalism in the age of automation and electronics, the "techno-scientific cadres" came to "decide everything." The new cadres have largely pigeonholed the *Foundations of Marxism-Leninism*, taking as guidelines to action the new discoveries of science and technology. And just as Lenin, in 1902, wanted to carry "social consciousness to the masses," the present-day Soviet leaders must ram ideology down the techno-scientific intelligentsia's throat to stem the tide of "de-ideologization."

The Soviet bloc's training aid policy for the backward peoples runs on a double track, is based on Soviet experience, and fits in with the overall strategy. The two tracks are:

1. Schooling of party, trade union, youth, and women functionaries, as well as the leadership cadres of other mass organizations, in doctrinal communism. These functionaries are trained to gain mass influence during the first phase of their country's development, to build up mass organizations, and to take over in the second phase.

2. Ostensibly nonideological training of a national elite of scientists, technicians, and engineers. This is initially to assure at least a techno-industrial psychological bond between the backward nations' technical intelligentsia and the Soviet bloc.

Party Schooling

So-called "Eastern Courses" were inaugurated at the Soviet People's Commissariat for Nationalities as early as 1918. Their primary purpose, however, was to train functionaries for the former Czarist regions in the Middle East. In May 1921 these "Eastern Courses" became the Communist University of Eastern Workers in Moscow (Russ. abbreviation: KUTV).[167] The student body of this university came partly from present-day Soviet Asia and partly from some of the Near Eastern and Southeast Asian countries. Except for the Union of South Africa, there were initially no students from any African nations south of the Sahara. No less than 700 students were enrolled at the end of 1921.[168] In 1925 Stalin spoke of fifty Eastern nations and national groups represented at this university,[169] a figure which he put at seventy-four in 1927.[170]

Until 1928, the leading communist functionaries for Asian countries were trained at the Communist University of Eastern Workers under a three-year program. With the expansion of the so-called Lenin School of the Comintern, which had been established at the end of 1926, this school took over the training of Party cadres for Oriental countries. KUTV henceforth largely trained medium-ranking functionaries under foreshortened programs.

Stalin, since 1925, had personally set the guidelines for the curriculum to be taught at this Eastern University. In a speech of 18 May 1925 before the student body of the old "Communist University of

---

[167] *Great Soviet Encyclopedia* (Russ.), 1938 ed., under: KOMVUSI.
[168] Walter Z. Laqueur, *The Soviet Union and the Middle East,* London 1959, p. 42.
[169] *Der Marxismus und die nationale und koloniale Frage,* Berlin 1953, p. 265.
[170] Stalin, *Werke,* East Berlin Vol. 9, p. 313.

Eastern Workers," he exhorted his listeners to attend to the main task, the struggle against a compromise-prone bourgeoisie and above all against India's Congress Party.[171]

Today, Soviet publications openly admit to the error in this university orientation. Thus the journal of the Soviet Institute of World Economics and International Relations wrote in April 1962: "Since 1920, there have been efforts afoot to deny an anti-imperialistic role to the bourgeoisie. Largely, these efforts were based on Stalin's misconceptions concerning the developmental prospects of the national liberation movement. In his 1925 speech, "On the political tasks of the University of the Eastern Peoples," Stalin, with India in mind, said: "The firepower must be concentrated on the compromise-prone bourgeoisie." He also assigned the proletariat of the colonies and dependent nations the task of "the buildup of a national-revolutionary bloc of workers, peasants, and the revolutionary intelligentsia against the bloc of the compromise-prone bourgeoisie and imperialism." The "compromise-prone bourgeoisie" was understood to mean "India's National Congress." [172]

Despite all criticism, not much has changed concerning the political practices of these universities. A 1959 demonstration, planned by African students at Moscow's Lomonosov University against the French atomic tests in the Sahara, was banned because Khrushchev at the time was preparing his Paris trip, hopeful of success. Students of the 1920s could have reported similar incidents. When Moscow sought to get on a good footing with Ankara, the teachers at KUTV got the word to soft-pedal their criticism so as not to endanger Turco-Soviet relations.[173]

The Communist University of Eastern Workers was closed in 1936, after its teachers and even students had been arrested during the Great Purges.[174]

A second "Eastern University" of early communism was the Sun Yat-sen University, whose first President was Karl Radek. This institution was the product of Russian Bolshevism and Chinese nationalism. Its founding dates back to 1925, the year of Sun's death. In 1927 the university boasted an enrollment of about 600 Chinese students.[175] In contrast to KUTV, the Sun Yat-sen University was open to the Kuo-

---

[171] Stalin, *Werke*, East Berlin, Vol. 7, pp. 115-31.
[172] *Mirovaya ekonomika i mezhdunarodnie otnosheniya* (Moscow), No. 4/1962, p. 81.
[173] Walter Z. Laqueur, *The Soviet Union and the Middle East*, p. 107.
[174] *ibid.*, p. 116.
[175] Mary A. Nourse, *400 Millionen—die Geschichte der Chinesen*, Berlin 1936, p. 319.

mintang, especially to its left wing. The curriculum was specially tailored for China, and the main objective of this institution was to improve the chances of a communist party that as yet boasted only a few members in the Kuomintang Party during the 1920s.

With the schism between Chinese nationalism and communism in 1927, and after Moscow had excommunicated even the Kuomintang's left wing, the Sun Yat-sen University was dissolved in the early 1930s. Its importance in the training of Chinese communist cadres is often overestimated. Since 1935, Mao Tse-tung has had his functionaries trained at home, and the Sun Yat-sen University today is no longer even mentioned in Chinese party literature.

With the closing of these two specialist schools for the training of communist functionaries, there was no centrally-organized East-oriented indoctrination center in all of the communist area for nearly twenty years. Even the Soviet Office of Oriental Studies hibernated until 1955. Training was limited in the USSR during these years (also in China since 1936) to larger groups of Eastern immigrants. For the USSR these included the Koreans that had settled in the region of the Uzbek towns of Chokand, Fergana, and Andishan since 1929-30, as well as the Kurds of the "Shorsh" organization (later the Kurdish Democratic Party of Iraq) who, under their leader Mulla Mustafa el Barzani, had left Iraq for the USSR after the abortive Kurd uprising of 1944. They too were temporarily settled in Uzbekistan and Turkmenistan.

The French Communist Party has attempted since 1946 to school the functionaries of its part-time ally in Africa, the *Rassemblement Démocratique Africain* (RDA).

Only since the mid-1950s has the Soviet bloc again taken up the centralized training of functionaries from the backward nations. These are to be schooled "to represent the future movement in the current (national) movement." The present-day program has assumed proportions that make earlier Soviet tries look puny by comparison. This type of schooling is in addition to the training aid furnished under economic assistance (schooling of scientists, engineers, and technicians within the Soviet bloc) and includes training of propagandists, organizers and "technicians of power," that is, of party, trade union, youth, student, women, as well as of cooperative functionaries from Asia, Africa and Latin America.

It is not true that party functionaries from backward nations largely receive their training at the Party's top level schools, such as that of the Soviet Communist Party's Central Committee or the Karl Marx University near Berlin. Only a few selected top-echelon functionaries of the (largely banned) communist parties of Afro-Asian countries have appeared at these schools in Soviet bloc nations. Only the communist parties of India and, until 30 September 1965, Indonesia trained their own functionaries in their own countries. Understandably enough, little information is available about these training sites for party functionaries from underdeveloped areas, for their existence is surrounded with conspiratorial secrecy. It has become known that the functionaries of Iran's Tudeh Party get their training at East Berlin and Prague schools and that Bulgaria is training Turkish, and China was training Algerian, functionaries. Czechoslovakia runs training schools for functionaries of Syria's Communist Party and the Institute for Latin American Affairs at the Central Committee of China's Communist Party is not only a research institution, but serves also as a place of study for Latin American Party students. Since the Twenty-Second Party Congress put heavy emphasis on a buildup of communist parties in the backward nations, it may be assumed that this type of cadre training will be expanded in the Soviet bloc.

Cuba, designated by Moscow as Soviet bloc nation No. 14, presents a more recent example of party schooling. Here, with Bulgarian help, a Georgi Dimitrov School was opened at Havana University in September 1961. Purpose of this school is to train budding functionaries for the new unity party. The same purpose is served by Havana's Carlos Marx School, for which East Germany's Karl Marx University is godparent and for which the East German government supplied the entire physical plant. Also schooled at these two party institutions are cadres for party and trade union work in the other Latin American republics. In addition, it is claimed that training schools have been opened in Cuba for some of the sub-continent's banned communist parties.

Training of Trade Union Cadres

"Never forget, the most important school for the worker functionary is the class struggle in which he and his classmates are engaged. That is the real university, whereas this is but a kind of evening school for apprentices." [176] In these words Louis Saillant, Secretary General of the World Federation of Trade Unions (WFTU) characterized the role of Budapest's WFTU Trade Union School. This "school of class warfare" was established in 1953. Directed by Jean Marillier, its instructors are furnished by the WFTU, as well as by the trade union centers of the Soviet bloc and France's communist CGT. Generally, this trade union school trains Afro-Asian and Latin American functionaries in three-month courses. "As early as 1953-55 a total of 140 unionists from Africa, Asia, and Latin-America had finished a three-month course, organized by the WFTU with the help of the Central Council of Hungary's trade unions . . . thirty-eight unionists from eleven African countries took part in the course run by the WFTU in Budapest from 31 August to 28 September 1959 for African trade union functionaries." [177]

Course titles reveal the training objective of this Budapest WFTU Trade Union School. The following subjects are taught:

1) *History of colonialism:* its evolution and inevitable breakdown; birth of the working class.

2) *The liberation struggle:* the national liberation movement, the role of the working class and the trade unions.

3) *Economic and social problems of the newly developing nations.*

---

[176] *Die Weltgewerkschaftsbewegung* (East Berlin), No. 11/1959, p. 17.
[177] *ibid.*, p. 15.

4) *Role of the trade unions and their organizational structures:* the democratic trade union, its methods of operating, its leadership.

5) *Unity:* prerequisite for successful class struggle.

6) *The importance, the themes, and the types of propaganda in the struggle of the working class.*

7) *Several forms of social action:* the role of the trade unions in organizing the workers' struggle for better living conditions.

8) *The role of trade unions in the safeguarding of social security within the framework of current Labor Law.*

9) *The situation of the agricultural laborers and small farmers:* the mass organizing of agricultural laborers, the close relation between the working class and the small farmers.

10) *Measures safeguarding and guaranteeing the rights and the freedom of trade unions.*

11) *The mission of the trade unions in the struggle for peace and peaceful coexistence.*

12) *The historical imperative of the establishment and development of the WFTU:* its role in the reestablishment of unity, international solidarity, social progress, peace, and national independence.[178]

At the graduation exercises of the aforementioned 1959 trade union course for Africans, Louis Saillant declared, entirely in line with Soviet bloc strategy: "On this African continent, where the young proletariat is arising and the young trade union movement developing, the bourgeoisie also has a goal that in its own eyes may well seem to justly protect its class interests: it seeks to spread obscurantism in questions relating to daily life, seeks to intensify the contradictions inherent in private life and daily work only to hide them again . . . In the heat of the great anti-imperialist battle, in which we stand shoulder to shoulder with all the people in the world to destroy imperialism and to oppose it with the most powerful force possible, *we must also never lose sight of the strengthening of our own special class forces.*"[179] An African graduate of another Soviet bloc trade union school summarizes the experience gained in these words: "First, to weaken the enemy camp, we must drive out the white capitalists. Next come the black capitalists. Sékou Touré and Lumumba are not bad for a beginning. With them, we can chase out the white capitalists. When that is done, we need other leaders."[180]

Other trade union training schools of signal importance are the FDGB Fritz Heckert University in Bernau near Berlin and the FDGB Institute for Foreign Students in Leipzig-Leutzsch. (Translator's note:

[178] *Deutsches Industrieinstitut* (Cologne), Berichte zu Gewerkschaftsfragen, (Hamburg), No. 5/1960, p. 12.
[179] *Die Weltgewerkschaftsbewegung,* (East Berlin), No. 11/1959, pp. 17-18.
[180] *Die Welt,* (Hamburg), 11 August 1960.

the FDGB or *Freier Deutscher Gewerkschaftsbund,* literally: Free German Federation of Trade Unions, is East Germany's government-sanctioned trade union organization.) Under the Soviet bloc's division of labor scheme, East Germany and the FDGB have been especially singled out for the training of African trade union functionaries. The Berlin FDGB Fritz Heckert University with its eighteen-month course schools African labor leaders. Though the university itself was opened in 1952, the first course for foreigners was given only in 1959.[181] The school's director, Professor Dr. Karl Kampfert, member of East Germany's Socialist Unity Party, has put the initial enrollment in 1959 at fifty African trade union students, a figure that is to have reached a hundred in 1960. In view of the school's limited capacity, a higher attendance figure of African students or students from any other underdeveloped area is unlikely, for also studying at this school in addition to the African and some Asian students are unionists from East Germany and some other Soviet bloc nations. At the time of the school's tenth anniversary in 1962 the East German news agency ADN reported a 60,000-volume school library, as well as an extensive building program that would permit an enrollment of 500, with a dormitory capacity of 450.[182] On 23 March 1963 the FDGB school at Bernau graduated its third eighteen-month Afro-Asian class. A "diploma of the Trade Union University Fritz Heckert" was presented to ninety-three labor leaders from twenty-one Afro-Asian countries. It was reported at the graduation ceremony that the school had successfully graduated about 200 students from more than twenty Afro-Asian countries since 1959. It should be said that the training program for Afro-Asian functionaries is entirely divorced from that of the courses for German and Soviet bloc labor leaders. The two groups come together only at political lectures during so-called social gatherings.

In July 1960 the East German labor union press had announced the founding in Leipzig-Leutzsch of an FDGB Institute for Foreign Students. Actually opened 1 September 1960, the school was officially dedicated 22 September 1960. It offers an eight-month course to functionaries from nearly every African nation. But unionists from Europe and Asia are also to study here, and plans called for a 300-student capacity by 1963. The seminar for African unionists is conducted in English and French.[183] "Seventy functionaries from eighteen countries attended the first class at the Leipzig school, among them labor leaders from Ghana, Guinea, Nigeria, the Congo, Togo, Cameroon, and Somalia, from Angola, the Ivory Coast, Senegal, and Niger,

[181] *Allgemeiner Deutscher Nachrichtendienst,* East Germany, 16 May 1962.
[182] *ibid.,* 9 January 1962.
[183] *Tribüne* (East Berlin), 26 July 1960; *Der Arbeitgeber,* 5 March 1961.

from Sierra Leone, Morocco, Mauritius, Zanzibar, and the Central African Republic. The lesson plan of the eight-month course, taught in English and French, included questions on international labor union solidarity and problems concerning youth work and mass organizations. At the dedicatory ceremonies on 22 September 1960 Herbert Warnke underscored the goal of the study course as exemplified in the curriculum: "The young African labor movement needs cadres that are familiar with the problems of union organizing and with the science-oriented interests of the working class." [184] The Africa seminaries at this institute, a report reveals, are not conducted only by propaganda experts and FDGB hacks but also by Africans themselves who have completed their studies at the FDGB Fritz Heckert University and are now assigned as instructors at the FDGB Institute for Foreign Students.

The Central Council of Soviet Trade Unions did not organize "Classes for the Training of Trade Union Cadres for the Countries of Asia, Africa, and Latin America" until 1961. These took the form of three separate courses, taught in Moscow, for African, Asian, and Latin American students. By early 1963 a total of over 100 unionists attended these courses.

The example of an "Africa Course" at the Central School for the Revolutionary Labor Movement in Czechoslovakia, located near Prague, shows the intensity and the methods with which this labor functionary training is conducted in the Soviet bloc. This five-week course was taught in the summer of 1961, with twenty-five labor leaders, between ages twenty and thirty, from ten African countries attending. Our description of the course follows the statements made by the man in charge, Jaroslav Thele, who said: "Preparations for this course took a full year." [185] Six months before the course started, a special training staff of thirty members was readied for the twenty-five students, to prepare lecture texts and translate them into English and French. These texts served as background for discussions, conducted in two language groups of twelve and thirteen members each.

This extraordinary outlay for only twenty-five students was certainly not made for the sake of thorough training. Rather, it points to the fact that here was trained a small group that, equipped with handouts and lecture texts, was to be enabled upon graduation to take over trade union schooling in their own countries. The trend of this schooling is revealed in the subject matter of the three lecture series at the Prague institute:

---

[184] Fritz Schatten, *Africa schwarz oder rot?*, *op. cit.*, p. 322; *Tribüne* (East Berlin), 23 September 1960.

[185] *Die Weltgewerkschaftsbewegung* (East Berlin), No. 11-12/1961, pp. 57-58.

1.) *Some indispensable basic principles:* a synopsis of the history of human society; analysis of imperialism; origin, present position, and significance of the socialist world system in international politics; the basic principles of capitalist and socialist economics.

2.) *Origin and mission of trade union organizations during the capitalist epoch in the struggle for economic and social justice, for progress, and for peace:* origin, development, and role of the WFTU and other international trade union organizations (especially from the viewpoint of trade union unity in Africa); the upswing in the struggle for national liberation and the disintegration of the imperialistic colonial system; the socialist world system and the nature of its aid to the economically retarded nations; Africa's agricultural problems and the position and tasks of the trade unions toward a solution of these problems in conjunction with the question of a tight alliance with the peasantry; an analysis of social forces from a class viewpoint and their role in the national liberation movement.

3.) *Position and tasks of the trade unions during the construction of Socialism:* basic principles of the structure and working methods of trade unions; planning and management of the national economy and the role of trade unions in mobilizing the wage earners for participation in management; role of trade unions in raising living standards and trade union activities in the fields of culture and public enlightenment.

The above instructional guide leaves no doubt that the Prague course is a "cadre factory," to which then as now applies Lenin's thesis: "Trade unions are schools of communism!" The aforementioned course director, Jaroslav Thele, points out that the organizers of the Prague trade union course drew on the experiences of the FDGB Fritz Heckert University, the WFTU, *and the international seminars of UNESCO.* These international seminars, within the framework of WFTU collaboration with UNESCO, are to assist "in the developing of trade union cadres that deal with cultural questions." It is openly admitted "that a thousand roads lead to unity of the workers." [186]

The first WFTU-UNESCO seminar was held in Bucharest as early as 1958. Interesting comments on it are found in several contributions to the communist trade-union journal *Die Weltgewerkschaftsbewegung* (literally: world trade union movement), including an address by Louis Saillant and a contribution by Monsieur Paul Lengrand, UNESCO representative, entitled "Collaboration between UNESCO and WFTU Continues." [187] A second WFTU-UNESCO

---

[186] *Die Weltgewerkschaftsbewegung* (East Berlin), No. 8/1961, p. 27.
[187] *Die Weltgewerkschaftsbewegung* (East Berlin), No. 4/1958, pp. 23, 24, and 26; see also No. 3/1958, p. 36.

seminar, under the motto, "The Workers' Road to Culture and Education," took place in Tashkent from 9-30 April 1961, with forty representatives of twenty-five countries participating. A total of twenty-two trade union centres were represented, among them five from Asia, five from Africa, four from Latin America, and eight from Europe. Thirteen organizations belonged to the WFTU, eight were listed as independent unions (among them Japan, Ghana, Mali, the UGTAN, and Egypt), the *Union Marocaine du Travail* was registered as a member of the International Confederation of Free Trade Unions (ICFTU). "Basis of discussion were seven addresses delivered by Professors A. Leontyev (USSR), S. Asimov (Uzbekistan), I. Teoreanu (Rumania), J. Mourir (France), A Forni (Italy), P. Lengrand (UNESCO representative), and A. Pizarro (FISE representative).[188] Six of the seven addresses were thus made by representatives of communist trade unions. Obviously, the WFTU and the Soviet bloc exploit this type of trade union seminar as a springboard for their Afro-Asian, and Latin American training programs.

But the Soviet bloc has also begun to establish trade union schools within the backward countries themselves. In Cuba the WFTU constructed a union school for the training of union functionaries from the Latin American countries. Better known is the UGTAN School of Dalaba, Guinea, established 1959 with help of the WFTU and serving to train trade union functionaries for six to seven French-speaking African countries. The "independent" UGTAN secretary general, Diallo Seydov, openly admitted to an intimate tie-up of this school with the WFTU. "Our plans," he said, "will succeed because we are not alone. There are other forces working with us, here in Africa and in the entire world. There is the fraternal force of the WFTU that stands beside us and supports us and that we clasp close to our hearts . . . you know the trade union school here in Dalaba, which the UGTAN has erected with the WFTU's fraternal help. Some of us have already attended it." [189] Instructors were exchanged between the Trade Union School Dalaba and East Germany's FDGB. The chairman of the latter, Herbert Warnke, in February 1960 lectured in Dalaba on "The role of the FDGB against the neofascist and neocolonial policies of the Bonn Government." In May 1960 Dialloy Seydov lectured on "Problems of trade union activity and trade union unity in Africa" at the FDGB Fritz Heckert University. During his trip to Guinea and Ghana in February 1960, Warnke made "concrete agreements for close collaboration with UGTAN. Similar agreements were also made with Guinea's trade unions as

[188] *Die Weltgewerkschaftsbewegung* (East Berlin), No. 8/1961, p. 27.
[189] *Die Weltgewerkschaftsbewegung* (East Berlin), No. 10/1960, p. 29.

well as Ghana's TUC . . . where it concerned advisory meetings on the training of cadres for the trade-union movement." [190]

The results of these agreements were not long in coming. After the model of the FDGB Fritz Heckert University, the *Université Ouvrière Africaine* was opened in Conakry on 3 December 1960. Professor Kampfert, director of the FDGB school, had rushed from Bernau to Conakry especially for the opening ceremonies. Up to August 1962, the Conakry school had trained a total of 275 African trade unionists from Angola, Mozambique, Cameroon, Nigeria, Niger, Senegal, the Congo, Ghana, and Guinea in the spirit of the Pan-African trade union ideas of the Casablanca group. In addition to African teachers, the university faculty included German, French, and English instructors of the WFTU.

After the *Université Ouvrière Africaine* had been enlarged (the new buildings had been built in Conakry with DDR and FDGB aid), the union school in Dalaba lost its international and Pan-African character. It too has been seeking to Africanize its teaching staff and to free itself of the influence of the WFTU in recent years. Other schools for the training of functionaries from backward nations for communist front and contact organizations may be briefly mentioned. The training of journalists from the African, Asian and Latin American countries is one of the tasks of the communist International Journalist's Organization (IJO) which has its headquarters in Prague. This organization equipped an International Center for the Training of Journalists from the Developing Countries in Hungary. Technicians and editors for African news agencies are being schooled in Roztes (CSSR).

The School of Solidarity, which is headed by the Association of Journalists of the DDR and is located in Buckow near Berlin, conducts special courses for African journalists. Altogether sixty-three Africans had graduated after the end of the first two courses. During the third ten-month course, completed 17 September 1965, twenty-two Africans participated, from Ghana, Kenya, Nigeria, Sierra Leone, Somalia, Southwest Africa, Uganda and Tanzania. The fourth course has thirty participants.[191]

Since spring 1961 Conakry also boasts an African School of Journalism, established with the aid of Prague's communist International Journalists Organization and including Czech, Polish, and Guinean press functionaries on its teaching staff. At the time of its establishment in May 1961 at Bamako, the Union of Pan-African Journalists decided to conduct further seminars for African journalists. Both

---

[190] *Die Weltgewerkschaftsbewegung* (East Berlin), No. 5/1960, pp. 20-21.
[191] *Neue Deutsche Presse* (East Berlin), No. 3/1965, p. 5, and No. 10/1965, p. 3.

the International Journalists Organization and the communist Organization of International Radio and Television agreed to support the founding of a second African school of journalism.

An Afro-Asian Youth College exists near Prague under the aegis of the International Union of Students (IUS) and the World Federation of Democratic Youth (WFDY). The WFDY has set up a specific scholarship fund for students from backward nations. "In the academic year 1958/59, the IUS, through its membership organizations, offered 132 scholarships to students from Africa, Asia, and Latin America. This was increased to 139 for the academic year 1959/60." [192]

The "Wilhelm Pieck Junior College of the Free German Youth" near Berlin, under the heading of Foreign Youth Education Program, has offered courses to young students from Asia and Africa since 1958. A special African class was inaugurated at this school in 1960. On 8 May 1962 the school began a six-month international course for African and Latin American youth leaders. Since 1958 this youth school has graduated 164 students from thirty-eight countries. The school library boasts 45,000 volumes in seven languages. A teaching staff of seventy and nine simultaneous interpreters conduct the training program. Subjects taught include political economy, history of the labor movement, and themes dealing with friendship among nations and peaceful coexistence.

The Leipzig German College of Physical Culture, founded in 1950, began to offer short courses in May 1961 in the training of African sport functionaries and in physical training. By the end of 1961, enrollment already included youth from Ghana, Guinea, Mali, Togo, Nigeria, Morocco, and Egypt, also from Cuba and Japan.

The Central Cooperative School of Jiloviste near Prague and the Consumers Cooperative School in East Germany's Blankenburg train cooperative functionaries from Algeria, Burma, Ceylon, India, Ghana, Kenya, Morocco, Mali, Togo, and Uganda.

The German School of Film Art in East Germany's Postdam-Babelsberg, as early as 1961, trained eighteen students from twelve foreign countries, including Ghana, Algeria, Sudan, Iraq, Jordania, Peru, and Brazil. A special study plan was designed for students from backward countries. "On graduation they can start work as directors or cameramen with dramaturgical film-technical know-how. Some 70% of the students come from worker and peasant families and receive a basic monthly stipend of 190 D-marks. About 40% are co-ed students." [193]

---

[192] *International Economic Organizations* (Russ.), *op. cit.*, p. 873.
[193] *Allgemeiner Deutscher Nachrichtendienst* (East Berlin), 12 March 1962.

Our outline of the Soviet bloc training measures for the schooling of party and front organization cadres for the backward nations is by no means exhaustive. It is clear, however, that an across-the-social-scale approach is in evidence in the bloc's political training program Additionally, the formal courses we listed are continuously supplemented by (usually) four-week international seminars, such as "international students seminars," "collectives seminaries," and the like. These seminars are conducted in Soviet bloc countries. Thus far, the Soviet bloc has met with no major trouble in its training program of young people from backward nations, who can serve as cadres in all phases of social life. Only a few cases are known where Asian or African students have dropped out of the schools listed. One reason, of course, is that the schools take in those who already are linked to communism or its front organizations; another, that few students were ever exposed to any other educational system. After all, student selection is entirely in the hands of Soviet bloc Party, trade union, youth, students, and similar organizations.

In the matter of cadre selection and training the Soviet bloc is vastly experienced. But, thanks largely to the USSR's industrial background, the bloc's capability of producing a technical intelligentsia of engineers and scientists for industry, agriculture, and the construction field is also nothing to sneer at. In the USSR alone some 190,000 engineers are currently trained annually. By 1970, this figure is to reach a quarter-million. In ten years the Soviet Union expects to produce an annual crop of some 2.5 million engineers and scientists. Still, where it concerns the education of a national elite in the underdeveloped countries, especially in its didactic methods, the Soviets— as their own pedagogues and development experts are bound to admit—are as yet a long way from their goal.

Schooling the National Elite

Even the Soviet bloc has come more and more to realize that engineers, technicians, and the budding scientific elite have a share in deciding the fate of the new national states. Through some few students from backward areas had studied in the USSR ever since 1956, it was not until 1960 that the Soviet bloc put real impetus behind its foreign training aid program. A series of agreements with Asian countries (Iraq, India, Indonesia) bear witness to this. And each and every USSR foreign aid agreement, made since 1961 with African nations, contains a training aid clause!

The following reasons account for the great importance attached by the Soviet bloc to the foreign training program today.

1. Politically, the Soviet strategists have come to see in the enlistment of the developing nations' intelligentsia in industry and technology, in Soviet training programs, working system, and methods, a key to political haymaking. For this reason, political indoctrination does not always rank first (as it does in the doctrinaire schooling of party and trade union cadres) in the training of backward nations' intelligentsia. Not illogically, the Soviet experts emphasize that man for man the Asian, but especially the African, intellectual (communist sympathizer is meant, naturally) carries more weight as an influencing factor over the masses, than does his Western counterpart.

2. The new view which the Soviet theoreticians have of the role the intellectual leadership strata plays in the developing countries. In contrast to standard communist doctrine, which holds that the working class is to determine the course of the development of society, the theoreticians have concluded that in countries with a generally

low level of education and widespread illiteracy the intellectual elite would fulfill this function and direct the activities of thousands and millions of people.[194] Therefore the Soviet bloc does not pursue the mass education of intellectual cadres in the developing countries but concentrates on the training of a small elite as a multiplier and transmission belt to the people.

3. Economic reasons are decisive. The Soviet bloc too has reached the conclusion that the effectiveness of economic aid is largely dependent on as rapid and complete an education of specialists as is possible.

We are in possession of the following figures about students from developing countries at institutions of higher learning in the Soviet bloc.

The Number of Students from the "Third World" at Universities
and Institutions of Higher Learning of the COMECON Countries[195]

School year	USSR	other COMECON countries	Total
1956/57	46	--	46
1959/60	929	916	1845
1960/61	1567	1932	3599
1961/62	4000	3800	7800
1963/64	6000	6000	12,000

We have the following figures about students being trained in the individual East bloc countries: USSR, school year 1964/65: "More than 900 boys and girls from more than 100 Asian, African and Latin American countries are studying at institutions of higher learning in the USSR at present";[196] school year 1965/66: "22,000 Asian, African and Latin American students are studying at the People's Friendship University Patrice Lumumba and other Soviet universities and institutions of higher learning";[197] China 1963/64: 2200; CSSR 1963/64: 300; DDR 1962/63: 1200; Yugoslavia 1964: 1000; Bulgaria 1962: 800; and Poland 1961/63: 850. A British source cites a figure of a

---

[194] DDR Wirtschaftshilfe contra Bonner Neokolonialismus, p. 127.
[195] Die Unterrichtshilfe des Ostblocks an die Entwicklungsländer kritisch betrachtet, mimeographed, December 7, 1961, pp. 3-4; Information about Education Around the World, U. S. Department of Health, Education and Welfare, International Educational Relations, No. 44, Washington 25, D. C., July 1960; Pravda, October 25, 1961; G. M. Prochorov, The Two World Systems and the Liberated Countries, pp. 130 and 147.
[196] Vneshnaya torgovlya (Moscow), No. 8/1965, p. 7.
[197] Voprosy istorii KPSS (Moscow), No. 4/1966, p. 21.

total of 18,500 students studying in the East bloc during 1962/63: 8000 in the USSR, 3000 in China, 2200 in the CSSR, 2000 in the DDR, 1300 in Poland, 1000 in Hungary, and 500 each in Bulgaria and Rumania.[198]

All these figures are quite contradictory, since the East bloc publishes no exact data about the number of students at the individual universities. Although these figures at best serve the purpose of general orientation, they do allow us to conclude that only a small minority of students from "Third World" countries take advantage of the opportunity of studying in the East bloc.

Admittedly, the number of Soviet bloc foreign students is still relatively small today. Enrollment of foreign students at British universities and technical schools alone is far higher than that of all of the Soviet bloc taken together. Yet, the comparison is exceedingly lopsided, for the effective range of communist influence over academic youth reaches far beyond the walls of the Soviet bloc universities and other training institutes themselves. Lenin's alleged *bon mot*, "I plan on taking your troops," in the aforementioned cartoon is called to mind by the claim reportedly made in a speech at the African Center of Social Studies in Léopoldville by Gilbert Pongault, Secretary General of the Pan-African Union of Believing Workers: "*An estimated 80% of African students studying in France are communists.*"[199] We are unable to check the validity of this claim. We do, however, have the results of a late 1962 poll of African students, conducted in Paris by a Senegalese sociologist in collaboration with the magazine, *Jeune Afrique*. To the question: "The aid of what country seems to you to be the least dangerous to Africa's independence?" 53.2% of all students asked replied, "The aid of the Soviet Union." Queried about the preferred *economic system*, 37.8% declared for "integrated socialism" after the Soviet and Chinese model, 29.3 for the African socialism of Léopold Senghor, 19.7 for Scandinavian socialism, Swedish-style, and 6.8% for a free-market economy.[200] It would be hasty to consider as convinced communists those 37.8% who declared for the Soviet and Chinese model. But the situation naturally sets the Foreign Bureau of the International Union of Students (IUS) in Prague up in hope. It is part of the duties of this bureau to cultivate contacts with foreign students at Western institutions, as well as to penetrate the organiza-

---

[198] According to *Das Studium der Ausländer im Ostblock, Sozialamt des Deutschen Bundesstudentenringes*, Bad Godesberg, November 22, 1962; *Die Welt*, September 15, 1962.

[199] *Labor* (Essen), 7th annual publ., No. 2/1960, p. 87.

[200] Report by Hans-Jürgen Wischnewski of the "EWP" Conference, Berlin 16 March 1963; *Frankfurter Allgemeine Zeitung*, 6 April 1963.

tions of students from backward areas. To this end, the IUS is in part employing the services of proven students from Africa and Asia who are studying in the Soviet bloc. It was thus no chance occurrence when an IUS representative appeared at the Second Congress of the African Student Union in Germany, held, in Munich, 26-30 April 1963. He came, accompanied by a Sengalese student studying at Leipzig, and several African students from Czechoslovakia. It was at this congress that IUS attempts at penetrating organizations of students from backward nations first came to light in West Germany. Not a single one of the many observers from Western student organizations, including the German Federal Republic, was allowed to take part in any of the congress' committee work. An authentic source reports: "*Except for the Committee on Relations to other Organizations, none of the observers and guests was permitted to attend committee deliberations. All resolutions were passed in camera. The only exception made was with the IUS representative. He was permitted to remain.*" [201]

The Soviet bloc has currently developed the following forms of educational assistance:

1. The training of youth from backward countries at Soviet bloc universities and technical institutes on the basis of government agreements.

2. Establishment of special technical institutes in Soviet bloc countries for the training of students from Asia, Africa and Latin America;

3. Technical training of engineers and other specialists for projects to be erected in the developing nations by the USSR and other Soviet bloc members.

4. Schooling in production management and techniquies of engineers and other specialists through on-the-job training in the factories, on the planning staffs, and with the scientific research institutes of the Soviet bloc.

5. Establishment of technical and trade schools in the developing nations.

[201] *Entwicklungsländer—Informationen, Nachrichten, Berichte, Dokumentationen für den Hochschulbetrieb, Weltstudenten—Dienst*, No. 9/63. Italics added.

Study at Universities
and Polytechnic Institutes

Up to 1960 the academic youth from the backward nations was generally trained only at existing Soviet bloc universities and polytechnic institutes. Only since 1960 have special schools for training of students from developing nations begun to appear in the communist bloc.

Many are the methods and means of recruiting youth for Soviet bloc study. UN scholarships and the student slots offered as part of cultural agreements are exploited. But by far the most commonly applied are those methods that guarantee from the very outset the application of communist selection criteria. This not only includes the scholarship-by-government-grant, but a whole network of organizations is enlisted in the recruiting of students for Soviet bloc study. The World Federation of Democratic Youth, the International Union of Students, and other front organizations not only send candidates of their choosing to Soviet bloc schools but grant scholarships as well. Scholarships are also distributed through tie-ins to the *Union Général des Etudiants d'Afrique Occidental* (Dakar), the *Fédération des Etudiants d'Afrique Noire en France* (Paris), the *Union Général des Etudiants d'Afrique Noire sur la domination Portugaise* (Rabat), and to the West African Student Union (London). Finally, in the more recent past, even those student organizations that came into existence in Soviet bloc countries, such as the Leipzig African Students Union, and also trustworthy students already in the Soviet bloc are enlisted to recruit new students in the backward nations or wean them away from Western institutions. In recent years in particular, communist bloc countries have successfully concluded cultural agreements with Afro-Asian and Latin

American nations that provide for free student berths. These cultural agreements are annually supplemented by concrete plans of the number of students to be sent.

The cultural agreement between the USSR and Ghana, concluded 25 August 1960, may serve as example. Here is stipulated that "each of the contracting partners, on the basis of an ancillary agreement, makes available at his country's institutions of learning an agreed number of spaces and scholarships for the students of the other partner. Each partner further agrees to assist to the best of his capabilities the citizens of the other country in all matters regarding their studies." [202]

The cultural agreement of 28 February 1960 between Indonesia and the Soviet Union provides that "The contracting parties, within the realm of their possibilities and requirements, shall accord the citizens of the other party, *who are selected by their government*, the right to study at each other's scientific, technical, and industrial institutes of learning. Both parties have agreed that those Indonesian students who have finished high school and are entitled to enter an Indonesian state university, shall be permitted, *under existing USSR laws and regulations*, to enroll in a USSR polytechnic institute. Soviet students, authorized to study at a USSR polytechnic institute, are allowed, according to existing Indonesian laws and regulations, to study at an Indonesian university." [203] Here it is especially underscored that the laws of the land are applicable to foreign students in the USSR. This is also brought out in the USSR University Ordinance, which states in regard to foreigners that "Foreign citizens enrolled at USSR institutes of higher learning enjoy all academic rights and responsibilities engendered by the given situation, unless other rights and responsibilities have been laid down for them in special agreement between the Soviet Government and the corresponding country . . . The enrollment sequence of foreign citizens living on USSR soil at institutes of higher learning is determined by the Ministry of Advanced Study and Undergraduate Polytechnic Training."

A special "Decree about the study of foreigners at the universities, intermediate technical schools, and scientific institutes of the USSR" was promulgated on 7 January 1964. This decree contains the following statements about the "duties of the foreign student":

"The foreigners who have been admitted to study at Soviet institutions of learning and scientific research institutes obligate themselves to obey the Soviet laws; respect the customs and the usual traditions of the Soviet people; to fulfill all demands made of them by the ordinances of the institutes of higher learning, intermediate technical

---

[202] *Vedomosty Verkhovnogo Soveta* (Moscow), SSSR, No. 28/1961, pp. 688-90.
[203] *Pravda*, 1 March 1960. Italics added.

schools and other institutions of learning; to obey the regulations about the travel and stay of foreign students in the USSR; to assimilate systematically and thoroughly the theoretical knowledge and practical know-how of their chosen speciality and to work toward raising their own scientific-technical level; to strictly observe school discipline, to attend all required courses (lectures, seminars, laboratory sessions) and to complete all work set forth in the schedules and programs at the designated time; to take the examinations and tests at the designated time; to strictly obey the regulations and the house rules of the communal life of the students and to participate in the self-service." [204]

Every student from the developing countries had to obligate himself in writing to obey these regulations. Moreover, the decree stipulates that any student who disobeys the decree, the school ordinance, discipline or house rules is punished and can even be expelled from the USSR.

Thus, the academic youth from backward nations, studying at USSR institutions, is put on an equal footing with his Soviet counterpart in all matters relating to study and student activities. This also largely applies to all learning establishments in the other Soviet bloc countries, and boils down to the fact that there is no academic freedom for the students from the underdeveloped nations, that all lectures are obligatory (we shall discuss Marxism-Leninism in the chapter on Political Education), that so-called "socials" are command performances, and that the Komsomol and Free-German-Youth rule and control at the universities and polytechnic institutes also apply to Afro-Asian and Latin American youth. Limitations on personal freedom and communistic dedication to the cause here go hand-in-hand with the "fight against the influence of bourgeois ideology," with which all foreign students must *a priori* be considered to be infected.

Students from the developing countries at Soviet universities and institutes are regarded, ipso facto, as asocial elements in need of re-education and retraining. It is said of them that "The young people from the developing countries come to a great extent from relatively well-to-do families . . . The majority of the students and auditors from the anti-imperialist national states come from bourgeois or intellectual circles, from a strata of the population that, by virtue of its social position at least, is divorced from productive work." [205]

Katharina Harig, the head of the Herder Institute in Leipzig, states: "The student brings with him a completely different conception of society, of the family, of the relation between man and woman, and

---

[204] *Bulletin of the Ministry for Higher Learning and Intermediate Technical Training of the USSR* (Russ.) No. 3/1964, pp. 1-5.
[205] *DDR-Wirtschaftshilfe contra Bonner Neokolonialismus*, p. 132.

very often also of work and the value of work, especially of physical labor." [206]

It is believed that these disadvantages which the students bring with them will be alleviated by regulating their studies, their life, and combining their training with "the practice of working socialistically," which is called polytechnical education.

Much is known about the disheartening experiences to which the "academic rights and responsibilities" exposed the African and Asian students at USSR, CSSR, Bulgarian, and East German universities.[207] The *Deutsche Bundesstudentenring* (a West German student organization) has compiled a listing of 228 former Soviet bloc students who entered West Germany during 1961-62. No less than 130 came from East Germany. The drop-out figures from other Soviet bloc countries are modest by comparison. It is no doubt apropos to publish the negative experiences of these students. Yet it must not be overlooked that new enrollments at Soviet bloc schools—as the statistics prove—far outnumber the drop-outs. It should also be realized that Moscow especially seeks to learn from mishaps.

Very few of the published critiques concerning the academic life at Moscow and Prague universities, especially that of African students, have taken a stand on the curriculum, on the educational system and instructional matters, or on the practical side of training methods. Looking at what the Soviet bloc pedagogues themselves, foremost those of Moscow, criticize, we find their primary objection is to the prevailing system of student selection. So far, this selection has been in the hands of several organizations and governments of disparate countries, with unequal criteria applied as concerns technical aptitude and educational level. Students from Asia and Africa arrived at Soviet universities educationally unprepared to meet the rather stiff requirements that Soviet schools put on their own students (mandatory lectures, seminaries, frequent examinations, and the like). Language difficulties are an additional serious handicap, as several Soviet publications point out. Concerning the disparity in prior education, a Soviet educator writes: "Many of them [i.e., students from Africa and Asia] came to the institute knowing almost no Russian, some of them have had no chemistry, others no trigonometry or geometry, and some know only the rudiments of physics and algebra." [208]

---

[206] "Nationaler Befreiungskampf und Neokolonialismus," East Berlin 1962, p. 417.

[207] Michel Avih, *Ein Afrikaner in Moskau*, Cologne 1961, "Afrikanische Studenten in der Tschechoslowakei," in *Neue Zürcher Zeitung*, 16 January 1962; Mahdi Ismail Ahmed, "My Communist Schooldays," in *Observer*, 18 February 1962.

[208] *Vestnik vizshey shkoly* (Moscow), No. 5/1961, pp. 110-12; quoted by Borys Levitskiy, *op. cit.*, p. 9.

Politically, the matter was even worse. For, although an official file on the student's aptitude and his, often inadequate, educational background would be submitted by appropriate authorities of the student's homeland, politically he was an unknown quantity and could be checked out only after arrival in Moscow or Prague. It was for these technical and political reasons, therefore, that nearly every Soviet bloc university and polytechnic institute after 1960 began to establish preparatory faculties for students from the developing countries. A turning point in the Soviet bloc's foreign aid educational program came with the establishment of the Patrice Lumumba People's Friendship University in Moscow, primarily because this step created a staff of specialists capable of dealing with all phases of educating the academic youth of Africa, Asia and Latin America.

The Patrice Lumumba
People's Friendship University

Nikita Khrushchev, to lend a special fillip to his early 1960 swing through India, Burma, Indonesia and Afghanistan, chose a suitable site for proclaiming a new Soviet government educational project. In Jogjakarta at Indonesia's national university Gadjah Mada, he announced: "The Soviet Government has decided to open in Moscow a university, dedicated to friendship among peoples . . . Many students from all countries of the world study in our country today. But most of them are sent by government agencies, and these agencies naturally cannot cater to everybody's desires. This prevents many talented young people from poorer families from indulging their wish to study in the Soviet Union. We believe not only those selected by government agencies, but also those voicing a personal interest, should study at the new university." [209]

The People's Friendship University was officially opened 1 October 1960 and solemnly dedicated 17 November of the same year. Since 1961 it carries the sobriquet "Patrice Lumumba." The university is described as an institution under public law, even though countless statements refer to it as government-created. Listed as "founders" are the Soviet Solidarity Organization of the Peoples of Asia and Africa; the Association of Soviet Societies for Friendship and Cultural Contact with Foreign Nations, and the Central Council of USSR Trade Unions. In March 1960 these "founders," together with the Committee of USSR Youth Organizations and the Ministry of Advanced Study and Undergraduate Polytechnic Training, organized the "university council." This "founder" fiction is, of course, of far-reaching importance,

[209] *Happiness and Peace to the Peoples!* (Russ.), p. 153.

both as concerns the university's relation to the governments of the backward nations, as well as student selection and political education. We shall return to this at another place.

As the university's first president the "founders" chose Professor S. V. Rumyantsev, doctor of applied sciences and member of the Soviet Solidarity Committee. "Professor Rumyantsev," reported *Pravda*, "for several years held a chair and was director of an institute. He was Deputy Minister for Higher Education in the USSR from 1955 to 1959 and more recently the Deputy Minister of Advanced Study and Undergraduate Polytechnic Training.[210]

The acceptance requirements of Patrice Lumumba University, which differ materially from student enrollment as generally practiced, merit a closer look.

"Enrollment at People's Friendship University is in the following faculties: Engineering (special fields: mechanical, mining, and construction engineering); Agriculture (special fields: agronomy and zootechny); Medicine (special fields: practical medicine and pharmaceutics); Physics-Mathematics, and Natural Science (special fields: physics, mathematics, chemistry, and biology); History-Philology (special fields: history, literature, and Russian); Economics and Law (special fields: economics, national-economic planning, international law).

"The university accepts, independent of race, creed, and nationality, male and female students up to thirty-five. Length of the course is four years, except five for medical students. Applications may be submitted by citizens of Afro-Asian and Latin American countries, either directly to the university, or through USSR embassies and consulates abroad. First-semester enrollment is predicated on an examination of the applicant's educational background by the university council. Applicants must possess a background in the higher education of their respective countries. Persons who lack the required educational background may be enrolled for a period of one to three years in the preparatory faculty. Also enrolled in the preparatory faculty for up to one year may be applicants who meet the educational requirements but lack Russian. Applications are accepted each year up to 31 July, inclusive. They must be addressed to the university president and include a personal history statement, with two passport photos; transcripts of school records, and a health certificate.

"An enrollment committee, composed of the president as chairman, with the vice-president in charge of studies, the dean of faculties, and the professors as members, examines all applications and passes its recommendations on to the university council for final decision. The

---

[210] *Pravda*, 24 March 1960.

test of the applicant's educational qualifications may be made in the applicant's own country, with the assistance of the universities and other institutes of higher learning of the respective country, or at the Lumumba University. The decision of the university council is final and will be made known to the applicant through university channels. Final enrollment date is 1 September and university classes begin 1 October. The university charges no tuition and grants scholarships to all students, including free medical care and dormitory accommodations (without family). The university defrays all expenses incurred by the student's journey to Moscow and return. Applications should be addressed: 16 Kalinin Street, Moscow, People's Friendship Building." [211]

These guidelines of admittance to the People's Friendship University bear strong resemblance to the student selection criteria of the Party and trade union schools. The decision on who is to study at the new university remains throughout in Soviet hands. Additionally, the Soviet embassies and consulates that accept and forward applications have a chance to check on the applicant's background and political reliability. This function is also carried out by the international contact organizations and committees that are part of the student recruitment network. Thus a report states: "The Soviet-Indian Friendship Society of New Delhi had to peruse hundreds of letters and applications of persons desiring to study in Moscow. The branch of the Society for Indo-Soviet Cultural Relations at Baroda alone received over 300 applications." [212]

Even the university council, final arbiter on all applications, contains a control point, for not only professors sit on this council, but also representatives of the political "founding organizations." Obviously, the Soviets endeavor to eliminate as much as possible the so-called "factor of uncertainty" that the student selection by the UN or the backward nations themselves contained.

Khrushchev's comments that the new university also offers students "from the poorer families" who are not sent by their governments the chance to study, as well as the setting up of a preparatory faculty for up to three years' schooling for "people who lack the required educational background," show a social selection principle at work. The intent, as in the case of the worker and peasant schools, is to educate faithful and able adherents of the system. As concerns governments sending students to the new university, only India has so far had any success. Professor Rumyantsev complained about the "odd attitude of several governments" toward the university who object

[211] *Pravda*, 24 March 1960.
[212] *Sovremeniy vostok* (Moscow), No. 9/1960, p. 59.

to the Soviet methods of student selection. He cited Burma, Nepal, the Congo, and Ethiopia in particular. "Burmese and Nepalese authorities prevented students from coming to the People's Friendship University." [213] Nonetheless, some 42,551 candidates allegedly applied for admission in the first year. In the second year the number of candidates exceeded the available places by only 6000.

About 3000 of the 42,551 applicants for the first school year were directed, at university expense, to appear in Moscow for entrance examination. Of these, 1800 passed but only 538 students from sixty-four nations were admitted to the university. The remaining 1262 were promised scholarships to other USSR and Soviet bloc universities.[214]

Students Enrolled at Patrice Lumumba University

During First Year [215]

	No. of students 1 Feb. 1961	No. of men	No. of women	of those under 25 years	25 and over
Total	597	530	67	478	119
From:					
Far East and Southeast Asia	112	92	20	93	19
Africa	140	134	6	98	42
Arab countries	95	87	8	72	23
Latin America	191	160	31	157	34
USSR	59	57	2	58	1

There were about 700 new enrollments, around 100 from the USSR, during the second academic year. A total of 1286 students are said to have been enrolled at Patrice Lumumba in 1961/62. More than 4000 applications were received for academic year 1962/63. During the 1964/65 school year more than 3000 students and 100 student candidates studied at the People's Friendship University. According to information supplied by S. W. Rumjanzev, the university rector, a total of 3800 students and 150 candidates were enrolled for the year 1965/66.

The figures reveal that 32.2% (538) of all students from underdeveloped countries studying in the USSR during 1960/61 (1667) were enrolled at the People's Friendship University. According to Mu-

---

[213] *Pravda*, 17 November 1960.
[214] *Die "Unterrichtshilfe" des Ostblocks*, p. 13.
[215] *Vizshee obrasovanie v SSSR*, Moscow 1961, p. 200; *Vierteljahresbericht der Friedrich—Ebert—Stiftung*, No. 7/1962, p. 8.

khitdinov, the number of students from backward 'nations at USSR schools in 1961/62 totaled 4000, of whom 1186 (not counting USSR citizens), or 29.65%, studied at Patrice Lumumba. There is no doubt the Soviets intend to concentrate the schooling of the underdeveloped nations' youth at this university. Ultimate success of this plan hinges largely on the outcome of the current experiment.

Actual instruction at the fourteen subdivisions of the six faculties listed did not start until the beginning of academic year 1961/62. The students who had enrolled in 1960 were first required to take a preparatory course in learning Russian. "From the very first lesson (October 1960) the students were broken down into groups of four to five people. Each group has its own classroom, equipped with tape recorder. It may be added that the Russian language department will be one of the largest of its kind in the world; even now it has more than 120 instructors. The teaching of Russian is tailored to the special subject areas of the individual student." [216] Rumyantsev also mentions this linking of language training to the student's study major. He stresses that "this combination of linguistic and technical training stimulates the students' interest, develops their initiative, and guides them on the road to personal mastery over their subject matter." [217] In November 1960 the word was that the university very soon would boast a training staff of 210—with an enrollment at the time of 597 students.[218]

In the 1963/64 school year the university had 723 instructors, among them 40 Ph.D's and 150 doctoral candidates. Nine hundred instructors taught 3000 students at the People's Friendship University in 1964/65, among them fifty-four professors and Ph.D.s and 296 doctoral candidates. At the end of June 1965 a total of 228 students from forty-seven countries had completed their course of study, among them fifty-seven from Southeast Asian and Far Eastern countries, thirty-eight from Africa, fifty-eight from Latin America, thirty-one from the Arabian countries and forty-four from the USSR. While the foreign students learned Russian, the Russian students devoted themselves to the study of foreign languages. Some of the Russian students became so proficient in these languages that they were able to write their examinations and their theses in them. These Soviet graduates are to be deployed as specialists in the developing countries.

At the end of the first academic year Professor Rumyantsev openly discussed the difficulties which Soviet teachers and pedagogues were hard put to overcome. Next to language difficulties, Rumyantsev lists

[216] *Sovremeniy vostok* (Moscow), No. 9/1960, p. 59.
[217] *Vestnik vizshey shkoly* (Moscow), No. 5/1961, p. 108.
[218] *Politika* (Warsaw), No. 45, 5 November 1960.

the difference in mental capacity of the students coming from three continents, to which must be added the students' disparate educational backgrounds and the lack of suitable textbooks.[219] "Even if these students gain an adequate knowledge of Russian, the normal textbooks found at Soviet universities and polytechnic institutes are of little use to them,"[220] for these textbooks are not tailored specifically to the needs of foreign students and the simplified training program of Patrice Lumumba University, but conform to the much more highly specialized standards of strictly Soviet universities.

But despite all difficulties, and even though the number of students at Patrice Lumumba University is small by Western count, the West must not overlook that here is trained an elite, selected after Soviet criteria and early examined for reliability. Politically, Patrice Lumumba University is part and parcel of "competition with capitalism." And in the same manner that the Soviet bloc's foreign aid program for politico-psychological reasons is oriented toward construction of monumental industrial works and nuclear experimental stations, the People's Friendship University "is to pioneer the entry of science into the underdeveloped countries" by means of Soviet-trained specialists. Rumyantsev leaves no doubt that the accent of the university's training program is in the fields of the natural sciences, technology, and the exact sciences, in the training of mechanical engineers, as well as specialists in radio electronics and automation. This explains why a doctor of technological science was called on to head the University."

The scholarships offered are not only by way of bait, but indicate preferential treatment of an elite, specially chosen by the Soviets. A Western visitor comments as follows: "Successful applicants receive a scholarship of a hundred dollars monthly, including vacations. This is over ten dollars more than the highest scholarship for Soviet students, the Lenin Scholarship, which is won by only a very few Soviet students in their junior year. Tuition, textbooks, medical care, and billets are free. Billeting is normally in student dorms of three-bed rooms near the university. Free also is winter clothing, an important consideration in view of Moscow's cold winters and the high Soviet clothing prices . . . Meals may be taken at the university student restaurant, which charges about $1.65 for breakfast, lunch, and supper together. To some extent, the restaurant serves typical dishes of the students' native lands."[221]

---

[219] *Vestnik vizshey shkoly* (Moscow), No. 5/1961, p. 108.
[220] Borys Levitskiy, *Vierteljahresberichte der Friedrich—Ebert—Stiftung*, No. 7/1962, p. 11.
[221] *Ifo-Schnelldienst*, 14th Year, No. 39, 27 September 1961, p. 3.

Other Soviet bloc countries have begun to imitate the Soviet example, in order to establish orientation centers for the training of students from Asia, Africa and Latin America. Czechoslovakia's University of 17 November and the Herder Institute in Leipzig are examples.

The University of 17 November

In mid-September 1961 Czechoslovakia's Council of Ministers decided to establish, in Prague, a university as part of the Czech foreign aid education program for underdeveloped nations. The name University of 17 November was chosen in commemoration of the day in 1939 when the Nazis closed the Czech universities and carried off their professors and students to concentration camps. The day has since been celebrated as International Students Day by Prague's International Union of Students. The university, pending erection of a new plant, was initially housed in the former Traffic Institute Building in Gorki Square.[222] The university was opened on 17 November 1961, with an enrollment of 1254 students from underdeveloped countries and Czechoslovakia.[223] In 1963 "more than 3000 students" studied there.

The school's director is Professor Dr. Jaroslav Martinic who was the Czech ambassador to Holland in 1949. In 1954 he became professor for Marxist-Leninist political science at Olmütz University and later on he occupied the same position at the Charles University in Prague. Martinic also was minister for education for a time.

The tasks assigned the University of 17 November reveals its cultural role in the academic youth training program:

1. The university is a preparatory faculty for students from backward countries. Emphasis is initially on learning Czech, with language instruction geared to the student's special study field. Graduates

---

[222] *Forschungsdienst Osteuropa*, Third Quarter Report 1961, pp. 29-30.
[223] *Die "Unterrichtshilfe" des Ostblocks an die Entwicklungländer*, p. 18.

of this preparatory faculty will continue their technical studies at Czech universities and polytechnic institutes.

2. The university is to serve as guide for other Czech language schools and study centers serving students from underdeveloped nations.

3. For academic year 1962/63 two additional faculties, a natural science-technical faculty and a sociological faculty, were opened.

4. The university was assigned politico-cultural and pedagogical supervision over all students from backward areas studying in Czechoslovakia. This makes the school the foreign students' center in the CSSR.

5. The new university is considered a central institute for the linguistic, technical, and cultural training of foreign aid experts who, upon completion of their studies, may be sent to Asian, African and Latin American countries.

The last item is a new Soviet bloc departure in the training of its own foreign aid experts. Here, two birds are to be killed with one stone. On the one hand, these native citizens, who study side by side with the foreign students, act as the latters' sponsors (of which more later). On the other hand, they are to become familiar with their foreign colleagues' mentality, customs, and mores. This "buddy system" is practiced in nearly all Soviet bloc countries today. At the time the students from the backward areas learn Russian or Czech at Patrice Lumumba University or the University of 17 November, their Russian and Czech fellow students receive instruction in English, French or Spanish. In the fall of 1963 the university established a translation and interpreting course for Czech citizens, a course which comprises eight semesters.[224]

Some kind of preparatory faculty is today installed at nearly every Soviet bloc institute engaged in training the academic youth of the young national states. The big problem is linguistic. The plan to present the instruction for academic year 1962/63 at least partially in a universal language, by which is meant English, French, or Spanish, met with great difficulties. These "universal" languages, taken for granted in the West, must first be learned in the Soviet bloc. And even though Soviet specialists, speaking Arabic or even Hindi, are met with in several backward countries, the USSR and CSSR nevertheless are short on foreign-language-speaking specialists for its far-flung foreign aid commitments. This is also the gist of a resolution, passed by the Soviet Council of Ministers in May 1961, "on the improvement of foreign language training in the USSR." The comments made about the Soviet Union undoubtedly also apply to the entire Soviet bloc:

[224] *Prace,* September 7, 1963; *Literarni noviny,* No. 43/1963.

"The great majority of graduates from institutes of higher learning have only a smattering of a foreign language. Possessing only a limited vocabulary and a nominal knowledge of grammar, they are not able to translate foreign texts without a dictionary. Conversational exercises of the spoken language are especially poorly organized. There are serious defects in the training of foreign language teachers." [225] Repeatedly, the Council's resolution stresses the discrepancy between the requirement and demand for foreign-language-speaking specialists and the low output of such specialists by universities, polytechnic institutes, and foreign language schools. This is one of the reasons—albeit a secondary one—why foreign students must still be taught Russian and Czech at preparatory faculties. The main reason is of course political: the language is looked upon as a bond. By learning Russian, Czech, or other Soviet bloc tongues the students are expected to become absorbed in the new language. Thus, their training at any of the Soviet bloc universities is not only technically oriented, but also slanted to arouse in the student graduates a predilection for the acquired language and its scientific, technical, cultural, and political literature.

We mentioned as one of the tasks of the University of 17 November the guidance of other Czech language schools and study centers. This may be assumed to include the following eight Czech-language schools for foreign students:

Two in Central Bohemia: Houstka(Prague) and Podebrady
Two in North Bohemia: Teplice and Liberec
One in West Bohemia: Marienbad
One in East Bohemia: Dobruska
One in North Moravia: Olomouc
One in West Slovakia: Senec

Most of these schools, which teach a language course of about one year, have classes for English-, French-, and Spanish-speaking students. Marienbad, largest of the language schools, even conducts classes for students whose mother tongue is Portuguese and Arabic.[226] Mostly, these institutes are small. The Dobruska school, for instance, enrolls an average of seventy-five students from Africa, Asia, and Latin America.[227]

---

[225] *Biyulletin Ministerstva srednogo spetsialnogo obrasovaniya* (Moscow), August 1961, pp. 22-24; German text in *Vierteljahresberichte der Friedrich—Ebert—Stiftung*, No. 7/1962. pp. 27-30.
[226] *Die "Unterrichtshilfe" des Ostblocks*, p. 19; cf. also *Aussenpolitik*, No. 1/1962, p. 46.
[227] *Neue Zürcher Zeitung*, 16 January 1962.

Of special importance as a preparatory school is the Institute for Economic Studies, opened in Prague in 1958. Of about 3000 students at this school, 200 came from Afro-Asian countries, with sixty from Mali, Guinea, and Somali. Students at this institute who pass their political, ideological, and technical examinations are sent to Moscow for further study in preparation for the most advanced careers.

The Herder Institute in Leipzig

In July 1956 the Institute for Foreign Students at the Karl Marx University in Leipzig was opened as a "preparatory school for foreign students in East Germany and a facility for teaching German." [228] This became the Herder Institute in 1961. First among the functions of this institute, which is headed by Professor (Mrs.) Harig, member of the Socialist Unity Party, is that of a quarantine station for all foreigners coming to East Germany for study. "Every foreign student desiring to study in East Germany, even though he speaks German fluently, is directed by East Berlin's State Secretariat for Higher Education to spend some time at the Leipzig institute. In this, it does not matter if the student is from a Soviet bloc country or from a 'capitalist' or 'anti-imperialist' state and plans to study only a particular technical aspect not yet known in his own land." [229]

An ordinance issued by the DDR State Secretary for Higher Education states the following about the institute's tasks:

"It prepares the foreign students linguistically and technically for their university studies. It supervises all universities and institutions of higher learning in their control of foreign students, and in this respect it works hand in hand with the assistant deans for students' affairs. It prepares the study material for the linguistic and technical instruction of the foreign students, and it develops teaching methods for language instruction of the foreigners. It heads the sections for

---

[228] *Allgemeiner Deutscher Nachrichtendienst*, 1 August 1961.
[229] Julian Lehnecke, "Die SED schult Farbige," SBZ-Archiv (Cologne), No. 24/1960 p. 382.

312

linguistic instruction at the universities and institutes of higher learning in all questions pertaining to the language instruction of foreigners." [230]

As a "German-teaching facility," the Herder Institute was established in competition to Munich's "Goethe Institute." It not only prepares foreign students for study in East Germany, but trains German language teachers for assignments abroad. This training is coupled with the establishment by the Herder Institute in the backward nations of so-called lectureships. Such lectureships for teaching German, supplied with instructors by the Leipzig institute, were opened during the past several years by the Herder Institute in India, Indonesia, Iraq, Burma, Ghana, Guinea and Egypt. Instrumental in setting up these lectureships was the Cairo switchboard of East Germany's Socialist Unity Party, the Office of the German Democratic Republics Plenipotentiary for the Arabic States, assisted by East German trade missions abroad. "Much meritorious work was done by the co-workers of this world-renowned institute [so the propaganda has it] in the preparation of modern training material for teaching German, a language much in demand abroad." [231]

"Modern training material" refers to the book *German, a Manual for Foreigners.* "In 1958 the Party directed a group of authors to compile Part One of this textbook. In the record time of six months the work was ready for the printer. This manual, aimed exclusively at foreigners, largely skips the imparting of linguistic rules or grammatical niceties but is often referred to as a 'masterpiece' of politico-psychological construction. A first edition of 10,000 went like hot cakes and a second, together with Part Two, appeared some time later. The book is not only used at the Leipzig institute (this would never account for the number of copies), but is disseminated to the four corners of the earth in the baggage of East Germany's cultural and trade missions, to be recommended at every opportunity as the 'most progressive' of German language training manuals." [232] In early 1963 appeared the third edition of the manual.

As early as Lesson No. 10 the manual drills into the students: "In the German Democratic Republic 90% of the students receive scholarships. In West Germany 8.5% of the students receive scholarships. In the German Democratic Republic .51% of the population are students. In West Germany .28% of the population are students. In the German Democratic Republic 60% of the students come from worker and peasant families. In West Germany 3% of the students come from

---

[230] *Das Hochschulwesen* (East Berlin), No. 10/1957, p. 57.
[231] *Allgemeiner Deutscher Nachrichtendienst* (East Berlin), 2 March 1962.
[232] Julian Lehnecke, *Die SED schult Farbige*, p. 382.

worker and peasant families."[233] More advanced students learn: "The workers suggested new production methods." . . . "On the initiative of the Socialist Unity Party wages were raised in many trades" . . . "The Soviet Union freed us from fascism." . . . "Socialism is a historical imperative" . . . "Germany's Communist Party has always fought for a common front between Communists and Social Democrats" . . . "The German Democratic Republic, established 7 October 1949, is the basis for a unified, peace-loving, democratic Germany" . . . and more of the like.[233] This manual is an example of how ideology is infused into language instruction, and shows how linguistic and political preparation for further study in East Germany go hand-in-hand.

Students from backward nations are enrolled at the Herder Institute either on the basis of scholarships, handed out by East German trade missions, or on scholarships granted by the East German authorities as per cultural agreements with the underdeveloped nations. Front organizations also (IUS, Free German Youth, WFTU) dispose over a certain number of student spaces.

The publication *Entwicklungsländer* notes that at the Herder Institute "German language instruction is conducted by an experienced staff and in accordance with time-tested didactic methods. The ten-month course is divided into two phases. The second phase concentrates on German grammar and syntax and builds up the student's vocabulary, in line with his speciality, in three separate groups of the arts, technology, or the biological and medical sciences. The curriculum provides for thirty-six to forty hours of instruction weekly and there are only from ten to thirteen students per instructor. With this intensive language instruction, foreign students know a considerable amount of German when they begin their technical study. Special three-month courses for groups of seldom more than six to eight have been organized for student candidates."[234]

In these "time-tested didactic methods" at the Herder Institute the politico-psychological goals are not overlooked, as witness the following guidelines worked out in 1958: "When this institute first opened in 1953 [from 1953-1957 there existed a department for aliens at the worker and peasant faculty of the Karl Marx University as a forerunner of today's Herder Institute] only students from People's Democracies were permitted to enroll. Today [early 1959] some 300 to 400 students, to a large extent from anti-imperialist states, study here . . .

---

[233] *Deutsch, ein Lehrbuch für Ausländer,* Part I and II, Halle 1959 and 1960, key I, p. 130; key II, pp. 62, 65, 82, 125, 139, 147-48.
[234] *Entwicklungsländer* (Bonn–Baden-Baden), No. 5/1961, 31 July 1961.

The institute has become the focal point of foreign studies in our Republic. This means that our institute must supervise all foreign students until the termination of their studies . . . We shall also extend our activities outside the borders of our Republic to work in socialist and capitalist countries beyond . . . We are going to confront the activities of Munich's Goethe Institute abroad . . . with the dissemination of our socialist ideology . . . During their studies in the German Democratic Republic the students . . . will not only acquire scientific knowledge, they will also become acquainted with life in a socialist country and carry their impressions home with them. We must see to it that these impressions are favorable to the cause of socialism. In this lies the important sociological mission of our institute . . . We must demand from each and every one of our instructors, whether Party member or not, not only a positive attitude toward our worker and peasant state, but an active collaboration in socialist reconstruction and a willingness to defend our achievements . . . Boldly and obedient to the party's dictates, we shall do battle against all inroads of bourgeois ideology . . ." [235]

Recently the Herder Institute has concentrated on "combining the course of study with an emphasis on the main problems of the respective country, and on imparting special know-how and capacities that the students will require upon their return to their homelands." [236]

However, not technical know-how and capacities are meant but social-political ones; for the document goes on to say: "However, the institute's task is not completed when it fills certain gaps in the student's education and makes him proficient in German. The educational effort that has been performed and continues to be performed is just as important. One of the institute's objectives is to educate the young people from the young national states, who in many cases belong to the socially higher placed strata, into people who will not regard their study as a private matter but as an important contribution in their country's fight for independence and the fight against imperialism and war. There is no doubt that such students who are not active in the fight for their nation's independence will not become a potent factor in their country's fight for political and economic independence." [236]

According to the *Leipziger Volkszeitung* of 26 April 1960 the Herder Institute as a transit station for foreign students has instructed 2000 students from more than fifty nations in the German language "since its founding four years ago" (1956). The East German news agency

---

[235] Cited by Julian Lehnecke, *Die SED schult Farbige*, p. 383.
[236] *DDR-Wirtschaftshilfe contra Bonner Neokolonialismus*, pp. 129 and 133.

ADN reported early in 1962: "Over 600 students from sixty-five countries are enrolled at the Herder Institute of Leipzig's Karl Marx University . . . Since 1953 this institute has prepared more than 4000 students from more than seventy countries for university study." [237]

Despite an increase of students from backward nations in the total number of East Germany's foreign students, the larger share today still comes from nations of the Soviet bloc itself. In the spring of 1958 the East German press reported a total of 1303 foreign students, 237 of them from Asia, Africa and Latin America. Previously we used a DDR source to arrive at the figure of 1200 students from the developing countries for the school year 1963/64. [238]

---

[237] *Allgemeiner Deutscher Nachrichtendienst* (East Berlin), 2 March 1962.

[238] *Entwicklungsländer* (Bonn–Baden-Baden), No. 5/1961, puts the figure of the backward nation students at 70% of 1800 foreign students, or 1250, in 1960. *Die Zeit* (Hamburg), of 10 November 1961 states: "There are currently some 2300 from Afro-Asian countries enrolled at East German universities and polytechnic institutes."

New Methods in the Political Education
and Indoctrination of Academic Youth

Khrushchev, in his 17 November 1960 dedicatory address at the opening of the People's Friendship University, set the tone for the new
type political education to be dispensed at Soviet schools to the youth
of the backward nations. "Naturally," he deadpanned, "we are not
going to force our opinions, our ideology on any students, for one's
view of the world is a most private matter. If you want to know my
own political convictions, I shall not deny I am a communist who is
deeply convinced that Marxism-Leninism is the most progressive of
all ideologies. If any one of you should come to find this ideology to
his taste, we shall not take this amiss . . . I repeat, if anyone becomes
infected with this 'disease' of our time, with communism, please do
not blame us for it." [239] Everything, we are told, is to be entirely voluntary. But man, in Khrushchev's words, "is the product of circumstances," and these may be manipulated by means and methods other
than direct political indoctrination. If the goal has not changed, the
means have become more subtle.

The following comment, made about East Germany, applies with
few exceptions to all Soviet bloc educational institutes: "The only
preferential treatment foreign students enjoy is that they need not
take any courses or pass any examinations in basic sociology (Marxism-Leninism, dialectic and historic materialism, and political economy). Yet, most foreign students regularly attend these lectures any-

[239] *Pravda,* 18 November 1960.

317

way." [240] This "preferential treatment" should not be interpreted as broadmindedness, nor as a sign that political indoctrination has been dropped from the curriculum.

As the documents show, the Soviets employed a dialectical trick in this instance. According to them, preparation does not constitute official study, and when they claim that the students from the developing countries have been absolved of the study of Marxism-Leninism and have to take no exams in these subjects, this claim does not hold true for the preparatory courses these students take. For example, a course on "An outline of social development" was made part of the program of the preparatory faculty of the People's Friendship University. What importance is accorded these lectures becomes clear from the fact that, although all general lectures at the university are held in Russian, this "special course" is given in English, French, Spanish and Arabic.

We are in possession of the manuals for these lectures on "An Outline of social development." They are published in Russian and the four aforementioned languages.

Part I has the subtitle "Pre-Capitalist Society"; Part II, "Capitalist Society"; Part III scheduled to be published in 1966, was announced under the title "The Inevitability of the Transition from Capitalism to Communism."

It is hardly necessary to point out that these lectures are written from the historical materialistic point of view of the development of society, something immediately evident from the preface to Part I, which says: "This is Part I of the textbook used for the Historical and Economic Survey, as taught in many languages for students from Asia, Africa and Latin America at Patrice Lumumba Friendship University.

The subject is the history of the development of human society. The topics discussed include the nature of this development, which is an historical transition from one socio-economic formation to the next, more progressive formation; also, an analysis is given of the level of the productive forces, the distinctive features of socio-economic relations, political institutions and ideological phenomena characteristic of the primitive-communal system, the slave and feudal systems, and capitalism and its final state—imperialism, the communist formation and its primary phase—socialism. There is a detailed review of the full-scale construction of a communist society in the Soviet Union, the development of the world socialist system, the strengthening of the international revolutionary movement of the working class, the

---

[240] *Entwicklungsländer* (Bonn–Baden-Baden), No. 5/1961, p. 130.

growth of the national liberation movement and the peoples' fight for peace." [241]

A Soviet author states in reference to "An Outline of Social Development" that "The course reserves a special place for such questions as the formation of the ideology of the proletariat, scientific socialism and its founders Karl Marx, Friedrich Engels, the founding of the first international organization of workers—The International, as well as the Paris Commune as a first attempt at a dictatorship of the proletariat.

"The foreign students, particularly those from countries that proclaim the construction of socialism as the objective of their development, are interested in Marxist-Leninist theory, and in the manual they cannot only become acquainted with the analyses of the historians and the components of Marxism but can also receive a general picture of the principles of dialectical and historical materialism and Marxist political science and the theory of communism." [242]

As everything written about this course shows, it is a question of elementary instruction in communist theory which every student at the preparatory faculty has to pass as a pre-condition for admission to the main course of study.

Moreover, all main subjects are more or less permeated with ideology, and the total cultural and social life at the universities are determined by it.

Finally, several new methods have been developed to make sure that the youth from the developing countries will be constantly exposed to Marxism-Leninism during their student days in the East bloc.

At nearly every Soviet bloc university and polytechnic institute the "buddy" system for foreign students has been introduced. Here too Khrushchev led off by saying, "The People's Friendship University is one of the Soviet universities, and our own students, citizens of the Soviet Union, are naturally also going to study there. What sort of people's friendship would this be if only foreigners were to attend the People's Friendship University? Fraternally, the Soviet people are helping their colleagues, the foreigners, in their studies. The mutually shared studies will promote lasting friendship among youth." [243]

At the Lomonosov University, for example, supervision and control over all students was in the hands of nonuniversity personnel, of the

[241] *An Outline of Social Development*, (Engl.) Patrice Lumumba Friendship University, Progress Publisher, Moscow.
[242] *Vestnik vizshey shkoly* (Moscow), No. 2/1966, p. 95.
[243] *Pravda*, 18 November 1960.

Party apparatus and the Komsomol bureaucracy. Today's mentors are fellow students, "buddies," who share rooms and study problems with the foreign students, who are themselves taking courses and who, on the Party's behalf, supervise and politically enlighten their foreign fellow students. "This personal service rendered foreign students by German fellow students [at the Herder Institute] is officially declared as directly supporting the training program that provides for—across-the-board—German language instruction for foreign students. Semi-officially, the German 'buddy' is to canalize conversational language drills into discussions of the superiority of the Democratic Republic and of West Germany's 'imperialist role.' Entirely unofficially, how-ever, word quickly spread among German students in Leipzig that volunteering for the foreign student 'buddy' service offered excellent chances to avoid other 'social' duties, at the same time greatly re-lieving the volunteer's food and billeting worries." [244] Especially the latter advantages may lead many a "buddy" conscientiously to carry out the Party's orders. Thus, the principle of selection is applied dur-ing the entire study period; which means that every student from a backward country who studies at the People's Friendship University undergoes three filtering processes: first, his selection by contact or front organizations, including consulates and embassies; second, the examination by the Admissions Office; third, the constant supervision by his "buddy."

In this way a constant weeding out process is at work, the useless goats being separated from the more willing and manageable sheep— a matter of greatest importance in political indoctrination. And, let us add, not all students who defected to the West came voluntarily. Quite a few were expelled, for which reasons are easily found.

The "buddy" system is also applied to on-the-job trainees from un-derdeveloped countries. As a matter of fact, the East German Plan-ning Commission retains a staff of such "buddies," who speak the language of their counterparts. They routinely visit the place of em-ployment of the latter, maintain contact with plant management, shop stewards, and Party cells, arrange for social activities that bring their foreign "buddy" in contact with other employees, and of course constantly report to the Planning Commission and the Central Com-mittee's foreign section on their charges. A report describes the rou-tine activity of a "buddy" in these words: "The man who was in charge of 1000 North Vietnamese on-the-job trainees also played 'buddy' to thirty Syrians. He managed the job alone, using his own car (a Skoda, costing 13,000 D-marks East). He was on the go all the time and seldom at home. Following a tight schedule, he would

---

[244] Julian Lehnecke, op. cit., p. 382.

cover all of Thuringia, visiting every plant even if it employed only one of his trainees. The interim and final seminars were like those conducted in West Germany. Those for Thuringia were held at Erfurt, with the program including discussions, sightseeing, and social events." [245]

In another area also, that of *organization*, the Soviet bloc learned the hard way. At the Lomonosov University the African students had established their own union of African students, which was banned, leading to serious altercations between the students and the university authorities. Now the Soviet bloc assiduously endeavors to establish officially sanctioned organizations for foreign students. To name but a few, there are the student associations by countries of origin; diverse student leagues; the International Student Committee, with branches in all bloc countries; the Herder Institute Cultural Group; the Committee of Iraqi Students in the German Democratic Republic; the Union of African Students in Leipzig; the Association of African Students in Czechoslovakia; and the Union of Somalian Students in the Socialist Camp. All of these organizations and committees are under the aegis of the Friendship Societies and Afro-Asian Solidarity Committees, co-founders and sponsors of the People's Friendship University. Thus, East Germany's Afro-German Society, with its president, Professor Walter Markov, in political charge, took part in the Second Congress of the Union of African Students in East Germany (President: Olga Oguntoye), held in Leipzig, 17-18 June 1961. "One hundred delegates of the more than 500 African university students" allegedly attended this congress. East Germany's German-Arabic Society is sponsoring the Committee of Iraqi Students which, among other things, tries to entice Iraqi students away from West German schools. In the Soviet Union the several student associations by countries of origin are centrally gathered under a Council of *Landsmannschaften*. This council, in collaboration with the "Soviet Solidarity Committee of the Peoples of Asia and Africa" and the "Association of Soviet Societies for Friendship and Cultural Contacts Abroad," directs the entire socio-political activity of the foreign student body in the USSR.

Indoctrination begins with the observance of national holidays and leads via cultural events to basic political indoctrination. The "advantages of the Soviet system" are hammered home to the young people from the underdeveloped nations through plant visits and excursions, carefully planned vacation and leisure activities, and the nurturing of

---

[245] *Das Vordringen der DDR in Südostasien—die ausländischen Praktikanten in der Ostzone,* Carl—Duisburg—Gesellschaft für Nachwuchsförderung e.V., 31 October 1961.

contacts with the Soviet Student Union, politicians, and creative artists. In addition, increasing familiarity with the Russian language and mastery of Soviet technical and pedagogical methods all serve to remold the views of the academic youth.

Yet another method is applied to strengthen the ties of foreign students to the Soviet bloc, a method at once serving Soviet purposes and remunerative to the students. No rosters are published of students attending the People's Friendship University. But a systematic newspaper reader and radio listener soon learns the names of hundreds of young Africans and Asians studying in the USSR. This comes about because, as part of the day's study activity, students from backward nations on propitious political occasions are called upon for radio commentaries and panel discussions for which the scripts—it is reported—are worked out collectively ahead of time. It is part of the method to pay for such "collaboration."

The above gives an idea of the lengths to which the Soviet bloc goes to arouse the interest of foreign students in socio-political activities. These students are not only expected to carry home with them Soviet bloc acquired scientific and technical knowledge, but to become activists at least in the communist front and contact organizations of their home country. Thus, the new methods also achieve the desired results and the grand gesture of waiving an otherwise obligatory study of Marxism-Leninism and other related disciplines for students from the backward nations serves only to avoid compromising the new Soviet bloc universities as training places for communist cadres.

The On-the-Job Training Program

In addition to the training of the backward nations' academic youth, the Soviet bloc's education program puts much emphasis on on-the-job training, refresher training, and retraining of engineers, technicians, and skilled workers. This on-the-job training may take place as a concomitant of Soviet bloc construction in the underdeveloped countries, or a kind of apprenticeship may be served by selected personnel from the backward nations in a Soviet bloc installation or institute. Nearly all "Agreements Concerning Economic and Technical Collaboration" provide for both types. This not only affords production training for a fairly large number of people, but at the same time —and this ranks high with Soviet bloc experts—a fairly large group of engineers, specialists, and technicians from technically backward areas become Soviet bloc oriented. Their familiarity with Soviet and Soviet bloc equipment, measurement systems, and technical standards, facilitate the introduction of bloc products and methods in the nations of Asia, Africa and Latin America. "As an example, all USSR-sponsored projects in Afghanistan call for the training of skilled workers and young technical personnel. In 1960 alone some 3300 Afghan workers and master craftsmen were trained.

"In Afghanistan 30,000 workers and specialists were trained in the process of constructing the various projects that were part of Afghan-Soviet cooperation between 1957 and 1963." [246]

In India, the construction of the Bhilai Steelworks is of great importance in the training of a native labor force. Soviet specialists

[246] G. M. Prochorov, *The Two World Systems and the Liberated Countries*, p. 181.

323

helped set up a technical school in Bhilai that turns out 500 qualified steelworkers annually. Here, too, thanks to Soviet aid, are erected the first state-owned assembly plants for electrotechnical and technological equipment, for refractory masonry, and partly for metal constructions. These plants employ 18,000 fitters, graduates of an excellent production school in Bhilai. These men constitute the priceless reserve of future construction under India's own steam.[247]

Between 1957 and 1964 more than 3500 engineers, technicians and specialists are supposed to have completed practical training courses in USSR plants. "Moreover, in the last five years more than 100,000 qualified workers and persons at the intermediate technical level were trained by Soviet specialists at plants in the developing countries that are being built with Soviet assistance." [248]

Some 15,000 engineers, technicians, and other skilled workers from backward areas (probably including Asian bloc members) allegedly underwent production training in USSR plants during the past six years. No figures are on hand for the entire Soviet bloc, but it is known that oil specialists from backward areas are engaged at the Ploesti oilfields. In Calbe (East Germany), Indian engineers are trained in blast furnace technique. The Lenin Works in Pilsen (CSSR) instructs selected personnel from backward nations in metallurgy, and Polish shipyards train shipwrights.

More important than mere numbers are the specialized training methods applied by the Soviet bloc. The Bhilai Steelworks, now completed, may serve to illustrate the point. On 2 February 1955 the construction agreement between the USSR and India was signed. On 8 March 1955 the Indian Government approved the initial Soviet plans, and by end of March 1956 the first equipment for Bhilai was shipped to India by the USSR. But already in March 1956 Soviet specialists had begun to set up the so-called Technological Institute in Bhilai. In courses of from two to nine months a labor force of 4500 unskilled and semiskilled workers was readied for later commitment at the steelworks. In a twelve-month course Soviet specialists trained 300 Indian technicians to serve as master craftsmen and shop foremen at the future plant. Additionally, 500 Indian engineers and technicians received on-the-site special training by Soviet experts in Bhilai.[249] But the future steelworks' top echelon personnel was taken to the USSR for on-the-job production training.

A total of 686 Indian engineers and technicians went through a

---

[247] *Mezhdunarodnaya zhizn* (Moscow), No. 3/1962, p. 104.
[248] *Voprosy istorii KPSS* (Moscow), No. 4/1966, p. 21.
[249] *Voprosy ekonomiki* (Moscow), No. 6/1957, p. 25.

three-year practical training course at such Soviet works as "Asov-steel," "Saparoshsteel," "Uralmach," and "Magnitogorsk."[250] More recent publications even put this figure at "more than 800."[251] Today's key personnel at the Bhilai Steelworks are graduates of this course. N. Shrivastava, director of the works, is also a graduate of a USSR production course. The purpose of these training measures was two-fold:

1.) India's self-esteem was to be flattered by having Indian specialists available at an early date to assume plant functions. For propaganda purposes the impression was to be created that the Indians themselves were doing the construction, with the Soviets only helping in the planning, through advice, and by supplying the machinery. Thus *Pravda* quoted an Indian journalist: "The first blast furnace was mainly built by Soviet specialists . . . The second was built by the Russians with a great deal of Indian assistance . . . The third furnace is being constructed entirely by Indian engineers, with the Russians only supervising."[252] It goes without saying that the Soviets were in firm control of construction from beginning to end. But their method of featuring the Soviet-trained Indian personnel as being in charge is noteworthy.

2.) Indian specialists became adept at Soviet techniques, at the same time helping to spread the word about Soviet economic aid. Some even learned Russian. A core of Indian specialists, skilled in Soviet techniques and working methods, will remain when the Soviet experts pull out of Bhilai. As a Soviet publication put it: "Now all production processes at the Bhilai Works are carried out without exception solely by Indian specialists."[253]

The Bhilai example was also applied in the construction of four Indian plants for surgical instruments, medicines, antibiotics, and fertilizers. For the construction of these projects, to be built with Soviet help under the agreement of 29 May 1959, the Soviet Union is sending 200 specialists to India. India, in turn, is sending 176 technicians to the USSR for training. The latter are to relieve the Soviet specialists six to twelve months after completion of the projects.

The Bhilai system of a combined training effort has largely been confined to India and Afghanistan. Some of the underdeveloped countries prefer to supply the key personnel for Soviet-built projects themselves. At the Aswan High Dam the Soviets still conducted on-

[250] *India. Economy and Foreign Trade* (Russ.), Moscow 1959, p. 323.
[251] *Mezhdunarodnaya zhizn* (Moscow), No. 3/1962, p. 98.
[252] *Pravda*, 24 December 1959.
[253] *Mezhdunarodnaya zhizn* (Moscow), No. 3/1962, p. 98.

the-job training for linemen, pipelayers, crane operators, hydro-mechanics, tractor operators, and laborers. But the Egyptian Ministry responsible for the Aswan construction assumed overall charge. This Ministry produced 200 Arabic engineers and technicians at the beginning of construction, who in February 1962 were working side by side with 400 Soviet specialists and 900 Egyptian laborers.[254] In May 1964 more than 30,000 UAR citizens and roughly 2000 Soviet specialists and qualified workers were working at the Aswan Dam.[255]

The USSR is out to expand further the program of training specialists of the backward nations. Thus, instruction courses in the installation, operation, and repair of machinery and equipment are to be tied in with the export of such items to the underdeveloped countries. Soviet export organizations are encouraged to have purchasers of Soviet equipment and their private middlemen establish technical courses in the underdeveloped nations. Also, Soviet firms that specialize in equipment for export—some 400 Soviet firms delivered equipment for the Bhilai Steelworks—are to be prepared to train equipment specialists from the backward areas.[256] Soviet industrial concerns interested in exporting their products have been directed to make up teams of qualified Soviet specialists (millwrights and repair experts) "who are specially schooled for work abroad, taught a foreign language, and are familiarized with the possible uses to which the machinery and equipment may be put in one or more countries." [257] Soviet exporters are told: "The preparation of training programs for foreign specialists visiting the USSR by the manufacturers and economic councils, the compilation of lesson plans, including textbooks and visual training aids, for the various groups of students and study courses, as well as the furnishing of instructors and program directors, is of great importance." [258]

Suitable technical training manuals, however, are still in short supply in the USSR today. Lumumba University, which has it own publishing house and printing plant, has published a total of sixty-five technical and instruction manuals so far. Some of them are language instruction books and dictionaries, and inasmuch as they are technical instruction manuals they are designed for the university courses, yet seem of little value for the technical courses. Here, too, the Soviet training plans still face formidable preparatory tasks.

---

[254] *Neue Zeit* (Moscow), No. 7/1962, p. 10.

[255] G. M. Prochorov, *The Two World Systems and the Liberated Countries, op. cit.,* p. 181.

[256] *Vneshnyaya torgovlya* (Moscow), No. 12/1960, p. 34.

[257] *ibid.,* p. 35.

[258] *ibid.,* p. 36.

Schools in the Underdeveloped Countries

The Herder Institute, in competition with Munich's Goethe Institute, and East Germany's lectureships in the backward nations show the Soviet bloc's readiness in its competitive struggle with the West to apply the same educational methods that the latter has used for years. Partly in envy, but partly also to exhort the functionaries to "do likewise," the journal of the Soviet Institute of World Economy and International Relations writes about the West German Federal Republic: "For thirty years there have been German schools in Teheran and Tabriz. Kabul has had a German trade school for fifty years. Until this day these schools employ German teachers, use German texts, and instruct in German. Since World War II the establishment of German institutes abroad has been systematically and rapidly expanded. German monopolists consider the buildup of schools as the most worthwhile of all 'technical aids' . . . West German monopolists are eager to extend their influence also to the instructional institutes already in being in the backward nations. Interest is especially shown in the physical equipment used in the training establishments of Asian and African countries, particularly where it concerns German-made equipment and apparatus. With the aid of these schools, West German monopolists seek to train people who are familiar with German equipment and know how to operate it." [259]

Only in recent years, and somewhat belatedly, has the Soviet bloc come to see one of the most effective means of foreign aid in the establishment of training institutes abroad, complete with Soviet equipment and Soviet instructors. Energetic steps are being taken to close

[259] *Mirovaya ekonomika i mezhdunarodnie otnosheniya* (Moscow), No. 1/1961.

this gap also. It is indicative that each new Soviet bloc school project in Asia and Africa gets top propaganda billing.

India. The Technological Institute, opened near Bombay in 1958, is touted in Soviet literature as an example of "selfless Soviet training assistance." Actually, this institute originated as a UNESCO project; that is, in 1955 it was agreed among UNESCO, India, and the USSR that the latter, as its share to the UN Expanded Program of Technical Assistance, would supply the equipment for the institute in the value of 2.5 million dollars. But in 1958 the USSR, for propaganda reasons, changed its UNESCO commitment to a bilateral agreement with India. Thus the USSR, in an agreement of 12 December 1958, pledged itself "during 1959-60 to supply India free of charge in gift form with the complete outfitting of the Indian Technical Institute in Bombay, to include the equipment for physics, electronics, radio, and television laboratories, as well as geodetic electronics equipment and the equipment for a central laboratory for scientific and technological research, in the amount of $750,000." [260] Nor was the Soviet Union loath to foot the bill and renew the five-year tenure of the Soviet professors in order to permit the latter to continue their Soviet-inspired activities at the Bombay institute. Also during this second five-year period the Soviets agreed to train "fifty Indian specialists at USSR expense in Soviet institutions." The new agreement also served to send, "in accordance with Indian desires, a group of Soviet professors and instructors, whose number, length of service, and technical field is to be worked out between the appropriate Soviet and Indian authorities, "at Soviet expense, to assume responsibility for translating Soviet technical textbooks into English for their use at Indian institutes, such books to be subsequently published by Indian organizations." [261]

The technological institute in Bombay is designed for 2000 students and 500 auditors. "Sixty-five professors and instructors from the USSR have taught here since the institute came into existence." [262] At present twenty Indian professors, who have completed their studies at Soviet universities, have replaced an equal number of Soviet instructors.

Burma. In July 1961 Burma's Soviet-built Technological Institute of Rangoon was opened. "The erection of Rangoon's Technological Institute, a gift of the peoples of the USSR to the Burmese nation, became known far and wide. One of the country's largest educational institutes, it will train Burma's young generations for the impending

[260] *Sbornik deystvuyushchikh dogovorov* . . . Vyp. XX, pp. 541-42, Moscow 1961.
[261] *Sbornik deystvuyushchikh dogovorov* . . . Vyp. XX, pp. 541-42, Moscow 1961.
[262] *Veshnaya torgovlya,* (Moscow), No. 8/1965, p. 6.

industrialization. Built for more than a thousand students, the institute is located on a nearly 150-acre campus, boasts four laboratory buildings, dormitories for the students, living quarters for the instructors, and other facilities." [263] At this writing fifteen Soviet Professors and instructors teach at the institute. [264]

Guinea. The Polytechnical Institute in Conakry was built with Soviet help and inaugurated in 1964. It is designed for 1500 students. Twenty Soviet instructors teach in four departments—electrical engineering, building engineering, geology and agriculture. The USSR donated the teaching plans and programs, the textbooks which are written in French, ten movie mobiles and a library of 10,000 volumes in French.

Cambodia. The name of the technical university that was opened in Phnom Penh in 1964 as a gift of the Soviet Union is Technical University-Institute of Khmer-Soviet Friendship. It is designed for 1000 students and fifty student candidates and has five departments: architecture, mining, electrical engineering, textiles and water improvement. Twenty to twenty-five Soviet instructors, assisted by five translators, constitute the teaching staff. The USSR underwrote the costs.

Ethiopia. On 11 June 1963 the USSR made the Ethiopian government a gift of a technical school in Bahard-Dar which the Ethiopian government gave the name Polytechnical Institute. The school is designed for 1000 students, with a new class of 250 entering each year on the four-year course of study. Chemists and laboratory analysts for industry, electricians, technologists for textile and wood finishing industries, and mechanics for agricultural machines are trained here.

Indonesia. The USSR is building a Technological Institute in the town of Ambon as part of a credit it granted on 28 July 1959. "The following is planned for the Ambon Institute: a department for shipbuilding, for oceanography and fish processing . . . The institute will form a little town by itself, consisting of a block of teaching facilities with an auditorium and lecture halls as well as laboratory buildings, instructional workshops, aquatic tanks for study purposes, a power plant . . . Apartment buildings, communal apartments, sports and communal projects will be constructed for the professors, instructors and students." [265]

Algeria. An Oil and Natural Gas Institute with a special technical school for the training of 2000 engineers and technicians was opened on 15 September 1964. It was a gift of the USSR. A Textile Institute

---

[263] *USSR Economic Collaboration with the Countries of Asia, Africa, and Latin America* (Russ.), p. 131.
[264] *Mezhdunarodnya zhizn* (Moscow), No. 3/1962, p. 105.
[265] *Problems of Aid to the Economically Underdeveloped Countries*, p. 109.

for the training of 500 engineers (a five year course of study) and technicians (a four-year course of study) was also constructed with help of the USSR and is supposed to have opened.

Tunisia. The USSR is constructing a National Technical Institute near Tunis University for 700 students.

Mali. The USSR equipped a Teaching and Study Center for 300 students that were to be trained as mechanics, electricians, mill operatives and foundry workers. The USSR also made Mali a gift of one high school, one medical school and one administrative college. On 15 June 1965 Mali and the USSR reached an accord whereby the USSR agreed to construct a Party University for the unity party of Mali, the *Union Soudanaise.*

Kenya. The USSR will build a Technical University for 1000 students that will train specialists in electrical engineering, automobile repairing, and building construction.

Uganda. The USSR is constructing a Technical School for 350 students who will be trained as agricultural mechanics.

UAR. So far the USSR has constructed twenty-three training centers that have the character of technical schools. By 1965 roughly 10,-000 specialists are supposed to have graduated from these schools. On 22 September 1965 the UAR and the USSR reached an accord that stipulated that the USSR would help build twenty more such schools in the UAR. Among them will be seven schools for workers in the metal industry, five for electrical engineering, one for automobile construction, one for coke-chemical production specialists, two for mining, one for precision mechanics, one for steel manufacturing, and two for energy production.

Ten trade school centers are on the Soviet program for *Iraq.* In *Ghana* the Soviet Union had promised to build a training center for 5000 to 6000 students to be trained as technicians for industry, building industry and agriculture. Toward the end of 1965 a total of ninety technical trade schools was on the USSR program for the developing countries. At that time roughly 300 Soviet training specialists are supposed to have been active in the training centers which the USSR constructed in the developing countries.[266]

Summarizing, we can say that the East bloc has recognized that training aid constitutes a decisive factor in acquiring influence in the Asian, African and Latin American countries. The East bloc not only regards "man's productive power" as the most important element in the control and development of material goods but also as the key that makes it possible to sway the course of the development of the societies in these countries.

---

[266] *Veshnaya torgovlya,* (Moscow), No. 8/1965, p. 5.

Just as the East bloc concentrates its efforts by means of foreign trade, credit grants and the construction of industrial plants and facilities in crucial areas of each country's economy, the East bloc's training program also seeks to achieve, with limited means, the greatest political-psychological effect, and to provide training equipment that will be of propagandistic value.

Crucial areas in the realm of training aid are represented by such undertakings as the People's Friendship University in Moscow, the University of 17 November in Prague, the construction of larger technological institutes and schools in the developing countries themselves, as well as by the training schools for the plants and facilities to be constructed in "Third World" countries.

Though still insufficiently prepared in many areas of its training program, the objective of the East bloc is clear: to use its newly developed sophisticated and adaptable methods to transform the leading elite, the technical intelligentsia and the workers of the developing countries into cadres that "decide everything."